Baseball Under the Lights

ALSO BY CHARLIE BEVIS
AND FROM McFARLAND

---

*Red Sox vs. Braves in Boston:
The Battle for Fans' Hearts, 1901–1952* (2017)

*Tim Keefe: A Biography of the Hall of Fame Pitcher
and Player-Rights Advocate* (2015)

Jimmy Collins: A Baseball Biography (2012)

Doubleheaders: A Major League History (2011)

*The New England League:
A Baseball History, 1885–1949* (2008)

*Sunday Baseball: The Major Leagues' Struggle to Play Baseball
on the Lord's Day, 1876–1934* (2003)

Mickey Cochrane: The Life of a Baseball Hall of Fame Catcher (1998)

Baseball Under the Lights

The Rise of the Night Game

CHARLIE BEVIS

McFarland & Company, Inc., Publishers

Jefferson, North Carolina

LIBRARY OF CONGRESS CATALOGUING-IN-PUBLICATION DATA

Names: Bevis, Charlie, 1954– author.
Title: Baseball under the lights : the rise of the night game / Charlie Bevis.
Description: Jefferson, North Carolina : McFarland & Company, Inc.,
Publishers, 2021. | Includes bibliographical references and index.
Identifiers: LCCN 2021013592 | ISBN 9781476680156 (paperback : acid free paper) ∞
ISBN 9781476642321 (ebook)
Subjects: LCSH: Baseball—United States—History—20th century. | Stadiums—
Lighting—United States—History—20th century. | Baseball attendance—
United States—History—20th century. | Television and baseball—United States—
History—20th century. | BISAC: SPORTS & RECREATION / Baseball / History
Classification: LCC GV863.A1 B479 2021 | DDC 796.357—dc23
LC record available at https://lccn.loc.gov/2021013592

BRITISH LIBRARY CATALOGUING DATA ARE AVAILABLE

ISBN (print) 978-1-4766-8015-6
ISBN (ebook) 978-1-4766-4232-1

Front cover: Wrigley Field at night during
Game 3 of the 2016 World Series (Arturo Pardavila III)

Printed in the United States of America

McFarland & Company, Inc., Publishers
Box 611, Jefferson, North Carolina 28640
www.mcfarlandpub.com

Table of Contents

Preface

This history of night baseball completes a trilogy of the three predominant scheduling techniques used by professional baseball to increase attendance at the ballpark, complementing my two earlier books *Sunday Baseball* (2003) and *Doubleheaders* (2011).

My previous research on Sunday games and doubleheaders had at its heart the creation of knowledge to fill the absolute void on those two topics in the baseball literature. Those two books largely contained factual information regarding the who, what, when, and where of those topics, with some analysis to explain the why and how they changed the nature of the ballpark audience.

Night baseball is the third piece of the trilogy because in the 1990s there was no immediate need for a factual history of that subject, since the literature two decades ago provided a basic understanding of the facts. The book *Lights On! The Wild Century-Long Saga of Night Baseball* by David Pietrusza (1997) provided some historical background and reviewed the initial home night games played by major-league clubs. Providing some context was "The Coming of Night Baseball," the fifth chapter in the book *Creating the National Pastime: Baseball Transforms Itself, 1903–1953* by Edward White (1996). The literature on night baseball remains relatively scant, with the addition of the book *Let There Be Light: A History of Night Baseball* by Robert Payne (2010), which focused on the first major-league night game in Cincinnati.

The main shortcoming of this existing literature on night baseball is its focus on factual information, i.e., the trees rather than the forest, in the classic arboreal metaphor. My book on night baseball examines not only the forest (baseball business) but also the motives and desires of the foresters (ball-club owners) and big-picture issues regarding the hikers in the forest (ballpark spectators and later television viewers). This history of night baseball provides a much broader perspective about the who, what, and how of the topic and deeply examines the why of its adoption, expansion, and saturation.

Several research projects following the publication of *Doubleheaders* piqued my interest to dig deeper into daylight baseball, since my perspective then on ballpark spectatorship was admittedly somewhat simplistic, along the lines of "more is better." What did not fall into that pattern was this question: why did the scheduling of poorly-attended daylight games continue for so long before club owners actively did something about it? My initial research to address this question was incorporated into my 2017 book *Red Sox vs. Braves in Boston: The Battle for Fans' Hearts, 1901–1952*.

The number of unresolved issues that came out of that project was the genesis of this book, since the adoption of night baseball at the major-league level most certainly did not follow the "more is better" principle. The factual foundation of night baseball in the literature did not seem nearly enough to truly understand the basis for its adoption and spread. Two big questions to address were: why was there a five-year gap between adoption in the minors and majors, and why was the spread so expeditious in the minors compared to the tortoise-like approach in majors? Other significant questions, previously unexplained, included: who created the seven-game restriction in the majors, why did it take so long before daylight games could be completed under lights, and why was the twi-night doubleheader so forgotten?

This book adds to the baseball literature by creating knowledge about the trends that impacted the adoption, expansion, and saturation of night baseball, both at the major-league level as well as the minor-league level. This book also adds factual information not already in the literature, especially regarding the progress of liberalization in major-league restrictions on the number of permitted night games and the disbanding of conventions to conduct night games on the premium daylight dates of home-opener, holidays, and Sunday. An additional new area of compiled knowledge is the competitive battle among three companies to engineer lighting systems in ballparks: General Electric, Westinghouse, and Giant Manufacturing.

Another contribution of this book to the baseball literature is that a comprehensive treatment now exists at both the major-league and minor-league levels for all three of the dominant scheduling techniques of night baseball, Sunday baseball, and doubleheaders. This book covers night baseball at both levels within its pages. While my earlier books about the other two techniques focused on the major-league level, the minor-league void on Sunday baseball now has been filled by my recent article "Sunday Baseball Adoption in the Minor Leagues" in *Base Ball 11: New Research on the Early Game* (2019) and doubleheaders at the minor-league level have a more expansive treatment in this book.

Introduction

Night baseball was the accelerant that completely transformed the business of professional baseball, as the audience for weekday games at night shifted to a larger, more economically diversified group of spectators than the smaller group of people that could attend afternoon daylight games.

From 1876 through 1929, daylight was the only option to schedule ball games, due to the inadequate lighting technology to conduct night games. Prior to the legal ability to conduct Sunday baseball, the audience at the ballpark consisted largely of businessmen, self-employed people, and a select few groups of people who had the time flexibility to attend ball games conducted in the afternoon on Monday through Saturday during the conventional six-day workweek that was the norm before the 1930s. Other than on holidays and Sunday, where legal, working people had little opportunity to attend a professional ball game, except if they were willing to forego a half-day's pay.

The explanation for the demise of the weekday daylight game, and the rise of night baseball that replaced it, requires a substantive understanding of the history of daylight baseball as well as the business foundation of the minor leagues, both of which were steeped in urban boosterism. Indeed, this book is as much a history of daylight baseball, which was an untold story in its own right until explored in this book, as well as an overview of the business of minor-league ball clubs from 1883 to 1941, before they essentially collapsed into being subsidiaries of major-league clubs and ceased to be independently owned. The impetus for night baseball began in the minor leagues, which had a higher adoption rate for night baseball and more quickly reached the night-game saturation point than did the major leagues.

During the 1920s, Sunday and holiday games began to subsidize the weekday daylight game, which suffered from dwindling attendance, especially the ball clubs in the minor leagues, which quickly latched onto night baseball at the dawn of the Great Depression as a salvation for their crumpled business basis. The minor leagues were the only practitioners of night baseball from 1930 through 1934, except for barnstorming clubs on the fringe of professional baseball, since the major leagues resisted the new technology.

While the major leagues initially adopted night baseball in 1935, league-wide restrictions on the number of night games exemplified the reluctance of ball-club owners to embrace the changing baseball audience. By 1948 all clubs but the Chicago Cubs had installed lighting systems to play night baseball. However, further expansion in the 1950s was stifled by the rise of television, and its intersection with other cultural trends, such as the population movement to the suburbs, as television viewership increasingly impacted the business basis of baseball. By the 1970s, night baseball became the predominant mode of conducting ball games, with two-thirds played at night and one-third in daylight.

The exploration of the changing ballpark audience resulting from the transition from daylight to night baseball must by its nature be pursued with a broad brush rather than with fine detail, due to the impossibility of a dataset to analyze the actual composition of the audience that attended ball games at the ballpark. Given the paucity of secondary sources regarding night baseball, primary-source newspaper accounts (particularly from *The Sporting News* and *New York Times*) and scholarly content on relevant topics were the research focus to develop the conclusions in this book.

Two tools are used to help examine this transformation. The first tool is the civic/profit business basis, which was implicitly used by ball clubs to balance profitability with civic boosterism, where changes in the revenue component of profitability are very instructive in understanding the conversion from daylight to night baseball. The second tool is the day-of-game mix, which was implicitly used by ball clubs in game scheduling to produce a total revenue stream from gate receipts (i.e., attendance) through the scheduling of games (and any promotions) on the available playing dates, which in baseball's early years were the trio of Sunday, holiday, and weekday (Monday through Saturday). Later, the day-of-game tool morphed into time-of-day, with its twin components of daylight and night.

One set of statistics, provided by the statisticians overseeing the Retrosheet database, is used to objectively illustrate the growth of night baseball in the major leagues. This data shows that what began as a seven-game experiment in 1935 slowly grew to be one-twentieth of all games played by 1941. In the postwar period, night games rapidly grew to one-quarter of all games played in 1947, one-half in 1961, and two-thirds in 1979. The two-thirds ratio was then remarkably consistent from 1980 through the 2015 season.[1]

This book is divided into two parts. The first part, consisting of the opening six chapters, provides essential background material during the period 1869 through 1929 to better understand the eventual adoption of night baseball. The second part, consisting of the subsequent ten chapters, examines in-depth the adoption, expansion, and saturation of night baseball during the period 1930 through 1990, culminating in a current outlook on night baseball in the last chapter.

In the first part of the book, the content alternates between the history of daylight baseball (Chapters 1, 3, and 5) and the early experiments in night baseball (Chapters 2, 4, and 6). Chapter 1 analyzes the original audience for professional baseball in the context of the urban development of American cities; Chapter 3 explores how civic boosterism impacted the development of the major leagues and the minor leagues, which institutionalized the daylight game; and Chapter 5 examines the economically fragile nature of the minor leagues in the 1920s amid societal changes, which set the stage for an immediate adoption of night baseball in 1930 and the rigid resistance to it in the major leagues. In the content about the early experiments in night baseball, Chapter 2 reviews the development of artificial lighting technology and the nineteenth-century baseball experiments, Chapter 4 explores the use of arc lighting for night games in the early twentieth century, and Chapter 6 examines the first practical applications of incandescent lighting to illuminate outdoor sports at night and the initial modern night baseball game in 1927.

In the second part of the book, the content proceeds chronologically to examine the adoption, expansion, and saturation of night baseball. Chapter 7 focuses on the rapid adoption of night baseball in the minor leagues in 1930, while Chapter 8 looks at the minor-league expansion over the next four years. Chapter 9 reviews the initial adoption in the National League, first by Cincinnati in 1935 and second by Brooklyn in 1938, both through the efforts of Larry MacPhail. Chapter 10 reviews the installation of lights in three ballparks in the American League in 1939 and four additional ballparks in 1940 and 1941 along with the transmission of night baseball throughout the minor leagues to a saturation point. Chapter 11 examines the escalation of night baseball during World War II, with new observations about how that was effectuated. Chapters 12 and 13 explore the expansion within the major leagues at a deliberate pace in the postwar years. Chapters 14 and 15 examine the rise of night baseball during the 1950s and 1960s during the relocation and expansion years. Chapter 16 reviews the march to saturation in the major leagues in the 1970s and the role of night baseball in fueling national television revenue in the 1980s, before observing the equilibrium state of night and daylight baseball in the twenty-first century.

◆ 1 ◆

Original Audience
for Daylight Baseball

During the inaugural season of the National League in 1876, baseball played during daylight hours was the only option to stage the ball games. Electric light was then merely an experimental technology, one barely noticed at the 1876 Centennial Exposition in Philadelphia where Moses Farmer and William Wallace exhibited their fledging lamp that used the arc lighting principle to create artificial illumination. Few people yet knew of Thomas Edison, who would soon toil away in his laboratory in New Jersey to try to perfect a viable incandescent light, the other predominant modern principle to create artificial illumination.

Daylight ruled the life of William Hulbert, the architect of the National League, as it did his contemporaries in the Chicago business world. Existing applications of artificial illumination in Chicago during the mid–1870s were barely tolerable to conduct a modicum of business after sundown and were hardly sufficient to enable a baseball game to be played at night.

At his office, Hulbert would have used an oil lamp at his desk if he needed to finish up the day's work in his grain business if it wasn't completed by mid-afternoon. At a luminosity of about five candlepower, or five times the light emitted by a single wax candle, the oil lamp was barely an adequate replacement for daylight through an office window to read or write, with the added displeasure of the odorous fumes from the burnt fuel. After sundown, Hulbert could travel the streets of the central business district with a degree of safety provided by the public gas lights situated at street corners. With a luminosity of about 20 candlepower, or four times the strength of an oil lamp, gas lights left numerous shadowy areas on the street that were only partially mitigated by oil lanterns sporadically hung outside shops, theaters, taverns, and hotels that operated at night.[1]

Darkness was generally feared in 1876, since it was "known by long tradition in Western society to be a time of crime, immorality, and sickness." Outside of the gas-lighted sections of the central business district, night time was considered to be a dangerous place, "where faces could not be recognized and shapes were only dimly discerned." In 1876 acceptable "night life" was the preserve of the wealthy few, who patronized first-class theaters and dined out in hotels, and the sporting crowd that spent evenings in taverns and music halls. Most other after-dark activities, especially if conducted beyond the gas-lighted business district, were considered illicit.[2]

While the development of artificial illumination by electric lamp would eventually dispel this fear of the night, urban darkness remained a safety concern for several decades. Initially, this fear helped to solidify the nature of daylight baseball; later, this fear helped to temper enthusiasm for the early experiments in night baseball.

Professional baseball was first recognized in 1869, when the sport finally acknowledged the existence of paid players, who had been increasingly utilized by many clubs during the previous amateur-only years and were paid under the table. In the traditional view of how baseball transformed from an amateur sport to a professional one in 1869, fraternal organizations of players converted into businesses run by owners due to the economic force of "an emerging impulse for profit" to be made from a sporting public that was willing to pay to attend competitions in a "search for winners" on the playing field. In his book *Early Baseball and the Rise of the National League*, Tom Melville characterized this transformation as an evolution from expression (participation) to achievement (championship), where "the former only recognizes winning *for* something, while the latter demands winning *as* something," thus forming the public's initial perception of professional baseball as the seemingly contradictory demand that "baseball's highest achievement level retain an obligation to, and accessibility from, locality." The "obligation to locality" was not the quaint notion of employing local ballplayers but rather the staging of games before local spectators at the ball grounds, while "achievement" included not just winning championships but also the business element of earning a profit (although far short of profit maximization).[3]

While some early professional ball clubs did attempt to cope with this twin-force combination as they converted from social organizations, one ball club in Cincinnati, Ohio, immediately redefined the two forces. By employing a city boosterism philosophy, the 1869 Cincinnati club focused on a national tour to stage ball games, not merely the local games, and barely earned a $1.39 profit, thus adopting a breakeven mentality and the possibility of underwriting losses if necessary in the short term. With its undefeated record in 1869, the Cincinnati Red Stockings achieved success by enhancing the city's reputation to be the "Queen City of the West" as a replacement for the derisive "Porkopolis," largely due to the efforts of a Cincinnati newspaperman who accompanied the team and telegraphed game scores and accounts from the tour cities to other large-city newspapers. Aaron Champion, the club president and "an enormous civic booster [who] believed that if the city prospered so would he," experienced increased business at his law firm and nearly won political office at the next city election.[4]

Since the business basis of the 1869 Cincinnati ball club was not pure profit making, a better characterization of its business mission would be a hybrid civic/profit basis. This was consistent with how businessmen viewed their role in American society during the middle decades of the nineteenth century.

The urban small businessman in mid-century America had "emerged from the concept of republican rural independent, self-sufficient landowning farmer or planter," which Thomas Jefferson had espoused as an ideal in the Declaration of Independence through the three fundamental inalienable rights of life, liberty and the pursuit of happiness. Back in 1776, though, "happiness" meant security, independence, and autonomy, not today's "joy" meaning of the word.[5]

By 1860, when one-sixth of the American population now lived in urban areas, up from just one-twentieth in 1820, Jefferson's rural version of the American Dream had morphed into an urban one, where initiative, hard work, and sacrifice could propel a man into becoming a merchant. However, the independent businessman in antebellum urban cities had a different approach to security than did the yeoman farmer. The merchant did not simply perform only mercantile transactions, but was also a "community maker and a community leader" whose "starting belief was in the interfusing of public and private prosperity."[6]

As Daniel Boorstin wrote in his book *The Americans: The National Experience*, "not to boost your city showed both a lack of community spirit and a lack of business sense," especially in cities in the Midwest, "where individual and community prosperity were so intermingled, competition among individuals was also a competition among communities." Businessmen during the mid-nineteenth century actively tempered their individualism to accept some societal obligations, because they could also serve their private interest, based on the concept that "the public good is the collected good of those individuals." This attitude transformed into a distinctive business ethic that was a "conflation of dynamic entrepreneurship with stable independence," colloquially referred to as civic capitalism by business historians to characterize the cohesive nature of ostensibly independent business owners concerning their city's position in the state and regional economies. This 1876 perspective on the local civic economy was distinctly different from the national capitalism that would eventually sweep across the nation in the early twentieth century.[7]

The desired audience for baseball games during the early years of professional baseball was a carryover from antebellum American society. The spectators at the ball grounds generally consisted of upper-income merchants and men of the "old" middle class, since "the hallmark of nearly all these occupations was the independence they afforded," which included going out to the ball grounds in the afternoon. According to Wright Mills, author of the book *White Collar: The American Middle Classes*, antebellum society essentially had two social strata: non-manual workers (merchants who worked with their head) and manual workers (mechanics who worked with their hands). There were distinct economic ramifications to the strata, as the merchants (owners) were the "haves" and the mechanics (laborers) were the "have-nots." In addition, there was a small "middling sorts" category, i.e., the "old" middle class, which consisted of sole-proprietor shopkeepers, intermediaries between merchants and shopkeepers, and clerks being groomed to become merchants.[8]

Mechanics, or manual workers, were not even a consideration at the dawn of professional baseball. Because they worked a 60-hour work week (10-hour days for six days a week), manual workers had no time to attend a baseball game during the workweek; on Sunday, their only day off from work, many states had laws that prohibited the playing of baseball games on Sunday.[9]

The nature of the spectators was indicated by the small number of home games played each season, only two to three dozen, and all erratically planned. There was also a distinct lack of games played in August, when ball clubs often took extended road trips, since most businessmen fled the city to escape the summer heat. With no formal schedule of games, spectators needed broad flexibility in their work schedule to attend the games. Since about 40 percent of the American workforce was self-employed in the 1870s, this was not a particular problem.[10]

Hulbert was part of the "old" middle class, since he was a broker in the grain industry. Six years before he established the National League in 1876, Hulbert, as an investor, helped to popularize the hybrid civic/profit business basis of professional baseball through the establishment of the 1870 Chicago ball club, which sought to promote the business interests of the city (similar to a modern-day chamber of commerce) and potentially make money while limiting financial loss to investors. The 1870 Chicago ball club was a corporation, not a business partnership, whose capital was supplied by local businessmen such as Joseph Medill, publisher of the *Chicago Tribune*, and Potter Palmer, owner of the Palmer House hotel, as well as Hulbert who bought a few shares. These investors were "less concerned about direct financial returns from the game than in employing baseball's high visibility as a means of advancing their political or commercial interests" as well as "to promote the city's reputation."[11]

During the early 1870s Chicago was not yet America's second city, as it competed with St. Louis, Kansas City, Milwaukee, and Minneapolis to become the city that was the regional economic center of the Midwest. Chicago bested these cities by deploying "advertising, mammoth commercial houses, rate wars, board-of-trade battles, and bids for cheap immigrant labor" to acquire recognition as the gateway city of the Midwest. Benjamin Rader, in his book *Baseball: A History of America's Game*, wrote that "uncertain about their city's status, but hopeful for its future, local newspapermen, merchants, and manufacturers frequently resorted to strident boosterism to bolster their extravagant claims in behalf of their cities." A winning baseball team was one of several "suitable institutions" to assist such boosterism.[12]

The best example of how boosterism could help convert a frontier town in the Midwest into a vibrant urban city occurred in Kansas City, Missouri, where in the 1860s a consortium of local businessmen built a bridge over the Missouri River. The bridge assured that the railroad would go west through Kansas City and thus secure the city's regional dominance, compared to bridge-less Leavenworth, Kansas, which ostensibly had a more favorable geographic location due to the shorter track mileage required to be built by the railroad.[13]

During the 1870s there was an intense competitive rivalry between Chicago and St. Louis. "Baseball competition became a metaphor for interurban rivalries," Steven Riess wrote in his book *City Games: The Evolution of American Urban Society and the Rise of Sports*, where a victory on the ball field symbolized the economic superiority of a city. "The baseball field was a comprehensible microcosm of the St. Louis–Chicago rivalry that was amenable to the promotion of civic pride," Gregg Carter wrote in his article "Baseball in Saint Louis, 1867–1875: An Historical Case Study in Civic Pride." Carter espoused that the

William Hulbert, the architect of the National League, created monopoly status for member ball clubs within their cities to connect with the civic boosterism of local businessmen who actively promoted the economic growth prospects of their city.

ball field was perceived to be a reasonable measurement of "the economic and cultural supremacy of the Midwest" due to its competitive, salient, and simple attributes.[14]

Professional baseball therefore served as a measuring stick of economic success to easily distinguish the future prospects of one city versus another. Since the local baseball team was a de facto part of civic boosterism, businessmen were expected to patronize the team's games at the local ball grounds. Thus, businessmen, the owner-operators of local companies in the civic capitalism community, became the original primary audience for professional baseball games in the 1870s, which became more prominent during the years of the National Association, a loose ballplayer-run confederation of professional ball clubs that competed for the national championship from 1871 through 1875.

Boston joined Chicago in forming a baseball club to leverage boosterism possibilities. The new 1871 Boston ball club, with Ivers Adams as its president, drafted off the blueprint of the 1870 Chicago club, as both clubs entered the National Association. The Boston club received its legal standing as a corporation in March 1871, after a protracted effort to marshal a bill through the Massachusetts legislature that had an articulated common good, "the purpose of promoting physical culture, and for the encouragement and improvement of the game of base ball." Initial stockholders in the ball club included Eben Jordan (department store owner), John Mills (hotel owner), and Henry Pierce (chocolate factory owner).[15]

Adams, an up-and-coming clerk in a family-owned carpet business and part of the "old" middle class, realized the potential that a professional baseball team could do for the Boston business community in an attempt to elevate Boston back into the same economic realm as New York City and Philadelphia. Boston's stature in the world of commerce had steadily slipped over the previous two decades, moving from being the nation's third largest city in 1850 to fifth largest in 1860 and down to seventh largest in 1870. In a classic execution of civic capitalism, a winning professional baseball team could elevate the overall prospects for all businessmen in Boston, not just the investors in the ball club. At the founding meeting of the Boston ball club, Adams defined the nature of desired spectators to watch the ball games as "shareholders, members of the club and those of our friends who may take sufficient interest in the success of this enterprise." Essentially, Adams codified the general audience for professional baseball during this era.[16]

By 1875 Boston and Chicago were the two clubs with the strongest financial backing in the National Association. However, insufficient revenue from road games with many other entrants for the championship made for dubious financial prospects and dulled a good deal of the positive impact desired from the boosterism component. Hulbert, now president of the Chicago club, put together a cabal of the strongest clubs to start their own organization, the National League.

A manifesto espousing a more financially vibrant baseball organization appeared in the *Chicago Tribune* in October 1875, highlighting four suggestions to put professional baseball on a sound business basis. The first suggestion was for every club to be "backed by a responsible association, financially capable of finishing a season" in order to eliminate gate-sharing-only "co-operative frauds" that often represented smaller cities. The second suggestion was that "no club should be admitted from a city of less size than 100,000 inhabitants, excepting only Hartford." The third suggestion was that "no two clubs should be admitted from the same city." The fourth suggestion was a $1,000 deposit to be forfeited if a club did not complete the season.[17]

While the four suggestions made by the *Chicago Tribune*, no doubt at the urging of Hulbert, were written in the context of improving the opportunity to make money at baseball, the advocacy of exclusivity in each city and a hefty population requirement were de facto "great city" requirements for league membership, in order to cast the National League as being comprised of the most prosperous cities of the United States. With the league members holding a monopoly in their cities, Hulbert could now better use professional baseball to promote civic boosterism at the national level. For the inaugural 1876 season, six of the eight National League clubs were in cities on the top-10 population list from the 1870 federal census: New York (1), Philadelphia (2), St. Louis (4), Chicago (5), Boston (7), and Cincinnati (8). The other two clubs were in Louisville (14) and Hartford, Connecticut (34).

The Chicago ball club, as champion of the National League in four of the league's first seven years, helped to boost the national stature of the city, during an era when ball clubs served as a measuring stick of economic success to distinguish the future prospects of one city versus another (Library of Congress, Prints & Photographs Division, LC-DIG-ppmsca-18390).

Six of the eight ball clubs in the National League in 1876 were named for the city where the club played its home games, thus tightly aligning with the boosterism goal originally fostered by Chicago. Only the clubs located in New York and Philadelphia retained their former social-club moniker, Mutual and Athletic, respectively. These two cities were already the largest in the country, so boosterism was not a primary motivation of either club.

The National League retained the same desired audience for ball games from the National Association days, which had been based on characteristics of antebellum America. However, in the now decidedly postbellum American society, a more sizeable middle tier emerged between the two polar antebellum groups of upper-income merchants and working-class mechanics. As Sam Bass Warner wrote in his book *Streetcar Suburbs*, this "new" middle class was not one homogenous category as was the "old" middle class of antebellum society, but rather consisted of three distinct segments: upper, central, and lower. The upper middle class was the antebellum "old" middle class, who were large storeowners, successful manufacturers, brokers, wholesalers, and prosperous lawyers. The central middle class consisted of small-store owners, successful salesmen, lawyers, school teachers, and large contractors. The lower middle class were skilled artisans (whose craft had not yet been eliminated by industrialization) and better-paid salaried office workers and sales personnel. While this "new" middle class would eventually outnumber the "old" middle class, during the 1870s the older version was still vibrant, outnumbering the newer one by a six-to-one margin.[18]

While Hulbert is often cited as establishing the National League for moral purposes, the espousal of eliminating gambling and drinking and prohibiting Sunday games came after the adoption of the monopoly principle. The moral doctrines were designed to appeal to the primary audience of the "old" middle class as well as to attract spectators from the central and lower segments of the "new" middle class, which often shared the civic mindedness of those wealthier businessmen. To cater to this desired audience, standard practices included a 3:00 mid-afternoon starting time and a 50-cent admission charge. A later time and lower admission price arguably could have produced a greater profit, but the standard practices maximized attendance to support civic boosterism. That was the tradeoff with the hybrid civic/profit business basis, which during Hulbert's tenure as league president resulted in most clubs losing money each year while many clubs struggled to successfully leverage the civic boosterism element.

Seating areas at the ball grounds were also segregated by economic means, to encourage attendance by the desire audience. The grandstand seats close to home plate required an additional charge to enter, typically 25 or 50 cents. The grandstand was designed to accommodate the desired audience of local businessmen and visiting out-of-town business customers, as well as to curry favor with politicians and government officials whose decisions might impact the future of the ball club.

People otherwise had to sit in the less comfortable bleacher sections located farther away from the action on the field. The bleachers existed to handle other people whose employment situation conceivably enabled them to attend a mid-afternoon ball game without losing pay. Many of these were night workers, who went to work after they had attended a ball game, including theater workers (actors, musicians, and stagehands), tavern workers (waiters and bartenders), newspaper workers (writers, telegraphers, and typesetters), and tradesmen with morning deliveries (milkmen and bakers). People involved in education, such as teachers and students, were also possibilities; illicit occupations such as prostitute and gambler were another prominent group of ball game spectators.[19]

By 1881 Chicago and Boston were the only cities left of the original eight franchises granted in 1876, as Hulbert actively pruned the league of laggards. At the end of the 1876 season, the Mutual and Athletic clubs were the first to be ousted (for not completing their schedules), followed by St. Louis and Louisville after the 1877 season (for gambling scandals) and Cincinnati after the 1880 season (for leasing its ball grounds for Sunday games). Four of the five ex-patriot cities that Hulbert jettisoned were among the nation's 10 largest cities in population in the 1870 federal census (note: Hartford voluntarily left the league after 1877). The "great city" boosterism goal seemed to only benefit Hulbert's Chicago club and his Boston rival, not the league as a whole.

Despite the elimination of clubs in cities that were among the nation's top 10 in population, boosterism kept the National League afloat because owners of many other ball clubs in regional leagues salivated to join the National League to better promote their city's economic prospects. To replace ejected or bankrupt clubs in the National League, there was no shortage of small-city recruits during the five years from 1878 through 1882: Providence, Indianapolis, Milwaukee, Buffalo, Syracuse, Troy, Cleveland, Worcester, and Detroit. Not one of these nine new cities was on the top-10 population list from the 1880 federal census; the largest were Cleveland and Buffalo, at number 11 and 13, respectively.

Most of these replacement franchises entered the National League expressly to leverage the potential boosterism element. While baseball clubs were an ancillary tool in civic boosterism relative to the primary efforts made by local boards of trade or other formal consortiums of business leaders, there almost always was a local businessman willing to operate a ball club to attempt to elevate his stature within the city's business community. Two replacement clubs were headed by city mayors (Detroit and Worcester) with the other clubs headed by one of the businessmen from the consortium of investors. These new franchises represented the perils of trying to balance the components of the hybrid civic/profit model in a rapidly changing American society. Among the businessmen-consortium clubs, Providence and Buffalo were the most successful, surviving in the league for eight-year and seven-year tenures, respectively, before both clubs were ousted from the league after the 1885 season.

Hulbert took monopoly status too far, though, elevating from city monopoly initially to an attempt to have the National League be the sole professional baseball league in the country. He intentionally sought to eliminate the nascent minor leagues that had evolved from 1877 to 1880. He also executed a "strategy of preempting the formation of competing leagues by absorbing their potentially strongest members," which resulted in the entry of two very small cities into the National League, Troy, New York, and Worcester, Massachusetts, which both barely made the top-30 list of most populous cities. While Hulbert had virtually eliminated the minor leagues (only one operated in 1881, none in 1882), this victory came at the expense of ravishing the great-city boosterism component of membership in the National League. In 1882, the league's eight clubs were certainly not in the eight cities with the largest population or best economic growth rate, and may not have even been the best baseball clubs, given the track record of the Metropolitan club in New York City.[20]

By the early 1880s the civic/profit business basis had collapsed, as neither component was working very well for ball clubs in the National League. The three-tier "new" middle class of American society was not as motivated by the boosterism element as was

The Buffalo ball club used its National League membership to advance the city's economic stature in the 1880s. However, by 1886, the city was relegated to minor-league status (Boston Public Library, Print Department, McGreevy Collection).

the "old" middle class. Attendance, for the most part, stagnated at the ball grounds, while the great city exclusivity of league membership no longer applied and thus eroded the potential benefit of boosterism. During the 1881 and 1882 seasons, Chicago and Boston were the only cities in the National League on the top-10 population list, rendering moot any benefit of boosterism to those two cities without the national comparison to New York and Philadelphia. While Chicago and Boston were clearly the largest in their own economic sub-regions, both cities sought national stature.

The value of boosterism became even more questionable when the American Association began operations as a major-league competitor for the 1882 season. Of its six cities, four were ranked on the top-10 population list, while Pittsburgh was ranked just outside it at number 12 and Louisville was the smallest city at number 16. Despite being in the populous cities, one-half of the American Association clubs adopted social-club nicknames rather than be known by their boosterism-friendly host-city names, which allowed the National League to retain some measure of boosterism advantage.

Profitability was also a problem in the National League, as generally only the championship club turned a profit and all other clubs lost money. The six-team league adopted a fixed 60-game schedule for the 1877 and 1878 seasons; after expanding to eight teams in 1879, the league then adopted an 84-game schedule. Even with more revenue-producing opportunities, a ball club had to mix in an enormous number of exhibition games between regular-season games in order to turn a profit.

Hulbert died in 1882 before the baseball season began, so he didn't have an opportunity to try to eliminate the American Association competition as he had the other earlier competing leagues. Arthur Soden, president of the Boston club, was the interim league president for the 1882 season. He orchestrated changes to the playing rules that made the ball game more exciting to spectators, thus putting greater emphasis on the profit component than the civic boosterism one. The National League also made peace with the American Association, by recognizing it as a second major league, and also recognized the Northwestern League as the first official minor league for the 1883 season.

This was the first move to a hierarchy of baseball leagues that distinguished cities by their relative economic positions on a national scale. The National League would not be the only league, but rather the number one league (or one of the two top-notch leagues, from the American Association perspective). This approach created the "big-league" city concept at the highest level, and drove the growth of minor leagues by encouraging each city with a professional ball club to strive for its highest position within the hierarchy of leagues. Civic boosterism naturally became an element of that competition among non-major-league cities.

The National League also welcomed New York and Philadelphia back into the league for the 1883 season, with both clubs run by highly motivated businessmen. This put the league at the top of the food chain in the new hierarchy scheme. By 1890 the National League essentially settled into its long-term great city format, having within its membership seven of the eight clubs that would comprise the league's never-changing franchise lineup during the first five decades of the twentieth century.

Boosterism drove the development of the minor leagues, beginning in 1883, where it had a much longer lasting impact than it did at the major-league level. In the long run, the minor leagues were the essential ingredient to the eventual widespread adoption of night baseball, while the major leagues clung to daylight baseball as a perceived essential element of their superiority. Boosterism also fostered the earliest attempts to play night baseball in the 1880s, when cities and institutions sought reliable outdoor electrical lighting to replace or augment the existing gas lighting used to illuminate outdoor space.

◆ 2 ◆

Premodern Night Baseball

In 1878, while Thomas Edison tinkered to make incandescent lighting commercially viable, Cleveland inventor Charles Brush perfected an arc lighting system for use by businesses and governments as an alternative to gas lights for outdoor lighting. Arc lights provided the illumination for night baseball experiments during the next 40 years. Even though it would be incandescent lights that turned night baseball into a practical endeavor, sportswriters for several decades thereafter continued to generically refer to night games as baseball played under the arcs.

Arc lighting differed significantly from incandescent lighting as a method to produce artificial illumination. In arc lighting, two carbon rods touch together and pull apart by a few millimeters to create a spark, or "arc," across the gap, which heats the carbon rods. The resulting vaporized carbon produces light that is very bright, typically 2,000 candlepower, which makes a good solution to illuminate large spaces, especially outdoors. In incandescent lighting, a filament in a sealed vacuum bulb is heated to throw off light until the filament breaks. The light produced by early incandescent lamps reached up to 25 candlepower, slightly better than gas lighting, but a much better solution for indoor lighting because there are no noxious fumes emitted from the enclosed bulb. At this dawn of artificial lighting, each approach required its own dynamo, or generator, to produce the electrical current that the lamp transformed into light.

Keeping the carbon rods at a constant distance from each other was the key to commercial success for a lamp using arc lighting, since the carbon rods burned quickly and at uneven rates. Brush, recognized as "the pioneer innovator in arc lighting," developed an efficient self-regulator for the carbon rods in his arc lamp, which he sold, along with a dynamo, to department stores in Philadelphia (Wanamaker) and Boston (Continental Clothing) in 1878. Brush, though, "did not confine his vision to establishments of moderate dimensions, but projected in his mind the lighting of the largest buildings and such outdoor areas as railway stations, docks, and streets."[1]

In the spring of 1879 Brush experimented with street lighting in Cleveland and by 1880 he had sold arc lamps to light public places in small cities such as Wabash, Indiana, and illuminate portions of large cities such as Broadway in New York City. These installations by the Brush Electric Company "heralded a new era in street lighting, in which gigantic strides would mark more progress in a few years than had occurred in all previous centuries." Other inventors soon imitated Brush's arc lamp, most notably Edward Weston, which unleashed a wave of competition among so-called electricians to convince institutions to install their particular arc light.[2]

The first baseball game played at night under artificial lighting occurred in 1880 strictly to illustrate the dramatic impact that arc lighting could have upon increasing the volume of people engaged in an outdoor evening activity, not to show how baseball could be played after sunset. In early September two teams of Boston department store employees demonstrated the utility of arc lights to play a game of baseball at the Sea Foam House on Strawberry Hill near Nantucket Beach in the seaside town of Hull, Massachusetts.

"What especially attracted the three hundred spectators to the balconies of the Sea Foam House was the promise of the exceedingly novel sight of a game of base ball in the evening, long after the sun's rays should be dispelled by natural darkness," the *Boston Daily Advertiser* observed, adding that "the real significance of the occasion, however, was the first public experiment in illustration of a new system of illuminating towns by electricity" produced by "thirty-six carbon lamps." As reported by the *Boston Globe*, "Three large towers had been erected, each 100 feet in height, and about 500 feet apart, from the tops of which twelve ordinary-sized Weston lamps were suspended in a circle. Each set of twelve lamps was supposed to have a power equal to the light of 30,000 candles."[3]

Two months later the Jordan Marsh department store, one of the two teams involved in the Hull exhibition, installed arc lamps on the front of its building in Boston's central business district, presumably those of inventor Weston, not Brush. The arc lamps "flooded that portion of the city with a light that equaled that of 50,000 candles" to encourage shoppers to purchase items in the evening, not just during daylight hours. In this manner, the night baseball game in Hull was a success, even if the ball game itself was played "with scarcely the precision as by daylight."[4]

Most baseball historians who have written about this inaugural night baseball game in 1880 have put its electrical component in the context of Edison, such as "just one year after Edison's invention of the incandescent lamp" which occurred in late 1879. These references all imply that the lighting at the Hull game in 1880 was by incandescent lamp, not arc lamp. Some references even inaccurately refer to the lighting as being by Edison's incandescent bulb, which would have been wholly inadequate to stage a ball game at the time. To truly comprehend the development of night baseball, it is vitally important to know that arc lighting technology, not incandescent, was deployed in all the nineteenth-century baseball experiments that used electricity to generate artificial light.[5]

During the early 1880s there was more widespread commercial value in outdoor lighting via

INTERESTING EVENT.

The great match between the Base Ball Nines of

JORDAN, MARSH & CO.

AND

R. H. WHITE & CO.

Will come off on THURSDAY EVENING, Sept. 2, at Strawberry Hill. They will play for the Purse offered by the

NANTASKET BEACH RAILROAD CO.

This will be the first Ball Match ever played in the evening, and it will be done under the new system of lighting by Electricity, now in operation at Strawberry Hill. The boats will leave Litchfield's Wharf, 466 Atlantic Ave., at 3.30, 5.30 and 6.30 P. M., and return after the match is over. Ladies will find pleasant accommodations, but they should go in the 3.30 and 5.30 boats if possible. ADMISSION FREE.

This advertisement in a Boston newspaper in 1880 provided publicity for the first experimental night baseball game played in Hull, Massachusetts.

arc lamps than there was in indoor lighting via incandescent lamps. In the journal article "Charles F. Brush and the First Public Electric Street Lighting System in America," Mel Gorman wrote that "by 1884 it was a rather backward city which had not replaced at least some of its gas lamps with electric arcs." Ironically, the desire of municipalities to install electrical street lighting to increase business activity at night helped to drive civic boosterism to include professional baseball that was played in daylight hours.[6]

In 1883 economic competition in the Great Lakes region among cities such as Grand Rapids, Michigan, Peoria, Illinois, and Fort Wayne, Indiana, helped to spawn the Northwestern League, the first minor league recognized as such by the major leagues. To help the city project a progressive image to attract industry, the Fort Wayne ball club staged the next experimental night baseball game in June 1883. James Jenney, proprietor of the Jenney Arc Lighting System that was a competitor of arc-light innovator Charles Brush, sought to increase his existing street lighting contract with the city of Fort Wayne, so he partnered with the ball club to stage an exhibition night game.

Jenney originally arranged to light the local baseball grounds for a night game to be played between the Fort Wayne and Indianapolis clubs on May 29. However, "baseball by electric light" had to be postponed because the 12 Jenney arc lights placed around the field "proved inadequate to properly light the center of the grounds." The remedy proposed was to "suspend lights in the center of the grounds by wires suspended on high poles on each side."[7]

On June 2, 1883, a seven-inning night game was played on the Fort Wayne grounds between the visiting ball club from Quincy, Illinois, and a local college team. As one of the smaller burgs in the league, the Quincy club probably thirsted to play the night game to gain the regional newspaper publicity of participating in the unique event. The Fort Wayne club, with little to gain from the arc-light exhibition (Jenney was reaping most of any rewards from the game), bowed out in favor of the college squad.

This first night game involving a professional baseball club was largely an artistic failure. "Seventeen electric lights were suspended and the heavens presented a weird appearance," the *Milwaukee Sentinel* reported on the night game. "The pitcher and catcher were enabled to work fairly, but the outfielding was unsatisfactory, owing to the insufficient number of lights used." Three arc lamps were attached to the grandstand and the rest were hung from wires crossing the field, with one hanging directly behind the pitcher. This array of arc lamps "seemed to light up the diamond splendidly," and beyond the infield it reportedly was "light enough to see the ball plainly in the outer field." However, the lights went out twice during the game, which interrupted the exhibition, and the ball had to be changed often, because "when the ball became dirty it could not be seen."[8]

The sportswriter for the *Milwaukee Daily Journal* was one of the first to note the potential to expand the audience at the baseball grounds beyond business owners to include lower ranking workers through night baseball: "Should the experiment prove successful, it will give an impetus to baseball, as many people who would like to see the games are unable to get away from business in the day time." The anonymous *Daily Journal* writer was also the first of many observers to prematurely proselytize a bright future for night baseball: "With between 25 and 30 lights there is no question but that electric light ball playing is an assured success."[9]

Professional baseball under electric lights proved from the beginning to be a tough sell to conservative businessmen, who bristled at the idea of expanding the baseball audience to include the lower social classes through night baseball. "There is something depressing in the news from the boundless West that a game of base ball is to be played at night," the *Boston Daily Advertiser* editorialized in 1883. "The electric current now comes in boldly and claims the right of lengthening indefinitely the hours during which this pastime may be practicable." The *Advertiser* pointed out that "the friendly shadows will assist the boys to purloin a view" and noted the distinct possibility "for the urchins to drop gently over the fence, and appear, ultimately, in the ranks of those who have paid for admission."[10]

Had there been further advancements in arc-lighting technology to allow baseball to be adequately played under artificial light, the social-class issue of ballpark attendance would have advanced more quickly than it did by provoking a chicken-or-egg booster-ism quandary of does a city first recruit an industry or the workers for that industry in its quest for increased urban status. This question was never thrust upon baseball executives, however, because the market for artificial lighting fundamentally changed during the mid–1880s to almost exclusively focus on the development of incandescent lamps and a consequent abandoning of advancements in arc lighting.

In 1885 Charles Brush's company was the dominant manufacturer of arc lamps, with more than three times the volume of its next competitor among arc-light inventors, Elihu Thomson's company, while Jenney was one of two dozen bit players and Weston had sold his company to end his involvement in arc lighting. However, the market had substantially changed in the seven years since Brush started selling arc lamps in 1878.[11]

Arc lighting had been "only partially successful in meeting the needs for better light-ing," Arthur Bright wrote in his seminal work *The Electric-Lamp Industry: Technological Change and Economic Development from 1800 to 1947*. "It gave off light of great strength and brilliance, effectively lighting large areas, but it could not be used with satisfaction in the confined space of a private home." As Bernard Carlson observed in *Innovation as a Social Process: Elihu Thomson and the Rise of General Electric*, "There was only a limited market for free-standing, isolated arc lighting systems. Only a few firms could afford to install a complete system with the required steam engine. To reach more customers, it was necessary to revise the marketing strategy … to move in the direction of the central station."[12]

The work of artificial lighting inventor Elihu Thomson in the 1880s led to the formation of the General Electric Company in 1892. In the twentieth century, General Electric developed the artificial lighting that could sufficiently illuminate a baseball field to conduct night baseball.

Edison's company had already successfully executed the central-station strategy to meet the bigger market demand for indoor lighting, where the incandescent lamp was clearly the better product compared to arc lighting. Edison's company was the dominant overall manufacturer of lighting products, having astutely executed the central-station strategy to spread the costs among a large number of potential consumers.

The two largest competitors in arc lighting, Brush and Thomson, had both started to diversify beyond arc lighting to develop incandescent products by mid-decade. While Brush had the largest market share, Thomson was the better innovator, despite his later start (1880) in the arc-lighting business than Brush. Fortuitously, Thomson's company sold an arc-lamp central station to a group of businessmen in Lynn, Massachusetts, in 1882, which then purchased the company, moved it to Lynn, and renamed it to be Thomson–Houston Electric. This infusion of business-minded owners, not inventors, gave Thomson a leg up on Brush as the artificial lighting market continued to change as it rapidly developed throughout the 1880s.[13]

The arc lighting versus incandescent lighting battle had basically concluded by 1885, with the incandescent approach being the victor. It is now largely a forgotten war, having been overshadowed in electrical history by the War of Electric Currents that pitted proponents of direct and alternating currents. This diversion from arc lighting to incandescent lighting stifled a potential earlier development of night baseball. However, even if better arc-lamp technology for outdoor lighting were available in the ensuing decades, ownership of baseball clubs would have ignored its potential in favor of continued focus on the existing audience at the ball grounds. There is no doubt that indoor lighting and the electric trolley were far more welcome innovations of greater utility to all, compared to the thirst for spectatorship at evening outdoor sporting activities.

This decline of arc-lighting technology is seen in the paucity of night baseball experiments during the second half of the 1880s. Two experiments at major-league ball grounds also illustrate issues that impeded additional advancements in night baseball.

During the spring of 1887, Erastus Wiman, owner of the New York Metropolitans of the American Association, consulted with Edward Johnson, vice president of the Edison Electric Light Company, about playing night baseball at Wiman's St. George Grounds on Staten Island, where night entertainment already complemented daylight baseball. Johnson astutely diagnosed that the failure of previous attempts to play baseball under artificial light was due to "the idea of placing the illumination at a great height above the field and throwing the original rays directly on it, thus either blinding the players by the glare, or casting shadows, either of which make it impracticable." To resolve this problem, Johnson proposed "to line the outside of the diamond, foul lines and extremes of the outfields with electric lights placed beneath the ground and projecting, by means of powerful reflectors, the rays upward through covering-plates of corrugated glass."[14]

Johnson was one of the first to recognize that the engineering of lamp positioning was as important as the volume of the artificial light itself, if not more important. Because the solution was much more complex than merely improving upon the lighting used in past experiments, Wiman ditched the idea of conducting night baseball at the St. George Grounds. Johnson's more lasting contribution to electrical history was his association with the first known electrically lighted Christmas tree.

During the late summer of 1888, John Brush, president of the Indianapolis club in the National League, sought to conduct night baseball at the Indianapolis ball grounds "with the grounds illuminated by natural gas." Brush apparently was sympathetic to the local gas company, which had controlled the public street lighting in Indianapolis until

July 1888 when the Brush Electric Company (headed by Charles Brush, no relation to John Brush) obtained a contract from the city for its arc lamps to replace the existing gas lights in the central business district. John Brush hoped to demonstrate that gas lighting was better than arc lighting, to dispel the prevailing notion that arc lighting was an improvement over gas.[15]

After a preliminary test of a few gas lights at the ball grounds in mid–August, John Brush "was much pleased with the results" as the Indianapolis players "seemed to get the balls as easily as in the daytime," especially balls hit high in the air that had posed some concern in earlier night game experiments. John Brush ordered additional lights to be installed and scheduled a night game for September 1 when the Chicago club would be in town. Charles Brush likely chuckled at the assertion that gas lights would enable an athletic event to be staged with improvement over the more brilliant illumination of arc lighting.[16]

The September 1 night game never happened, as "the projected game by natural-gas light has been postponed, in as much as the lights have not been put into position." Charles Brush, the lighting expert, was correct, not John Brush, the baseball promoter. "It was quite evident that the illumination was by no means sufficient to light the grounds for playing at night," the *Indianapolis Journal* reported, adding a suggestion that "it might be well to leave the lights where they are, as the park might be rented for summer evening exhibitions of some kind."[17]

Baseball at night was thus relegated to novelty status, confined to be associated with the circus and other low-brow events conducted during evening hours under artificial light. It was a negative connotation that took decades to overcome before night baseball was considered acceptable.

By 1888 Elihu Thomson's company had adapted far better to the changing artificial lighting market than had Charles Brush's company, since its managers favored marketing and product development as the key components of its overall business strategy, rather than technical improvements in the products. In fact, Thomson–Houston Electric soon acquired Brush's company along with a number of other small competitors, including Jenney's company in Fort Wayne, Indiana. By 1890 Thomson–Houston and its acquired companies controlled two-thirds of the arc-lighting market. More importantly, Thomson–Houston had expanded rapidly within the incandescent lamp market and in 1889 aggressively entered the new market of electric railways. The electric trolley quickly became an urban necessity, as cities of all sizes sought to replace the outmoded horse-drawn streetcar system with the faster, more efficient electric trolley.[18]

The lighting industry's two largest competitors, Edison General Electric based in Schenectady, New York, and Thomson–Houston Electric based in Lynn, Massachusetts, merged in 1892 to form the General Electric Company. While Edison's company was larger than Thomson's company, the management at Thomson–Houston was vastly stronger and thus dominated the executive ranks of the merged organization.[19]

While electrical engineers at General Electric in the 1920s would ultimately create the lighting apparatus necessary to successfully stage night baseball, further attempts until then to play baseball under artificial light simply languished in futility. There were sporadic attempts during the last decade of the nineteenth century to stage night baseball games in professional leagues, in both state leagues (Spokane, Washington, in 1891 and Galveston, Texas, in 1892) as well as the recognized minor leagues (Stockton, California, in 1893 and Wilmington, Delaware, in 1896).[20]

The night game in Wilmington on July 4, 1896, is a good example of how night baseball was viewed as just a low-class curiosity, not a serious endeavor, at the end of the nineteenth century. The Wilmington team in the Atlantic League played a holiday twin bill that day with the Paterson, New Jersey, team, which attracted 4,500 spectators. The exhibition night game was the third game on the holiday card. As the *Wilmington Daily Republican* reported, "The night game was played by electric light, and while it was not a success, was an interesting exhibition. About 200 people were out [to see it]."[21]

While the writer for the *Daily Republican* might have more accurately labeled the night game a "horrifying spectacle" rather than "an interesting exhibition," the newspaper was as concerned as the minor-league baseball club about conveying a positive message that Wilmington was a good place for business activity. Civic boosterism was a major driver of minor-league baseball development in the last two decades of the nineteenth century.

Small cities in the minor leagues did not race to try to embrace night baseball, since night games did not serve the ultimate objective for the local baseball club to be a tool within a city's overall boosterism effort to enhance the city's economy through industrial growth.

◆ 3 ◆

Boosterism and Baseball

Professional baseball was played exclusively during daylight hours in the nineteenth century and the first two decades of the twentieth century. This institutionalizing of daylight baseball impacted the eventual acceptance of night baseball in the 1930s, with a different impact to the major leagues than to the minor leagues. Daylight baseball injected complacency into major-league baseball, which established a resistance to the potential for night baseball, while introducing desperation into minor-league baseball, which produced a stampede to adopt night baseball.

Professional baseball, though, first had to become economically viable. By 1882, the old model of reliance on merchants and members of the "old" middle class to fill the grandstand at major-league ballparks was less viable than it had been in the 1870s. An attendance analysis of games staged in Boston, published by the *Boston Globe*, indicated that the average game attendance of 1,000 people was comprised of just 100 people in the grandstand, with the other 900 people in the lower-priced seats. The "new" middle class was making some inroad into the weekday attendance at major-league ballparks, although largely via non-grandstand seating and on a less frequent basis, since most of these men did not have nearly the same flexibility in their work schedules as did the original preferred audience.[1]

On holiday dates during the playing season, working-class men also attended baseball games, when mills and factories were closed to provide a reprieve from their six-day workweek. "The seating capacity of the grounds was taxed to its utmost, crowds of people surging in at the several entrances," the *Chicago Inter Ocean* reported on an Independence Day game in 1881. "Almost the entire field was covered with people when the players stepped onto the field a little before 3 o'clock."[2]

In the early 1880s there were two national holidays during the baseball season, Decoration Day on May 30 (now known as Memorial Day) and Independence Day on July 4. Leagues generally divided these lucrative holiday dates evenly among the clubs in the league, so that each club had one home game and one road game on the holidays. When Labor Day, celebrated on the first Monday in September, was established in the late 1880s, holiday scheduling became more politically complicated with three holiday dates to divvy up.

Ball games on holidays normally attracted an attendance three to five times higher than the typical crowd for a weekday game. Holiday dates were lucrative for the club owners, even if many of the additional admissions came from people not within the preferred audience of middle-class businessmen. In effect, working-class attendance at holiday games helped to subsidize the mid-afternoon ball games attended by businessmen on Monday through Saturday during the workweek.

The first attempt to attract a more diverse audience to the ballpark was to schedule a morning game on a holiday date as a supplement to the normal mid-afternoon holiday game. In 1881 the Detroit and Buffalo clubs in the National League both staged morning games on Independence Day, playing the first game of the day at 10:30 as a prelude to the second game at 3:30. These morning matches were done on an ad hoc basis, by moving up the scheduled game on July 5 between the same teams. The total attendance from two games on the same date with separate admissions was viewed so favorably that in 1882 twin bills were played by a few National League clubs on Decoration Day and by all eight clubs on Independence Day. For the 1883 season the National League and the competing American Association both arranged their schedules to pre-plan twin bills on the two holidays.[3]

Holiday twin bills, a staple of league scheduling for the next several decades, became the first component of a constantly evolving day-of-game mix, which drove a club's controllable attendance potential and thus consequently the club's success, whether via profit or boosterism measures. This day-of-game mix helps to explain the economic viability of ball clubs at both the major-league and minor-league levels.

In the National League during the 1880s, the first iteration of the day-of-game mix was two-fold: (1) weekday games on Monday through Saturday and (2) holiday twin bills. Sunday baseball was prohibited by the league constitution, as it was perceived to be anathema to the desired audience. There could be a small inherent variation in attendance during the six weekdays, since a Saturday half-holiday during the summer months in many cities would swell ballpark attendance on that day and Ladies Day promotions would elevate attendance on those selected dates. Neither was large enough to warrant isolation as a separate factor in the day-of-game mix for this era.

Daylight baseball in the afternoon on weekdays became institutionalized within professional baseball during the 1880s. This may seem obvious, since there was no other reasonable time to stage ball games other than in the mid-afternoon. Certainly, night baseball was not remotely viable given the electrical technology available in the nineteenth century. However, later afternoon start times could have been explored, although this alternative would come at the expense of disrupting dinner time and thus likely alienating the preferred business audience.

Daylight baseball became an institution not because it was particularly lucrative, but because it attracted the type of spectator that club owners wanted to have associated with their club, to earn the civic respect of the city's business community. In this way, club owners accepted lower profit potential for greater boosterism impact. Profit potential in the early 1880s was not especially significant in the initial iteration of the day-of-game mix. It was challenging to earn money from six weekdays of similar-sized crowds from the business community, which was only augmented by larger crowds on a holiday. A championship-caliber baseball team, or at least a winning team that had a chance to win the pennant, was required to attract larger audiences at the ballpark. For decades, the rule of thumb in professional baseball was that a team's winning percentage directly related to the profit potential of a ball club.

While boosterism had been a positive factor in the development of professional baseball during the 1870s, the reality was that it had merely maintained the existence of a league, not necessarily made its clubs profitable. During the mid–1880s profitability became a more paramount factor in the operation of a ball club. In general, for the next several decades, the major and minor leagues began to diverge in their application of the civic/profit business basis, with the major leagues leaning toward profit, while the minor leagues leaned to civic boosterism. In this manner, an overbalance toward booster-ism became a negative factor in determining the respect accorded a league within the universe of professional baseball.

During the three years from 1883 to 1885, a broad outline developed of a multi-tier hierarchy of professional base-ball leagues, which coalesced further in the 1890s and solidified by 1903. It was not sim-ply a bifurcation between the more-talented major leagues at the top of the hierarchy and the less-talented minor leagues at the bot-tom. There were multiple tiers based on the balance that ball clubs strove for in the civic/profit business basis. The larger the booster-ism component, the lower was a league's stat-ure in the hierarchy; vice versa, the larger the profit component, the higher the ranking.

For the 1883 season, the National Agreement developed in the aftermath of William Hulbert's death established two major leagues (National League and Amer-ican Association) and one minor league (Northwestern League). There were 16 com-bined ball clubs in the two major leagues, representing 14 different cities (New York City and Philadelphia had clubs in both leagues). Seven of these cities were in the top-10 of population in the 1880 federal cen-sus (all except Brooklyn, New Orleans, and San Francisco), while six other cities made it into the top-20. The smallest major-league city was Columbus, Ohio, at number 33 on the population list. Among the eight clubs in the Northwestern League, the Toledo, Ohio, club was the most populous city, at number 35; all other league cities had a population outside the top-50, including Quincy, Illi-nois, and Fort Wayne, Indiana, the two cities involved in the 1883 night baseball experi-ment, at number 73 and 74, respectively.

The success of the local minor-league ball club was viewed as a barometer of a city's economic growth prospects in the 1880s. Posters were displayed to encourage busi-nessmen to attend the ball games, which began mid-afternoon, as indicated at the bottom of this 1885 poster for a New England League game (Library of Con-gress, Prints & Photographs Division, LC-DIG-pga-08978).

There was a flurry of activity in 1884 for cities to be recognized as having a major-league ball club to promote not only the city's quest for baseball stature but more importantly to help boost the city's image to improve its overall economic growth prospects. At the beginning of the 1884 baseball season, there were 28 different ball clubs in three major leagues, with the addition of the Union Association as a third major league and the expansion of the American Association to a dozen clubs. However, there were just five new cities represented in the major leagues: Brooklyn, Toledo, Indianapolis, and Washington in the American Association and Altoona, Pennsylvania, in the Union Association. Five other cities abandoned their minor leagues to become midseason replacement clubs at the major-league level: Richmond, Virginia, in the American Association and Milwaukee, St. Paul, Kansas City, and Wilmington, Delaware, in the Union Association.

Clearly, there were far too many cities competing for major-league recognition. This situation immediately sorted itself out during the 1885 baseball season with the demise of the Union Association and the contraction of the American Association back to eight clubs. Major-league status was now accorded only to the 13 cities with a ball club in one of the two major leagues (New York, Philadelphia, and St. Louis each had a club in both leagues), to form the top tier of the baseball hierarchy. At the next lower level were regional minor leagues that represented three large geographic sections of the country: Eastern League, Western League, and Southern League. At the lowest level were the single-state minor leagues such as the New York State League.

This three-tier structure was the basic architecture of professional baseball for the rest of the nineteenth century, with a few slight adjustments before the 1892 merger of the National League and American Association. Prior to that merger, the major-league level was in practicality sub-divided into two spheres, the high-brow National League with its more esteemed Sabbatarian audience and the low-brow American Association that attracted a lower-income audience with its less respectable policies of Sunday games, 25-cent admission, and beer sales at the ballpark.

The American Association was more similar to the emerging minor leagues in the middle tier of the baseball hierarchy of 1885, where several ball clubs staged Sunday homes games and nearly all clubs participated in them on the road. Both tiers deployed a modification of the day-of-game mix used in the National League, which included a Sunday factor to augment the holiday and weekday components. An analysis of ticket-sale data for 1886 to 1888 in Cincinnati, which has survived to the present day, indicates that the Sunday attendance was about triple the size of the average weekday crowd. However, since the sales pattern on Sunday among the three sections of the ballpark was very similar to the percentages on a weekday, the small difference in lower grandstand sales and higher bleacher sales "is hardly indicative of a massive influx of working-class fans attending their only game of the week." Despite a preponderance of white-collar workers at the ballpark on a Sunday, the National League still did not partake in Sunday baseball.[4]

In the National League there were several new ballpark facilities built in the 1880s, which exemplified the profit leaning of major-league clubs, as new ballparks were constructed in Chicago (1883), Philadelphia (1887), Boston (1888), and New York (1889) to accommodate the crowds seeking to watch afternoon baseball. "There was a greater shift toward special semi-permanent structures, which cost more and were significantly larger and more complex than their predecessors with amenities such as small manual scoreboards, clubhouses, betting areas, ladies sections, grandstand seating, and some limited luxury accommodations." In the few surviving photographs of these new ballparks, the desired audience of local businessmen is quite evident, as the spectators seated in the grandstand section are virtually all men dressed in business attire of hat, coat, and tie.[5]

The new ballparks often came with a special section for newspaper writers, perhaps the most important of the improvements beside the additional seating capacity. Typically, there had been only brief coverage of a team's games in the Republican newspapers of a city, such as the *Boston Herald* or *Chicago Tribune*, which were targeted to an audience of businessmen. With the introduction of the specialized sports section at the *New York World*, Democratic newspapers took a greater interest in covering sports, leading more central and lower middle-class men to become baseball enthusiasts. The rise of weekly baseball publications in the 1880s also encouraged the development of a more diversified audience, such as *Sporting Life* (1883) and *The Sporting News* (1886) and in New York City the short-lived *Sporting Times* (1888).

Following the successful introduction of indoor incandescent lighting in 1883 by Thomas Edison's electric company, boosterism was rampant in cities during the last two decades of the nineteenth century. With the level of the nation's population living in urban areas crossing the 28 percent threshold in 1880 on its way to 39 percent in 1900, cities competed to be the most progressive in the use of electricity so that they could attract new industry for economic growth and make life easier for residents. "The market for electric light grew in part because Americans embraced the idea that their town's standing on the great ladder of civilization could be measured by its ability to provide residents with the latest technological conveniences," Ernest Freeberg argued in his book *The Age of Edison: Electric Light and the Invention of Modern America*. "Each time one town or city unveiled the light, boosters in neighboring municipalities felt the sting of inferiority and fretted that their town might be doomed to bring up the rear of history's march."[6]

Having electric light was one thing; using it to attract new industry was another matter. "Urban growth was spurred by an open competition among promoters interested in achieving regional domination for their city," William Flanagan wrote in his book *Urban Sociology: Images and Structure*. "The competition stemmed from the recognition that a city's economic prosperity was tied to the relative importance that could be achieved for the city within the developing national system of inter-metropolitan dominance and subordination." The competition spanned different sized regions, from large multi-state ones to small slices of a single state, creating a good fit to the emerging hierarchy of minor-league baseball.[7]

Baseball was part of the boosterism strategy, which kept alive the civic element in the civic/profit business basis pursued by professional baseball clubs. "Any leading late-nineteenth-century metropolis was expected to have such cultural institutions as art museums, symphonies, and universities, as well as public parks and major-league baseball teams," Steven Riess observed in his book *Sport in Industrial America*. Boosterism, though, was most potent at the minor-league level.[8]

"There were contests between New York City and competing metropolitan centers, between these giants and their regional rivals, and between warring factions within each center," Blake McKelvey wrote in his book *The Urbanization of America*. In comparison to the diversified economies of large cities with ball clubs in the major leagues, regional cities often specialized in a single industry, such as Minneapolis in the milling of wheat, Kansas City in meat packing, and Milwaukee in brewing, which "strengthened their positions by developing accessory industries and by extending urban economic services to a hinterland which they constantly endeavored to expand." This enabled the minor-league ball clubs in these three cities to maintain a strong position for decades, first in the Western League and then in the American Association, to the effect of even incorporating the industries into club nicknames, such as Milwaukee Brewers and Minneapolis Millers. Interestingly, from a night baseball perspective, the New York State League had a franchise known as the Schenectady Electricians, based on the location there of a large plant of the General Electric Company.[9]

Urban economic rivalries predated baseball rivalries. "Rivalry among competing urban centers for transportation and for commercial and manufacturing enterprises constituted a central theme of American urban history," historian Charles Glaab concluded. Geographic advantages such as river access or proximity to natural resources was no longer enough, as promotional savvy now ruled the day. "The character of promotional activity [by organized private groups] within aspiring urban centers was frequently influential in determining which community became a successful urban enterprise and which remained a failure." Fear of failure was a great motivator in those times, which fostered the passion for businessmen to root for the local minor-league ball club that served as a proxy for their city's future growth.[10]

This rivalry made strange bedfellows for many minor-league ball clubs, which competed against the other clubs in the league for supremacy in civic boosterism, yet still needed those cities to remain viable economically to keep the league in business. "Minor-league baseball teams are, in part, business organizations (they must make a profit for continued existence) and, in part, cultural and leisure institutions (they embody general cultural values and symbols, provide entertainment, and have consumers, namely, fans)," Kenneth Land wrote in his paper "Organizing the Boys of Summer: The Evolution of Minor-League Baseball, 1883–1990." In his paper, Land discussed a "structured mutualism" concept that summarizes the conflict inherent in many minor leagues of the era. "Minor-league baseball teams cannot be successful unless they have other existing minor-league teams to play. There is an intrinsic structural force that impels teams to cooperate with other teams within a league," not just defeat them on the playing field and possibly put them out of business. This situation differed from the usual competitive nature of an industry, in which "one firm may profit from the demise of another through increased sales."[11]

By the 1890 season four ball clubs had transferred from the American Association to the National League (Pittsburgh in 1887, Cleveland in 1889, and Brooklyn and Cincinnati in 1890) to establish seven-eighths of the National League's long-term future as an eight-club major league that would not have a franchise change during the first half of the twentieth century (St. Louis would eventually replace Cleveland in that lineup). After the American Association tried to muddle through with replacement clubs in minor-league outposts such as Syracuse and Rochester, New York, the league opted to merge into the National League after the 1891 season, with four of its eight clubs transferring to the National League.

For the 1892 season, the 12-club National League was the sole major league at the top tier of the baseball hierarchy. These dozen clubs could focus on profit and have less consideration for civic boosterism. Eleven of the 12 cities were in the top-15 of population in the 1890 federal census, with Louisville the smallest city at number 20 in population. The National League was well on its way to having a "great city" lineup of ball clubs, paving the way for the major leagues, as the top tier of the baseball hierarchy, to unquestionably contain the best ball clubs as well as represent the largest cities in the nation.

Following the merger, the National League authorized Sunday baseball where legal, which introduced a third component to its day-of-game mix that had previously been comprised of just holiday and weekday games. In 1893 there were a dozen clubs in the high minor leagues that staged Sunday games, compared to just four major-league clubs, a pattern that would persist for the next four decades. Eight of the 12 major-league clubs played Sunday games of some fashion, with four clubs playing Sunday both at home and on the road and four clubs playing only road games on Sunday. Of the four clubs abstaining from Sunday baseball, two adopted Sunday play on the road in 1898 (New York and Pittsburgh) and the other two did so in 1903 (Boston and Philadelphia).[12]

Advancements in electricity first directly impacted professional baseball in 1889 with the introduction of the electric trolley, which quickly replaced horse-powered streetcars that had dominated the urban transportation scene. The electric trolley made it easier for businessmen to travel from the central business district to the ballpark. On the down side, the electric trolley also facilitated the creation of the suburbs, where many businessmen soon moved to, which reduced ballpark patronage by making the trek home too long of a trip to do often during the playing season.

The success of the National League encouraged the emergence of minor leagues to attempt to emulate similar status on a regional basis. During the 1890s, though, the lower two tiers of the baseball hierarchy were less robust, with a half dozen minor leagues struggling to survive. The three big regional leagues comprised the middle tier, while the lower tier consisted of a few single-state and bi-state (small regional) leagues. All minor leagues in the nineteenth century were founded on, and many were slave to, civic

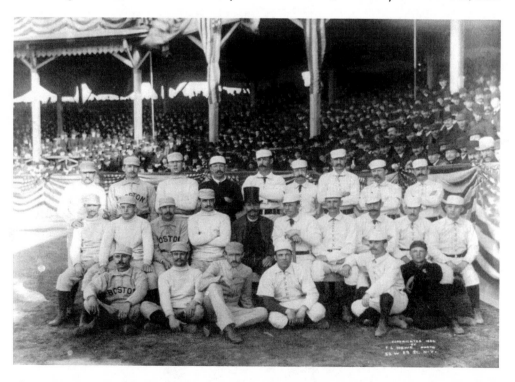

The predominant audience of businessmen is demonstrated by this rare photograph showing the spectators in the grandstand in 1886 at the Polo Grounds in New York City. In the foreground are players of the New York Giants team (right) and the Boston team (left) (Library of Congress, Prints & Photographs Division, LC-DIG-ds-11798).

boosterism, where the city's ball club was an integral component of the city's hopes to be viewed as a modern urban society.

Businessmen in Seattle, Washington, believed that "their claim to being an important city" in their economic battle with the nearby city of Tacoma "relied in part on its support for and the quality of its baseball enterprise." Atlanta newspaperman Henry Grady used the pages of the *Atlanta Constitution* to become "the herald of the New South" in post–Reconstruction years, where "the Southern League provided a material example of the South's progressive nature." Grady sought to shape Atlanta into a thriving city by attracting investment and encouraging workers to immigrate there from the North.[13]

While the confluence of baseball and boosterism could work out well, as it did in Seattle and Atlanta, success required that investors in a ball club finance the enterprise "not for their own personal profit, but for the advertising and entertainment value to the city," since few ball clubs in the minor leagues "returned sufficient profit to justify the exorbitant sums of money invested in baseball." For example, the wealthier backers of the minor-league club in Williamsport, Pennsylvania, "donated land for playing fields, financed players' salaries, underwrote baseball operations, and often absorbed gate losses in times of economic downturn."[14]

Boosterism without sufficient backers often was a recipe for financial disaster. In 1891 a group of businessmen in Lowell, Massachusetts, formed a ball club in the New England League because they wanted to position the city as "no longer a mere workshop and an adjunct to Boston." They saw the club as a form of "advertising the city" and thus "bolstering the region's view of the city." However, rather than sell stock in the ball club, they financed the team only by ticket sales. By the Independence Day holiday the club was losing significant money. The real bad news was that "the nine weeks between Independence Day and Labor Day in 1891 represented an interminable period for a shaky minor league ball club to survive in the 19th century." Alas, the Lowell club went out of business in late July. The *Lowell Daily News* accurately opined that "the one plain and unvarnished conclusion that can be drawn from this year's experience is that baseball in New England is a very poor money making business." It wasn't all that good for boosterism either.[15]

It was not unusual for minor-league clubs to seek a bailout from local businessmen to keep afloat a baseball enterprise to support their booster efforts. "There has been a mass meeting called for Friday night in the city hall to see if the businessmen and merchants care to continue having a baseball club," a Wichita, Kansas, newspaper reported in 1898. To develop support for the local ball club, the newspaper noted that 100 businessmen in the rival city of Topeka had each pledged $5 per month to keep that ball club operating. As further incentive, the newspaper exhorted that "Wichita certainly won't be behind Topeka." Alas, the Wichita ball club soon went out of business.[16]

Although night baseball was still decades into the future, this focus on boosterism in the minor leagues during the 1890s was a set-up for the shaky financial foundations that existed at many minor-league clubs in the twentieth century. This created a more immediate demand for a diversified day-of-game strategy in the minors than was employed at the major-league level. Sunday baseball in the minor leagues in the 1890s was vital to the boosterism effort. As early as 1887 New Orleans in the Southern League staged Sunday twin bills, with separate morning and afternoon games. Sunday-hosting clubs in the Western League engaged in similar scheduling of doubleheaders to maximize attendance on the one day during the workweek that the working class could attend a ball game.[17]

The three regional minor leagues that covered a broad geographic area (Eastern, Western, and Southern Leagues) could better survive the perils of the civic/profit business basis that was largely inherent in minor-league baseball. For minor leagues that operated in more constrained geographic areas, the civic/profit balancing act was more precarious, even before considering the shady characters that all-too-often embezzled funds to contribute to minor-league ball's negative, fly-by-night image.[18]

The majority of minor leagues that operated in the 1890s were single-state leagues, stocked with ball clubs that had evolved from their roots as a town team, which were clearly boosterism oriented. "In many towns, the local baseball team was an important source of community pride and unity," Mark Eberle observed in his book *Kansas Baseball, 1858–1941*, "perhaps even a surrogate for the competition among towns vying for advantages in economic growth and prosperity." In Kansas in the 1890s, the fervor for town teams elevated into professional teams and propelled the creation of the Kansas State League.[19]

While some single-state leagues, like the Kansas State League, subscribed to the National Agreement and thus were official minor leagues, many other organized single-state leagues decided to forego the umbrella of the National Agreement. A significant reason for these defections was to avoid paying for a bond to guarantee payment of player salaries, the most tangible benefit for a ball club (to recruit better ballplayers) to be part of the National Agreement beyond the avowed respect by major-league clubs for the minor-league club's rights in player contracts. Obviously, the economic pressure within the civic/profit business basis was a major factor in staying outside of the National Agreement. There were far more non-signatory single-state leagues than signers before the turn of the twentieth century.[20]

Many of the best minor-league ball clubs barely broke even. For example, the Cortland club in the New York State League finished in second place in the 1900 season, edged out for the championship by only a two-game margin. Yet the club only made a $39 profit on $11,661 of total revenue. Midway through the 1901 season, the backers of the Cortland club gave up and transferred the club to another city where investors there hoped to more successfully execute the profit-boosterism balance.[21]

Within the larger cities of the nation, civic boosterism had run its latest course by the beginning of the twentieth century, since the competition for regional dominance in certain industries had sorted out the winners and losers. "By the end of the nineteenth century, all of the major American cities were busy widening their tributaries and extending their zones of influence," according to city-planning historian John Thomas. While the composition of the regional minor leagues had settled upon certain large cities, a flurry of boosterism activity continued among smaller cities for recognition and ranking within the emerging economic hierarchy of "tributary" cities and consequently sub-regional or single-state minor leagues.[22]

For tributary cities, though, boosterism had changed, moving from the efforts of an ad hoc group of businessmen to the control of a formalized board of trade or chamber of commerce, which often had close ties to local political officials. These groups used more subtle tactics to encourage urban development and were more amenable to a balance of business and social improvements than the earlier incarnation of civic promoters.[23]

This change in promotional strategy was a natural outgrowth of the general move of the urban economy "from civic capitalism, or entrepreneurial individualism, to bureaucratic corporatism, or national capitalism, [which] began in the late nineteenth century ... and engulfed the United States in the first half of the twentieth century." The transition from civic to national capitalism radically altered a city, including its relationship to the ball club, as "national capitalism with its home offices and stockholders and managers and self-generating finances eclipsed civic capitalism's local entrepreneurs."[24]

The measure of a city, which boosterism hoped to impact, now swerved from industrial might to that of electric light, with that prowess in electricity displayed wisely in the central business district as well as in residential neighborhoods. "Electricity was coming of age, no longer a curiosity, but a mass commodity, delivered by a sophisticated and heavily capitalized industry," Freeberg wrote in *The Age of Edison*. "Boosters pointed with pride to their town's new 'white way,'" where "rows of bright lamps neatly lining their Main Street served as a visual symbol of the town's progressive spirit, its participation in the era's embrace of urban improvement." The centerpiece of the well-lit "white way" was street lighting that was "not only functional but appealed to the senses of beauty, harmony, and art."[25]

Electricity slowly reshaped public perception of the evening hours in the city. "The electric street lights had gone a long way toward purging 'nightlife' of its aura of licentiousness," one amusement historian has noted, since the presumption was that "the electric street lamps were removing much of the danger that had lurked in the dark." Still, at the turn of the century, there was little competition from entertainment or sporting activities in the evening that made daylight baseball seem out-of-place or might stimulate ball clubs to consider ways to conduct their games at night. Most outdoor entertainment was considered low brow, such as the traveling circus, or at least suspect, such as amusement parks like Coney Island in New York City that sprouted at the end of electric trolley lines. Indoor entertainment such as vaudeville theaters offered "something for everybody" programs, which many people found tawdry if not akin to the devil's workshop.[26]

There were few other professional team sports that played games during the evening hours. Basketball was played in dimly lit YMCA gymnasiums and militia armories, while ice hockey was played in expensive, specially built facilities such as the St. Nicholas Rink in New York City. One professional team sport that did experience some spectator popularity when played indoors at night under artificial light was roller polo. Now a long-forgotten sport, roller polo was a hockey-like game played on roller skates that involved seven-man teams of men hitting a ball with a stick along the floor into a goal. Games were staged in roller-skating rinks, where typically open skating was held from 7:00 to 9:00 followed by a one-hour polo match. "On nights when polo is played, the rinks are crowded, not only with skaters, but with people who go only to see the game," one sports historian noted. Given roller polo's blend of skill and speed with blood and violence, though, professional baseball had little interest in this spectator base, even if it could overcome the technical challenge of effective artificial lighting at the ballpark.[27]

After the National League contracted to eight clubs for the 1900 season, its seven cities (Brooklyn having been absorbed into New York City in 1898) were all ranked in the top-12 of population in the 1900 federal census. Pittsburgh was its smallest city, at number 11. Three of the four cities dropped by the league (Baltimore, Cleveland, and Washington) found their way into the nouveau American League, which became a major league for the 1901 season. The fourth, Louisville, dropped into the minor leagues.

The major-league American League grew from the Western League, one of the three regional minor leagues, which had experienced a dramatic three-year transformation under the leadership of Ban Johnson. In 1898 all clubs in the league were in Midwestern cities. In 1899 the league added Buffalo, New York, and in 1900 added clubs in Chicago and Cleveland. The league changed its name to the American League for the 1900 season, signaling its intention to soon compete with the National League, which it did in 1901. Detroit and Milwaukee were the only survivors from the 1898 season; the Baltimore and Washington castoffs from the National League joined the American League in 1901 along with clubs in Boston and Philadelphia. By 1903 Baltimore and Milwaukee had been replaced by New York City and St. Louis, respectively, to form the eight-city lineup that the American League would maintain uninterrupted for five decades.

When peace was achieved in 1903 between the two warring major leagues, the minor-league consortium deal negotiated in September 1901 was folded into the new National Agreement, which established a formal mechanism for the ranking of leagues within the baseball hierarchy. This also formulated the last element of boosterism in the maturity of major-league baseball, which partitioned the 10 cities with a major-league club into a three-tier structure. During the next 50 years, there were no changes in these 10 cities that had major-league franchises, a remarkable period of stability.

At the top was New York City, which was a three-club city (Giants, Yankees, and Dodgers). At the next rung down were the four two-club cities (Boston, Chicago, Philadelphia, and St. Louis). Below them were the five single-club cities (Cincinnati, Cleveland, Detroit, Pittsburgh, and Washington). This three-tier structure juxtaposed perfectly with the population rankings of the ten cities in the 1900 federal census. New York City was the number 1 city in population, as well as the acknowledged economic leader among American cities. The four two-club cities were ranked number 2 through 5 in population, while the five single-club cities were ranked within the banding of numbers 7 to 15. All 10 major-league cities had populations within the 15 most populous cities in the nation.

In the five cities with multiple ball clubs, there was a baseball game nearly every day of the playing season, because the two major leagues integrated their schedules to avoid, as much as possible, the conflict of having two teams with home games on the same date. In multi-club cities, there was a ball game nearly every day of the workweek, providing a plethora of opportunity for businessmen to watch a ball game without having to make a patronage choice between the ball clubs.

In the minor leagues, there were four classification levels, Class A to Class D, based on the population of league cities. The classification system tied right into the boosterism motivation behind the original formation of minor-league clubs. Indeed, the classification system fueled growth of new minor leagues, movement of leagues within classes, and movement of clubs among leagues, as cities sought to have a ball club that provided the highest reflection of the city's perceived progressive character. "A city was not viewed as much of an urban area unless it had a professional team," Steven Riess wrote in his book *Touching Base: Professional Baseball and American Culture in the Progressive Era.* "The club should be in the best possible league since that was a sign that the city was progressive and growing. But if the team was in an association that included smaller cities, then the town might be regarded as stagnant."[28]

The Class A leagues, originally the Eastern League, American Association, Southern Association, Western League, and Pacific Coast League, were regional leagues that tried to emulate major-league baseball in its business mix of profit and boosterism. Class B leagues were sub-regional or multi-state leagues, like the New England League or the Central League, where boosterism and profit were generally evenly balanced. The Class C and D leagues were single-state and sub-state leagues, where boosterism was primary.

Because cities now needed to be in a recognized minor league to be seen as relevant, the minor leagues rapidly expanded from 21 leagues in 1903 to 34 in 1905 to 52 in 1910, according to data in *The Encyclopedia of Minor League Baseball*.

Warning signs for the future of night baseball were on the horizon, though, in major-league baseball. The first objective of the preamble to the 1903 National Agreement called for the "perpetuation of baseball as the national pastime of America, by surrounding it with such safeguards as will warrant absolute public confidence in its integrity and methods." This opening statement of the philosophy of professional baseball led to entrenched positions relating to the sanctity of the regular season to determine a champion and the special nature of daylight baseball, a diversion largely available only to the businessman with time flexibility to attend an afternoon ball game during the six-day workweek. This re-enforced that the sport was a unique, special product, not entertainment but rather a status symbol, available to a favored audience. This hubris delayed the eventual embrace of night baseball by major-league baseball.[29]

The World Series, which matched the champions of the National League and American League, exemplified this fixation with daylight baseball. After becoming a fixture of major-league baseball in 1905 (following the 1903 experiment with an inter-league series), the World Series continued to be played entirely in daylight games through 1970, long after night baseball represented more than one-half of the baseball games played during the regular season.

League champions were the ball clubs with the highest winning percentage over the course of the regular season, a standard established back in the 1880s. The best-record format became firmly entrenched in major-league baseball's mindset as club owners sought to emulate the winner-take-all nature of the leading industrialists of the Gilded Age, John D. Rockefeller and Andrew Carnegie, who, due to their monopolies, were the recognized champions of the oil and steel industries, respectively. This Darwinian philosophy cemented the best-record format within major-league baseball for nearly a century.

By 1905 two-thirds of the Class A minor-league clubs hosted Sunday games, compared to just one-third of major-league clubs. Sunday crowds were so much larger than those for weekday games that it was becoming essential to engage in some form of Sunday baseball, even if simply on the road to gain a visitor's share of the immense gate receipts. Clubs did whatever it took to make the Sunday/holiday/weekday day-of-game mix work to the club's financial advantage to support its operation to pursue a pennant and maximize the businessmen audience for weekday games.[30]

For major-league clubs constrained by state laws and not able to stage Sunday home games, many played exhibition games at nearby minor-league sites that did permit Sunday games, such as Hoboken, New Jersey, and Bridgeport, Connecticut, outside of New York City and Providence, Rhode Island, not far from Boston. Some minor-league clubs utilized Sunday-only ballparks, including Minneapolis at the Minnehaha Driving Park, Scranton in neighboring Minooka, and Providence at the Rocky Point amusement park.[31]

Another option for Sunday baseball was the one-day road trip amidst a long homestand, which was practiced by Pittsburgh often traveling to Cincinnati for a Sunday game or Cleveland going to Chicago or St. Louis. Because Sunday baseball was so lucrative, the Providence club often engaged in this tactic, once traveling in 1907 from Rochester, New York, to Rocky Point for an exhibition game against the Chicago Cubs and returning that evening to Buffalo, New York, to resume its road trip. Neutral sites were also an option, which were used several times from 1903 to 1905 by major-league clubs at minor-league ballparks in Columbus, Ohio, and Fort Wayne, Indiana.[32]

While many major-league clubs were not overly hampered financially by a state pro-hibition on Sunday home games, minor-league clubs needed Sunday games to survive. "Sunday baseball is necessary to the success of many minor league organizations," F.C. Lane wrote in *Baseball Magazine* in 1911. "The whole existence of the minor league struc-ture is threatened and the surest way of turning ruinous deficits into profits lies in the profits of Sunday baseball. The very existence of many minor league organizations seems to depend on the inauguration of a system of Sunday games, when the largest crowds may be expected and the greatest financial returns obtained." One big problem was that many states in the South still prohibited professional Sunday baseball.[33]

While the audience for daylight afternoon ball games on weekdays was entrenched in the business community, the nature of that audience underwent substantial change during the early years of the twentieth century. Individualism as an owner-operator of a business had declined during the Industrial Revolution of the last quarter of the nine-teenth century, as large corporations (or trusts in parlance of that era) established near monopolies in many industries. "Hundreds of once-proud family firms succumbed to the blandishments or assaults of the trust-makers and disappeared into corporate ano-nymity," one historian described the upheaval of the Industrial Revolution on the once ubiquitous independent small-business owner, who had been not only a fixture of the American economic landscape but also the preferred audience at the ballpark.[34]

A mixture of middle-class men comprised the overflow crowd for the final game of the 1908 season at the Polo Grounds to watch the playoff game between the New York Giants and Chi-cago Cubs for the National League championship (Library of Congress, Prints & Photographs Division, LC-DIG-ggbain-02322).

This decline in individualism continued into the twentieth century. According to *A History of Small Business in America*, the percentage of self-employed workers steadily declined from one-third of the workforce in 1900 to just one-quarter in 1920. This produced a consequent increase in salaried and wage workers, who very often had much less flexibility to leave work to attend an afternoon ball game than did self-employed people. This was particularly bad news for the minor leagues, where many ball clubs primarily existed for civic boosterism, not necessarily to be a profit-making business.[35]

This decline in self-employed individuals was a natural outgrowth of national capitalism's industrialization of the American office that was then occurring. In his book *The Genesis of Industrial America*, Maury Klein described this change as "transforming a society of individuals into one of organizations," which possessed "hierarchical management structures and specialized departmental functions." Besides being the "harbingers of the age of bureaucracy," this transformation of employment had little "reliance on rugged individualism" that had been the foundation of self-employment. The good news was that "an enormous number of people edged their way into the middle class by serving as foot soldiers of the corporate economy in jobs that required less education and training." However, these foot soldiers could only attend ball games on Saturday or Sunday, due to the naturally shrinking corps of businessmen with the time flexibility to go to the games on Monday through Friday.[36]

The decline of individualism in corporate employment changed the nature of the American Dream. "The robber barons of the age, men like Andrew Carnegie and John D. Rockefeller, believed that their tremendous economic success was evidence that the law of competition produced the survival of the fittest through a sometimes painful but always efficient process of natural selection," Cal Jillson wrote in his book *Pursuing the American Dream*. While there still remained the possibility for a rags-to-riches rise like those of a Horatio Alger novel, Darwinian-style natural selection left the common man with "only the slimmest chance of winning against much more powerful actors."[37]

The definition of success changed from independent businessman to well-paid corporate employee, from "rugged individualism in the business world to clawing one's way up the hierarchy." Growing corporations operating in national markets required armies of office workers, managers, and salespeople. The products generated by those corporations required distribution within multiple geographic markets, which created the need for wholesalers, jobbers, and agents to deal with the increasing number of stores that sold the goods.[38]

The former entrepreneurship found in the independent businessman was still found in the small capitalism of retailing, which supplied a large segment of the "new" middle class to complement "the ascendance of clerical and managerial work" in the corporation. The "proletarianization of artisans," who became wage labor in unskilled factory jobs, were largely confined to the working class, moving down from the "old" middle class. Middle class at the turn of twentieth century was not as much the observable economic wealth and social status that had defined that ranking in the nineteenth century, but rather a "code of civility" based on the moral values of hard work and centrality of home. This created increased social mobility into the middle class via perceptions, based on "the ease of acquiring cultural codes of middle-class behavior and lifestyle, and the loose fit between affluence and the wherewithal to ape middle-class decorum in public places."[39]

By 1910 civic boosterism had advanced beyond mere business growth, as "civic and business groups across the nation began to commission City Beautiful plans," which devised park and recreational systems, municipal building complexes, and grand railroad stations all with architectural beauty. According to city-planning historian Jon Peterson, the goal now was to have "the manufacturer with his $10 million plant and 500 employees locate in the city which furnishes the greater number of attractions in the way of good schools, clear water, parks and boulevards, broad avenues, civic centers, and beautiful public buildings." Cities such as Scranton, Pennsylvania, Davenport, Iowa, and Little Rock, Arkansas, also established industrial development corporations, staffed by specialists, not local businessmen, to pursue their economic growth plans. Since "beauty became a coin of industrial rivalry" and campaigns were run by professional city planners, the local minor-league ball club soon played far less of a role in civic boosterism campaigns.[40]

With the limited supply of indoor spectator sports during evening hours in the early years of the twentieth century, and a consequent limited demand, it was not surprising that the development of safe and efficient artificial lighting failed to transfer to a rise of night baseball before World War I. There was, though, some experimentation with the lighting of ballparks to stage night baseball during the first decade of the twentieth century. Given the precarious financial situation with the Cortland, New York, minor-league club, as described earlier in this chapter, it was seemingly natural for some of the earliest night-baseball experiments to occur in Upstate New York, where many ball clubs like Cortland were anxious to stage events that could contribute to both the profit and boosterism aspects of the club's business basis.

◆ 4 ◆

Night Games
by Cahill's Arc Lights

Beyond replacing existing gas lights on streets, there was little effort exerted in the early years of the twentieth century to adequately illuminate outdoor space for sporting activities. Arc lighting, the only technologically feasible way at the time to attempt to play baseball under artificial light, had proven to be a dismal artistic failure during the 1890s. However, there were a few rudimentary signs that night baseball one day might become a viable option to supplant the daylight game.

In June 1901, following the collapse of the semipro Pennsylvania State League, Alfred W. Lawson, manager of the Easton club, set out to stage baseball at night. Lawson commissioned the American Fire Engine Company to manufacture some portable lighting equipment that could be easily transported from one city to another. The first game using Lawson's portable lights was played in Seneca Falls, New York, in August 1901. Lawson then traveled by railroad with the equipment to stage games in other small cities in eastern Pennsylvania and northern New Jersey.[1]

It would be tempting to say that Lawson recognized an untapped market to provide evening entertainment to working men, who normally could not attend baseball games in the afternoon like the businessmen that he had tried to attract to Pennsylvania State League games. However, Lawson's motivation was surely to tap into the inherent boosterism exhibited by businessmen who desired to attract interest to their small city and bolster its economic future.

For one thing, the actual game exhibited under Lawson's arc lights was far different from the usual baseball game played during daylight hours. The ball used in the night game was six inches in diameter, about twice the size of a regular baseball, and much softer. There was "no lightning speed" of pitches and "no heavy hitting" due to the use of a lighter bat. Only part of the diamond was utilized. "The scheme is to have about twenty arc lights arranged around the field close in toward the diamond," one writer explained the setup. "The infielders play in close around the pitcher and the outfielders [are] where the infielders usually play."[2]

It is unclear how Lawson, an inveterate entrepreneur and promoter, came upon the idea that night baseball could be a profit-making venture. One distinct possibility is communication that Lawson had with his former associates in the Central League from the 1900 season, where Lawson had been the manager of the Peoria, Illinois, club. After the Central League disbanded in early September, the Decatur and Bloomington clubs played a postseason series, which included a night game using portable lights on September 12 in Decatur.[3]

Lawson continued the portable lighting experiment during the 1902 season, when he was manager of the Scranton club in the revived Pennsylvania State League. He started promoting the idea before the baseball season began. The *Scranton Tribune* reported that "Manager Lawson is the owner of a $6,000 portable electric light plant, which includes dynamo, lamps, poles, and all the other appliances for illuminating a field."[4]

The first use of the lighting plant in 1902 came on May 14 when Scranton played a night game against Lancaster. With 2,000 spectators in attendance, Scranton defeated Lancaster, 8 to 6, as the *Tribune* reported that "extra powerful arc lights, on twenty-foot poles, at short intervals, surrounding the playing space of the field, made the diamond, not as bright as mid-day to be sure, but bright enough to make the ball playing possible." A more sobering account appeared in the *Scranton Times*, which reported that the game was "a farce comedy" played in "murky darkness." Given that there were "eighteen arc lamps, having a total of 3,600 candlepower," the *Times* had the more accurate depiction of the illumination power.[5]

A few days later Lawson's portable lighting system, with "sixteen arc lights, gerry-rigged around the perimeter of the infield," was used in Williamsport, Pennsylvania, although "the game was not a howling success," according to the *Williamsport Gazette & Bulletin*. "The exhibition quickly degenerated into a comic spectacle when fielders careened into poles and lost fly balls that went beyond the range of the lights."[6]

In early June, Lawson demonstrated his portable lights in ballparks of the New York State League, a Class B minor league. The game on June 9 in Binghamton against the Amsterdam–Johnstown–Gloversville team was reported nationwide through the Associated Press wire service. "The electric lights did not work as well as expected," the AP report glumly noted. "While the infield was fairly lighted, it was impossible to judge a fly that went above the lights or into the outfield." The next day the system of the Lawson Portable Electric Light Company was used in Ilion, New York, for a game against Utica. Lawson's night baseball experiment soon fizzled out, though, and he sold his portable system to a traveling circus.[7]

Formerly an itinerant ballplayer who played for numerous minor-league clubs (and a short three-game stint in the National League in 1890), Lawson was "an adept innovator of baseball economics, promotion, and marketing." He was best known for organizing and promoting the Union League in 1908, a formative, though pretender to become, third major league. After that venture, Lawson turned his attention to promoting the nascent industry of commercial aviation, where he more successfully envisioned commercial airlines to fly passengers as a replacement for independent operators of aircraft.[8]

Lawson's most lasting impact on night baseball was having his idea adopted around 1905 by two Native-American traveling baseball teams. The Nebraska Indians team, which barnstormed the Midwest under the management of Guy Green, had many talented players, but also entertained fans "with a combination of Wild West showmanship and zany baseball antics." The Cherokee Indians team, headquartered in Michigan but traveling extensively along the East Coast, was managed by John Olsen, also an entertainment-oriented promoter who considered himself "both a baseball man and a circus man." Both teams transported themselves and their portable lighting equipment by railroad, while also carrying a portable grandstand and fencing.[9]

Both Native-American teams played the same game as previously demonstrated under Lawson's lights, using a ball that was larger than a regular baseball and made of soft material coated with glistening white enamel. While Alfred Lawson had been selling outdoor lighting to help businessmen boost their city's economic growth prospects, the Native-American teams were selling working-class entertainment, similar to basketball and roller polo that were played indoor under lights at night.

In the summer of 1907, the Cherokee team made an extensive trip throughout New England to play night games in minor-league ballparks and on September 11 made one appearance in a major-league park. "The first game of baseball ever played in Boston after dark" was staged under 20 arc lights hung on poles at the Huntington Avenue Grounds used by the Boston American League team, where 1,000 people saw the local Dorchester town team defeat the Cherokee team.[10]

Night baseball as a funny novelty act created an immense negative image, however, which stayed lodged in the minds of baseball fans and ball-club owners for many years. This was one reason that excessively delayed the introduction of night baseball at the major-league level. It didn't help that newspaper headlines such as "Baseball by Electric Light" focused on the electrical component rather than the audience-focused evening component to night baseball.

Those attitudes shifted a bit in August 1908. A wire service report published in newspapers across the country (one headlined "To Try Baseball at Night") announced the expected trial of night baseball in Cincinnati, using an idea devised by inventor George F. Cahill of New York City. "Cahill has devised a lighting system which he believes will flood a ball park with sufficient artificial light to make is possible for games to be played at night as well as by day," the wire report stated. "The proposition has progressed so far that President Herrmann will be ready to test it within a few weeks at the Cincinnati ball park." The lighting scheme was said to "revolutionize baseball and enable clubs to play to larger crowds than at present, when many fans cannot get away from their daily round of work to attend the games."[11]

Francis Richter, editor of the weekly *Sporting Life* publication, was the behind-the-scenes matchmaker between August Herrmann, the owner of the Cincinnati ball club, and Cahill, an inventor. Richter wanted to democratize the audience for professional baseball, since the daylight game Monday to Saturday leaned heavily toward businessmen. With the availability of night games, baseball fans would no longer be docked a half day's pay for sneaking out to the ballpark to take in an afternoon game.

Cahill was the one person at this juncture who was seriously interested in the science of playing baseball under artificial light. In March 1904 he was granted patent number 755,447 by the United States Patent Office regarding a "System for Illuminating Fields So That Games May Be Played at Night." Unfortunately, Herrmann and other lords of baseball were just using Cahill to make money through non-baseball ventures conducted in the evening at their ballparks under artificial light. The Night Baseball Development Company that Herrmann established to invest in Cahill's patented approach to lighting a baseball field was the forerunner to a broader strategy that several ball-club owners implemented two years later.

As Cahill described the process in his patent application, "My invention relates to the illuminating of a field or area, so that base-ball and other games may be played at night; and the object of my invention is to render it possible to play such games at night in substantially the same manner as they are played in daylight and to make it convenient and enjoyable for spectators to watch the playing of the game." In order to accomplish these goals, Cahill specified three necessary factors: "First, that a powerful light or lights be thrown upon the field and players; second, that the space above the field for a

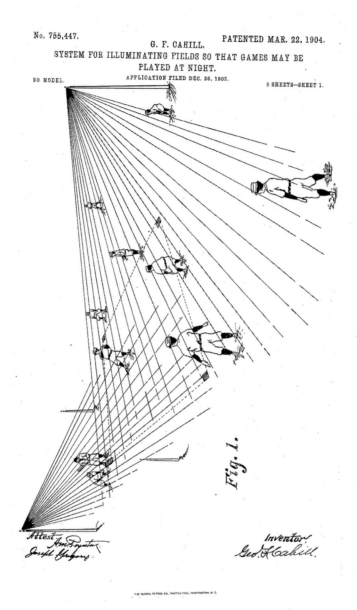

George F. Cahill was the one person at the turn of the twentieth century who was seriously interested in the science of playing baseball under artificial light. In March 1904 the United States Patent Office granted Cahill a patent for his lighting system, which was illustrated by this schematic in his patent application.

considerable distance into the air where batted balls may pass be brightly illuminated; and, third, that so far as possible the eyes of the players be screened or shaded from the glare of the powerful light or lights before mentioned."[12]

The idea of playing baseball at night first came to Cahill during the early 1890s when he was playing baseball at Oberlin College. "One afternoon in my college days, as a number of us were going home from the ball field, we passed some boys about our own age working on a house," Cahill recalled in 1909 the genesis of his thinking about night baseball. "As we sauntered by, one of the boys looked up from his work and said to his companion in a half-weary, half-plaintive way, 'Wish we could play ball this afternoon.' The words and tone aroused the thought in me: Too bad those boys have to work while the rest of us are having a good time. And this in turn led to the reflection: Why can't baseball be played at night?"[13]

After his college graduation, Cahill went to work in Washington, D.C., where he attended some afternoon games played by the city's ball club in the National League. "I saw the great interest in baseball there and the multitude of people who could not get away to attend the games, and noted they were the people most interested in the sport and most in need of fresh air and recreation. Then it struck me with great force: Man does almost everything else he wants to at night, so why wouldn't it be possible to play baseball at night?"[14]

Cahill thought of using a lighted ball to play at night, but quickly discarded that thought. "Why not light the whole field brilliantly enough so that every one can see the ordinary ball? Artificial lights have been greatly strengthened and I believe I can illuminate the whole field without the light shining in anybody's eyes," he concluded. "Erect a high tower on the grandstand directly behind the catcher and batter and pour a powerful light over the space between the grandstand and the diamond, and over most of the diamond, but trained on the ground before it reaches the basemen who face that direction. Then erect another high tower in deep centerfield and pour a powerful illumination on the outfield and over most of the diamond, but trained to the ground before it reaches batter and catcher, who face that direction. Thus every player will occupy a position lighted from above and behind him, while the light in front of him is trained to the ground before it reaches him, so he is not dazzled by its powerful rays."[15]

Cahill was effectively one of the first lighting engineers, who could skillfully direct the light emitted from several lamps to illuminate an object. As it turned out, Cahill's 1904 patent was just the first step toward solving the difficult puzzle of how to adequately illuminate a baseball field. Cahill realized it was not merely as simple as putting up lights around the field, but he underestimated the challenge of determining an appropriate illumination pattern, which was a process far more complex than he initially imagined.

It was four years before Cahill acted to implement his patent, though. He was sidetracked by a bigger project he was working on with his brother Thaddeus, to develop electric music (what we know today as a music synthesizer) into a commercially viable product. They called their invention the Telharmonium, an extremely large instrument with "complex tones such as musical instruments produced directly from electrical dynamos" that could "send music anywhere electricity could be transported," especially "over a network of telephone lines." The two brothers perfected a version of the Telharmonium in 1906, but their company foundered in 1908 when investors abandoned the project, freeing up Cahill to work on his lighting system for night baseball.[16]

While Cahill began installation of lights at the Cincinnati ballpark in September 1908, an experimental night game was postponed until the following season. Initially slated as a preseason exhibition game on April 11 between the Reds and the visiting Chicago White Sox, technical issues delayed the experimental game to June 18.

One of those technical issues was the filing of a patent application for the lighting system, since Cahill had made significant improvement to the approach detailed in his original 1904 patent. Cahill applied for a new patent on June 1, 1909, which paved the way for the June 18 exhibition night game. However, the United States Patent Office did not immediately grant approval in 1909 and Cahill had to wait eight years for its approval, which came long after professional baseball had discarded interest in his arc-lighting system.[17]

Cahill's system was to erect five towers around the ballpark, each 100-foot tall and holding two lamps, supplemented by a bank of four lamps mounted atop the grandstand, for a total of 14 lamps that produced artificial light through the principle of arc lighting. The carbons in Cahill's arc lights were enormous, one and three-eighths inches in diameter, with an estimated length of 10 inches, based on the published photo of the bell-shaped hood covering the carbons, which had a diameter that ranged from the nose to the waist of the workman standing next to it.[18]

The experimental night baseball game received coast-to-coast publicity through a wire-service article that reported "the players had no difficulty in keeping their eyes on the ball" and they "seemed to perform as well as if it had been bright daylight." However, Herrmann was more circumspect in his comments: "Night baseball has come to stay. It needs some further development, but with proper lighting conditions—better than this experiment provided—will make the sport immensely popular." Cincinnati manager Clark Griffith was even more doubtful: "I don't believe night ball is destined to rival the daylight article, but I will say I was much surprised at the ease with which the game was played under tonight." Griffith would become a consistent critic of night baseball over the next three decades, before embracing the concept in the 1940s as owner of the Washington Senators.[19]

In the next issue of *Sporting Life*, Richter heralded the night exhibition game a success with the front-page headline "Cahill Triumphant," but eventually admitted that "it will be some time before the National and American Leaguers are fighting for championships under the glare of electric lights." *The Sporting News* was downright hostile to the idea of baseball

This front page of the *Sporting Life* in June 1909 heralded the effort of George F. Cahill to light the Cincinnati ballpark for a night baseball game. Following two subsequent night baseball experiments in 1909 and 1910, the idea failed to be accepted by owners of professional baseball clubs.

not played under what it considered "natural conditions" in the daylight. "We had our first taste of night baseball last week and it can't be said that anyone has gone daffy over it," the baseball weekly commented. "The rays of the good, old sun were missing, the grass didn't take on the right hue, and you couldn't see the inside workings of the minds of the spectators."[20]

Technical issues also continued to dog Cahill. While the infield lighting seemed adequate, there were several problems with Cahill's lamps in the outfield where the lighting was not strong, often flickered, and a few times extinguished. When one batter struck a home run over the fence, the outfielders reportedly heard the crack of the bat, but never saw the ball.

More important than the technical issues with the arc lights was the revealing of Herrmann's disingenuous public motive to stage the night game, when he nixed using major-league players in the night game, opting instead to deploy teams comprised of amateur players who were members of local Elks lodges. The majority of the 5,000 spectators at the game were also from Elks lodges, who helped fund Herrmann's trip to the fraternal order's national convention where Herrmann was a candidate for a leadership position.

More troubling were the reports that the lights would be used to conduct not just night baseball but also "endurance races and outdoor meets of all kinds." In fact, since the Reds soon left for a four-week road trip, the Cincinnati ballpark was used to house a carnival. Obviously, Herrmann was more interested in the profits from these non-baseball ventures than he was in conducting professional baseball under artificial lighting, a conclusion supported by the non-existence of future night games.[21]

Cahill next took his invention to Grand Rapids, Michigan, for a July 7 experimental night game in the minor-league Central League between Grand Rapids and Zanesville, Ohio, where a hokey atmosphere overshadowed the night game sponsored by a local civic organization, which used the ball game as a fund-raising event. Cahill modified his lighting layout to add some searchlights so that fly balls could more easily be detected by the outfielders, but "the illumination was much better for the batters than the fielders," as only three fly balls were caught for an out. All in all, this night game was a dismal failure as an artistic example of baseball well played under artificial illumination.[22]

Later in July Cahill traveled to Pittsburgh to oversee the execution of his lighting system, which had been installed in the spring, for the first hippodrome night at the newly built Forbes Field. The ballpark was being used to stage vaudeville acts and concert performances during evening hours when the Pittsburgh Pirates baseball club was on the road, to generate additional revenue beyond the gate receipts for home baseball games. Theater promoter Harry Davis orchestrated the hippodrome events at Forbes Field.[23]

At least Pirates owner Barney Dreyfuss had been upfront with Cahill about the actual use of his lighting system at Forbes Field, having early on announced that "it was not the intention of the [Pirates] management to have night [baseball] games." What Cahill didn't realize at the time was that wherever his lighting system was installed the hippodrome events would not only be the primary purpose for the lighting, but also virtually the only reason for the lighting. Night baseball was not the driver of the lighting system installations.[24]

Cahill's lights would get one more chance at night baseball in 1910.

The hippodrome strategy became public in September 1909 when Davis announced his plan to strike deals with 20 ballparks to stage evening hippodrome events. By the

August Herrmann (right), owner of the Cincinnati ball club, was less interested in conducting night baseball and more interested in using artificial lighting to stage hippodrome entertainment when the Cincinnati team was on the road. Herrmann is shown here talking to concessionaire Frank Stevens (Library of Congress, Prints & Photographs Division, LC-DIG-ggbain-14970).

spring of 1910 Cincinnati Reds president Herrmann and a group of theater promoters announced the formation of company to run the hippodrome events at the various ballparks, in which "baseball parks are to be turned into moneymakers when the national game is not played on them." In addition to the parks in Cincinnati and Pittsburgh the venture was expected to soon include the American League ballpark in St. Louis and the minor-league park in Indianapolis.[25]

This hippodrome usage was ostensibly good news for Cahill, as there would be an increased demand for the installation of his lighting system at ballparks. But there was a tradeoff for Cahill, who was more interested in advancing the science of lighting a complex baseball game than in merely performing a rudimentary function of shining lights on simple theatrical events. Cahill may have justified this tradeoff by viewing the broader audience possible for the evening hippodrome events in comparison to the typical audience for a daylight ball game in the afternoon.

Chicago White Sox owner Charles Comiskey was also in on the Davis hippodrome consortium, as Cahill soon installed his lighting system at the newly constructed Comiskey Park. In August 1910 Cahill had one more try at exhibiting night baseball, which was the third leg of a three-day trial of the lighting system on August 25 to 27. A soccer game was planned for Thursday night, a lacrosse game on Friday night, and the baseball game was on Saturday night. Unfortunately, the trio of sports demonstrated that artificial lighting worked best for lacrosse and soccer, not baseball.

Richter maintained his public relations campaign for night baseball with another front-page article in *Sporting Life*, this time headlined "Electric Light Ball" with the sub-head "The Interesting Details of a Very Successful Experiment in Playing Base Ball at Night Which Will Have Far-Reaching, and Possibly Revolutionary, Effect on the National Game." However, the baseball game on Saturday night between two Chicago semipro teams received scant mention in the Sunday newspapers across the country, while the lacrosse game on Friday night received more national press than did the baseball game.[26]

For the Chicago night baseball game, Cahill made several modifications to his arc lighting system that he had used in 1909. He utilized both elevated and ground lamps to light Comiskey Park, and added to each lamp "a reflector of parabolic form [that] directs the rays downward in the roof and tower lamps and upward in the ground lamps." Additionally, "All of the lamps are screened by a strip of black cloth, which keeps the glare out of the eyes of the players," the Chicago newspapers reported. However, "the screening also throws a shadow across the diamond, between the outfield and where the infield stops." This deficiency, along with continued trouble with some of the lamps going out of service, rendered this experimental night game another artistic failure.[27]

A final nail in the coffin of baseball by arc light was a *Chicago Tribune* editorial, which used the term "unholy enterprise" to characterize Comiskey's use of artificial lights. "It is enough to cause mental goose flesh to arise showing our disgust," the *Tribune* concluded. "Athletic sports, healthy ones at least, demand daylight. They are absurd in artificial light. No self-respecting game will last under such conditions."[28]

The hippodrome events were soon abandoned at all professional ballparks, as were experimental night baseball games. Cincinnati, the smallest city in the National League, and the Chicago White Sox, competing in a two-club city, were natural candidates to explore night baseball (and supplemental hippodrome events) to augment Sunday games as a way to adjust to waning attendance at afternoon games during the workweek. However, professional baseball remained wedded to daylight baseball for the next two decades.

Cahill was also consigned to the sidelines. In the long run, the accolades that Cahill received for his effort to advance the plausibility of night baseball were few and largely posthumous. *The Sporting News* in its obituary of Cahill in 1935 called him "the pioneer exponent of night games, inventing a special projector that first solved the problem of lighting large fields without blinding players and spectators."[29]

One substantial problem for Cahill was that arc lighting was quickly on its way to becoming an obsolete technology. The General Electric Company, in 1901, created a research laboratory in Schenectady, New York, to focus on basic research that executives hoped would evolve into new product development. One fruitful market that research might bridge at the time was the gap between the 100-candlepower incandescent lamp for indoor use and the 2000-candlepower arc-light lamp for outdoor use. At the turn of the twentieth century there were no lamp sizes in between. There were significant downsides to arc lighting, which limited its potential uses, such as flickering, humming, ash spent from the burning carbon rods, and bleached colors from the resulting light. The development of a larger size enclosed incandescent lamp would solve these arc-light deficiencies.

Scientists at the General Electric research laboratory perfected an incandescent lamp with a tungsten filament, which produced a much brighter light than the previous carbon-filament lamp. General Electric trademarked this new product as the Mazda light bulb, which became commercially available in 1907. Mazda was the Persian god of light (also the inspiration for the modern-day automobile of the same name). By 1911 the scientists at General Electric had improved the original Mazda bulb, and began selling it as the Mazda B bulb. The marketers at General Electric coincidingly replaced the candle-power ratings of its light bulbs with watt sizes, to emphasize the electricity required to power the bulb rather than the luminosity of the light emitted. The Madza B bulb came in 25-watt and 100-watt sizes.[30]

The research breakthrough that impacted night baseball came in 1913 when General Electric introduced the Mazda C light bulb, which encased the existing ductile-tungsten filament in nitrogen gas. This enhancement enabled the creation of a 1000-watt incandescent lamp that provided illumination similar to a lamp using arc lighting, and less powerful 250-watt and 500-watt versions that were useful in targeting light to different distinct areas of the surface being illuminated. Irving Langmuir was the lead scientist in the creation of the Mazda C concept and was granted a patent for his work in 1916 (which he assigned to General Electric). Eventually the Madza C bulb was filled with argon, instead of nitrogen, and was produced in larger wattage sizes, which made arc lighting virtually obsolete for most outdoor lighting purposes.[31]

One of the first high-profile uses of the Mazda C bulbs was in 1915 to externally light the Woolworth Building in New York City, which at the time was the world's tallest

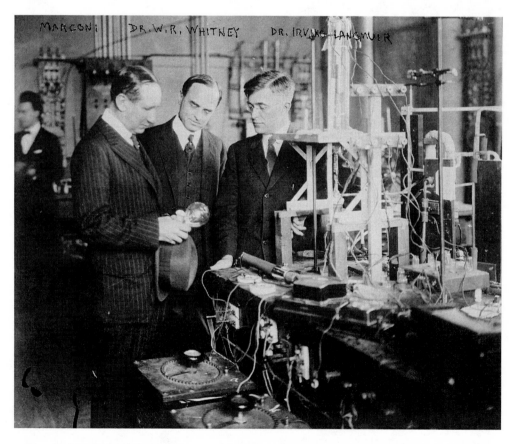

Irving Langmuir (right) led the team that created the Mazda C light bulb in 1913. Langmuir was a scientist at the General Electric Company research laboratory, shown here with Italian inventor Guglielmo Marconi (left) and GE scientist Willis Whitney (middle). The Madza C incandescent lamp enabled the efficient artificial lighting of outdoor spaces for evening activities (Library of Congress, Prints & Photographs Division, LC-DIG-ggbain-34476).

building. To illuminate such a large surface area, General Electric electrical engineers, led by Henry Magdsick, utilized 550 Madza C lamps, most of the 250-watt size but also two dozen 1000-watt lamps at the top of the building. While the explicit objective was to provide an even floodlighting of the building during evening hours, the implicit reward to Woolworth executives was "to intensify awareness of the Woolworth brand and to heighten consumer desire" to shop in its chain of retail stores across the country. Outdoor lighting was not just utilitarian, as it now served an aesthetic architectural purpose as well as advertising and marketing rationales. The skill to expertly light the Woolworth Building became a foundational skill needed to properly light a baseball field.[32]

The lighting of the Woolworth Building may have inspired George Cahill to take one more try at lighting a field for night baseball.

In September 1915 the Brooklyn ball club in the Federal League installed lights at its ballpark to play a few night games in late September and then schedule a full slate for the upcoming 1916 season. What would have been the first regular-season night game played in a professional league was set for September 29 against the Buffalo club. However, the game was canceled, since it was "impossible for them to have the electric light plant so completed that night baseball will become a reality for this season."[33]

While the *Brooklyn Eagle* reported few details regarding the lighting technology, or its provider, being installed at the ballpark, the scant information reported for the semi-pro game played under the lights in late October strongly hints that Cahill was likely involved. The 24 "huge lights" noted atop the towers indicate the use of arc lights, not the more modern Madza incandescent lamps, and the "patented screens" on the lights that needed adjustment during the game also imply the involvement of Cahill. In December 1916 Cahill renewed his never-approved 1909 patent application for lighting a baseball field to enable games to be played at night, which the United States Patent Office approved in July 1917.[34]

When the Federal League collapsed after the 1915 season, the night baseball experiment expired as well, relegated to a few boxing matches staged under the lights in Brooklyn in 1916. Even if the Federal League had survived into 1916 and night games were conducted in Brooklyn, it was unlikely that the National League or American League would have adopted night baseball earlier than it did two decades later in the 1930s.

If not for the entry of the United States into World War I during 1917 and 1918, the market for commercial applications for floodlighting of competitive sports likely would have developed much sooner than it did during the 1920s. Given this slow adaptation, professional baseball held fast to its fixation with daylight ball games on weekdays.

◆ 5 ◆

Attendance Decline
at Weekday Games

Brutal competition in 1914 and 1915 from a third major league, the Federal League, and the dire economic impact in 1917 and 1918 of the U.S. involvement in World War I profoundly changed the civic/profit business basis of professional baseball. These conditions challenged ball clubs to respond to the significant societal changes that occurred during the 1920s in the nature of the traditional audience for weekday afternoon games, especially in the minor leagues and the two-club cities in the major leagues.

By 1920, the day-of-game model was increasingly concentrated on Sunday and holiday games, with Saturday games making a more important contribution to overall ballpark attendance. These were the days when a greater segment of the public could get to the ballpark. The single weekday game on Monday through Friday was losing its patronage allure, given the changing nature of urban employment. Without an incentive to attend, such as two-for-one doubleheader or discounted-admission promotion, attendance began to wane at weekday games.

Although all ball games were played in afternoon daylight, there was a more diverse audience by social class for the greater-attended games conducted on Saturday, Sunday, and holidays, than the businessman-concentrated audience for the lesser-attended games on the weekdays. Since the ball-club owners preferred the audience for the lesser-attended weekday games, a holdover from the boosterism era, the club owners were implicitly using the gate receipts from the Saturday, Sunday, and holiday games to subsidize the lesser-attended weekday games.

The first movement toward non-afternoon professional baseball occurred in 1918 when many ball clubs experimented with twilight games that began after dinnertime in the early evening, typically between 6:00 and 7:00. This starting time was more feasible than before the war, since the nation converted to "war time" by advancing clocks one hour to have more daylight hours for outdoor work activity. Today, we know this as daylight savings time.

Minneapolis in the American Association was one of the first ball clubs to conduct a twilight game in the minor leagues, staging a "night game" on May 24, 1918. The game started at 6:45 and ended at 8:05, about half an hour before sunset, and drew a good-sized crowd to the ballpark. Soon many other minor-league clubs adopted the same technique to try to attract spectators to the ballpark during wartime, including Wichita in the Western League and Binghamton in the International League.[1]

The Boston Braves even tried twilight ball in the National League with its July 1 game against Brooklyn. While twilight games in the minor leagues attracted decent crowds, the major-league version was "not a howling success in point of attendance," as just 1,500 people went to Braves Field for the 6:00 game, including the soldiers and sailors who were admitted free. "Twilight games are not likely to become a fixture," the *Boston Globe* forecast.[2]

Twilight baseball did not receive a long enough trial period, though, as most minor leagues shut down prematurely in July due to wartime restrictions, while the major leagues managed to play into early September before concluding their season. With the uncertainty associated with the 1919 season, one baseball writer used the twilight-game experiment to suggest an abbreviated wartime schedule should the war continue into the following year, comprised of 112 games by playing a doubleheader on Sunday, a single game on Saturday, and two twilight games on selected weekdays.[3]

However, after the armistice to end the war in November 1918, no ball clubs tried twilight games during the 1919 season. The big winners in twilight baseball were the adult men's leagues that formed in cities after the war, which provided both exercise for the ballplayers and entertainment for hundreds of friends, family, and neighbors. Some of these twilight leagues were considered to be semipro; several later elevated into minor leagues. Urban twilight leagues in 1919 were a leading indicator of the changing nature of ballpark attendance in professional baseball that occurred during the 1920s.

By 1920 "a second and equally profound transformation had seriously eroded the nineteenth-century industrial city, the postindustrial revolution," John Mollenkopf wrote in his book *The Contested City*. "If labor and capital concentrated into factories defined the industrial city, the postindustrial city was characterized by the geographic diffusion of production and population. The office building, not the factory, now provided the organizing institution for the central city." This second urban revolution, as described by sociologist Mollenkopf, dissolved the old order that was based on the industrial revolution. As historian John Cumbler phrased it, civic capitalism was eclipsed by national capitalism and "it became more and more difficult for the city to control its own destiny," as locally-owned companies consolidated into national corporations controlled by non-local management that was less responsive to local conditions.[4]

Minor-league ball clubs suffered the brunt of the postindustrial revolution, and consequent demise of civic capitalism, since the small cities where these ball clubs were located had less diverse economies than did the larger cities with major-league ball clubs. Some cities comprising a minor league in the lower classifications had just one industry (or even just one company) that was the engine of the city's economy, which when merged into a national corporation severely hampered the civic boosterism of local businessmen that had financially supported the local minor-league ball club.

The postindustrial urban revolution also coincided with several cultural changes in American society, which further challenged the continued operation of minor-league baseball during the 1920s.

The downtown area of a city where once everyone worked, shopped, and sought entertainment underwent rapid change in the 1920s. One of the reasons that the weekday element of the day-of-game model had worked so well for ball clubs the previous decades was that a large percentage of the spectators at a weekday afternoon ball game worked in or visited businesses in the downtown area of the city. However, this natural connection between downtown business and ballpark attendance disintegrated during the 1920s.

During the first two decades of the twentieth century, "downtown was synonymous with the business district virtually everywhere in urban America," according to urban-studies professor Robert Fogelson in his book *Downtown: Its Rise and Fall, 1880–1950.* "The retailers and wholesalers worked there, as did the bankers, financiers, insurance, utility, and corporate executives, the lawyers, realtors, architects, engineers, and accountants, the clerks, typists, salesmen, salesgirls, and messengers, and many craftsmen and laborers. The courts, government agencies, and post and telegraph offices were located downtown, as were most hotels, restaurants, places of popular amusement, and institutions of high culture." Nearby were railroad stations and manufacturing facilities.[5]

Every city "boasted a conspicuous core business district," city-planning expert Jon Peterson observed in his book *The Birth of City Planning in the United States, 1840–1917.* There were "department stores, banks, hotels, theaters, restaurants, and all manner of street-level specialty shops topped by floor after floor of professional and small-business offices." All these buildings "drew a daily crush of patrons and clients to the downtown streets," in addition to workers, all of whom provided the spectator base for weekday games at the ballpark, which generally was located within a short trolley ride of downtown.[6]

However, by the 1920s most middle-class workers in the downtown area lived in the suburbs, five to ten miles from downtown, and were dependent on automobiles for transportation rather than the electric trolley that required a home to be two to three miles from downtown. First, there was a gradual diminishing of downtown workers at ball games, given the long weekday commute and availability of Saturday and Sunday ball games as well as other amusement and entertainment options. Second, as the nature of businesses changed to be more corporate (nationally managed and owned by non-local investors) and less independent (locally owned and family businesses), businessmen had less time flexibility in their jobs and were precluded from often attending weekday ball games. Then, throughout the 1920s many of these businessmen no longer had their place of employment in the downtown area, because they worked in the suburbs.

Another factor in the decreased audience for daylight baseball on weekdays in the 1920s was the changed nature of downtown in the evening. No longer were there "two Sixth Avenues, by day sober and honest, but at night a raffish mixture of ordinary citizens, streetwalkers, pickpockets, and ruffians." In a now well-lighted downtown, "the perception of darkness was vanquished" by electrical lighting, according to David Nye in his book *American Illuminations: Urban Lighting, 1800–1920.* Because people flocked to the new entertainment options, such as the movie theater, "going out on the town, once a luxury, became commonplace." Baseball during the day now had to compete with other options in the evening as American society increasingly became a consumer culture.[7]

The gradual change in the 1920s that greatly impacted weekday daylight baseball was downtown no longer being the "only" business district in the city, but rather the central business district, or "main" business area. The growth of outlying business districts was not only significant, but, as Fogelson observed, this change "reflected other changes in urban America at the time, among them the increasing dispersal of residences, the growing decentralization of industry, the decline of mass transit, and the proliferation of private automobiles." Downtown became less important during the 1920s, as industrial enterprises moved from the downtown periphery to the outlying areas, soon followed by cultural institutions, stores, and offices.[8]

City planners, now directing civic strategy more than business owners, no longer considered that downtown would be an "inevitable and desirable" section of a city in the future. The boards of trade transformed into downtown associations, which focused on maintaining, not expanding, business through "improvements that would make downtown a more attractive place to work and shop." Industrial development corporations were formed to entice businesses to locate in a city. Suddenly, the specter of decentralization of business was seen as a positive factor. This meant a challenging environment for professional baseball, before the arrival of the cataclysmic economic events in October 1929 and the early 1930s.[9]

The possibility for upward social mobility from low-paid worker to wealthy owner also began to change its characteristics in the 1920s, even as the middle class continued to expand its presence in American society. There were fewer opportunities for business ownership, while the chance to move into corporate management increased. While the income derived from both business tracks may have been roughly equivalent, there was a significant difference in the independence to make decisions, which included the flexibility to take an afternoon off to attend a ball game. During the previous 50 years, the decline in self-employed individuals had dropped from 40 percent of the workforce in 1870 to 25 percent in 1920, and continued to decline over the coming decades.[10]

The transition from civic capitalism to national capitalism further reduced the number of people who could attend a weekday afternoon ball game due to the rapid expansion of the "chain store" concept. Grocery stores, gas stations, and variety stores were the largest segments of the urban economy affected by chain stores. Since "retailing merchandise through store units owned and controlled by a corporation" forced many independent businessmen to shut down, James Palmer argued in his journal article "Economic and Social Aspects of Chain Stores" that chain stores not only "produced a nation of clerks" but also "to the extent that these retailers are desirable citizens and a valuable part of the social life of the community, the community suffers."[11]

The concept of the American Dream to achieve upward social mobility, while reinforced by the upward movement in stock-market values during the 1920s, reached a turning point. "Despite rapid social and economic change, conservatives argued for adherence to the competitive individualism that they believed underlay the nation's evident growth and prosperity," Cal Jillson observed in his book *Pursuing the American Dream*. "Alternatively, reformers argued that these changes demanded careful thought and detailed planning to assure social order and economic efficiency."[12]

To conservative advocates, "the American Dream was the patrimony of the man who rose by the dint of his own effort, improved his talents, and succeeded by their application." To liberal thinkers, this was much harder to accomplish as a corporate employee. Yet, the "dint of his own effort" philosophy continued to be the mantra for upward social mobility throughout the 1920s. Early in the decade, Herbert Hoover tried to bridge these two perspectives in his book *American Individualism*: "While we build our society upon the attainment of the individual, we shall safeguard to every individual an equality of opportunity to take that position in the community to which his intelligence, character, ability, and ambition entitle him ... while he in turn must stand up to the emery wheel of competition."[13]

In professional baseball, upward mobility was exemplified by Charles Comiskey, Connie Mack, and Clark Griffith, since all three men were "reminders of an age in which a player might become an owner and join the magnates of industry." That had become a dying trend, though, by the 1920s. As historian Jules Tygiel mourned in his book *Past Time: Baseball as History*, "In modern America, success would assume different incarnations."[14]

These larger trends had a diminishing impact throughout the 1920s on ballpark attendance at games played Monday through Friday. Other societal trends contributed to masking this impact, as seen through an analysis of the day-of-game mix trends at both the major-league and minor-league levels.

In major-league baseball, Sunday baseball legislation in New York (1919) and District of Columbia (1918) had a tremendously positive impact to the general day-of-game mix of revenue balancing, particularly in the American League where the Babe Ruth Effect had its greatest impact, when attendance surged at ballparks throughout the league to watch the potential home runs hit by Ruth and players of the New York Yankees. In cities such as Chicago and St. Louis where Sunday baseball had been conducted for three decades or more, Sunday doubleheaders became increasingly prevalent to stave off the observable decline in attendance for single games on Sunday.

The increased volume of Sunday games helped to offset the decline in audience for holiday and weekday games. Over the course of the 1920s, the holiday twin bill for most ball clubs converted from two separate-admission ball games to a two-for-one doubleheader, as the morning game became much less popular. More doubleheaders were slated for weekday games, to offer a "bargain bill" to attract more businessmen to the ballpark. Many were created to make up a rainout or tie game (the one quirky need that night baseball would ostensibly solve). About one-quarter of all major-league ball games were staged via doubleheaders during this decade, becoming an early example of the modern buy-one-get-one-free marketing technique, designed to induce a full-price purchase in the future.[15]

By mid-decade, several ball clubs sought women and children as new customers for weekday ball games, since they were another segment of the population that had the time flexibility to get to the ballpark on a weekday. Women received discount admission at Ladies Day and children could attend with a Knothole Gang pass. In 1921 the Chicago Cubs revived the concept of Ladies Day (which had been discontinued in the majors around 1910), but instead of requiring women to have a male escort (who paid for his ticket) the new Ladies Day policy was free admission. By 1923 all the clubs in Chicago and St. Louis conducted frequent Ladies Day promotions, as did the two clubs in Boston. At the end of the decade most major-league clubs had a regular Ladies Day to minimize the negative impact of declining audiences for afternoon ball games during the workweek.[16]

Radio broadcasts of ball games beginning in 1925 helped to generate enthusiasm among women and children (and suburbanites) to instantly follow a ball game, which might encourage them to attend a weekday ball game. "Fans who only a few years earlier could never have hoped to attend a major league game, yet followed its progress assiduously through newspaper reports, suddenly could hear live radio broadcasts that placed them at the games," Tygiel related in *Past Time: Baseball as History*. "For most fans major league baseball still entailed an act of imagination. But the process had changed, transformed from belated newspaper coverage, to instant telegraphic recreations, to detailed broadcast descriptions." While helping to democratize the following of baseball, "the process had become more familial or individualistic, replacing the communal experience with a more isolated one." The community aspect would eventually become much more of an issue as it related to ballpark attendance.[17]

Washington Senators manager Bucky Harris (left) signs scorecards for women attending a Ladies Day game in 1925. Ball clubs offered discount admission to women on Ladies Day to offset the declining attendance of male businessmen at weekday ball games (Library of Congress, Prints & Photographs Division, LC-USZ62–51270).

Saturday became a separate component of the day-of-game mix, especially for the clubs in Massachusetts and Pennsylvania, where Sunday home games were still prohibited by law. The "weekend" was becoming a more common term, as the workweek for most people had shrunk to at least five and a half days and for many was down to just five days. Attendance on the Saturday and Sunday non-work days now greatly eclipsed the volume of spectators for games on Monday through Friday. Having a winning team was no longer a sufficient draw in itself for weekday ball games. The "build it and they will come" attitude, which had worked reasonably well in the late nineteenth and early twentieth centuries, could still enhance crowds for weekend games, but could not appreciably elevate the number of people in the stands for weekday games.

Baseball was increasingly becoming a weekend game, when it came to gate receipts at the ballpark, which during the 1920s was responsible for producing at least 90 percent of a club's revenue, and often 95 percent or more. The attendance relationship between Sunday and weekday games was roughly six-to-one, with Saturday games four to five times greater than a typical crowd during the workweek. For example, in the four-day homestand of the St. Louis Cardinals from May 18 to 21, 1922, the Thursday game attracted 3,000 people, the Friday game 2,000, the Saturday game 12,000, and the Sunday game 15,000. A doubleheader during the workweek might draw 5,000 spectators, about twice the attendance of the typical weekday game.

In the minor leagues, the weekend issue was particularly troublesome during the 1920s, which exacerbated an already precarious profit-making environment. From the lowest Class D leagues up through the Class AA leagues (the new top ranking added to the classification system in 1912 that housed the International League [formerly the Eastern League], American Association, and Pacific Coast League), revenues from gate receipts were increasingly difficult to generate from weekday afternoon ball games. The situation was especially acute for leagues located in southern states, where 100-degree summer afternoons easily dissuaded potential spectators from going to the ballpark.

Sunday baseball was more pervasive in the minor leagues, as 96 percent of the clubs in the three Class AA leagues in 1920 could stage Sunday home games (23 of 24), while just 69 percent of major-league clubs could (11 of 16). All eight clubs in the American Association conducted Sunday baseball, as did the eight clubs in the Pacific Coast League. Because Sunday games were so ingrained in the West Coast culture, the PCL began scheduling regular two-for-one Sunday doubleheaders in 1919, coincident with the move to weekly seven-game series with opponents rather than shorter series during the week. Seven of the eight clubs in the International League hosted Sunday baseball, with Toronto the lone exception, due to the Lord's Day Act in Canada.[18]

For those minor leagues with clubs located in states that still prohibited Sunday baseball, such as Virginia, Maryland, and Massachusetts, financial survival was often unlikely. Indeed, in 1928 both the Virginia League and the Eastern Shore League disbanded in mid-season after a half dozen years of trying to eke out survival without Sunday games. The New England League survived into 1929, its first year of legal Sunday games, but soon disbanded early in 1930.

The bulk of attendance for the minor leagues came from the weekend games on Saturday and Sunday. Doubleheaders on Sunday, though, were prevalent in most minor leagues by mid-decade. For example, on July 12, 1925, doubleheaders were a preponderance of the Sunday schedule in the high minors. All clubs in the Pacific Coast League and Western League engaged in Sunday doubleheaders on that day, as did six of eight clubs in the Eastern League, four of eight clubs in the International League and American Association, and two of eight clubs in the Southern Association and Texas League. No major-league games that Sunday were played as doubleheaders. By 1928 some clubs, notably Houston in the Texas League (a farm club of the St. Louis Cardinals), were regularly canceling Monday games and rescheduling them as the second game on Sunday.[19]

Holiday twin bills continued in the minor leagues, with morning and afternoon games still the usual fare to optimize attendance rather than stage a two-for-one doubleheader. Twin bills were especially prominent when two clubs could stage a home-and-home series on the holiday, such as Minneapolis vs. St. Paul in the American Association and Newark vs. Jersey City in the International League.

Discount admission was rampant for afternoon games staged Monday through Friday. In addition to many doubleheaders, Ladies Day was a frequent promotion in the minors in 1920, as seen in Buffalo in the International League and Indianapolis in the American Association. Booster Day, which offered a doubleheader to encourage attendance by local businessmen at regular ticket prices, was already a mainstay at several minor-league ballparks by 1922, as seen in Rock Island, Illinois, of the Three-I League and Joplin, Missouri, of the Western League. By the end of the decade, both promotions were nearly ubiquitous in the minor leagues; Los Angeles of the Pacific Coast League even offered Ladies Day admission for every ball game in 1928, which the club amended in 1929 to apply only to games on Monday through Friday.[20]

Many minor leagues in the 1902s also adopted a postseason scheme to improve the championship hopes of multiple ball clubs, in order to encourage greater attendance during the hot summer months of the regular season. The split-season format was the most common, where the season was divided into two halves, the first half ending at the Independence Day holiday and the second half running from there to September. The first-place teams in each half then met in a postseason playoff series to determine the league champion.

The split-season format was controversial due to its lack of correlation to a club's full-season won-lost record and the associated undesirable outcomes. A strong club could win both halves of the season and thus negate most of the benefit of the split season (like Fort Worth did in the Texas League in 1925); the first-half winner could tank during the second half while awaiting the postseason playoff, making a mockery of the split season (like Attleboro did in the New England League in 1928, finishing next-to-last during the second half); or a club could have the best record over the entire season but not win either half and thus be deprived of an opportunity to win the championship (like Alexandria did in the Cotton States League in 1929).[21]

As this analysis of day-of-game trends shows, major-league baseball was better positioned to respond to the postwar challenges of the 1920s than was minor-league baseball. During this period, the civic/profit balance of major-league baseball also improved by increasing its focus on both profit-making and boosterism (although in a new way to a national perspective, not city or regional). Minor-league baseball, on the other hand, was hamstrung by movement in both components of its civic/profit balance, increasing its emphasis on profit-making and decreasing its reliance on boosterism, which both served to its detriment. By the end of the decade in 1929, the future of the minor leagues was much more perilous than was publicly perceived at the time, while the major leagues retained a solid foundation.

Major-league ball clubs in the postwar era were very profitable. The second wave of new major-league ballparks from 1909 to 1915 showcased that profitability. Indeed, the new concrete-and-steel stadiums in Boston, Philadelphia, Pittsburgh, and New York City (in the Manhattan and Brooklyn boroughs), were shrines to American entrepreneurism on the urban landscape. For example, as Bruce Kuklick described in his book *To Every Thing a Season: Shibe Park and Urban Philadelphia*, "Shibe Park was to have an abiding element; it was a lasting monument, built to endure, with a grandiose beauty that should express continuing prosperity and assured advance."[22]

During the 1920s, 9 of the 16 major-league clubs were profitable in at least 9 of the 10 years of the decade, while two clubs (both St. Louis clubs) were profitable in 8 of the 10 years. The five clubs that showed more overt weakness were the Cleveland Indians, Cincinnati Reds, Philadelphia Phillies, and both clubs in Boston. The American League clubs were slightly stronger than the National League ones due to the Babe Ruth Effect.[23]

Ball clubs did not attempt to maximize profits, however, as they continued to forego profits in the name of traditional civic boosterism through a full slate of weekday daylight games. Given the dynamics of declining attendance at these weekday ball games, clubs would have been better off scheduling doubleheaders to eliminate games on certain weekdays (much like the 1918 proposal concerning twilight games). Because the major leagues were founded on the concept of city boosterism with the consequent desired audience of businessmen, this conflict over the appropriate profit strategy would dog ball clubs into the 1950s. In essence, major-league ball clubs were subsidizing weekday games through the profits from weekend games.

Not all was rosy on the profit front, though, as there were some distinct cracks, particularly regarding the two-club cities. Suddenly, major-league baseball was no longer purely a "great city" lineup. The Boston Braves, Philadelphia Phillies, and St. Louis Browns would never thrive as the weaker franchise in their two-club city, while the small-market city of Cincinnati had dim prospects until it could conduct night baseball in the mid–1930s.

Since 1903 the five multi-club cities had held top-tier status within major-league baseball, by demonstrating sufficient spectator demand for a ball game nearly every day of the playing season, while in the other five single-club cities ball games were staged only half the time. That perceived elite collection of cities began to crumble when the 1920 federal census indicated that the five multi-club cities were no longer the top five cities in terms of population. New York City, Chicago, and Philadelphia continued to be the three most populous cities; however, St. Louis dropped to number six and Boston to number seven, both behind Detroit and Cleveland at number four and five, respectively.

By the end of the decade the two-club situation had deteriorated further, when the 1930 federal census indicated that St. Louis and Boston had slipped on the top-10 list to numbers seven and nine, respectively, while the top three remained intact. While eight of the top 10 cities still had major-league ball clubs, only nine of the top 15 cities could make the same claim. It was arguable whether the top tier of professional baseball was indeed the top slice of American cities, the largest of the large, to represent the national pastime. The weakest clubs in the two-club cities were dragging down the prestige of major-league baseball, as was its smallest city, Cincinnati, which had dropped from number 13 in 1910 to number 17 in 1930.

These fissures represented a renovation on the civic side of the civic/profit balance for major-league baseball, which largely replaced the classical perspective of city-specific or regional boosterism with a national perspective via the elevation of the national pastime from a marketing slogan to a heart-felt philosophical belief. Legally, this zeitgeist originated in 1902 during the contractual fight between the Philadelphia ball clubs of the American and National Leagues over the services of Nap Lajoie. In ruling on that case, the Pennsylvania Supreme Court concluded that professional baseball was a business with a "peculiar nature and circumstances." In 1922 this concept was solidified in the minds of major-league club owners by a ruling of the United States Supreme Court in *Federal Baseball Club of Baltimore v. National League of Professional Baseball Clubs*.[24]

The Federal League challenged the monopoly status of major-league baseball in American League and National League cities, both on the field (with ball clubs in Buffalo, Kansas City, Baltimore, and Newark) and in the courts (with several lawsuits). To win in court, the Federal League needed to prove that major-league baseball was a monopoly in violation of the Sherman Antitrust Act of 1890, which defined a monopoly as "every contract, combination or conspiracy, in restraint of trade or commerce among the several States." As observed by legal historian Stuart Banner in his book *The*

Baseball Trust: A History of Baseball's Antitrust Exemption, "The National Agreement was no doubt a contract, but was it a contract in restraint of trade?" Club owners in the major leagues readily acknowledged that baseball was a monopoly, but they argued that it was a good monopoly, one that promoted trade, since without its restraints the business would not exist.[25]

Major-league baseball did not do well in the initial lawsuits filed by the Federal League. In the first lawsuit in 1914, the judge ruled in favor of the Federal League. Famously, the second lawsuit in 1915 was assigned to Chicago federal judge Kenesaw Landis, who interminably delayed his decision to force the two sides to settle out of court. During the hearing in February 1916 to officially drop the suit, Landis signaled to the lawyers that his decision would have sided with the Federal League. While the league had dropped its lawsuit, the Baltimore ball club in the Federal League continued to pursue damages resulting from that settlement. Judge Stafford in that case ruled that major-league baseball "constituted in law an attempt to monopolize the business of com-

petitive baseball exhibitions for profit," and thus had violated the Sherman Act. Upon appeal, though, the District of Columbia Court of Appeals ruled in favor of major-league baseball. Judge Smyth wrote in the decision that baseball was "not trade or commerce; it is sport," so the Sherman Act did not apply. Smyth further stated that if baseball were commerce, it was a local activity that should not be construed as being "interstate" simply because the ball club sometimes travels to another state.[26]

When the Baltimore club appealed that decision, the United States Supreme Court unanimously agreed with the Court of Appeals that baseball was neither commerce nor an interstate activity. Justice Oliver Wendell Holmes wrote in the opinion that "the business is giving exhibitions of baseball, which are purely state affairs," that the exhibitions "although made for money would not be called trade or commerce in the commonly accepted use of those terms,"

Oliver Wendell Holmes, associate justice of the U.S. Supreme Court, wrote the decision in 1922 that legally established major-league baseball as an institution that was a sport, but not a business. This ruling made the national pastime a key element in the business basis of baseball, which fostered a resistance to night baseball (Library of Congress, Prints & Photographs Division, LC-DIG-npcc-26413).

and that crossing state lines to conduct such exhibitions "is not enough to change the character of the business."[27]

Therefore, major-league baseball was a legal monopoly, and its ball clubs essentially a cartel, which cemented its legal standing as a "peculiar" institution in the American business world. "The enterprise of major league baseball was 'peculiar' in that, at some level, it was valued even more highly than making money," Edward White observed in his book *Creating the National Pastime*. "It was not simply a business, or a sport, or a means of getting rich; it was the national pastime." Baseball was an enterprise that contradictorily was "at once more light-hearted, more trivial, and also more engaging, more culturally significant, than other American enterprises." White observed that while "Holmes's insistence that baseball games were 'local' and not 'trade or commerce' was jurisprudentially orthodox" for the 1920s, "looked at from almost any other perspective, the *Federal Baseball* decision was extraordinary." How could anyone doubt that the framers of the National Agreement "were combining to interfere with free competition in interstate commerce?" White asked. "Their entire agreement had been predicated on doing just that."[28]

This U.S. Supreme Court decision spawned the "sanctity of the ballpark spectator" mentality. Baseball was special and a privilege to watch, contrary to the newspaper accounts that baseball was a democratizing force, which was largely a publicity campaign orchestrated during the 1920s to enhance the image of baseball in the wake of the Black Sox Scandal in 1919. "The financial support of baseball is provided by the so-called 'moneyed class' and not the 'working class' to whom that honor is too frequently accorded," Edgar Wolfe wrote in *Literary Digest*. "If an accurate poll were taken of the attendance at any big-league ball game, the ratio would be around 80 percent of business officials, office employees, and men of leisure to 20 percent of the actual 'working class.'"[29]

The World Series was a critical element in portraying this national civic nature of major-league baseball. In 1922 the World Series was broadcast on radio for the first time, which enhanced the national reach of major-league baseball. The World Series was the Super Bowl of its era. This national element of boosterism ultimately helped to foster major-league baseball's resistance to night baseball. The decline of city or regional boosterism in minor-league baseball during the 1920s ultimately created a desperation attitude for night baseball.

While major-league baseball was thriving in the 1920s, minor-league baseball was showing increasing cracks in a sustainable model moving forward. Because the minor leagues were founded on civic boosterism, the changing nature of civic duty dramatically impacted that component of the civic/profit business basis of a minor-league ball club.

Minor-league baseball almost did not survive the twin threats of the Federal League and World War I during the 1910s. The downturn began in 1910, at the height of boosterism-infused growth within the minor-league system, when 52 leagues started the season. In the state of Kansas that year, there were 24 minor-league teams, 22 of which were at the Class D level, spread among three intra-state leagues (Kansas State, Central Kansas, and Eastern Kansas). By 1915 there were only two Kansas-based teams remaining in the minor leagues, its two Class A teams, Topeka and Wichita. Similar contractions occurred elsewhere in the minor-league system. By 1918 only ten minor leagues started the season; just one completed that season, the International League.[30]

After the postwar revival in 1919, the minor leagues were on shaky ground, as the 1920s challenged the ability of the minor leagues to cope with its rapidly changing civic/

profit business basis. Although the minors ostensibly "enjoyed a measure of prosperity during the decade," the erosion of their traditional boosterism foundation forced club owners into a greater focus on profit than they generally had in the past. If the financial gains by major-league clubs "were less impressive than those of the motion-picture industry," a big competitor in the entertainment space, what were the hopes for minor-league ball clubs to achieve reasonable profits, when "year after year local capital would grimly dig down into its jeans and pay its debts and come back for more with a smile on its face the following year?"[31]

The changing nature of downtown in a city, and its business inhabitants that had always financially supported minor-league baseball, forced a downsizing of the civic component of the business basis of a ball club. Civic more and more related to city residents rather than the businessmen who worked in the city. Within the business basis, civic began to relate to the allure of financial support from a major-league ball club for a minor-league team to be its "farm club." During the late 1920s and into the 1930s, major-league baseball replaced local businessmen as the financial angels of minor-league baseball, to put a whole new meaning on the civic component, where historically businessmen were stewards of the city and used the minor-league ball club to help promote the city's regional economic vitality.

In 1926 Joe Carr became president of the Columbus minor-league ball club in the American Association. Since the ball club was nearly bankrupt and hopelessly mired in last place of the league standings, Carr helped to facilitate the sale of the ball club to Sidney Weil, an owner of the Cincinnati Reds, since local businessmen could not raise enough capital to purchase the club and continue to operate it as a civic endeavor. Carr

Aerial view of downtown Columbus, Ohio, a city that was at the leading edge of change in minor-league baseball, as the Columbus ball club shifted from ownership by local investors to being a farm club owned by a major-league club. Columbus also nurtured baseball executives Joe Carr and Larry MacPhail, both instrumental in developing night baseball during the 1930s (Boston Public Library, Arts Department, Tichnor Brothers Collection).

stayed on to run the Columbus team as a farm club for the Reds through 1930, but he struggled to balance the player-development element of minor-league baseball with the traditional boosterism aspect.[32]

Carr had two other jobs in addition to running the Columbus ball club, which helped to inform his later perspective on improving minor-league baseball to attract more ballpark spectators. As the president of two other sports leagues, the National Football League, still a fledging operation that had begun in 1920, and the American Basketball League, a start-up in 1925, Carr explored new ways to determine a league champion beyond the oft-scorned split-season format.

Both the NFL and ABL played their games when working-class people could attend, unlike professional baseball that was played predominantly in the afternoon on workdays. The spectator audience for both professional football and basketball was largely working-class fans, as the NFL usually played its games on Sunday afternoon and the ABL staged most of its games at night on indoor courts. As it turned out, these sport leagues were important testing grounds for the future of minor-league baseball.

In 1927 Carr proposed that the NFL divide its teams into two divisions, with the division winners meeting for one game to decide the NFL championship. He perceived that this split-league format was better than the split-season one, because it retained the best-record principle over an entire season and there was always a postseason game to determine the champion (no common winner of both halves). Carr had better luck selling the split-league idea to the ABL owners. After using the split-season format for two years, the ABL split for the 1927–28 season into two geographic divisions of four teams each and matched the two division champions in a best-of-five-games series for the ABL championship.[33]

Neither innovative idea went over well at the time. When the NFL club owners could not agree on the best way to organize into two divisions, the league simply pared the field to a more manageable 12 teams. The ABL experiment lasted just one season before the league reverted to the split-season approach.

Accepting a financial subsidy as a farm club introduced a new wrinkle into the civic/profit perspective of minor-league clubs. In essence, the major-league ball club, as the owner or at least controller through a working agreement, became the civic entity since it covered the losses of the minor-league club. This was the ultimate tradeoff for a farm club. For the clubs that wanted to remain independent of a farm system, their owners needed to adopt more of a major-league perspective to concentrate on the profit-making element. This was a big challenge for the independent-minded minor-league ball club, which was now thrust from being a sporting operation into the entertainment business while retaining baseball's financial uncertainties of player acquisition and consequent sale of their contracts to a higher-level league.

While never a wildly profitable business, minor-league baseball did enjoy a few heady years in the early 1920s after the draft rules were relaxed to allow some clubs to sell ballplayer contracts at market prices rather than the traditional fixed draft rate. By 1925 this resulted in inflated values of minor-league clubs. An editorial in *The Sporting News* heralded the hefty sum paid by the new owners of the St. Paul club in the American Association as demonstrating "the passing of the time when operating a club in the average minor league was regarded as a sort of civic duty without thought of a profit, rather with the prospect of financial loss to be endured for sport sake." Big-ticket sale prices for minor-league clubs in the mid–1920s, though, were more a signal of the top of the market, as owners seemingly sold out while the getting was good. Indeed, by 1928 *The Sporting News* lamented the plight of the backers of minor-league clubs, who were then "deep in the red" and were engaged in "a happy game of fooling each other, just pretending," as they suffered losses "for the pleasure of providing entertainment for the faithful fans, the glory of putting the home team on the map, and beating, or trying to beat, some rival town for the thrill of it all."[34]

By the end of the decade, a number of minor-league clubs were experiencing serious conflict trying to balance the traditional boosterism with the new profit-making focus in the civic/profit business basis. The crossroads faced by minor-league baseball were illustrated in the International League by the flurry of ownership transactions in 1927 related to the Jersey City, Newark, and Rochester ball clubs, as profit struggles encouraged existing owners to sell while optimistic buyers continued to line up, many intending to continue the traditional civic aspect of the ball club.

Four different outcomes emerged in the 1927 ownership transactions in the International League. In Jersey City, the new owners bought the club to transfer it to Montreal, Canada, in order to put that city back on the minor-league map. In Newark, a local newspaper publisher bought the club out of receivership to keep it in Newark. In Rochester, local businessman tried to bail out the club after golfer Walter Hagan defaulted on purchasing the club, trying to utilize the Rochester Industrial Development Corporation to invest in the club, before the St. Louis Cardinals purchased it to be a farm club. Back in Jersey City, a group of local businessmen bought the Syracuse ball club (from the St. Louis Cardinals) to transfer it to Jersey City and keep that city on the minor-league map.[35]

By the end of the 1930s, the farm clubs would significantly outnumber the independent clubs throughout all levels of the minor leagues, thus initiating what one writer termed "the transmogrification of the minor leagues from a wild and wooly showcase for boosterism at its best into a wholly owned subsidiary of corporate America."[36]

The 1920s are considered to be the Golden Age of Sports, with the exploits of Babe Ruth in baseball, Red Grange in football, and Jack Dempsey in boxing. Ruth and Grange conducted their sports heroics only in the daylight; Dempsey, though, often fought during the evening under artificial lights in outdoor stadiums. Professional boxing helped light the way for improved applications of lighting systems for ballparks in order to effectively stage baseball games after sunset.

◆ 6 ◆

Birth of Modern
Night Baseball

The new profession of illuminating engineer came to life in the postwar era. The Madza C light bulb invented by General Electric before the war created several newly viable commercial markets for exterior lighting in the postwar years following Armistice Day in 1918. These new markets, which included sporting venues, required the skills of an illuminating engineer to design complex patterns to focus the light emitted from the new generation of high-powered incandescent lamps to best illuminate a specific area. Lamps also needed to be fitted with appropriate reflectors to best execute the engineer's design.

Following the lead of the Woolworth Building in New York City in 1915, corporations rushed to emulate the advertising benefits and civic attributes of architectural lighting. In 1921 exterior lighting was added to the Wrigley Building, which made it stand out on the Chicago skyline during evening hours. The floodlit Wrigley Building shed light not just on the chewing gum business, but also the newly named Wrigley Field after William Wrigley became majority owner of the Chicago Cubs. This turned out to be irony in later years once night baseball became acceptable scheduling in the National League, because the Cubs ownership did not install artificial lighting at Wrigley Field until 1988.[1]

Railroad yards were another early market for incandescent outdoor lighting, so that trains could be repaired around-the-clock to limit disruption to daylight operations. The Union Pacific Railroad, with its headquarters in Omaha, Nebraska, and its rail yards across the Missouri River in Council Bluffs, Iowa, was one of the first to take advantage of artificial lighting in its rail yards. Not surprisingly, the Giant Manufacturing Company in Council Bluffs became a major supplier of outdoor lights, which propelled the firm to become an early, major provider of lighting systems for ballparks.[2]

Perhaps the largest burgeoning market for the new incandescent lamps was automobile headlamps and the coincident need for improved street lighting for safe travel at night. Parameters for acceptable levels of street lighting were established by the National Electric Light Association, with the goal of eliminating shadows and reducing glare to make large objects and surface irregularities discernible to drivers at night. Engineers created different street classifications with differing lighting needs, from brighter illumination for heavily traveled streets (such as in business districts) to lower illumination in suburban residential areas.[3]

While sporting arenas were not yet an immediate new market for exterior lighting in the early 1920s, the training ground for how to appropriately illuminate a baseball field was the lighting of corporate buildings, railroad yards, and automobile-filled streets, where illuminating engineers cut their teeth on how to create the best lighting patterns to illuminate a particular space.

George Cahill, the one person interested in lighting baseball parks in the prewar years, turned his attention to recreational markets in the postwar era. Although he never used his 1917 patent to light another professional baseball field, Cahill did successfully apply his ideas to illuminate other outdoor sporting facilities in the booming postwar economy. By 1922 George and his brothers had established the Cahill Bros. Company, which provided indoor theatrical lighting as well as outdoor athletic lighting for small areas such as playgrounds and tennis courts. These relatively small surface areas required only basic illuminating engineering to adequately light them for use in the evening hours.[4]

In 1923 Cahill provided temporary lighting for a sporting event at the Polo Grounds in New York City; however, the sport involved was boxing, not baseball. On the night of September 14, 1923, the heavyweight title fight between boxers Jack Dempsey and Luis Firpo was witnessed by 90,000 spectators at the Polo Grounds. While only the boxing ring was illuminated by Cahill's lights, promoter Tex Rickard did demonstrate the commercial possibilities for professional sports conducted in the evening hours, based on attracting a new audience, working-class people, beyond the conventional audience for afternoon sports staged during the workweek.[5]

Rickard was a huge proponent of staging professional sports during the evening hours. He purchased Madison Square Garden, the indoor arena in New York City, razed the aging structure and built a replacement in 1925 to be a 17,000-seat indoor sports palace that would be "the twentieth century version of the Roman Coliseum." Rickard replaced the previous fare of circus acts and six-day bicycle races with year-round boxing, pro basketball games of the American Basketball League, and pro ice hockey games of the National Hockey League. Many of these sports contests were staged at night. More college basketball games were also played at night, due to improved indoor lighting at college gymnasiums. Another Dempsey heavyweight title fight under the lights at Philadelphia's Municipal Stadium in 1926 drew a huge crowd. These advancements all helped to expand the potential audience for night games contested indoors by team sports, as well as expand the horizon for their application to outdoor sports. Baseball, though, was slow to embrace that future.[6]

The genesis of modern night baseball came in the summer of 1923, when the street lighting engineers at the General Electric plant in Lynn, Massachusetts, were asked to light the General Electric Employees Athletic Association field for a company event. As engineer Fred Ralston recalled four years later, "The lights were turned on for adjusting and focusing on the night preceding the affair, and we were surprised to see the boys of the neighborhood play a baseball game. That gave us the definite idea of lighting a baseball diamond."[7]

In August 1923 two experimental night baseball games were conducted under the lights at the General Electric baseball field. On August 24 employees of the company played a few innings to test out the new lighting pattern for the baseball field and management determined that "every play was observable and the players found no difficulty in making hits and fielding properly." On August 27, two amateur teams played a night game at the General Electric field, which drew 5,000 curious onlookers. "Baseball by floodlight was played last night at the new General Electric field, but the demonstration proved that Old Sol has no need to worry," the *Lynn Evening Item* reported. "The rays of light were centered on the diamond and balls hit to the infield were handled almost as well as in the daylight. High batted flies to the outfield proved hard to follow."[8]

The lighting fixtures used to illuminate an athletic field were called floodlights based on the non-water definition of flood that means to overwhelm with an abundance or excess, since the lamps flooded a broad area with high-intensity light.

While Ed Riley, business manager of the Boston Braves, slammed the idea ("I hardly believe that night baseball will affect the regular sports to any great degree"), Bob Quinn, president of the Boston Red Sox, prophetically told sportswriters, "People said the airplane could never be, but they were wrong, and the same may be true of night baseball."[9]

While the General Electric engineers ruminated on how to modify the lighting system to better illuminate fly balls on the baseball field, a challenge that Cahill could not solve in previous decades, other sporting activities took place at night under the lights at the General Electric athletic field. During the fall of 1923, football and soccer, sports where the ball does not rise as high above the field as it does in baseball, were successfully conducted in night games.[10]

General Electric generated a bit of newspaper coverage about its initial effort to light a baseball field for night games. In December 1923 a large article, accompanied by several photographs, appeared in the *Schenectady Gazette*, which was a natural outlet given the location of the General Electric research laboratory in Schenectady. An adaptation of that article was distributed through a Midwest wire service in March 1924.

"Two games of baseball and a game of football, played between the hours of 7 and 10 o'clock in the evening, exhibited all the thrills of a fast daylight game and tolled the dirge on the sun's supremacy as an aid to outdoor sports," the *Schenectady Gazette* reported in an article headlined "Sun Outwitted by Electricians." The *Gazette* added that it was now "perfectly practicable, from an engineering viewpoint, to play both baseball and football in the evening unhindered by any restrictions due to darkness." For the August 27 game, the General Electric engineers set up three light poles to deploy 20 floodlights to illuminate the ground of the field with 1000-watt Mazda lamps, along with three searchlights to illuminate the air canopy over the ball field.[11]

To improve the lighting situation for experiments in 1924, General Electric engineers increased the number of poles to five, the number of floodlights to 31, and the number of searchlights to five. One lighting station was near home plate (100 feet back) with two lighting stations near first and third bases (125 feet from home plate), each of which supported five floodlights and one searchlight. Two lighting stations were near the right- and left-field foul lines (175 feet from home plate), each with eight floodlights and one searchlight. All lamps on the poles were placed 40 feet off the ground.[12]

Over the next three years, teams comprised of General Electric employees and engineering students predominantly used the company's lighted athletic field for night games of football and soccer. By 1926 high-school football and amateur soccer teams also regularly used the lighted field. On the baseball front, Lynn-based amateur and semipro teams occasionally used the lighted field, especially in 1926 when General Electric entered a team in the semipro Greater Boston Twilight League.

Lynn also had a minor-league team in 1926 in the recently revived New England League. The team president was Gene Fraser, an executive at the Lynn Gas & Electric Company, who was a long-time baseball fan and civic promoter of the city of Lynn. In 1927 the engineers at General Electric worked with Fraser to have his team play an exhibition baseball game under the lights at General Electric Field. The exhibition night game was initially slated to be played on June 20.

After a dress rehearsal of the final lighting strategy on June 17 in a Greater Boston Twilight League game, the General Electric engineers thought things looked promising for a night game contested among professional ballplayers. There now were six poles set around the perimeter of the baseball field, each topped with 12 floodlights that were 50 feet off the ground. The 72 floodlights for the 1927 game were triple the number of lamps used in the initial night game experiment back in 1923. To form a canopy of light 500 feet high to illuminate fly balls, 25 floodlights were aimed to the sky, compared to the mere three so used in the 1923 game. The engineers estimated that the light emitted equaled a brilliance of 26 million candlepower, or 500 times brighter than moonlight.[13]

The June 20 game was postponed by rain and had to be rescheduled for June 23. This new date coordinated with the getaway day of the New York Yankees leaving Boston after its series with the Red Sox at Fenway Park, which would enable Babe Ruth to play in the exhibition game and help attract more spectators to the experimental night game. Weather again interfered with the plan, though, as rain on the night of June 23 forced another postponement to the following evening, June 24. Ruth, however, had another commitment that day to play with the Yankees in an exhibition game in Springfield, Massachusetts. "A sudden downpour of rain robbed Babe Ruth of his opportunity to try for a home run by electric light," the *New York Times* proclaimed.[14]

Goose Goslin, outfielder of the Washington Senators, attended the 1927 experimental night game conducted in Lynn, Massachusetts. "I didn't believe they could do it," Goslin told reporters after the game. "It's just as good ball as they could play by daylight" (Library of Congress, Prints & Photographs Division, LC-DIG-ggbain-37505).

With the weather finally cooperating on June 24, the Lynn and Salem teams in the New England League took their positions under the lights at General Electric Field "under an arrangement of projections that approximated daylight conditions" in the "first night game ever attempted by organized league teams." Players of the Boston Red Sox and Washington Senators, who were in Boston for a series at Fenway Park, attended the June 24 game in Lynn, which is just ten miles north of Boston. Washington outfielder Goose Goslin spoke very favorably about the night game. "I didn't believe they could do it," Goslin said. "It's just as good ball as they could play by daylight."[15]

Other Washington players also had encouraging thoughts about the future of night baseball. "I'll do my baseball playing in the day time, but I'm willing to admit that I was surprised to be able to follow the ball all during the game," manager Bucky Harris told sportswriters. "I will not be foolish enough to say that baseball cannot be played by electric light and played well." Outfielder Sam Rice moved from his seat in the stands mid-game to get a better view of the playing conditions from behind the outfield fence, where "he had no trouble keeping his eye on the ball when he stood back of the outer line of defense."[16]

In September 1927 the Lynn team in the New England League played a second experimental night game, against a local semipro team, before 2,500 spectators at General Electric Field. "The G.E. engineers have made considerable improvements on the lighting effects," the *Lynn Evening Item* reported. "The lighting arrangement on the field was more efficient than in the previous game the Lynn club played three months ago and the spectators could follow the ball a mite closer."[17]

There were 84 Mazda lamps mounted on eight poles for the September night game, with six of the eight poles each holding 12 lamps and the two poles closest to home plate each holding six lamps. With two additional poles to the six used for the June game, one was added to the infield alignment and the other to the outfield array. The 12-lamp groupings were arranged in three rows of four lights, with the bottom row 47 feet above ground, the middle row 49 feet up, and the top row 53 feet up. Most of the banks had eight lamps directed down toward the field and four directed into the air.[18]

With the Mazda incandescent lamps manufactured by General Electric, each lamp could be individually angled, giving the incandescent lamps greater flexibility and precision in directing light beams than George Cahill could using arc lights in his earlier night baseball experiments. Once night baseball became acceptable in professional leagues, the term "under the mazdas" became an oft-mentioned phrase to describe night baseball games, as sportswriters converted the proper noun for the trademarked lamp product (named for the Persian god of light) into a common noun for a floodlight.

The science of illuminating engineering uses the factors of lamp size, mounting height of lamp poles, space between lamp poles, and the angle positioning of lamps to determine an optimal pattern for how artificial light reaches a coverage area. The lighting of a baseball game is one of the more complex applications, because the field has a non-standard shape and the game occurs both on the ground and well into the air above (fly balls), making the coverage area a three-dimensional, irregularly shaped expanse to be illuminated. In comparison, lighting a rectangular parking lot is much simpler, since the coverage area is basically a two-dimensional surface of standard shape. The basic strategy of the illuminating engineer is to crisscross light from the lamps to provide an even lighting pattern over the coverage area, eliminating shadows and glare as much as possible. Each square foot of the playing field receives light from multiple lamps.[19]

After the June 24 night game in Lynn, New England League president Claude Davidson issued an optimistic prediction: "Within five years the big leagues will be playing regularly scheduled baseball games at night under artificial light. And within less time than five years the New England League will be playing its regulation games by electric light." However, the traditional-bound baseball world did not embrace the novel idea right away. *The Sporting News* called that night game "the stunt" in a brief note buried in agate type far from the front page. New England League club owners were not in a financial position to invest in lighting systems for their ballparks, as they devoted their attention to securing a new law in Massachusetts to legalize Sunday games, which they saw as the more cost-effective approach to increasing ballpark attendance.[20]

As a measure of its impact, the Associated Press story on the night game in Lynn was carried throughout New England, but appeared only sporadically in other newspapers nationwide. Predictably, the first real night baseball game did not gain much traction with executives in major-league baseball, but less understandably there was no perceptible traction within the minor-league ranks either. General Electric also didn't push the issue, presumably because its engineers knew that there was more work needed before professional baseball could be competently played under artificial lights multiple times during a playing season. In effect, General Electric had a solution that was seeking an acknowledged problem. Daylight baseball was just fine with the baseball establishment, even if attendance at weekday ball games was much smaller than at Saturday and Sunday games.

"The introduction of lights into baseball was a collision of two cultural systems openly at odds with each other," Sheila Schroeder diagnosed the situation in her article "When Technology and Culture Collide: The Advent of Night Baseball" published in *NINE: A Journal of Baseball History and Social Policy Perspectives.* "Meaning within the game was dependent on associations with past traditions, but growth was only possible because of its alliance with modernity. Modernity as symbolized by the lights and the disruption of the daytime schedule was an encroachment on the traditional afternoon game which was as old as baseball itself."[21]

Schroeder's observation of the complex problem that actually needed to be tackled, as articulated in her 1994 journal article, was not so evident to the baseball world in 1927. How to solve that cultural problem involved even greater perplexities. The introduction of any new technology never happens in "an ideologically neutral process," but instead occurs within a "discussion of the utopian hope and dystopian fear that surrounds the introduction of technology." In the case of night baseball, its potential acceptance "occurred within a charged atmosphere filled with tension brought on by culturally bound meanings surrounding lights and baseball." Indeed, in 1927 dystopian fears greatly outweighed utopian hopes for night baseball.[22]

There were, however, other promising venues besides baseball fields for the artificial lighting of athletic contests, which could be more immediately implemented. By 1926 the Cahill Bros. Company had expanded into supplying lights for larger athletic areas such as soccer and football fields, using the firm's flagship product, the Cahill Giant Duplex Projector. It appears that George Cahill now specialized in producing reflectors that fit over conventional incandescent lamps, to better aim the emitted light, rather than fashion his own lamps as he had done when he experimented with arc lighting 20 years earlier to illuminate baseball games at night.[23]

Football and soccer fields were much easier to illuminate than a baseball field, since they were akin to the parking-lot example mentioned above as basically a two-dimensional rectangular area. Lighting the airspace above a football or soccer field was less essential than in baseball, since only a few high kicks occurred during a game and there were few passes thrown in football during the 1920s. Both games also transpired largely in the middle of the field, making shadowy areas more tolerable in the corners and on the sidelines.

The first college football field to install the Cahill lights was Lewisohn Stadium at the City College of New York, when the namesake of the stadium donated more money to purchase 30 Cahill reflectors, 20 placed at the top of the stadium and 10 put on poles along the playing field. In the fall of 1927, City College of New York and William & Mary University were among the first colleges to stage football games at night under lights. In the spring of 1928, the Cahill lights were used at the Polo Grounds to illuminate professional soccer games played at night. On May 2 the New York Nationals defeated the team from Fall River, Massachusetts, in an American Soccer League match, where "the greater part of the game took place under the light shed by sixteen huge Cahill reflectors, which together gave out more than 1,000,000 candle power."[24]

In September 1928 Drake University, located in Des Moines, Iowa, announced that its football team would play several football games at night that season. "With larger attendance expected to patronize evening games," Drake looked to expand the type of spectator at its home football games, since the night games would "enable thousands of people who are employed afternoons to attend." The first night football game at Drake's stadium was held on October 6 against Simpson College, with a second game played two weeks later against Grinnell College. The first night game drew 8,200 spectators, nearly triple the 2,800 attendance at the afternoon game in 1927 against Simpson. The 20 projectors, each with two 1000-watt lamps, emitted light rays that "were scientifically crossed in four different directions, leaving no possibility of shadows."[25]

The night football experiment at Drake in 1928 was so successful that numerous colleges installed lights for their football team to play night games during the 1929 season, including Syracuse, Duquesne, and Detroit. There was even a National Football League game played at night in November 1929 at Providence, Rhode Island. Drake expanded its night football ambitions in 1929 by announcing it would play college football powerhouse Notre Dame in a night game at Soldier Field in Chicago.

College football played under the lights at Drake University was particularly inspirational to Lee Keyser, owner of the Des Moines minor-league baseball club in the Western League. By 1928 he was seriously investigating the possibility of playing baseball at night, hoping to reverse the precipitous decline he saw in attendance at non–Sunday afternoon games. Keyser had been looking into night baseball since the summer of 1927, when he learned of the experimental night game played in Lynn, Massachusetts.

Keyser credited night football in Des Moines and a brochure from General Electric as the instigators of his "studying the proposition with engineers who claimed it could be done successfully, contrary to the belief of most in baseball." To become educated about night baseball, Keyser brought General Electric engineers from Schenectady, New York, to Des Moines and he personally visited General Electric Field in Massachusetts to view a demonstration of the lighting system there.[26]

By the fall of 1929 Keyser was sold on the idea of night baseball. He announced that the Des Moines ball club would install lights in its ballpark and conduct night games during the 1930 season. With that bold decision, Keyser stepped into a great unknown and became the pioneer of modern night baseball.

◆ 7 ◆

Minor League
Introduction

Three ball clubs initiated night baseball within five days of each other at the beginning of the 1930 season, each with its own degree of impact on the adoption of the substitute for daylight games. Many writers over the years doing a retrospective on night baseball have tried to place each of these three clubs in the context of "being the first" at staging some aspect of night baseball, such as the first night game under "permanent lights" or "adequate illumination." This often results in trivialities or parsing of facts. More important is what each club's widespread impact was to night baseball.

The long-term impact came in Des Moines, Iowa, where Lee Keyser installed a top-of-the-line lighting system at his ballpark in the Class A Western League. The short-term impact came in Independence, Kansas, where Marvin Truby financed a low-cost, adequate lighting system at the ballpark there in the Class C Western Association. A medium-term impact came in Kansas City, Missouri, where James Wilkinson purchased a portable lighting system that was used for barnstorming by his ball club in the Negro National League, which stoked a desire among residents of small cities in the Midwest to watch night baseball.

In Des Moines, Keyser took a technology-oriented approach to night baseball. After Keyser worked with the lighting engineers at the General Electric Company, he borrowed $22,000 to purchase lights and install them on 100-foot-high steel towers whose four legs were imbedded in concrete. "I could have gotten the lights for one-third that amount," Keyser said a few years later. "But if baseball failed to be a success under them I'd always think it might have succeeded under the better lights, so I'm taking a chance and am getting the best there is."[1]

All too often writers of baseball history have proclaimed that the minor leagues adopted night baseball because of the negative economic impact of the Great Depression. That's not what directly motivated Keyser, however. He had been studying the idea since the 1927 experimental night game in Lynn, Massachusetts, and more seriously since Drake University, the local college near the Des Moines ballpark, installed lights at its football field to play night games in 1928. Keyser was intrigued because attendance at the weekday afternoon games of his ball club had been declining for several years, despite a booming economy during the latter years of the Roaring Twenties. The stock market crash in October 1929 might have been the push-point, forecasting a bigger downturn in attendance for the 1930 season. More likely, though, Keyser had been plotting to install lights based simply on the business potential of the new technology to change the economics of minor-league baseball.

When Keyser announced at the annual minor-league meeting in December 1929 that he would try night baseball in Des Moines for the 1930 season, "many of the magnates who heard of his plan refused to take him seriously at first," *The Sporting News* reported on the perceived insanity of his idea. Other than engineers at the General Electric Company, no one was remotely considering the concept of night baseball at the time. Keyser saw the distinct potential for a new audience at the ballpark. "A great many of our fans belong to the working classes who cannot get away from their duties during the day time," Keyser said in 1929. "But that trouble would be eliminated with night baseball. Look at what it has done for [college] football. It can do the same for baseball."[2]

Keyser used a business argument to convince the other club owners in the Western League to approve his use of night baseball. Based on an analysis of the increased attendance for night games of college football, Keyser forecast that attendance at weekday ball games would be at least two or three times higher than the dismal level of the daylight games in 1929. "An increase of 100 percent for baseball games will make the night experiment not only worthwhile, but a profitable one," Keyser concluded, "which would convert baseball into a financially successful business."[3]

Dale Gear, president of both the Western League and Western Association, was also a big proponent of night baseball as a means to reverse the low attendance at weekday games that had been silently lurking in the background to undermine the operation of many minor leagues since the middle years of the 1920s. Gear never received his due historical credit for helping to expand the installation of lights in the minor leagues. "I don't believe there is a question but that night baseball is the exact solution to the attendance problem in the minors," Gear said in March 1930 after Western League club owners approved the playing of night games in Des Moines. "Many dyed-in-the-wool fans, who are kept from the parks in the afternoons by their labors, would be able and eager to go to the park at night."[4]

In their advocating for night baseball, Keyser and Gear sought to focus the business of minor-league baseball on a new audience for weekday ball games, the working class rather than the businessman. This was heresy in professional baseball, which for decades had built a brand around the special nature of daylight baseball. Modifying the balance in the civic/profit equation of the minor-league business basis was equally heretical, since the slant of the minor leagues had always been toward boosterism of a city, not profitability. It was a brave new world for club owners in the minor leagues to be largely focused on profits. Boosterism, at best, now had a different form, focused on the general population of a city rather than its businessmen, following the decline in civic capitalism experienced in the 1920s. For many ball clubs, this new world was not a good fit.

On May 2, the first night game in Des Moines drew 12,000 spectators to watch the game against the Wichita club under the 146 floodlights atop six light towers that produced a luminosity of 50 million candlepower. Keyser invited a number of baseball executives to view this inaugural night game, but Commissioner Landis was notably absent, having telegraphed that he was "keenly interested in the night baseball idea and regretted his inability to attend." Landis, who shared the conservative ideology of many major-league club owners, despised the idea of night baseball, and was thus more "keenly interested" in seeing the idea fail.[5]

The general feedback from the invited dignitaries was positive, especially that "outfielders invariably started in the right direction at the crack of the bat," signaling the sufficiency of lighting fly balls hit to the outfield. Cy Slapnicka, a scout for the Cleveland

Indians, was the most effusive in his remarks: "Within another year every Class A and B ballpark in the country will be equipped with lights. The playing of both teams indicates that everything can be done under artificial light that can be done in daylight games."[6]

Keyser also arranged to have NBC do a radio broadcast of a portion of the ball game, so that listeners across the country could vicariously share in the excitement and help prime the pump of consumer demand for the adoption of night baseball. "My reaction to night baseball is that it is glorious and wonderful," Keyser told the radio audience during the broadcast. "The players are happy, the crowd perfectly satisfied, and it means that baseball in the minor leagues will now live."[7]

The engineers from General Electric, led in Des Moines by Robert Swackhamer, had greatly improved the lighting technology from the 1927 experimental night game in Lynn, Massachusetts. While the tower locations were similar, each tower in Des Moines held more lamps, 36 lamps for several towers compared to a maximum of 12 lamps in Lynn. The lamps also produced greater brilliance, nearly double the candlepower, 50 million in Des Moines compared to 26 million in Lynn.

The use of high-end lighting technology was both a positive and negative for Keyser. It was positive in the long term by showing that the night game could replicate the condition of daylight games, which provided a significant impetus, albeit five years later, for the major leagues to adopt night baseball. It was negative because the vast majority of minor-league clubs during the next five years did not follow his lead and instead bought low-cost lighting, which hampered the image of night baseball.

The identification of a new audience for the ballpark, one that was not as elite as businessmen, was also both a positive and negative for Keyser. The new audience was a long-term positive, as it became the predominant audience for professional baseball following the end of World War II. That was 15 years into the future in 1930, though. For the remainder of the 1930s, it was negative, very disruptive, as the minor leagues shod their classic emphasis on civic boosterism and now largely focused on profit making. This rubbed the elders of Organized Baseball the wrong way, especially those at the major-league level, by actively courting a lower-income crowd at the expense of the more socially prominent businessman. However, within the next few years, there would be a connection between these short-term changes in minor-league baseball and the New Deal focus of President Franklin D. Roosevelt, which will be explored in the next chapter.

Keyser expected to make money not only from the night ball games in Des Moines, but also by convincing other ball clubs to install lights, through a partnership with General Electric called the Outdoor Sports Illuminating Company. General Electric ran advertisements in the May issues of *The Sporting News* to try to generate business, directing readers to contact their nearest office of General Electric or to mail Keyser in Des Moines. One advertisement touted Keyser as saying "a great night, a great game, and a great gate" after the May 2 night game where he "had floodlighted the field with 146 General Electric Novalux projectors and had scheduled the game *for the evening*," thus making the ball field "a segregated section of daytime, brilliantly lighted from home plate to deep field, from the pitcher's mound to the sky."[8]

Expectations were high, but results were low. "We tried to get a patent or a copyright on the idea," Keyser recalled years later. "But we found out quickly there was no possible way of doing it. We were informed that anyone could obtain lights and do anything they wanted with them." Also derailing Keyser's plan to sell numerous General Electric lighting systems was the intense competition from another Iowa business. The Giant

Manufacturing Company of Council Bluffs, Iowa, had a lower cost lighting system, which the company sold to illuminate the minor-league ballpark in Independence, Kansas.[9]

Night baseball in Independence, Kansas, had the greatest short-term impact to minor-league baseball. The Independence club took the inexpensive route to equip its ballpark with lighting by purchasing an $8,000 system from Giant Manufacturing. One of the city's leading businessmen, wealthy oilman Marvin Truby, loaned the ball club the money to buy the lights. The club also skimped on the infrastructure to position the lights. The mayor of Independence marshaled local resources to scavenge metal pipes from the local oil fields to fashion into 60-foot-high poles on which to hang the lights.[10]

The end result in Independence was five poles circling the foul lines and outfield fence, with additional lights mounted atop the grandstand behind home plate. Given the illicit fear that darkness still instilled in many people, lights were also installed in the parking lot to "prevent the borrowing of automobiles" during the night ball games. The lighting system was tested at an April 17 exhibition game between the Independence Producers and the barnstorming House of David novelty team. The first regular-season night game was slated for Saturday, April 26, but rain forced a delay to Monday, April 28, when

The first regular-season game played under artificial lighting occurred at Independence, Kansas, in the Class C Western Association. The low-cost, low-light, nature of lighting systems installed at many lower-classification minor-league ballparks contributed to a widespread negative image of night baseball (Independence Historical Museum).

1,500 people watched Independence play its first regular-season night game against the team from Muskogee, Oklahoma.[11]

Compared to the lighting system in Des Moines, the lights in Independence were decidedly less brilliant in illuminating the baseball field. It was the low-cost, low-light, nature of lighting systems installed at many lower-classification minor-league ballparks that contributed to a widespread negative image of night baseball. Portable lighting systems helped to further that negative perception.

James Wilkinson, owner of the Kansas City Monarchs ball club, used a portable lighting system in 1930 to play a substantial barnstorming schedule against white semipro and black independent teams beyond its games in the Negro National League. In addition to spreading the concept of night baseball within the Midwest, Wilkinson's most immediate impact to professional baseball was stimulating the Class A Texas League to become an early adopter of night baseball. Later in 1930 Wilkinson also staged the first night game conducted at a major-league ballpark.

For $7,000 the Giant Manufacturing Company built Wilkinson a portable lighting system, which was similar to the one used by Al Lawson back in 1902, only this one used incandescent lamps, not arc lights. Wilkinson's system was "powered by a portable generator that fed electricity to floodlights secured to telescoping poles fastened to trucks; the poles elevated to a height of forty-five to fifty feet and supported six floodlights each." The trucks would be parked in foul territory along the infield and behind a canvas fence in the outfield (inside the normal outfield fence). The smaller actual playing area required special ground rules for batted balls hitting the temporary canvas fence. While the makeshift system and its mediocre light intensity contributed to a carnival atmosphere that did not help elevate the image of night baseball, it did expose numerous people to the concept of night baseball.[12]

The first night game under Wilkinson's portable lights was slated for April 26 in Arkansas City, Kansas, but it was rained out. Two days later the portable system made its debut on April 28, when the Monarchs played under the lights in Enid, Oklahoma, against a college baseball team. On May 5 the Monarchs played a night game at the minor-league ballpark in Waco, Texas, where the lighting system intrigued several Texas League executives, who could envision it as a solution to the torrid summer heat that usually drew tiny crowds to the ballpark for afternoon daylight games played on weekdays.

Ollie Biedenharn, owner of the Shreveport, Louisiana, club in the Texas League, arranged to rent Wilkinson's portable lighting system for a test game on May 8 at his club's ballpark in Shreveport, contested between two Louisiana clubs in the Class D Cotton States League, Baton Rouge and Alexandria. This regular-season game in the league standings attracted 3,500 spectators, seven times the typical 500 admissions for a weekday game in Shreveport. Emulating the approach taken by Keyser in Des Moines, Biedenharn contracted with General Electric to supply high-quality lighting and Shreveport inaugurated night games on July 10, the first of 15 such home games during the 1930 season. Shreveport was the second Texas League club to install lights for night games, as the Waco club played its first home night game on June 20.[13]

In mid–May, following the debut of night baseball in Des Moines and Independence, two more minor-league clubs staged night games at their ballpark, the Decatur, Illinois, club in the Class B Three-I League on May 14 and the Lincoln, Nebraska, club in the Class D Nebraska State League on May 19. Somewhat appropriately, the visiting team for the Decatur night game was from Quincy, Illinois, whose ancestor club back in 1883 had participated in the one of the first experimental night games. Drafting off the success of the Cotton States League night game played in Shreveport earlier in May, the league's Jackson, Mississippi, club installed lights and played its first night game on May 29.[14]

By the end of May, Gear's two minor leagues, the Western League and Western Association, had multiple clubs with lighting systems at their home ballpark. Joining Independence in the Western Association were Muskogee, Oklahoma, and Joplin, Missouri; joining Des Moines in the Western League was Omaha, Nebraska.

Given the uncommon nature of baseball at night compared to the daylight version, newspapers reported the scores of night games in their summary of league standings and results with a parenthetical "(night game)" or "(night)" label immediately following the score, as in "Des Moines 14, St. Joseph 6 (Monday night game)." This convention persisted for decades, well into the 1960s, as a relic of the conservative attitude of professional baseball as it struggled to fully embrace the concept of night baseball.[15]

Despite the leadership of Keyser to install a top-of-the-line General Electric lighting system in Des Moines, all these other early adopters of night baseball instead followed the example of Independence and purchased a lower-cost lighting system. During the first month of night baseball in the minor leagues, Giant Manufacturing captured the vast majority of the nascent market for lighting systems at baseball parks. General Electric was involved only in the installation at Des Moines. Giant Manufacturing touted this advantage in its advertising, claiming in late May that by having supplied the lighting systems for 14 of the 15 ball clubs staging night games in the minor leagues that "certainly is sufficient proof as to which system is superior for the playing of night games."[16]

Giant Manufacturing was "superior" definitely when it came to low cost, which could translate into quick profits for ball clubs, but the company was not necessarily superior in its technical knowledge of lighting. In fact, Giant used the Mazda lamps invented by General Electric, which were licensed to be manufactured by several other companies. What most tangibly differentiated Giant Manufacturing from its competitor General Electric was the housing around the light bulb, i.e., the projector, which had what Giant characterized as "an interior finish with ultra-reflecting quality." What Giant Manufacturing was selling was its projector, while its advertisements subtly implied there could be a difference in the actual light bulbs used, vis-à-vis those in a General Electric lighting system.[17]

The other big difference between Giant Manufacturing and General Electric was the engineering consulting ability. General Electric had an advantage here, having a better understanding of the science of illuminating an athletic field. Giant liked to recommend that the poles holding the lights be erected in front of the stands, to minimize the loss of light efficiency due to the distance traveled from the lamp. This gave Giant a cost advantage, since placing lights on the roof of a grandstand usually required reinforcing the roof to handle the additional weight. It also minimized the effort needed to engineer a lighting pattern. However, poles placed in front of the stands blocked the view of spectators, a big downside.

Between the Decoration Day holiday on May 30 and the Independence Day holiday on July 4, all three Class AA leagues had at least one ball club install lights to play home night games.

The Pacific Coast League was the most enthusiastic adopter of night baseball, with six of its eight clubs installing lights in their home ballpark during the 1930 season. The

Sacramento club led the way, playing its first home night game on June 10. The ball clubs in Oakland, Los Angeles (two), Portland, and Seattle quickly followed suit. Night baseball would have completely swept through the league if the stadium in San Francisco, which housed both the Seals and Mission Reds clubs, had not been slated for demolition after the 1930 season, since both clubs were slated to play in the new Seals Stadium beginning in 1931.[18]

Night baseball was so popular among club owners in the Pacific Coast League because it gave them an advantage to retain their independence from the major leagues. "Optimistic owners predict the Coast league will see a better brand of baseball," newspapers reported following the 1930 season. "The added receipts will enable them to keep their star players, whom they might otherwise sell at a profit to the majors."[19]

The International League was the next largest adopter of night baseball among the top-tier minor leagues, with five of its eight clubs installing lights during the 1930 season. The Buffalo club initiated night games on July 3, followed later that month by Jersey City and in August by the Newark and Reading, Pennsylvania, clubs. The Baltimore club began night games in September, initially hosting an exhibition game with the major-league Philadelphia Phillies.[20]

The American Association had just one of its eight ball clubs install lights in 1930, the Indianapolis club, which staged its first night game on June 7 before 4,000 spectators. Owner Norman Perry, an executive at the Indianapolis Power & Light Company, utilized the services of General Electric rather than Giant Manufacturing, one of the few ball clubs that followed Keyser's example to install a high-quality lighting system. The meager expansion of night baseball within the league was partially due to the prevalence of cities with a northern climate (which did not stop Buffalo in the International League), but more prominently because the league saw itself as more major-league caliber than other minor leagues.[21]

Indianapolis left its mark on night baseball by ushering in the solution to the initially vexing issue of how to make up a rainout of a night game. On June 11 the club initially tried what today is known as a day/night doubleheader, playing the rained-out game as an afternoon game and keeping the scheduled night game as a separate-admission event. By August, though, Indianapolis was using what today is known as a twi-night doubleheader, a two-games-for-one-admission event where the first game starts at dinner time and the second game begins 15 minutes after the conclusion of the opener. While technically this is not a night doubleheader, the twin bill could easily result in a five-hour event and might even stretch beyond midnight.[22]

In July numerous minor-league ball clubs installed lights to commence night baseball. All leagues in Class A were now playing some night games with the addition of Allentown, Pennsylvania, in the Eastern League and Little Rock, Arkansas, in the Southern Association. Major inroads were made at the Class B and C levels, with the debut of night baseball in Binghamton, New York, in the New York–Pennsylvania League; Wheeling, West Virginia, in the Middle Atlantic League; and High Point, North Carolina, in the Piedmont League.[23]

The Mississippi Valley League in Class D was a fervent believer in the value of night baseball, with six of the eight clubs having lights in 1930, with the other two joining in 1931 so the entire league played night ball. With its clubs in small cities in Iowa and Illinois, this league was a remarkable example of forward thinking with its belief in the financial payback of using such an expensive new technology, with the clubs in Rock

Island and Moline, Illinois, also using the services of General Electric to engineer their lighting systems.[24]

Keyser's working-class audience model was a great fit for many industrial cities in the mid-level minor leagues, since there was an inherent limited volume of businessmen that could reasonably attend daylight games during the workweek. "Omaha is primarily an industrial town and a large portion of the fans are working during the daytime," the owner of the Omaha ball club told *The Sporting News*. "Our Saturday and Sunday crowds have always been good, indicating the baseball followers were here, if games could be played at a time when they could attend." Giant Manufacturing advertised nearly every week in *The Sporting News*, appealing to ball clubs in small industrial cities to install lighting systems. By the end of July, Giant Manufacturing was claiming that "more than 90% of all night baseball is being played under Giant Projectors."[25]

Also in July 1930 Wilkinson's portable lighting system was set up at Forbes Field in Pittsburgh, where a night game was played on July 18 between two black teams, the Kansas City Monarchs and Homestead Grays. This first night contest at a major-league ballpark helped to elevate the discussion of potential night baseball adoption among major-league executives.[26]

By late July three ball clubs in the National League were actively exploring the idea of night baseball. The St. Louis Cardinals were the earliest public advocate of the idea, meeting with Keyser in May and then installing a lighting system in the ballpark of its Houston farm club in the Texas League. The Cincinnati Reds were the first major-league club to play a night exhibition game, on July 30 at Indianapolis of the American Association.[27]

Charles Stoneham, owner of the New York Giants, was the most active major-league executive to explore night baseball. The Giants announced that the temporary lights at the Polo Grounds would be used to stage exhibition night baseball games between semipro teams in the summer and for college football games at night during the fall. The Giants also played an exhibition game on August 6 at Bridgeport, Connecticut, against the club there in the Eastern League.[28]

The initial experimental baseball game on August 1 at the Polo Grounds was a flop, since the lighting system normally used for soccer games and boxing matches at night was not nearly brilliant enough for baseball. Improved lighting for semipro night baseball games at the Polo Grounds in September proved more successful. However, the games under temporary lighting there were no comparison to the semipro games conducted by the Bushwick club under lights at Dexter Park in Queens, where regular night games were staged beginning in mid–July.[29]

This flurry of activity by three National League clubs occurred despite the public dismissal of night baseball by the league president, John Heydler: "I find there is no demand in the major leagues to get away from baseball and all that it means as a great sport through tradition and development and get it into the show business, which, after all is said and done, is all that night baseball is or can be." When Heydler referred to "no demand," he meant by the club owners, not by baseball fans, as he kept tightly to the major-league mantra that baseball was meant to only be played in the daylight and that it was a sport, certainly not entertainment. He also strongly implied that daylight baseball during the six-day workweek was meant largely for businessmen, not the masses.[30]

American League ball clubs displayed little interest in exploring night baseball at this time. New York Yankees owner Jacob Ruppert issued a bland statement, with many

National League president John Heydler dismissed night baseball in 1930, saying that "show business ... is all that night baseball is or can be," in the midst of rapid adoption of the night game in the minor leagues (Library of Congress, Prints & Photographs Division, LC-DIG-npcc-17316).

qualifiers, at the inaugural night game in the New York City area at Jersey City: "I imagine night baseball will prove a great benefit to the minor leagues and if it becomes definitely popular in the minors I don't see why some day it should not become part of major league baseball." Owners in both major leagues likely bristled when postseason playoff series in several minor leagues were conducted via night games, in stark contrast to entirely daylight nature of the vaunted World Series.[31]

The forecast made by Keyser back in February 1930 for increased attendance at night games came to fruition. In the Pacific Coast League and American Association, the number of spectators at night games tripled the level at daylight games during the workweek. A similar comparison in the Western League showed that night attendance doubled the daylight average.[32]

During the 1930 season, 19 of the 23 minor leagues had at least one ball club that installed a lighting system at its ballpark to stage night games (see Appendix A). All four leagues that competed without the availability of night baseball in 1930 disbanded before the start of the 1931 season. Ironically, two minor leagues with a history of involvement in experimental night games did not engage in night baseball during 1930, due to financial woes, which inhibited clubs in those two Class B league from purchasing lighting systems. The New England League, which had clubs participate in the 1927 night game in Lynn, Massachusetts, failed to make it to mid-season before the league disbanded; the

Central League, with clubs involved in the 1909 night game in Grand Rapids, Michigan, barely survived to the end of the 1930 season.

Night baseball seemed necessary to survive as a league, although it was not a universal savior of minor-league baseball, since three of the 19 leagues with night-baseball clubs failed to return for the 1931 season (South Atlantic, Southeastern, and Blue Ridge). The other 16 leagues that embraced night baseball in 1930 formed the foundation of minor-league baseball in 1931, which had effectively suffered a 30 percent reduction in the number of leagues from the 23 that began the 1930 season (all three new leagues in 1931 disbanded by mid-season that year).

Night baseball forestalled a complete liquidation of the minor-league system. Without night baseball, it is doubtful than more than eight minor leagues would have survived the entire 1930 season, with a half dozen Class AA and A leagues (all except the Eastern League) and perhaps one or two Class B or C leagues. Night baseball, though, did not have many friends in high places.

Commissioner Landis was a champion of the independence of minor-league ball clubs, but he was not a proponent of night baseball. "I've talked with a lot of players who have participated in games at night, and they all seem to like it," Landis lukewarmly told *The Sporting News* after the first year of night baseball in the minor leagues. "People can go see games at night when they couldn't get away from their work in the daytime."[33]

The conservatism of Landis and major-league club owners would stymie the growth of night baseball in the minor leagues over the next four years, as professional baseball grappled with the detrimental effects of the Great Depression.

◆ 8 ◆

Divergent Views

Among the 19 minor leagues that began the 1931 season, the ability to conduct night baseball was highly correlated to survival. The 16 carryover leagues from 1930 all had at least one club that could host night games; these 16 leagues all survived to the end of the 1931 season. The three new minor leagues, all in Class D, had no clubs with lighting systems; these three leagues all disbanded by mid-season.

In 1931 at least 50 minor-league clubs had a lighting system at their ballpark to stage night baseball. One newcomer to night baseball in 1931 was San Francisco in the Pacific Coast League, where Seals Stadium, "the first ballpark built since the night ball vogue started," had light towers specifically incorporated into the stadium design to produce a more brilliant illumination of the playing field. The first night game at Seals Stadium in San Francisco was held on April 23, 1931.[1]

All eight ball clubs in the Pacific Coast League hosted night baseball during the 1931 season. Night ball was also pervasive in four leagues where at least six of the eight clubs hosted night games: Texas League, Three-I League, Piedmont League, and Mississippi Valley League. Among the higher classification leagues, the fewest lighted ballparks were in the American Association (just Indianapolis) and the Southern Association (Little Rock and Atlanta).[2]

The Middle Atlantic League was also a hotbed of night baseball in 1931, as 75 percent of that 12-club league had stadium lighting for night games to appeal to the largely working-class population of the cities in the league. The Beckley, West Virginia, club was even featured in an advertisement for the Giant Manufacturing Company. "After several months of thorough investigation of all different types of light equipment for playing satisfactory night baseball, my directors and I decided to purchase and install your Giant 4500 watt projector," the president of the Beckley club wrote in a letter to Giant, which was prominently displayed in the advertisement. The purchase was consummated "not withstanding the fact that the Westinghouse and General Electric Companies offered and recommended lighting systems at from two to three thousand dollars less in price."[3]

Giant Manufacturing was the leader in ballpark lighting systems at this early stage of night baseball, providing the lights for two dozen minor-league clubs. The company's advertisements boldly emphasized that "90% of all night baseball is played under Giants" and noted that its larger customers included the Pacific Coast League clubs in Sacramento, Oakland, and Seattle. The General Electric Company, which used more understated advertising lines such as "floodlighting has made better business for baseball," provided lighting systems to one dozen ball clubs, including Baltimore and Reading in the International League and Indianapolis in the American Association.[4]

During the early 1930s Giant Manufacturing and General Electric competed on the design of the projector surrounding the light source, since both firms used the same high-wattage Madza lamps. Giant Manufacturing sold open-type projectors, which it claimed produced no glare and were most economical; General Electric sold closed-type projectors, which it claimed better protected the product from the weather and reflected the greatest amount of light (with minimum glare). General Electric also emphasized the human element of engineering the lighting pattern onto the field, not just a product that produced light.[5]

At this early stage of night baseball, minor-league clubs tended to purchase a Giant Manufacturing lighting

MORE NIGHT BASEBALL Under Giant Projectors

The whole baseball world is in a unit on the superiority of Giant Projectors — and this confidence is expressed by the added orders daily for the illumination of baseball fields.

During the past week the following have contracted for Giant Projectors to play night games:

Binghamton, N. Y., in the New York-Pennsylvania League; Akron, Ohio; Seattle, Wash., in Pacific Coast League; Topeka, Kans., in the Western League; Wheeling, W. Va., in the Middle Atlantic League; Portland, Oregon; in the Pacific Coast League; Danville, Ill., in the Three-I League.

Among the clubs to play night baseball with huge success under Giants are the following:

Winston-Salem, High Point and Durham, N. C., all in the Piedmont League; Spokane, Wash.; Phoenix,

Ariz., in the Arizona State League; Waterloo, Iowa, in the Mississippi Valley League; Waco, Tex., Texas League; Montgomery, Ala., Southeastern League; Springfield and Decatur, Ill., in Three-I League; Jackson, Miss., Cotton States League; Omaha, Nebr., Western League; Lincoln, Nebr., Nebraska State League; Muskogee, Okla., and Independence, Kansas, in the Western Association; and many semi-pro teams.

More than 80% of night baseball is played under Giants and the outstanding successes with night games everywhere is further proof of the superiority of Giant Projectors for night baseball.

Write or Wire for Complete Details

GIANT MFG. CO.

Division N-B

COUNCIL BLUFFS, IOWA   TRENTON, N. J.

During the formative years of night baseball in the early 1930s, Giant Manufacturing Company of Council Bluffs, Iowa, provided the majority of lighting systems for minor-league ballparks, which the firm prominently noted in its advertisements during that period.

system because it had the lowest cost in the short term. This was particularly the case in the Class C and D leagues, where finances were the most difficult to manage. General Electric had the cost advantage in the long term, though, given the lower maintenance cost of the closed-type projector. It arguably also had an engineering advantage for ball clubs seeking better lighting of a baseball field. General Electric gradually made inroads into the early market dominance of Giant Manufacturing, particularly as the downside of the open-type projector became more evident, as bugs, dirt, and other debris clogged the projectors and resulted in diminished lighting. In essence, the projector from Giant Manufacturing cost less, but, if not periodically cleaned, it reflected increasingly lower levels of light over time.

Night baseball was now a significant aspect of minor-league baseball. During the 1931 season about 40 percent of all minor-league clubs staged night baseball; excluding the Class D leagues, that ratio rose to about 50 percent. However, to the major leagues, night baseball was a mere curiosity, something not remotely considered to be a future possibility for regular-season play.[6]

Progress on night baseball at the major-league level was minimal in 1931. The New York Giants did play two exhibition night games with the Chicago White Sox during spring training, on March 21 in Houston and March 25 at San Antonio. Typical of the derisive attitude toward the innovation, the *New York Times* reporter wrote, "For a reason not at all clear, the Giants and White Sox allowed a perfectly fine afternoon of brilliant Texas sunshine to go to complete waste here today in order to demonstrate once again the marvels of night baseball."[7]

Major-league ball clubs had numerous objections to the concept of night baseball. At the top of the list was the philosophical argument that baseball, by its very nature, was a daylight game. "I do not like night baseball," Pittsburgh owner Barney Dreyfuss said in 1930. "The national game is a daylight game. Any attempt to take it from its natural surroundings, where it has always been played, is to destroy its appeal as an open game where the ball can be followed every second and every play can be seen by every spectator." Related to this inherency was the benefit to ballpark spectators. "There is no chance of night baseball becoming popular in the bigger cities," Washington owner Clark Griffith said. "People there are educated to see the best there is and will stand for only the best. High-class baseball cannot be played at night under artificial light." According to Griffith, the benefits derived from attending a daylight game "are largely due to fresh air and sunshine," so therefore "night air and electric lights are a poor substitute."[8]

Another oft-noted objection was that night baseball was just a novelty or passing fad. As late as 1933 baseball writers were still connecting this argument to the daylight argument, in newspaper headlines such as "Popularity of Night Baseball Wanes" and "Night Ball Wearing Off."[9]

Many were also concerned about the difficulty of judging the skills of minor-league players as they developed to play at the major-league level, where no night games would be played. "Playing baseball at night is quite different from playing it in the daytime," Cleveland general manager Billy Evans said. "A player trained for night baseball might not be so successful in the sunlight." Some pitchers thought they had an advantage, since their pitches might not be seen as well by batters, although many batters reported being able to see the ball better under lights. Fielding was nearly universally seen as suffering in night baseball, as fielders had some difficulty picking up line drives and ground balls rolled differently through the dew-soaked grass.[10]

The uneven nature of the lighting systems between the high and low minor leagues made these player development judgments harder to make. Different lengths of the season where night ball was feasible, not burdening spectators and players with cold weather, added to this

"There is no chance of night baseball becoming popular in the bigger cities," Washington Senators owner Clark Griffith said in 1930. "People there are educated to see the best there is and will stand for only the best. High-class baseball cannot be played at night under artificial light" (Library of Congress, Prints & Photographs Division, LC-DIG-npcc-14297).

conundrum. The Pacific Coast League began to play night games in April, while minor leagues in the South commenced in early May and leagues in the North in late May. Some leagues even delayed the first night game of the season until June. Hot-weather leagues understandably tended to play the most night games, as did leagues with ball clubs located in working-class cities.

The one very positive attribute of night baseball was given short shrift by major-league executives. "A far greater number of people are able and eager to attend ball games at night than is the case in daytime," Cardinals owner Sam Breadon often said. "The introduction of an occasional night game into the league schedule might not prove a bad idea." A larger number of people could attend night games, since they worked a fixed schedule during the day and thus had no opportunity to go to the ballpark to watch an afternoon game during the workweek (unless they wanted to forego a half-day's pay). This attitude indicates that there was a bias toward businessmen and others with time flexibility in their work schedule, who frequented the higher-priced seats at a daylight game, rather than simply customers who could afford the basic admission price, who could only attend a game on Sunday. However, because Breadon wanted to expand the diversity of the weekday audience for major-league baseball, his fellow club owners generally ignored his comments about night baseball.[11]

Objections to night baseball seemed to be irrationally connected to the nineteenth-century fear of the darkness in the gaslight era of illumination, which would ostensibly soil the integrity of the twentieth-century national pastime. "There appeared to be something sinister, something artificial, something destabilizing about the night," White noted in *Creating the National Pastime* to explain the resistance to night baseball. "It was an atmosphere of the circus, the opera, the hippodrome. It was more sophisticated, more contrived, and more dangerous than baseball merited." The major leagues had an inherent obliviousness to, if not disdain for, the broader audience interested in baseball but unable to attend a weekday afternoon ball game. It was an early sign that the major leagues had an unhealthy reliance on the national boosterism component of their civic/profit business basis, a mythology that White referred to as "a timeless, even magical, phenomenon, insulated from the rest of life." Unfortunately, this characterization meant that "the sport had become a metaphor for the past itself."[12]

Baseball in the early 1930s was caught in the clash of tradition and modernity. While baseball executives had earlier embraced the improvements in telegraph and trolley, the technology of electric floodlights stymied the imagination of major-league club owners, who were failing to cope well with the radio (to broadcast games or not) and the automobile (where people could park for the game). All these new technologies that permeated American society during the 1930s channeled the major leagues to a dystopian fear of night baseball, as Schroeder observed in her journal article "When Technology and Culture Collide: The Advent of Night Baseball," rather than the utopian hope that it would better the baseball business. Major-league baseball chose the safety blanket of national boosterism rather than grapple with how to best use new technology to sustain their profits.[13]

For the 1932 season minor-league baseball essentially took a breather on the expansion of night baseball, as Americans experienced the depth of the Great Depression when unemployment rates reached 25 percent and hundreds of bank failures plagued the country. In December 1931, a five-man executive committee was appointed to study the fundamental problems impacting the growth and stability of the minor leagues and recommend a plan to fix those problems. One of the five committee members was Joe Carr, former president of the Columbus ball club, who would have a prominent role in implementing the fix-it plan to revive minor-league baseball.

While 19 leagues started the 1932 season (16 holdovers plus three new ones), only 11 leagues completed the season. Seven leagues disbanded midseason, including the Three-I League and the Cotton States League, which had been night-baseball stalwarts. The dissolution of the Eastern League was a particularly disturbing clarion call, since it was a Class A league, six of its eight clubs staged night games, and three of its eight clubs were associated with the nascent farm systems of the three major-league clubs based in New York City. Once that financial assistance was withdrawn in July, though, the Eastern League discontinued operations. An eighth league, the Western Association that had inaugurated night baseball back in 1930, limped to the finish line with just four clubs, barely alive and basically disbanded; the league did not operate the following year, given its financial distress.

Clearly, night baseball was no magic bullet for minor-league baseball, given the huge number of potential ballpark spectators who were unemployed and the many other people who were underemployed or scared of losing their job. In a broader context, there was also fear that night baseball indeed was merely a fad and not a precursor of the future.

A few minor-league clubs did commence hosting night games during the 1932 season, although it was not close to the pace of the previous two years. Demand for new lighting systems had demonstrably declined, as evidenced by the complete lack of advertisements in *The Sporting News* by General Electric and Giant Manufacturing. The two companies had been prodigious advertisers when they provided the vast majority of lighting equipment for ballparks in 1930 and 1931.

General Electric worked with the Williamsport ball club in the Class B New York–Pennsylvania League to install lights at Bowman Field in 1932 through a civic effort by the local community. The project was jointly financed by several wealthy directors of the ball club and the Williamsport School District, since the high school also played its games in the stadium. General Electric also worked with the three clubs in the American Association that initiated night baseball in 1932, bringing the level of lighted ballparks in that Class AA league up to four (one-half of the league). Consistent with the league's approach to emulate major-league baseball, the Columbus, Kansas City, and Louisville clubs took a conservative approach to scheduling night games, but yet spared no expense to purchase a top-of-the-line lighting system. Both Louisville and Kansas City announced they would limit night games to the slowest weekdays for attendance. Columbus pursued the most radical approach to rationing night baseball.[14]

At Columbus, Larry MacPhail, in his second year as president of the ball club, quietly announced a strategy to stage just seven night games during the playing season, one against each other club in the American Association. The seven-game strategy was unique in minor-league baseball, during a period when most clubs sought to conduct as many home games as possible under the lights.[15]

MacPhail was an inveterate entrepreneur, who had owned a variety of business enterprises in Columbus during the 1920s. As a man who "embodied the consumer component of modern capitalism," MacPhail was characterized as having "great imagination and completely fearless." However, his self-destructive tendencies also illustrated that "there is a thin line between genius and insanity and in Larry's case it was sometimes so thin you could see him drifting back and forth." MacPhail was a maverick, which put him on a circuitous path through three stops in major-league baseball where he instigated tempestuous rifts with many people. Still, his contributions to night baseball resulted in his selection to the Baseball Hall of Fame.[16]

MacPhail left no written record regarding how he arrived at this strategy to market night baseball as a "special" event that would encourage greater attendance at daylight ball games. Since Columbus was a farm club of the St. Louis Cardinals, it seems likely that MacPhail consulted with Cardinals owner Sam Breadon or general manager Branch Rickey about restricting night games in Columbus to serve as a pilot program for the Cardinals to eventually propose night baseball in the National League. The Cardinals fronted the money for the new ballpark in Columbus as well as its lighting system. Both men had experience watching Sunday games in St. Louis transform from a special event into a necessity to conduct two-for-one doubleheaders on Sunday, which they wanted to avert with the eventual introduction of night baseball.

Attendance at the first night game in Columbus on Friday, June 17, was 21,000 people, which exceeded the 17,000 capacity of the stadium. MacPhail, though, was more interested in expanding the audience more into the middle class. In a 1933 interview published in *The Sporting News*, MacPhail barely mentioned night games as he talked about his other promotional activities. "The game is no longer a semi-civic sport monopoly," MacPhail avowed, believing that baseball "is in the amusement business and therefore highly competitive" and that he operated under the "theory of giving fans a good show, in a clean seat, and they'll come back." He implemented a number of goodwill gestures to foster that strategy, including appreciation days when unemployed fans were admitted free, lower ticket prices for women and children, and coupons for free Ladies Day admission to encourage family attendance.[17]

The seven-game restriction did not stop MacPhail from playing a few additional night games as "special" exhibition games in addition to his abbreviated night-game schedule against American Association clubs. The Cincinnati Reds played an exhibition game under the lights in Columbus in September 1932.[18]

In 1932 a few more major-league clubs also gingerly experimented with night baseball by playing exhibition games under the lights. The New York Giants played two exhibitions in 1932 under permanent lighting, at Seals Stadium in San Francisco in late March against the minor-league Seals and at Dexter Park in Queens in late September against the semipro Bushwick club. The Boston Braves and St. Louis Cardinals played exhibitions in their home ballparks under the portable lighting equipment of the barnstorming House of David baseball team.[19]

The House of David was a quirky religious colony based in Benton Harbor, Michigan, which required men to sport a beard and long hair as a pre-condition of the faith. In the 1920s the House of David fielded a talented semipro team comprised of faith members. By 1932 this ball team had converted into a traveling novelty act, which included non-faith pitcher Grover Cleveland Alexander, who was not required to sport a beard. The team traveled with a portable lighting system, similar to the one used by the Kansas City Monarchs, to play night games in small cities across the country. Their trucks were even emblazoned on the side with the promotional tagline "House of David Night Baseball."[20]

The Boston Braves played the House of David in August under its portable lights at Braves Field. Only a sparse crowd of 2,500 people showed up that evening to watch the nocturnal spectacle. "Six floodlights, set at sporting distances like cuspidors in an old-fashioned hotel, illuminated the field, and made the ball visible to a certain degree," the *Boston Globe* reported. "But when all is said and done, baseball is a national pastime only when the sun is hot and high, and the clouds scud off the Charles [River]." The *Globe* further editorialized: "It is hard to believe that the big leagues will ever abandon the sunlight for the arc light. As a novelty, night baseball is all right. As a permanent diet, its value is at least doubtful."[21]

In September the St. Louis Cardinals hosted the House of David for an exhibition game at Sportsman's Park. Breadon used the portable lights to pump up interest in the night baseball concept among St. Louis baseball fans. The night exhibition game attracted 10,000 spectators, while merely 400 people had bothered to pay to watch the National League ball game that afternoon. "At Columbus, where we have the latest thing in floodlights, there is not a shadow or a dark spot," Breadon told a sportswriter after the game. "In some respects the visibility is greater than by daylight. The ball is highly illuminated by the lights, and really is more easily followed."[22]

While the traveling House of David team may have helped to expand popularity of night games among residents of small cities, the low-quality lighting and comedic pre-game warm-up act did little to burnish the image of night baseball among sportswriters and most major-league executives, who questioned the sense of dignity in night games and periodically used the term "travesty" to characterize night baseball.

Breadon was the sole club owner in 1932 to express enthusiasm for the possibility of playing night baseball at the major-league level. Given his club's dependence on Sunday doubleheaders, he was an exuberant proponent of night baseball. Unfortunately, Breadon was stymied by the St. Louis Browns, since the Cardinals were a tenant of the Browns at Sportsman's Park. While he continued to discuss the issue with Browns owner Phil Ball, Breadon expanded night baseball in 1933 within his own minor-league farm system beyond Houston and Columbus to include its Rochester, New York, club in the International League. Upon the death of Ball in 1933, however, the seemingly hill-like obstacle to considering night baseball in St. Louis turned into a mountain, as protracted negotiations with the Ball estate as well as with the new owners of the Browns excessively delayed the adoption of night baseball in St. Louis.

By 1933 the day-of-game mix in the major leagues had effectively defaulted to simply doubleheaders on Sunday and holidays. Weekday afternoon games drew an inconsequential attendance, which was often discounted through promotions such as Ladies Day or another doubleheader and thus provided only a marginal supplement to revenue. The "synthetic" doubleheader on Sunday became a staple of the major-league calendar in 1930, as clubs actively eliminated a low-attendance weekday game to add it as the second game of a Sunday doubleheader, rather than wait for rain to postpone a game to naturally construct a twin bill on Sunday. Major-league clubs had unwittingly replicated the minor-league day-of-game model of the 1920s, by extensively utilizing promotions to drive ballpark attendance.

Breadon had initiated the synthetic doubleheader in St. Louis, but other ball clubs quickly adopted the approach. During the early years of the Great Depression, the volume of Sunday doubleheaders rose in direct correlation with the increase in the unemployment rate. Sunday doubleheaders increased in volume from 27 in 1929 to 69 in 1931 to 107 in 1933, while the unemployment rate spiked from 5.5 percent in 1929 to 16 percent in 1931 and topped out at 25 percent in 1933. Sunday doubleheaders in 1933 routinely comprised one-half to two-thirds of the Sunday card.[23]

Sunday attendance produced the vast majority of ball-club revenue due to a large proportion of suburban fans, since the population of suburbs in most cities was growing faster than the inner-city population. People also had more free time during the Great Depression, as many employers reduced the hours of their employees to minimize the impact of unemployment rather than lay off large portions of the workforce. The "weekend" was becoming the norm for many people, with both Saturday and Sunday as days of rest; at worst, the workweek had slimmed down to five and a half days, with just a half-day of work on the sixth non-full day (usually Wednesday or Saturday morning, depending on occupation). Therefore, job-holding suburban residents, whether white-collar or blue-collar, had more time to devote to amusement activities.

"Considerable criticism of synthetic double-headers is being heard over the land and the fear is being voiced in some quarters that baseball is going to become a weekend sport, instead of a daily affair," *The Sporting News* astutely observed in an editorial in the spring of 1933. "Its possibility does counsel serious consideration of the probable effects of the arbitrary shifting around of weekday games to make possible doubleheaders on Sunday. It is a fact that some people in cities where it is known that twin bills will be held on Sunday, deliberately stay away from the weekday games." The newspaper suggested the "solution for slim weekday crowds is to reduce the price of admission on the poorer days of the week to make them as attractive as double bills on the weekend holiday." Unfortunately, the newspaper was less astute in comprehending the problem, as the solution was abysmally short-sighted in understanding that most Sunday spectators did not have the employment flexibility to take the afternoon off to attend a ball game during the workweek.[24]

The two major leagues actually imposed a curtailment of Sunday doubleheaders in a club-owner vote conducted at the winter meeting in December 1933, which prohibited such promotions before June 15 of the playing season. Similar restrictions remained in effect, generally phrased as the third or fourth home Sunday date, throughout the rest of the 1930s. Clearly, the major-league club owners neither understood the attendance problem, nor cared to learn from the four years of night baseball exhibited in the minor leagues. One owner at least effectively used radio broadcasts to try to stem the decline in attendance at weekday games.[25]

While Ladies Day was a staple at most ballparks by 1932, in Chicago at Wrigley Field it was an effective multi-purpose promotion, where Ladies Day on Friday afternoon often drew 20,000 women with a complimentary admission, filling the seats that otherwise would remain as empty as they were every other day of the workweek. Ladies Day was effectively advertising for the weekend games, giving away samples of baseball, similar to what Wrigley did in his chewing-gum business. "Saturdays and Sundays brought yet more women," Robert Ehrgott noted in his book *Mr. Wrigley's Ball Club*, "this time as paying customers who had learned baseball on Friday afternoons or by listening to the broadcasts during household chores and now attended with spouses and families." The influence of radio broadcasts also encouraged fans to flock to Chicago from the hinterlands to attend the weekend games, initiating a long-lasting link between baseball and the mass market.[26]

Traditionally, the proletariat occupied the cheapest seats at the ballpark, the bleachers behind the outfield walls, where the shirt-sleeved crowd distinguished itself sartorially from the coat-and-tie assemblage in the reserved grandstand and box seats. Increasingly, though, the unreserved grandstand seats were being occupied by the non-elite in shirt sleeves, and accompanied by a family, who now mingled with the stature-clothed attendees. Attracting a regional following had its downside, though, for professional baseball as a whole, since these weekend crowds started to cannibalize the audience for minor-league games. Suddenly, a family in Decatur, Illinois, could travel by automobile to Chicago on the weekend to watch a game rather than stay at home to attend a Three-I League game.

In the minor leagues by 1933 the day-of-game mix had gravitated to a time-of-day mix that contained just two components: night games and day games with promotions. The term "daytime baseball" had even made its way onto the sports pages to denote the increasingly rare afternoon ball game during the workweek and even on Saturday. The Buffalo club in the International League did double promotions for all of its 13 Sunday dates in 1933, staging both a doubleheader and an automobile giveaway to one lucky ticket-holder in a random drawing of ticket stubs.[27]

To make the ubiquitous Sunday doubleheader more fan friendly, many minor leagues pre-planned the twin bills on the season schedule and shortened the second game to seven innings to enable the crowd to get home earlier for the popular Sunday-evening radio shows. Promotions even entered the night-game sphere, as Ladies Night was a fixture, door prizes became popular, and night doubleheaders were fairly common (what were later called twi-night doubleheaders). To decrease the chance of the second (night) game running past midnight, the first (twilight) game was usually limited to seven innings so that the night contest would generally start at its usual time.

In the national election in November 1932, Franklin D. Roosevelt was elected president. Few at the time envisioned the impact that newly elected FDR would have on the country as he took unprecedented action with his New Deal legislation to propel the country out of the Great Depression. Even fewer foresaw the impact that FDR would have to increase the audience for professional baseball and the impetus this would have to increase the adoption of night baseball.

Adolf Berle was Roosevelt's chief economic theorist during the 1932 presidential campaign. A corporation lawyer and not a social reformer by nature, Berle provided the intellectual underpinning for the New Deal. He perceived the existing American policy of pure individualism to be an "oligarchic concentration of economic power," represented by 200 companies that controlled one-half of the national wealth, run by "a dictatorship of unscrupulous corporation interests" that had precipitated the Great Depression. Berle advocated a middle ground between laissez-faire treatment of big business via capitalism (individualism) and government operation of big business via socialism (collectivism), by advocating government regulation of business. Berle wanted big business to provide economic benefits to the rest of society as the price for its prosperity. "It cannot be individualism, pure and simple, as we used to know it. It must not be either regimented socialism or fascism as we ordinarily think of it," Berle wrote. "Surely, there must be the middle ground which permits individuals to fulfill themselves in their lives, without leaving the bulk of the population merely sport or prey of passing economic ambition." It was a radical idea, especially to those steeped in individualism (like owners of major-league baseball clubs). Many then perceived Berle's ideas as communism; today, it is simply liberalism.[28]

During the interim period between the election and inauguration of Roosevelt, a novel idea, loosely premised on Berle's thoughts, was introduced into minor-league baseball for the 1933 season to increase attendance at the ballpark. The idea was to conduct a postseason series to determine the league champion rather than continue with

President Franklin D. Roosevelt, shown here throwing out the first ball on opening day of the baseball season in Washington, redefined the American Dream through his New Deal legislation, which had a far-reaching impact to expanding the ballpark audience (Library of Congress, Prints & Photographs Division, LC-DIG-hec-47402).

the conventional best-record format, after runaway pennant winners in several minor leagues had eviscerated attendance during the 1932 season. From the Berle perspective, this approach was a balance between individualism (survival of the fittest) and collectivism (beneficial to many). However, this approach was heresy to traditionalists in professional baseball.

In the American Association, Larry MacPhail introduced a split-league approach, where the league was divided into two divisions and the division winners played each other in a best-of-seven-games series to determine the champion. While the innovation was heralded as a "radical move to help baseball," its downside was prominently noted as "the plan makes it possible for a team finishing fifth in the general averages to win the pennant in the championship series."[29]

In the International League, Frank Shaughnessy of the Montreal club convinced the other club owners to adopt a multiple-team postseason series to determine the league champion, what today we call a playoff format. Because he saw how successful the Stanley Cup postseason format was in the National Hockey League, Shaughnessy pitched a replica of the NHL approach to the club owners to conduct a playoff among the top four clubs in the league. Shaughnessy also convinced the Texas League to adopt a variation of the NHL format, the now familiar playoff approach where the first- and fourth-place clubs play a series while the second- and third-place clubs meet, with the series winners meeting for the league title.[30]

The Shaughnessy Plan was nearly scuttled after just one year of existence, when Newark was eliminated in the first round, after finishing with the best record during the season, and Buffalo was crowned champion by winning the playoffs after finishing the regular season with a sub–.500 record. The Shaughnessy Plan was roundly criticized as a joke, which created intense opposition to continuing it for the 1934 season. However, since Buffalo had led the International League in attendance, the playoff scheme continued in 1934 with a few modifications to increase the odds that the club with the best won-lost record might become the champion. The version of the Shaughnessy Plan used in 1933 by the Texas League became the standard playoff format used in professional team sports.

For the 1933 season, 14 minor leagues began operation, the 11 leagues that had finished the previous season and three new leagues. Joe Carr was named promotional director of the minor leagues in January 1933 to help rebuilt the minors. His role was not to be merely an evangelist to start up leagues, but to deploy a businessman's mind to organize leagues to survive more than one season. While this was a tall order in the midst of the Great Depression, Carr had its own New Deal program for the minor leagues, similar to how FDR was revamping the American economy. "We are working on a five-year program and by the end of 1937 we hope to have 50 leagues in operation," Carr stated his ambitious goal.[31]

Carr used many approaches to convince people to invest in minor-league baseball. He emphasized night baseball to tap into the daytime-worker population, touted the Shaughnessy playoffs to maintain fan interest throughout the season, and acted as matchmaker with major-league club owners to arrange for farm-club status. Carr used the traditional civic-responsibility angle to enlist investors to promote their city's economic growth, not bashful about noting the badge of shame associated with a city that was unable to support a professional baseball team. He even helped lobby the Roosevelt administration to build new ballparks with WPA money from that New Deal program.

As Carr assisted leagues with how to best grapple with the money-making component that was an expanding focus of the civic/profit business basis in the minor leagues, the major leagues had their own challenges with making money as well as a surprisingly strong tug from the boosterism component. Suddenly, the national pastime element that largely drove the civic element was transformed from tacitly promoting the club's location as a "great city" to actively arguing that the location was still a "big city" that continued to qualify for major-league status.

Several newspapers in the 1930s reported that night baseball was the "salvation of the minor leagues." Certainly, that was temporarily the case during the early years of the decade. However, as demonstrated by Carr, night baseball was just one of three factors that helped the minors survive, the other two being playoffs and farm-system affiliation. Longer term, farm-club status was the ultimate savior of the minor leagues, as these subsidies were the only mechanism to ensure financial soundness of ball-club operation in light of the evaporating support of civic-minded investors. Much like the systemic conversion of the independent retail store into part of the chain-store model, minor-league ball clubs, outside of the Pacific Coast League, were destined to be controlled by major-league clubs. Night baseball provided enough of an economic foundation to operate a farm club for player development purposes. By 1937 roughly one-half of minor-league ball clubs had some kind of affiliation with a major-league club.

While the minor leagues were resolving their issues with the civic/profit business basis by using night baseball to actively appeal to a new audience to fill their ballparks, the major leagues were struggling with how to readjust the civic/profit balance that had worked so well for them the previous three decades. During the three-year period from 1931 to 1933, more than half of all major-league clubs lost money; in 1933 alone, 14 of the 16 clubs lost money.[32]

Commissioner Landis told reporters in the fall of 1933 that there was nothing wrong with major-league baseball other than the impact of the Great Depression. He downplayed the need for the new audience that attended night games in the minors, such as office workers, working-class occupations, and farmers. Pointing to the double-digit unemployment rate, Landis assured sportswriters that fans "will return as paid customers as soon as they have any money." Indications of a changing workforce, though, were on the horizon. New Deal legislation pushed by President Roosevelt to rescue the nation from the Great Depression would have a far-reaching impact to expand the audience for professional baseball—for ball games played at night—as FDR redefined the American Dream.[33]

James Truslow Adams popularized the term "American Dream" in his 1931 book *The Epic of America*, which he defined as "that dream of a land in which life should be better and richer and fuller for every man, with opportunity for each according to his ability or achievement." Adams went on to amplify his meaning: "It is not a dream of motor cars and high wages merely, but a dream of social order in which each man and each woman shall be able to attain to the fullest stature of which they are innately capable, and be recognized by others for what they are, regardless of the fortuitous circumstances of birth or position." Adams sought to reduce economic inequality in America, a Democratic political stance that few major-league executives then aligned with, preferring instead the Republican political stance that advocated rugged individualism within a free-market economy.[34]

"Roosevelt argued that common people were more vulnerable in an urban, industrial society, where they worked for wages or ran small businesses, than they had been when most lived on farms and in rural villages," Jillson observed in his book *Pursuing the American Dream*. "Roosevelt explicitly sought to redefine the American Dream for the urban and industrial America of his day and to make the national government responsible for restoring broad access to it." In crafting the New Deal, Roosevelt "looked beyond unconstrained individualism and unregulated laissez-faire" to create a broader American Dream that provided "greater freedom and greater security to the average man" and not just opportunity to be an enterprising businessman.[35]

New Deal legislation increased unionization, which led to blue-collar workers entering the middle class through increased wages, shorter hours, and stable employment. New laws also increased the regulation of publicly-held corporations, which led to more white-collar jobs such as accountants. Growth in the number of corporations led to demand for managers, office workers, and salesmen. To achieve upward social mobility, the acceptance of stable corporate employment replaced the previous aspiration to be a business owner as the typical means to improve social status. Since more people could rise above their earlier station in life through hard work as a corporate employee, they were receptive to a similar concept deployed in professional sports.

All these beneficiaries of the New Deal and the revised American Dream were a natural middle-class audience for night baseball. In the minor leagues, the Shaughnessy playoffs resembled the emerging concept of the American Dream, since a ball club did not need to be at the top to achieve success (e.g., the first-place club with the best record) and with hard work a second-, third-, or fourth-place club could become the league champion. Major-league baseball, with the World Series, was much slower to adopt a playoff format than other professional sports leagues, which negatively impacted its ability to tap into the new audience for sports and successfully grow the business in the forthcoming postwar era.

By 1934 night baseball in the minor leagues was well established as a long-term strategy. Ten minor leagues had operated continuously during the five years from 1930 through 1934; all used night baseball to survive. Three were Class AA (American Association, International League, and Pacific Coast League), four were Class A (Southern Association, Western League, Texas League, and New York–Pennsylvania League), one was Class B (Piedmont League), one was Class C (Middle Atlantic League), and one was Class D (Nebraska State League).

During the 1934 season, 67 ball clubs had the facilities to conduct night games, about two-thirds of all minor-league clubs above the Class D level. Edgar Brands, in his article "Minors' Night Game Experience Lights Way for Majors," expressed the opinion that "most of the objections raised have been refuted" and "the theory baseball is a day sport and not a night game is merely a prejudice, built on tradition." Lighting did remain one of the lingering concerns about night baseball, despite numerous improvements in the lighting systems installed in 1933 and 1934. The chief issues concerned improved focusing of lamps, reduced tarnishing or dimness of projectors, and reduction of glare. "The most-needed improvement, however, seems to be uniform lighting throughout a league," Brands wrote. "While it is impossible to make this absolute, even with a minimum wattage requirement, the same relative intensity would remove much criticism that has followed from players shifting from a well-lighted to a poorly-illuminated [ballpark]."[36]

At the Class AA level, the International League joined the Pacific Coast League with 100 percent night-game capability, where it was not unusual for all eight clubs to engage in four night games on a weekday evening. Buffalo played a complete night-game schedule Monday through Saturday beginning in June, except for one "bargain day" afternoon game during the workweek. Montreal and Toronto installed lights to expand night baseball to Canada. Montreal even staged a Sunday night game.[37]

In the third Class AA league, the American Association slowly inched its way to full night-baseball capacity, now with five clubs with lighting systems (Toledo added lights in 1933). Norman Perry, president of the Indianapolis club, scheduled as many night games as he could, rather than attempt to ration the evening encounters. Perhaps his role as an executive at the Indianapolis Power & Light Company gave Perry a more prescient perspective on how important night baseball would be in the not-too-distant future.

At the Class A level, all Western League clubs and seven of the eights clubs in the Texas League had lighting systems, while the Southern Association (three clubs) and the New York–Pennsylvania League (two clubs) had less than one-half full capability. Leagues at the Class B and C levels with widespread lighting adoption were the Middle Atlantic League (all eight clubs), Western Association (five of six clubs), and Piedmont League (four of six clubs). The Nebraska State League was the only Class D league with a club equipped with lights.[38]

A 1934 survey of three dozen minor-league ballparks with lighting systems revealed that 14 were engineering by Giant Manufacturing, 12 by General Electric, three by Crouse-Hinds Company in Syracuse, New York, and seven by other firms. The top four ballparks rated as having the best lighting systems were all at the Class AA level, in Columbus (American Association), Syracuse and Rochester (International), and San Francisco (Pacific Coast League).[39]

Larger minor-league cities that continued to completely stage daylight home games included Minneapolis and St. Paul, Minnesota, in the American Association; Beaumont, Texas, in the Texas League; New Orleans, Louisiana, in the Southern Association; and Norfolk, Virginia, in the Piedmont League.

While an estimated 33 percent of all minor-league games at Class C and higher levels were played at night, the comparable ratio of major-league games was 0 percent. During the summer of 1934, however, initial discussions about night baseball began to occur at the major-league level, unbeknownst to the public. In Chicago, Bill Veeck unsuccessfully pitched Cubs owner Phil Wrigley on the idea of installing lights at Wrigley Field. Larry MacPhail, late of Columbus and now general manager of the downtrodden Cincinnati Reds, had more success with Reds owner Powel Crosley, who in his radio and refrigerator businesses produced products "for the masses, not the classes" and understood the value of promotion. MacPhail secured Crosley's buy-in to night baseball by convincing him of the marketing value of having his radio station broadcast Reds games, renaming Redland Field to be Crosley Field, and putting a giant image of his Shelvador refrigerator atop the scoreboard.[40]

While Crosley was comfortable with baseball for the masses, MacPhail knew that convincing the other National League club owners to approve night baseball by the Reds was yet another matter. He had to maneuver within their Byzantine thinking on night baseball. Fortuitously, the National League elected Ford Frick to be its new president at the league meeting in December 1934. Frick's last job, publicity director for the National League, made him well acquainted with the issues related to night baseball.

◆ 9 ◆

National League Adoption

After five years of night baseball in the minor leagues, the first proposal to conduct night games in the major leagues was submitted for league approval in December 1934, when the Cincinnati Reds asked the National League club owners to approve night baseball for the 1935 season.

Larry MacPhail, general manager of the Cincinnati club, was the man behind the proposal, which he based upon his earlier experience with night baseball in the minor leagues when he was general manager of the Columbus club in the American Association. MacPhail was hired during the fall of 1933 to revive the financially distressed, habitually last-place Reds by the ownership group, led by the bankers at Central Bank & Trust Company that held the ball-club stock that had served as collateral for loans, now long delinquent, made to the ball club's previous president, Sidney Weil. MacPhail then convinced local businessman Powel Crosley to acquire a controlling interest from the bankers in February 1934 to become president of the ball club.[1]

MacPhail had an exceptionally challenging assignment to revive the Cincinnati ball club. Cincinnati was then the smallest city in major-league baseball, listed at number 17 in size on the top-20 list of the most populous cities in the 1930 federal census. Half a dozen minor-league cities had a larger population. Cincinnati was also one of the three southernmost major-league cities (along with St. Louis and Washington, all at approximately the same latitude), which had hot summer months that naturally suppressed interest in attending a ball game, especially those hosted by a losing team.

Public reports about the league meeting on December 12 focused on the meager attendance at weekday afternoon games in Cincinnati. Crosley, "fortified with weighty statistics which showed the tremendous disadvantage under which clubs of the smaller cities in the circuit operated, apparently carried the day by the sheer force of his argument." The thrust of the argument was that 70 percent of the 206,773 total attendance at Reds games in 1934 came from just 15 dates: 12 Sundays, two holidays, and the opening game of the season (considered a holiday in Cincinnati). This indicated a very poor attendance for weekday games, at about 1,200 spectators for each weekday afternoon game.[2]

Left unsaid in public reports, since it was a fact readily understood by all at the meeting, was the importance of maintaining the traditional audience for weekday games, primarily local businessmen and other non-laborers with time flexibility in their work schedule. Declining attendance at weekday afternoon ball games was not a unique problem in the National League, as every ball club experienced that reduction in the early 1930s. Cincinnati may have experienced the worst decline among the eight clubs in the league, but the situation was not unique to the Reds. What was unique was the ball club in bad economic shape had an ancestor that was the original professional baseball club during the 1869 season.

This intangible argument regarding attendance was the set-up to the proposal to resolve the tangible financial losses from the meager weekday attendance. After Crosley presented the attendance analysis to his fellow club owners, MacPhail discussed the proposed solution, which was contained in a 40-page report provided during the meeting. If the real issue was simply reversing the declining attendance at weekday games, the report would have been much shorter, since the simple solution, as executed throughout the minor leagues, would be to allow night games on an unlimited basis.[3]

There was much more to MacPhail's plan than simply requesting approval to conduct night baseball. If he had followed the minor-league model, the National League club owners would have immediately dismissed the proposal. MacPhail had to craft a major-league strategy that was within the confines of the league's accepted civic/profit business basis, in order to convince the other club owners to approve night baseball. MacPhail used Sunday baseball as the foundation of his proposal for night baseball.

In 1934 Cincinnati had six fewer Sunday dates than the 18 Sundays it had staged home games in 1933, because the Pittsburgh Pirates could now host Sunday games following the legalization of Sunday baseball in Pennsylvania in November 1933. For many

Cincinnati Reds owner Powel Crosley manufactured products "for the masses, not the classes" in his radio and refrigerator businesses, so he was receptive to Larry MacPhail's idea to conduct night baseball and expand the audience at the ballpark (Library of Congress, Prints & Photographs Division, LC-DIG-hec-33925).

years Pittsburgh had engaged in one-day road trips to Cincinnati to play on Sunday. Often that visit would be in the midst of a Pittsburgh homestand and sometimes it would be in the midst of a Cincinnati road trip. During the 1933 season, Pittsburgh had played on Sunday in Cincinnati six times (four doubleheaders and two single games), nearly its entire road schedule with the Reds.[4]

MacPhail wanted the club owners to authorize replacement of those lost Sunday dates with night games on a weekday. In essence he asked to replicate Sunday dates since he could not willy-nilly create more Sunday dates on the calendar. The owners could buy into the Sunday-style philosophy for limited night baseball because they already understood that revenue from Sunday games was used, in part, to subsidize the declining attendance at weekday games. Maintaining the traditional audience for weekday games was a paramount concern to club owners, who knowingly pursued this boosterism objective and accepted lower overall profits. This was the nature of the baseball business at the major-league level, with what one baseball writer called the engrained belief that "the dignity of the national pastime must be upheld at all costs, even if this means parading the national pastime before thousands of empty seats." MacPhail argued for seven night games, which was comparable to the six lost Sunday dates.[5]

The seven-game restriction was not an abstract thought, though. MacPhail had devised this same limitation when he was general manager at Columbus in 1932, to play one night game against each other club in the American Association. He was a counter-culture advocate while at Columbus, not following the herd that wanted to maximize attendance with unlimited night baseball. His philosophy back in Columbus was to ration night baseball as a special event, which he could document as a profitable technique (likely through several pages in that 40-page report) that had met the approval of Cardinals owner Sam Breadon and his general manager Branch Rickey, since Columbus was a farm club owned by St. Louis. Columbus was still using the seven-game limit in 1934 after MacPhail had left the ball club.

Importantly, MacPhail avoided advocating a diversification of the ballpark audience, which was the underlying outcome of unlimited night games in the minor leagues. The limited number of night games in Cincinnati kept the businessmen as the target audience, and was not, per se, an encouragement of working-class spectators to populate the ballpark. This connection to the traditional ballpark audience was essential in obtaining club-owner approval of MacPhail's proposal. If he had taken the same philosophical route as Lee Keyser did in Des Moines in 1930 by economically diversifying the weekday audience through night baseball, MacPhail's proposal would not have been approved.

Also important was MacPhail's promise to invest the profits from the additional revenue from night games to obtain better ballplayers to build a winning team, not just flow the profits through to ownership. This adhered to the major-league sporting mantra of fielding a winning team as the business basis of the enterprise. A winning team would also produce greater attendance at weekday afternoon games, a secondary benefit of night baseball.

A third selling point to the owners was that the Reds would install the best lighting system that was technologically available, to maintain the integrity of the game. MacPhail would bring in the experts from General Electric, not buy a low-quality system from Giant Manufacturing, which was still advertising its "glare-free" projectors in its competition with General Electric and exhorting ball clubs to "install Giant Projectors so that fans may enjoy their favorite sport at its best."[6]

As the clincher, MacPhail told the club owners that he would disband the experiment after the 1935 season and dismantle the light towers if night baseball did not produce the financial results he forecast. MacPhail was betting his job on night baseball and Crosley was betting tens of thousands of dollars of his own money. Both men had their reputations at stake.

MacPhail essentially pursued a "light up or fold up" strategy, although he unlikely was heavy-handed about it, by overtly threatening bankruptcy or the need for another league takeover to add to the Boston Braves situation already confronting the league. Relocation also was not an option, given the prohibitive cost to purchase another ball club and its territory in a sizeable minor-league city that would be acceptable to the National League owners.

Because MacPhail's persuasive arguments made it virtually impossible for the club owners to vote down the proposal, the owners voted to approve night baseball for the 1935 season. A few conditions were added to MacPhail's seven-game maximum. No opponent could be compelled to play a night game; it was an option for the visiting club, not a requirement. And a $15,000 fine, per game, would be levied by the league if a club played more than seven night games in a season.[7]

MacPhail billed himself as the savior of daylight baseball. "I've been called the father of night ball in the majors. It isn't true. I'm not. I'm probably the best friend of day baseball in the whole world. Maybe I'm planning to save day baseball. Maybe that's in the back of my mind," he told John Lardner in an interview in March 1935. To provide some evidence to back up his assertion, MacPhail said, "I've safeguarded day baseball against the menace of night baseball with various little protective measures. For instance, it's been fixed so that further plans for night baseball in the National League can be defeated by a single vote of any member. When the league decides to go in for night baseball on a big scale, it will have to be unanimous. I hope it never happens."[8]

If MacPhail had not experimented with a seven-game restriction for night games in Columbus back in 1932, it would have taken many more years for major-league baseball to embrace the night baseball concept.

St. Louis owner Sam Breadon was the one National League owner that aligned with Cincinnati's stance on night baseball. But since the Cardinals were a tenant in Sportsman's Park, owned by the St. Louis Browns of the American League, the idea of night baseball in St. Louis was stillborn for the 1935 season. "We probably will go along just as we have done," Breadon told baseball writers about the lighting situation at Sportsman's Park, which would require extensive alterations to the existing grandstand structure to enable the positioning there of light towers. Since the Browns were engulfed in uncertainty in the midst of the settling the Phil Ball estate, the ball club was not interested in night baseball: "I have no idea what the company owning the park would do even if approached on the subject by the Cardinals."[9]

New York Giants owner Charles Stoneham now hated the idea of night baseball, despite having been an early experimenter with exhibition night games in 1931 and 1932. "Baseball never was, is not now, and never will be a night game," Stoneham said. "It costs $40,000 to install a good lighting system for night baseball. It seems to me that any club that has that much money to spend might do better spending it on ball players." Stoneham was insistent that the Giants would not play any night games in Cincinnati. They were the only National League club to forego the opportunity for a big payday from the visitor's share of the night gate. Indeed, the Giants would not play a night game until 1940 when lights were finally installed at the Polo Grounds.[10]

Most sportswriters ridiculed the idea, labeling the National League a burlesque circuit. "MacPhail was looked down upon as something of a charlatan, trying to breathe fresh life into the corpse of the Cincinnati franchise with the methods of a quack," Lee Allen described the reaction in his book *The Cincinnati Reds*. Many writers dismissed the experiment, such as Dan Daniel who wrote in *The Sporting News* that the Reds were "likely to be alone in the experiment with night baseball." Even Cincinnati writer Tom Swope took a swipe at the idea, proclaiming that "a more certain way for Crosley and MacPhail to raise their weekday attendance is to get a winning team."[11]

A connection was quickly made between night baseball in Cincinnati and the financial plight of the Boston Braves, the other big issue at the league meeting in December 1934, where the Braves ownership had unsuccessfully proposed to conduct dog racing at Braves Field to increase revenue. "Night baseball will bring the game closer to dog racing," one commentator observed. "When the fans take to yelling 'put in a new rabbit,' the situation will have become intricate." However, the phrase "night baseball is just one step above dog racing" soon became a common refrain among the opponents of the concept.[12]

There was a consistent negative reaction from those associated with the American League. New York Yankees manager Joe McCarthy told the Associated Press: "Everyone knows baseball should be played in the daytime. I don't believe it is necessary for the big leagues to resort to the night game." Boston Red Sox manager Joe Cronin concurred with those thoughts by calling night baseball "a circus side show" and "just a big joke," among other spicier descriptions. "Sure, I know it will draw, so would football on roller skates. It still doesn't make night baseball a good game, in my opinion," Cronin added. "If the National League wants to go switch on the lights, let it go to it. That will make the American League the only real big league in the country."[13]

Cronin's bosses echoed those thoughts. "I am now, and always have been, opposed to playing baseball in artificial light. Baseball is a daylight game," Red Sox general manager Eddie Collins said. "We want no part of it, nor do I think the fans want it." Red Sox owner Tom Yawkey was even more adamant: "I certainly hope I will never live to see the time when I shall see a major league night baseball game at Fenway Park."[14]

Connie Mack, owner of the Philadelphia Athletics, was unenthusiastic. "Night baseball, in my opinion, would be a very tiresome spectacle for the fans. To watch a game, especially on damp nights in late August or September, won't be any fun." He also expected the game on the field to be negatively impacted, with the likes of speedball pitchers Dizzy Dean and Schoolboy Rowe. "It's tough enough to stand up at the plate against men like that in broad daylight."[15]

Ford Frick, the new president of the National League, also did not whole-heartedly support night baseball in his public remarks. In a January 1935 article authored by Frick, he wrote a bland "we look forward with special interest to the experiment with night baseball," while backstopping the club owners with his comments that "the league owners were unanimous in deciding to try the experiment" and that those clubs unwilling to actually engage in night games "are entirely agreeable to having others try out the idea." Describing the deliberations at the meeting of club owners in December 1934, Frick biographer John Carvalho wrote: "In the discussion that day, Frick established his leadership style, offering no opinions of his own while explaining the differences between a resolution that would allow clubs to experiment with night baseball and an amendment to

Boston Red Sox owner Tom Yawkey (left) was an adamant opponent of night baseball, saying in 1935: "I certainly hope I will never live to see the time when I shall see a major league night baseball game at Fenway Park." By 1938 American League president Will Harridge (right) had a different tone: "Night baseball is coming to the majors, there's no question about it. It's coming just as radio came to the game" (courtesy Boston Public Library, Leslie Jones Collection).

the by-laws that would have made the innovation something permanent." In a circuitous manner, Frick seemed to imply he supported the effort to experiment rather than offer an endorsement that night baseball was a good idea.[16]

In February 1935, the National League put further restrictions on night baseball, when MacPhail was not available to attend the special league meeting. No night games were permitted on Saturday, Sunday, or holidays. No doubleheaders could be played at night. No daylight game could be completed under the lights. No exhibition night games were allowed.[17]

The prohibition on exhibition games nearly kyboshed the installation of lights in Cincinnati, since MacPhail was counting on additional revenue from exhibition games with American League clubs as well as minor-league clubs that had not yet installed lighting systems. This was something he did do while in Columbus, but probably did not divulge in the proposal meeting in December. His consternation at this limitation shows the true motive of the National League owners to focus on sustaining the businessmen audience and improving the talent of the ball club. The additional exhibition night games seemed just too much of a line-your-pockets tactic.

The board of directors of the Reds voted to proceed forward, even though MacPhail himself recommended that the project be abandoned, since without the exhibition-game revenue the venture was much more risky. The board rejected MacPhail's recommendation.[18]

Due to the restriction that no daylight game could be completed under the lights, the National League drew a bright line to distinguish a night game from a daylight game. Start times therefore had to be after sunset, which could be as late as 9:00 in cities like Cincinnati that were located at the western edge of the Eastern Time Zone. This was not the most fan-friendly of restrictions, since a game could end near midnight.

The first major-league night games were not so designated on the National League schedule released during the winter, but rather were arranged on-the-fly during the playing season, much like how Sunday doubleheaders were then handled. The first night game in Cincinnati was announced by the ball club on April 23 to be played one month later on May 23 against the Philadelphia Phillies.

To execute the promise to have the best lighting system available, MacPhail established the goal for the lights at Crosley Field to be twice as bright as the best-lighted baseball field in the minor leagues. Cincinnati spent $50,000 to procure lighting equipment, have the Cincinnati Gas & Electric Company install the lights, and hire General Electric Company illuminating engineers to oversee the entire project. Robert Swackhamer was the lead engineer from General Electric. Having worked on the lighting installation in 1930 at Des Moines, he brought five years of baseball illumination experience to Cincinnati to achieve MacPhail's lighting objective.[19]

Crosley Field was lighted by 632 floodlights, which were 1,500-watt lamps marketed by General Electric as AL-51 and AL-34 Novalux. One lighting innovation deployed in Cincinnati was to illuminate all parts of the playing field relatively equally, rather than concentrate more light on the infield and less in the outfield, which was then the usual mode of illumination in the minor leagues. The illuminating engineers created a detailed plot plan for Crosley Field that had a maximum intensity of 70 foot-candles over the entire field, with a minimum of 62 foot-candles at any one point.[20]

Candlepower was now an obsolete terminology for the measurement of illumination, especially for outdoor areas, since the resulting number routinely was expressed in hundreds of thousands and easily ran into the millions for large areas such as athletic fields. The replacement measurement of foot-candles produces a more digestible number for consumers, since it measures the illumination upon one square foot of the surface area.

Rain canceled the inaugural night game slated for May 23, which was rescheduled to the following night, May 24. Many dignitaries were invited to the festivities, including President Roosevelt who, from his office in Washington, flipped an honorary switch to turn on the lights at Crosley Field for the 8:30 start to the ball game. The one-day delay did not deter attendance, as 20,422 people paid their way into the ballpark to watch the historic event along with about 5,000 honored guests, which swelled the overall spectatorship to 25,000 people.[21]

"Lovers of tradition may wail and those who cannot bring themselves around to accepting baseball at night may condemn it," *The Sporting News* editorialized about the future of night baseball, "but nothing short of a phenomenal outpouring of fans for the daylight games during the rest of the season and the failure of the Cincinnati experiment can stay the inexorable hand of electricity from enveloping the sport in the majors for at least one night a week during the hot season."[22]

Six of the seven National League ball clubs participated in a night game at Cincinnati during the 1935 season, all except the New York Giants. The St. Louis Cardinals, the only other avowed proponent of the concept, played two night games in Cincinnati.

Total paid attendance for the seven night games in Cincinnati during the 1935 season was 130,337 spectators, for an average night-game crowd of 18,619. General Electric used this data to advertise its lighting expertise during the fall of 1935, and added another data point for comparison to the alternative to a night game: "The average paid attendance at the 48 day games, from beginning of the season to the time of the final night game, was only 5,495." Recognizing that a larger number of potential buyers existed in the minor leagues, General Electric also advertised the attendance comparison under the lights engineered by the company at the ballpark at Milwaukee, where "eighteen night games averaged an attendance of 2,340 against an average of 672 for daylight."[23]

During the 1936 and 1937 seasons, General Electric broadened the appeal of its baseball advertising to both major-league and minor-league ball clubs. The GE advertisement moved beyond the tripling of attendance for night games to focus on the composition of the potential audience being downtown office workers, not just anyone, for night games, an important consideration to major-league ball clubs. "Some of them, many of them, like baseball but unfortunately have to spend their afternoons making a living," the advertising copy stated. "This is the group of people that make up the record-breaking Saturday and Sunday crowds—and who will pack your stands when games are played at night." Another advertisement accentuated this potential with the title: "At 5:00 O'clock Millions of Baseball Fans Leave Work: You Can Attract Them with Night Baseball."[24]

For the 1936 season, the National League club owners approved continuation of the night baseball experiment, while the American League owners maintained their disdain of night baseball. However, no other club owners in the National League expressed a desire to install lights and expand the experiment beyond Cincinnati.

There was new ownership of the Boston Braves, under the leadership of Bob Quinn, the former owner of the Red Sox, who had put together a consortium of investors to acquire

NIGHT GAMES

PUT BASEBALL IN REACH OF ALL

Attendance Figures Reach New Peaks

Enthusiasm Grows

Profits Increase

WITH NIGHT BASEBALL

THE General Electric Company offers you floodlighting equipment that has been designed and developed especially for night sports—floodlighting that provides the right illumination to meet every requirement for night play. Actual installations in all parts of the country have thoroughly tested and approved this equipment.

To help you in selecting the proper equipment for your particular needs, General Electric extends the service of its lighting specialists. Write or phone today to your nearest G-E sales office. Or if more convenient, write direct to General Electric Company; Schenectady, N. Y.

GENERAL ⊕ ELECTRIC

During the 1937 season, General Electric broadened the appeal of its ballpark-lighting advertising to both major-league and minor-league ball clubs, by focusing on downtown office buildings and the potential audience of middle-class office workers, not just anyone, for night games.

the Braves. Quinn, though, was not a proponent of installing lights at Braves Field to play night baseball. "I'm enough of an old-fashioned baseball man not to like night ball," Quinn told the *Brooklyn Eagle* in October 1935. "The game itself is a peculiar mixture of business and sport. Its success is founded upon the fact that the sporting end has been predominant before the public down through the years." As a dyed-in-the-wool daylight baseball guy, Quinn opted to change the name of the Boston ball club from Braves to Bees, hoping that approach would attract more customers to the club's weekday afternoon ball games.[25]

The National League did not pursue a sale of the bankrupt Braves to an avowed proponent of night baseball, George Preston Marshall, owner of the Boston Redskins football club in the National Football League. Marshall was a bit too flamboyant for the National League, since he advocated not only playing night games at Braves Field but also selling beer there. Marshall became more famous as the man who moved the Redskins to Washington, D.C., for the 1937 NFL season.[26]

The National League schedule released in February 1936 contained seven asterisks for the Cincinnati home games to be played as night games. One informal restriction self-imposed by the Reds in 1936 was to have an off day following a night game. This scheduling was more from the spectator perspective, not the ballplayer, in order to avoid the tiny crowd at the weekday afternoon game that was played just 16 hours after the conclusion of a night game. This restriction contributed to more Sunday doubleheaders. In 1936 the seven night games in Cincinnati attracted a paid attendance of 136,722, for an average of 19,532 per game.[27]

The greater attendance for night games in 1936 compared to 1935 demonstrated that night baseball was not just a fad. One prescient sportswriter in January 1937 concluded that the two years of night baseball in Cincinnati signaled a long-term trend, writing that the recent concession by ball-club owners to recognize the benefit of having an extensive farm system "must lead to almost universal adoption of night baseball by the organizations that now frown upon such activities." MacPhail's forecast of how limited night baseball would improve the Cincinnati ball club had proved accurate, as the Reds reversed their financial plight and the team moved up to fifth place in the 1936 standings. "The Reds are [now] rich. They do not acutely need night ball for the financial support," the writer continued his observation. "They need it because the people of Cincinnati would not tolerate its abandonment."[28]

In November 1936, when the sale of the St. Louis Browns was finalized, the American League club owners approved night baseball for the Browns, contingent on the new owners reaching an agreement with the Cardinals to install lights at Sportsman's Park. This seemed to establish a hardship basis for a need to play night baseball, not simply a desire, roughly akin to how the National League had originally approved night games for Cincinnati. However, when those negotiations fell apart by October 1937, the American League rescinded its approval of night baseball and returned to its more Neanderthal policy on the concept.[29]

Breadon, the king of the Sunday doubleheader, tried his best to accommodate the desires of the Browns. Since the new owners of the Browns wanted to spend their money to acquire ballplayers rather than lights, Breadon offered to cover the full cost of purchasing a lighting system if the Browns would sign a nine-year lease to rent the lights for their night games. Even that offer was too big of a financial commitment for the Browns.[30]

Connie Mack, the septuagenarian owner of the Philadelphia Athletics, was the next

American League club owner to pursue staging night baseball. While his ball club was not as financially desperate as the Browns, Mack suffered ill effects from so many years of having to conduct daylight games only from Monday to Saturday, since Pennsylvania law prohibited Sunday baseball played by professional athletes. The failure to convince the Pennsylvania Supreme Court to permit beer sales in Shibe Park was the initial impetus to the pursuit of night baseball, since Mack had hoped to use that concession revenue to augment his club's finances from the second year of legal Sunday baseball during the 1935 season.

After reading about the success of the Cincinnati Reds with their seven night games, Mack became more of a believer in night baseball. During the 1936 season he observed the big crowds to watch night games played in a Philadelphia sandlot league and had the Athletics play a couple of exhibition games with nearby minor-league teams under the lights to get a feel for the impact to the game on the field. After an August exhibition night game in Allentown, Mack seemed convinced to proceed forward. "I was impressed with the attitude of the other owners, who willingly consented to cooperate and play night games," Mack said in November 1936 after the American League club owners gave the Browns permission to conduct night baseball. "This was a departure from their attitude in the past, which always has been strong against night contests."[31]

At the American League meeting in December 1936, after the club owners had ratified their earlier decision to allow night games for the St. Louis Browns in order to facilitate the sale of that moribund franchise, Mack raised the proposition of the Philadelphia Athletics also conducting night games during the 1937 season. "I would like to see how the clubs feel about Philadelphia if we decide to put in the lights," Mack asked his fellow owners. "I am thinking seriously about it. I may not want to. I have just an idea that possibly we would like to put the lights in over there." After just St. Louis and Cleveland indicated a willingness to play a night game at Shibe Park, Mack resumed his pitch. "I do not believe in standing still. I believe in moving on. If it is going to pay us to play night ball, why, I say let us play night ball." Clark Griffith, the Washington club owner and staunch opponent of night baseball, spoke for most of the other owners. "You will never stop once you start," Griffith told Mack. "I wish you would try it another year without it. I may be in the same boat in another year, too. But I am firmly convinced we shouldn't go to this thing until we are forced to it."[32]

Mack's proposal to play night baseball was voted down by the American League club owners. The 73-year-old patriarch of the Philadelphia ball club, however, had more visionary thinking than his younger brethren.

While no major-league clubs installed lighting systems during the 1936 and 1937 seasons, General Electric and its top lighting engineer Robert Swackhamer were very busy with installations at 20 minor-league ballparks in 1937, including Minneapolis and St. Paul, Minnesota (the remaining two unlighted ballparks in the American Association); Mobile, Alabama; Tallahassee, Florida; Owensboro, Kentucky; Tacoma, Washington; and Wilkes-Barre, Pennsylvania.[33]

The installation of lights in Minnesota was particularly noteworthy for two reasons. The twin cities of Minneapolis and St. Paul were the last outposts of all-daylight baseball not only in the American Association but also in all of the Class AA minor leagues. Now all ball clubs in the highest level of the minor leagues conducted night baseball. The lights were also significant because these systems would get less usage than clubs in more southern locations, due to the cooler spring nights in Minnesota, making the financial return a riskier proposition and also a longer process. Night baseball debuted in the Minneapolis–St. Paul area in July 1937.[34]

The enthusiasm for night baseball in the minor leagues was greatly abetted by Joe Carr, the publicity director for minor-league baseball when he wasn't absorbed in his duties as president of the National Football League. As a result of Carr's efforts, during the 1935 season there were 21 minor leagues, a 50 percent increase over the 14 leagues that operated in 1933. Carr lined up five new leagues for the 1936 season, including his beloved Ohio State League following a 20-year hiatus. "Today, the structure of most of the minor leagues is at a point where the men who had the courage and faith to put time and money into the game can realize on their investment," Carr told a wire-service writer. Most of the new leagues were at the Class D level, where Carr could most easily deploy the selling points of player development and civic responsibility for new clubs that would be part of a major-league farm system, play its games at

The St. Paul, Minnesota, ball club in the American Association was one of the last clubs in the top level of the minor leagues to install lights, due to its location in a northern climate. Night baseball debuted in St. Paul in July 1937 (Library of Congress, Prints & Photographs Division, LC-USF33-011288-M2).

night under lights, and compete for a championship in the Shaughnessy playoff format. The city might also be able to build a new WPA-funded ballpark.[35]

Following the completion of the 1937 major-league season, the Cleveland Indians were ready to play night games at the city's Municipal Stadium, which had an existing lighting system, or spend $75,000 to put in a lighting plant at League Park. Municipal Stadium, with its 78,000 seats, would produce a high-revenue night game. However, at the American League meeting in December 1937, Cleveland owner Alva Bradley admitted that there was no financial emergency, so the American League club owners turned down the Cleveland proposal, since "the league took the stand that night ball was an emergency measure for a club in financial straits."[36]

The American League was more adamant against night baseball than the National League because half of the league owners were traditionalists for daylight baseball. Jacob Ruppert (New York), Walter Briggs (Detroit), Clark Griffith (Washington), and Tom

Yawkey (Boston) were all dead set against night ball, since they viewed themselves as sportsmen whose investment was in the national pastime, not in a business. All but Griffith had other profit-making enterprises that generated their wealth.

Civic boosterism that fueled the desire by traditionalists for the downtown businessmen audience at weekday daylight ball games was in serious decline by the 1930s, though, due to the de-industrialization of the urban economy in American cities. "The growth of downtown's daytime population came to a standstill because most cities grew very slowly in the 1930s," Fogelson observed in his book *Downtown: Its Rise and Fall.* "Many Americans now worked, shopped, did business, and amused themselves in the outlying business districts. Some stopped going downtown and others went much less often." Parking lots replaced demolished empty buildings downtown as "more Americans now used automobiles rather than streetcars," during an era when "it was clear downtown was in trouble," replaced by an older, seedier, and less frequented vestige of its former prominence. Using Sunday game profits to subsidize the losses from the small audiences at weekday daylight games was no longer a sustainable strategy for the ball-club owner who was not a wealthy sportsman.[37]

At its league meeting in December 1937, the National League owners approved night baseball for the fourth consecutive year. On January 1, 1938, Cincinnati was still the only major-league ball club hosting night baseball. However, night baseball in the major leagues would receive a much needed stimulation during the 1938 season.

Larry MacPhail, who had left the Cincinnati Reds after the 1936 season, resurfaced in January 1938 when he was named general manager of the Brooklyn Dodgers. Despite expectations by sportswriters that he would immediately announce the playing of night baseball in Brooklyn, MacPhail initially dismissed that idea. "That doesn't mean I've changed my attitude toward night ball," MacPhail told the *Brooklyn Eagle.* "Seven night games a year are great for Cincinnati, but that doesn't mean it would be a great thing for Brooklyn, or even desirable." By May, though, the idea of night games in Brooklyn was moving forward, as the Dodgers became the second major-league ball club to stage night baseball.[38]

As general manager of the ball clubs in Columbus, Cincinnati, and Brooklyn during the 1930s, Larry MacPhail conducted night baseball as a special event by rationing night games to just seven home games each season. In this way, MacPhail executed his goal to subsidize the continuation of daylight baseball on weekdays, not replace it (National Baseball Hall of Fame Library, Cooperstown, New York).

Unlike his coy public statements when he introduced night baseball in Cincinnati, MacPhail was more vocal about his true thoughts in Brooklyn. His $110,000 investment in a lighting system would produce attendance the equivalent of seven Sunday games, thus allowing him to purchase better ballplayers. He was increasing the bottom line not just in the short term, but also in the long run. Just as he did in Cincinnati, MacPhail promised "the best lighting plant science can produce and the best money can buy" would be installed at Ebbets Field. He immediately hired General Electric to oversee the installation of a state-of-the-art lighting system.[39]

General Electric engineered a lighting pattern that produced an average illumination of 100 foot-candles at Ebbets Field, which was 40 percent brighter than the 70 foot-candles of light in Cincinnati. Most minor-league ballparks had illuminations of 30 to 50 foot-candles, with Class AA ballparks ranging from 50 to 60 foot-candles.[40]

In early June MacPhail announced the dates for Brooklyn's first six night games, with the initial contest slated for June 15 against the Cincinnati Reds (the seventh night game was a wild card, since the New York Giants continued to refuse to play at night). He followed the pattern he had used in Cincinnati to arrange an off-day following each night game, which required the scheduling of additional Sunday doubleheaders to compensate for the lost game dates during the workweek. Attendance in Brooklyn topped the biggest night-game crowd in Cincinnati, as 38,748 people watched the first night game at Ebbets Field.[41]

Total attendance for the seven night games in Brooklyn topped 190,000 people, for an average of 27,159 spectators at each night game. "The medicinal value of night baseball in Brooklyn might be estimated at 150,000," *Brooklyn Eagle* sportswriter Tommy Holmes reported that September. "On average, a single game on a weekday evening has outdrawn a single game on a weekday afternoon by almost 22,000 and has proved more attractive than even a Sunday doubleheader by a margin of more than 4,000." Night-game attendance in Brooklyn was five times the crowd at a weekday single game, which averaged just 5,400 paying customers, and was nearly triple that of a Saturday afternoon game, which averaged 10,300 spectators.[42]

The experience in a large city such as Brooklyn seemed to spur the naysayers into being more flexible about night baseball at the major-league level. Night baseball could work in the "big time," not just the smaller cities of the minor leagues. But MacPhail was insistent about rationing night baseball. "I don't think of night baseball as a substitute for baseball in the afternoon," he said. "But I do believe that there is a definite place for seven night games a season."[43]

As a result of his success with night baseball in Brooklyn, MacPhail opened the minds of other major-league club owners. MacPhail single-handedly revised the day-of-game model to add an influential night-game component to complement the significant Sunday doubleheader driver of attendance and further offset the deficiency of the weak weekday element. The MacPhail modification was an early version of what today we would call a disruptive innovation. The day-of-game model was on its way to becoming a time-of-day model, but for a few years it lingered as a time/day-of-game model, before the more volcanic disruption would occur eight years in the future.

During the summer of 1938, the first serious movement towards night baseball in the American League started to materialize, when its league president, Will Harridge, told a baseball writer for the Associated Press: "Night baseball is coming to the majors, there's no question about it. It's coming just as radio came to the game. Not so many years ago major-league owners thought radio would ruin the game. They've changed their minds and I think they'll change their minds on night baseball." Although Harridge adeptly did not specifically point his finger at the American League club owners as the stonewalling faction, he strongly implied that sentiment, since the National League already had three and a half years of experience with night baseball.[44]

By the end of the 1938 season, just 1.1 percent of all major-league ball games were played at night (14 of 1223 total games). That statistic shot up to 3.4 percent during the 1939 season when four more ball clubs began to conduct night games.[45]

The St. Louis Browns and Philadelphia Athletics continued to struggle financially in the American League. The Athletics were late to Sunday baseball, not able to legally stage Sunday games until the 1934 season. Sunday baseball in St. Louis was old hat, having been a staple there since 1882, so even Sunday doubleheaders for the Browns were nothing special. Both clubs were canaries in the coal mine of the two-club city baseball dilemma and desperately needed night baseball to survive.

During the fall of 1938, a proposal to approve night baseball in the American League seemed to be in the offing, when Connie Mack told sportswriters, "Night baseball has its place in the scheme of the major leagues just as much as day baseball." Conceptually, Mack was on board. Now he needed to exercise his most polished political skills to convince four of the other seven club owners to see things his way.[46]

◆ 10 ◆

American League Adoption

After four years of observing the National League successfully create "another Sunday" on the baseball calendar with night baseball, the American League club owners finally approved night baseball at their league meeting in December 1938. The owners of the Philadelphia Athletics and Cleveland Indians ball clubs immediately announced they would stage night games during the 1939 season, seeking to replicate Larry MacPhail's success in Cincinnati and most recently in Brooklyn to increase box-office revenue and build a winning team on the playing field.

Connie Mack, the venerable owner of the Philadelphia Athletics who had been the league's most staunch advocate for night baseball, pulled no punches in his night-baseball argument to his fellow owners. "We must progress the same as any other sport and night baseball is one of the steps forward that baseball has taken," Mack said. "Night baseball has its place in the scheme of baseball as much as day games. We cannot dictate to the public. Those who work during the day want night games."[1]

The majority approval for night baseball in the American League passed by a whisker after the tentative vote count ahead of the league meeting was deadlocked at four clubs for and four clubs against. Washington owner Clark Griffith switched sides after Cleveland owner Alva Bradley blocked waivers on Griffith's proposed trade of first baseman Zeke Bonura to the New York Giants for $20,000 and two players. In what is politely called log-rolling, the side agreement called for Griffith to vote yes on night baseball if Cleveland would drop its claim on Bonura. In more sinister lexicon, that agreement might be termed extortion as a more apt description for why Griffith reversed his rabid opposition and voted for the league to adopt night baseball.[2]

Restrictions on night ball in the American League were the same as those imposed by the National League (seven-game maximum, never on Sunday or holidays, optional for visiting team), with the exception that Saturday night games were allowed in the senior circuit. One additional restriction for the American League was that no inning could be started after 11:50 in the evening, to avoid overly late conclusions to night games. This became known as the night-game curfew.[3]

There were actually 14 night games played at Shibe Park in Philadelphia during the 1939 season, since the Phillies of the National League also conducted night ball, since they were now a tenant at Shibe Park. With three ball clubs hosting 21 night games in 1939, the National League took the opportunity to put both Sunday doubleheaders and night games on the league schedule released in February. Since an open date traditionally followed a night game, it made sense to pre-plan the associated Sunday doubleheader that would pick up that aborted game. Twelve Sunday doubleheaders were slated on that

original schedule, five in Philadelphia, four in Cincinnati, and three
in Brooklyn.[4] Sunday doubleheaders not related to night-game open
dates soon began to populate the
pre-planned league schedules
rather than be created on the fly
during the season.

While he believed in a more
egalitarian audience at the ballpark to save his business, Mack
remained sensitive to the fundamental tenet of major-league club
owners that baseball was a daylight game, which served as a
foundational philosophy for those
American League club owners
who had voted against night baseball. "Now night baseball opens
another chapter," Mack told baseball writers a week after the league
approval for night games. "If judi-
ciously handled, it will be a life-
saver, but it must not be abused
by playing too many games," he
added in a nod to MacPhail's reasoning that the rationing of night

Connie Mack, the septuagenarian owner of the Philadelphia Athletics during the mid–1930s, was the
American League's most staunch advocate for night
baseball, leading the movement for the league to adopt
night baseball for the 1939 season (Boston Public
Library, Print Department, McGreevy Collection).

baseball would save the daylight game. Will Harridge, the president of the American
League, echoed Mack's thoughts: "Baseball is a daylight, sunshine game. If it's kept as a
spectacle, night baseball will be an attraction. If it's not overdone and remains a novelty,
the clubs ought to benefit." In accordance with the national pastime conviction, neither
man mentioned the increased profits from night baseball.[5]

General Electric was not as diplomatic about the business aspects in its advertising for ballpark lighting systems. "Baseball at night has proved profitable to the
approximately 150 professional clubs which are playing at least a portion of their
games under the lights," the company's January 1939 advertisement noted. "They have
thrown over the tradition that baseball is a daylight game, to take advantage of the
additional profits from games at night. You, too, can gain those added profits playing
under the lights."[6]

Baseball as an inherent daylight sport was never an evidenced-based argument,
merely a philosophical one. The argument was, at its core, grounded in the civic component of the civic/profit balance that itself was founded on the national pastime concept.
However, as night baseball expanded within major-league baseball, the daylight argument increasingly became more of a platitude. Mack had been out in front of this issue,
but it was Bradley in Cleveland who more brazenly pushed the financial angle, given the
immense seating capacity available in Municipal Stadium for night games. Bradley's public motivation to advocate for night baseball was to build a winning team, not per se to

build profits, since the Cleveland ball club had no burdensome financial hardship as did the Philadelphia Athletics and St. Louis Browns.

Interestingly, the money-making element of night baseball was publicly masked by the newspaper coverage of the more economically diversified audience at the ballpark, as reflected in a focus on attendance figures. In the midst of the New Deal economic recovery from the Great Depression, this diversification was viewed as a benefit for American society, since workers without time flexibility (middle- and low-level office workers and those in the working class) could now attend ball games on weekdays, not just on the weekend. While the minor leagues had recognized this societal good since the dawn of night baseball, it would take several more years before the major leagues reluctantly adopted this more progressive posture.

The profits were not just in ticket sales, but also at the concession stands. As Westinghouse illuminating engineers were finalizing the $100,000 lighting system at Shibe Park, with its 780 1,500-watt floodlights, Mack renovated the concession area to add more spacious cafes that served a real meal before the start of a night game, not just the usual ballpark cuisine of hot dogs and peanuts.[7]

Griffith, the vote-switcher on night baseball, attended the inaugural night game at Shibe Park between the Athletics and the Indians on May 16. While he may have changed his vote, he hadn't changed his mind on the topic. "This game wasn't meant to be played at night. It was meant to be played in the Lord's broad sunlight," Griffith said after the game. "There's more to a ball game than just a ball game. There's fresh air and sunshine and everything that goes to make up a fine afternoon. I don't want night baseball at Griffith Stadium. I won't put it in unless I have to, at least. Not unless I'm driven to it."[8]

However, Griffith was not averse to playing night games on the road to pick up a lucrative visitor's share of the gate, compared to the less substantial haul from a weekday daylight game. The three other clubs opposed to night baseball (Boston, Detroit, and New York) all proceeded with caution before committing to play night games in 1939, waiting to see how the experiment played out in the American League. All were convinced after the May 16 game in Philadelphia.

The New York Yankees, after initially firmly declaring that the ball club would not participate in the night games planned at Philadelphia and Cleveland, reversed that position the day after the inaugural night game at Shibe Park. "The fall of the McCarthymen to the appeal of the electric light bulbs leaves the Giants as the only major-league club adamant in their determination to play their baseball solely in the afternoons," the *New York Times* described the evolving situation in night baseball in New York City. Ed Barrow, now president of the New York Yankees after Jacob Ruppert's death in January 1939, softened the ball club's position on night baseball, primarily as a money-making proposition to benefit the Ruppert estate (still the majority owner of the ball club), not from any change in ideology about night baseball. Barrow also agreed to an open date following each night game, so that weakly-attended afternoon game could be moved to create a Sunday doubleheader in another series between the ball clubs.[9]

The seven night games played by the Athletics in Philadelphia in 1939 attracted a total attendance of 121,000 people, which represented 30 percent of the club's total attendance of 395,000 for the full season. Sunday games (161,000) and holiday games (46,000) combined to represent 50 percent of total attendance. Only 67,000 spectators attended the remaining daylight games, for an average of just 1,500 spectators per game, indicating that the weekday afternoon game was heavily subsidized by Sunday and night games, which combined accounted for nearly three-quarters of the total attendance during the 1939 season.[10]

Attendance in Cleveland was even better, as the initial night game on June 27 drew 55,000 people and the August 30 game against the Yankees drew 35,000. The Indians played their seventh, and last, night game on September 4 against the White Sox as the nightcap in a Labor Day doubleheader, following an afternoon game that day. This was a single-admission event for both games (with a several-hour intermission between games), so the Indians technically did not violate the no-holiday rule for night games. As it turned out, though, the afternoon game was rained out, so just the night game was actually played.

The Chicago White Sox became the third American League club to play night baseball, when that ball club made a mid-season decision to install lights and play several night games during a two-week August homestand. The top attendance was the night game with the Yankees when 50,000 people packed Comiskey Park. On September 27, the White Sox played the first major-league doubleheader that included a night game, combining a scheduled night game with the Cleveland Indians with an afternoon contest to make up a postponed game. Technically, it was a single-admission day-night doubleheader, where spectators could leave Comiskey Park at the conclusion of the daylight game and use their rain check to return for the night game.[11]

With big attendance figures generated at the night games staged during the 1939 season, Larry MacPhail felt compelled to issue a warning mid-season about the lure of expanding the seven-game limitation on each club's night baseball venture. "The Dodgers this year passed the 500,000-mark in home attendance, with the season just half over. I estimate nearly 200,000 of these as new fans for which night baseball is chiefly responsible," MacPhail told baseball writers. "A limited number of night games brings in new patronage and whets the appetite of the fans for the day game. But increase the number of night games and you are bound to kill off the daylight game, and once the fans tire of the night game, where will baseball turn next? What we must never lose sight of is that night baseball is still only an artificial stimulation and that major league baseball must basically remain a daylight game."[12]

MacPhail was adamant that a night game be considered another premium scheduling date, like Sunday and holidays, which was to be implicitly used to subsidize the deficiency in attendance for afternoon weekday ball games largely attended by business clientele. He insisted that night ball in the major leagues was not to be used to cater to a lower-income audience through an expansive nighttime schedule, as had happened in the minor leagues.

Baseball writers had already noticed that the typical audience at a night game was different from the one at weekday daylight games. "Night ball has developed a new clientele for the game in the majors," columnist Dan Daniel observed during the summer of 1939. "The night fan reacts to the game in a different way. He apparently attends less often than the daylight customer, and gets quite excited over things which the sunshine client takes more or less as a matter of course." Most sportswriters focused on the sporting-knowledge difference in spectator composition, as there was little reporting at this time on the contrast in socio-economic status.[13]

Neither MacPhail, the baseball executive, nor Daniel, the sportswriter, wanted to explicitly recognize that major-league baseball was now in the entertainment business and thus had to compete for customers who had other options for evening amusement during the workweek. Their preference that the national pastime be considered a special diversion for afternoon consumption was an outdated belief, one that the two men only very reluctantly relinquished during the next few years.

Part of the belief system of baseball traditionalists was that paying to watch a ball game at the ballpark should correlate to the spectator's interest in the sport, i.e., baseball fans rather than consumers of entertainment. One basic way to categorize baseball fans is to group them by level of interest, such as high, moderate, and low. These three levels can then be mapped to the enthusiasm level to attend ball games at the ballpark, with high-interest people being frequent attendees, moderate-interest people being periodic attendees, and low-interest people being occasional attendees.[14]

Prior to the inception of night baseball in 1930, the ballpark audience for daylight-only baseball in the 1920s essentially had a two-part composition: frequent and occasional. The occasional customers were largely tolerated by ball clubs for Sunday games, in order to subsidize the declining audience of spectators who could frequently attend games on weekdays. The middle ground of periodic customer, which had persisted before World War I, was much less apparent in the 1920s and had no obvious replacement for weekday daylight games.

For weekday daylight games in the 1930s, as the Great Depression gripped the nation, there was just a small group (medium size in a few cities) of potential frequent and periodic attendees, which was largely dependent on the home club being a winning team that was contending for the league championship. For Sunday and holiday games, there was a large group of potential occasional and periodic attendees, which was largely dependent on their desire for entertainment, rather than sport, but which could expand in frequency to watch a contender for the league championship. By 1939 the small group of frequent attendees was shrinking in size, while the large group of occasional attendees was increasing in size.

Minor-league clubs, recognizing that they were in the entertainment business, more rapidly viewed the baseball business in the three-tier, level-of-interest manner and thus embraced a greater schedule of night baseball to capture occasional customers in order to survive. Major-league clubs, on the other hand, wedded to their unique civic/profit dynamics, conducted night baseball as a special event in their sporting philosophy of the baseball business that highly valued the frequent spectator at weekday daylight games.

Ebbets Field in Brooklyn had the brightest illumination, as measured by lamp wattage, among the four major-league ballparks hosting night games at the start of the 1939 season, all with more than one million of wattage. Brooklyn's lighting capability measured 1,210,000 watts, slightly higher than the 1,196,000 watts in Cincinnati and the 1,170,000 watts in Philadelphia, while Cleveland came in at 1,062,000 watts. Because Chicago did not make a decision to pursue night ball until mid-season, its lighting capability had not yet been determined at the time of the survey.[15]

General Electric, which had devoted a dozen years to developing the technology to illuminate ballparks for night baseball, was now losing ground in the competition to secure contracts to engineer the illumination of major-league ballparks. The company had an initial monopoly for four years when it was tapped to engineer the lighting of Crosley Field in Cincinnati and Ebbets Field in Brooklyn. However, in 1939 General Electric was awarded only one of the three lighting projects instituted that year (Cleveland) while Westinghouse secured the other two (Philadelphia and Chicago). Giant Manufacturing, the original market leader in the lighting of minor-league ballparks, seemed to be a non-existent factor in the competition for major-league lighting contracts.[16]

During the fall of 1939, General Electric countered this competition from Westinghouse by actively promoting Robert Swackhamer, the company's lead illumination engineer, as an expert not just in the current lighting challenges but also on the future of ballpark lighting. Swackhamer was well-versed in the reflective properties of Alzak finishes versus porcelain-enameled surfaces, the relationship between mounting height of lamps and number of towers needed, and the proper angling of lamp beams. He also had startling views on the future of night baseball. "I believe club owners in the majors eventually will build bigger and better stadiums to accommodate from 100,000 to 150,000 fans for night games," Swackhamer told newspaper reporters. He also forecast a future that involved night games played in domed stadiums, where the lighting would be projected from concealed locations below the roof up to the ceiling of the roof, where the light would then be reflected downward to the playing surface. While his forecast for six-figure seating in stadiums failed to materialize, Swackhamer's thoughts about domed stadiums did prove to be accurate just 25 years later.[17]

The New Deal programs of President Roosevelt were instrumental in fueling attendance at night games during the 1930s at both the major-league and minor-league levels, as lower-income Americans could now more often enjoy a trip to the ballpark, not just fans in the middle class. "President Roosevelt used the national pastime to ward off despair and retain American pride and morale during a period of crisis," Ron Briley wrote in his article "Don't Let Hitler (or the Depression) Kill Baseball: Franklin D. Roosevelt and the National Pastime." Briley added that "Roosevelt and his speechwriters cleverly manipulated baseball metaphors to explain the New Deal and gain political support."[18]

Ever the master politician, Roosevelt made ample use of the public political platform available to presidents not only to mouth familiar platitudes about sport and patriotism but he also used baseball imagery and symbolism to identify himself with the national pastime. During the 1936 re-election campaign, he exhibited his political astuteness to use baseball for political gain by delivering speeches at ballparks, asking attendees there to compare the box score of their current life with that of four years earlier in 1932 during the depth of the Great Depression. Roosevelt also made ample use of the opportunity to attend the season-opening ball game at Griffith Stadium in Washington, where he threw out the first pitch for six consecutive years from 1933 through 1938.[19]

Following the outbreak of war in Europe in September 1939, when Germany invaded Poland, Roosevelt enhanced the country's military preparation, ostensibly to avoid being drawn into a global armed conflict. Roosevelt's actions further heightened the intersection of baseball and politics, which would soon encompass night baseball.

Using funds provided by the Works Progress Administration agency of the Roosevelt administration, numerous minor-league ballparks were built in the late 1930s. One of the largest WPA ballparks was located in Jersey City, New Jersey, and named after the president, Roosevelt Stadium, which began operation in 1937 in the International League. Two well-known WPA stadiums built for minor-league baseball in the 1930s that have survived into the twenty-first century are Riverview Stadium in Clinton, Iowa (when the club was in the Three-I League) and Carson Park in Eau Claire, Wisconsin (when the club was in the Northern League). Most WPA stadiums were built with lighting systems, which helped to foster the rebirth of minor-league baseball during the 1930s.

Roosevelt Stadium in Jersey City, New Jersey, with multiple light towers surrounding the ball-park located in a suburban location, was considered the best-lighted ballpark in the minor leagues during the late 1930s (Library of Congress, Prints & Photographs Division, HABS NJ,9-JERCI,16–39).

An unsung hero of night baseball is Joe Carr, whose efforts as minor-league promotion director grew the minors from 11 leagues at the end of the 1932 season up to 40 leagues in 1939, before he died that spring. Carr vigilantly pitched night baseball to potential organizers of new minor leagues and the investors in their ball clubs, and counseled them on how to obtain WPA funds to build a ballpark. While the lighting for major-league ballparks required at least 1,000,000 in lamp wattage, the best minor-league parks had at least 250,000 and the minimum was 100,000. Of the three WPA stadiums noted in the previous paragraph, Roosevelt Stadium in Jersey City was the best-lighted ballpark in the minors, with 750,000 in lamp wattage; Clinton and Eau Claire had decent lighting, with 198,000 and 175,000 in wattage, respectively.[20]

Except for afternoon games on Sunday and the rare ball club that did not play in a stadium with a lighting system, the minor leagues operated almost exclusively through night games by the late 1930s, with many night games conducted through promotions. Night games on Sunday were popular in the high minors, as were appliance raffles and social-organization nights (e.g., American Legion) in the lower minors, to optimize attendance. Among the more hokey promotions, a chicken chase was conducted by the Huntington, West Virginia, club in the Middle Atlantic League, where a dozen chickens, each with a ticket to a future game tied around its neck, were set loose on the field for spectators to hunt down. The Lafayette, Louisiana, club in the Class D Evangeline League

As was typical for the lower minor leagues, the ballpark in Marshall, Texas, where the club in the Class C East Texas League played its games, had a low-quality lighting system that produced barely passable illumination of ball games (Library of Congress, Prints & Photographs Division, LC-USF33-012166-M1).

drew a capacity crowd one evening in 1937 to witness the wedding of pitcher Truett Richardson during the game.[21]

In 1940 major-league baseball began its transformation into a time-of-day model from the day-of-game mixture it had employed for decades, emulating the minor leagues except for the rampant promotions used there for night games. Night doubleheaders, especially, likely scared major-league clubs owners into believing their early fears that night baseball was just a fad that would eventually peter out and make night games no more popular than their under-attended daylight games. For example, the Rochester club in the International League staged a flurry of night-game promotions in July 1937, where "Rabbit Maranville Night, July 9, and Tony Kaufmann Night, July 26, brought out bumper crowds, and a twilight-night twin bill against the Newark Bears, July 28, was viewed by the season's biggest mob."[22]

As its name implies, a twilight-night doubleheader was a single-admission twin bill consisting of a twilight game starting around 6:00 followed by a night game that began around 8:30. To keep the evening manageable for spectators, the twilight game was usually capped at seven innings, while the main event of the night game went the usual nine-inning distance. Originally, in the early 1930s these twin bills were called a "night" doubleheader, but by mid-decade the moniker "twilight-night" had replaced the descriptor of an after-dinner doubleheader. During the forthcoming war years, the term would be shortened to "twi-night" doubleheader.[23]

Twilight-night doubleheaders were problematical for major-league clubs, since a daylight game (including one in twilight) could not be completed under an artificial lighting system without it counting as a night game for purposes of the seven-game limitation on night baseball. There were no such restraints in the minor leagues, which were happy to eliminate a poorly attended daylight game (whether naturally rescheduled by weather or artificially moved by choice) by converting it into the twilight opener of an evening doubleheader. The two-games-for-the-price-of-one promotion helped to attract even larger crowds for night baseball in the minors.

The first-place finish by the Cincinnati Reds in 1939, having gone from worst to first over the previous five years, coupled with the third-place finish of the once-downtrodden Brooklyn Dodgers, convinced several more National League clubs to adopt night baseball for the 1940 season. The Reds announced that attendance equaled 703,192 for the club's 35 night home games during the previous five seasons, a little more than 20,000 per game. Revenue from night baseball enabled the club to secure better ballplayers to lift the club to the top of the National League standings. Such an escalation would never have occurred by playing an all-daylight schedule.[24]

The New York Giants were the first club to jump on the night-baseball bandwagon for the 1940 season, announcing a few weeks after the 1939 World Series that the club would stage night games at the Polo Grounds, after vociferously decrying the idea for five years and refusing to play in any night games as the visiting team. Horace Stoneham, the Giants president who had succeeded his late father Charles, elevated the lighting-system arms race by investing $135,000 to install 836 1,500-watt floodlights on towers 150 feet above the field and have Westinghouse engineer the field lighting in order to promote the Polo Grounds as the best lighted ballpark at 200 million candlepower.[25]

Night baseball was now so routine that there were no announcements at the league meetings in December 1939 regarding night-game renewals (now just a formality) or any discussion regarding the seven-game limitation. Both leagues did vote to permit night games on a Saturday. Later, at a rules committee session in February 1940, both leagues decided to apply the 11:50 curfew for night games to games in both leagues, adjusted for daylight savings time where applicable.[26]

The Pittsburgh Pirates and St. Louis Cardinals joined the New York Giants by announcing the clubs would also conduct night baseball in 1940. The Cardinals finally reached an agreement with the Browns to share the cost to install lights at Sportsman's Park. With the St. Louis Browns now set to play night games, the Washington Senators investigated the cost to install lights at Griffith Stadium to play night ball in 1940. However, the club backtracked after receiving bids for the project and abandoned the idea. "I won't be held up on the price like some club owners were," Clark Griffith declared. "The lowest bid we got for lighting equipment was $124,000 plus about $6,000 more for the engineers."[27]

To provide the lighting system at the Polo Grounds, Sportsman's Park, and Forbes Field to begin conducting night games in 1940, Westinghouse was chosen over General Electric. Of the eight major-league ballparks that now hosted night games, Westinghouse was the leading lighting engineer, having worked on five ballparks while General Electric had done three ballparks.[28]

It is not clear why Westinghouse became the industry leader in major-league ballpark lighting in 1940, after it had been awarded contracts in multiple competitions with General Electric. Prior to being selected for the 1939 lighting project at Shibe Park in Philadelphia, Westinghouse had been a peripheral competitor for ballpark lighting in both the majors and the minors. Westinghouse had bid unsuccessfully on the 1935 lighting project at Crosley Field in Cincinnati and its largest minor-league project was the 1931 installation at Seals Stadium in San Francisco.[29]

Westinghouse did advertise its "VHR–20 floodlight developed especially for baseball parks." However, the advertising copy provided no technical details why its floodlight might be superior to General Electric products, instead relying on more florid text that the Westinghouse floodlight was "sturdy, dependable, and stands up in every kind of weather." The 1939 World's Fair in New York City may have played a role in the sudden competitive position of Westinghouse in ballpark lighting, as part of a strategy to increase its overall outdoor lighting business. The company spent millions of dollars in the promotion of its electrical capabilities not only in its Westinghouse exhibition building but also in the general lighting of the fair grounds in the Queens borough of the city.[30]

Mack "invited Westinghouse executives to come to Shibe Park" to evaluate the lighting situation there in the months preceding the American League meeting in December 1938, according to one biographer of Mack. With no mention of General Electric, it appears that Mack had an existing relationship with Westinghouse or had received a recommendation from a trusted associate. Through whatever means the company obtained the lighting contract for Shibe Park, Westinghouse leveraged the success of that project into an additional opportunity later in 1939 at Chicago and with three more ballparks for the 1940 season.[31]

The 1940 season was the tenth anniversary of the commencement of night games in professional baseball. Ten major-league clubs now conducted night games, six in the National League and four in the American League. The six abstainers that clung to daylight baseball were the New York Yankees, Washington Senators, Chicago Cubs, Detroit Tigers, Boston Braves, and Boston Red Sox. Within the 40 minor leagues that operated in 1939, night baseball was conducted in 37 leagues by 196 ball clubs. Only a few cities in leagues at Class B or higher did not have lighted ballparks, such as Asheville, North Carolina, Hartford, Connecticut, and Knoxville, Tennessee.[32]

As Westinghouse became the lighting vendor of choice for major-league ballparks and Giant Manufacturing focused on minor-league ballparks, General Electric took the opportunity in 1940 to promote the fact that "they've been playing under G–E lights for 17 years." The company's advertisements traced its long history in providing ballpark lighting technology, from its beginnings for amateur games in 1923 at Lynn, to the first minor-league night game in 1930 at Des Moines, to the first major-league night game at Cincinnati, to lighting Cleveland's Municipal Stadium in 1939, which enabled the company to have "a complete knowledge of light control" through reflector contours, lamp research, and field experience. Despite its breadth of knowledge, General Electric continued to lag behind Westinghouse as the premier engineer of major-league ballpark lighting systems.[33]

The New York Giants and St. Louis Browns played their initial night games on May 24, while the St. Louis Cardinals and Pittsburgh Pirates opened night play on June 4. All four clubs drew an audience of more than 20,000 spectators, with the St. Louis Browns drawing the largest attendance figure, at 24,827 people. During the early part of the 1940 season, night games staged by the ten clubs with lighting systems averaged 24,000 spectators, in comparison to the average for daylight games of only 3,000 to 4,000 spectators per game experienced in 1939.[34]

In mid–June the American League club owners very quietly gave the St. Louis Browns an exemption to conduct 14 night games during the 1940 season. While contemporary newspaper reporting on the exception was very spotty, eventual accounts of that league meeting cited "financial expediency" as the reason for the decision to allow the Browns to play twice as many night games as the other three night-hosting clubs in the league.[35]

The 14-game exception for the St. Louis Browns did help the club stave off its financial problems, but it was not an overwhelming success. With the Cardinals playing seven night games, the 21 total night contests in St. Louis were an overload to the city's baseball interest. While the attendance at the initial night game for the Browns represented 20 percent of the club's total daylight attendance in 1939, the attendance for some of the later night games dipped below 10,000. Night games did represent one-half of the Browns' total attendance for 1940.

Overall night-game attendance for the ten night-hosting clubs during the 1940 season was 1.5 million spectators, for an average audience of 20,700 spectators. Cleveland and Chicago had the highest average game attendance, at 33,000 and 32,000, respectively, as each club drew more than one-quarter of a million spectators to their quota of seven night games. Brooklyn (28,700), Cincinnati (25,400), New York (24,000), and Pittsburgh (23,800) rounded out the top six clubs. The other four night-hosting clubs all averaged less than 15,000 per game, as the two-club cities of St. Louis and Philadelphia essentially split the night-game audience. The two Philadelphia clubs together averaged 24,000 and

The Boston Braves, one of the last six major-league clubs to install lights, barely survived financially on small crowds at weekday afternoon ball games, such as this one in 1940, presumably a Ladies Day promotion since five women are standing at the railing in front of empty box seats (courtesy Boston Public Library, Leslie Jones Collection).

the two St. Louis clubs 22,700, providing substantive evidence that two-club cities were doomed to failure in the civic/profit business basis.[36]

Several days after the re-election of President Roosevelt to a third term in November 1940, Griffith announced that the Washington Senators would install a light system to play night games at Griffith Stadium during the 1941 season. Westinghouse was hired for the lighting project, following the recent trend by other club owners to use that firm rather than General Electric. Westinghouse commenced a small advertising campaign that touted the slogan "6 parks out of 9 lighted by Westinghouse."[37]

The timing of the announcement seemed to indicate that Griffith was resigned to accepting four more years of Democratic political influence in Washington, during which night baseball would be good for business. The $130,000 cost for the lighting, deemed exorbitant just eight months earlier, was now considered acceptable. This was just one example of how Griffith was fluid on the issue of night baseball.

Griffith had a long, often contradictory, history regarding night baseball, as related by Francis Stan in his 1940 article "Now Arc Addict, Inconsistent Griff Is a Man of Mystery" published in the *Washington Evening Star*. For most of the 1930s, Griffith had devotedly despised night baseball, loudly proclaiming that "there is only one time to play ball and that is in the daytime." After the American League belatedly adopted night baseball for the 1939 season, Griffith stunned people when he then advocated that the majors dedicate the months of June, July, and August to night games in order to make maximum use of lighting systems. When he finally seemed agreeable to the seven-game limitation, he then abruptly reneged on purchasing a lighting system in March 1940 as he balked at paying the six-figure cost. It did not surprise many that Griffith soon after his November 1940 announcement publicly began lobbying for the ability to conduct a dozen night games during the 1941 season.[38]

At the league meetings in December 1940, the National League pushed for a uniform rule to limit night games in both leagues to seven home games per club, while some American League club owners were lobbying for a 14-game restriction similar to the exemption given the St. Louis Browns six months earlier. Cardinals owner Sam Breadon reportedly pushed for the common limit, after his fellow National League owners had rebuffed his request during the summer for the Cardinals to host 14 night games to equal the policy under which the Browns were operating. While he no doubt felt that a higher limit for the Browns gave that club an unfair advantage in competing for St. Louis baseball fans, Breadon diplomatically justified his position at the meeting with an argument "to the effect that twenty-eight night games in any city would ruin the daytime attendance."[39]

The seven-game limitation, applied equally to both leagues, was adopted. In the joint-league meeting, where leagues voted as a block and not individual clubs, the National League voted for the restriction to be seven games and the American League voted for it to be 14 games. The deadlock was broken "with Commissioner Landis casting the deciding vote," the *New York Times* reported, without elaboration. Landis gave no public explanation why he sided with the National League and the seven-game restriction, leading one historian to conclude that Landis was "frozen in time and impervious to the cultural changes that had occurred during his tenure as commissioner." Landis, though, voted his personal belief that excessive night baseball was not in the best interests of baseball, which was his purview as commissioner, notwithstanding the cultural changes then in motion. Left to his own desires, Landis would have voted for zero night games, but he had to choose one of the existing votes, so he picked the lowest number.[40]

Landis was an avowed baseball traditionalist who whole-heartedly believed in the contradictory civic/profit business balance that *New York Times* sportswriter John Kieran laid out in a June 1940 "Sports of the *Times*" column. "It stands to reason that there are more prospective customers on the loose in the evening than in the daytime, and in business it's sensible to bid for the largest market," Kieran wrote. "But the Supreme Court of the United States held that professional baseball was not like other businesses and those who know the game will agree with that decision by the learned justices." In other words, subsidize the weekday daylight game for the perpetuation of the ballpark audience for the national pastime as it existed four decades earlier. Landis was just one of "the sun-worshipers [who] have the charts to show that night-life in baseball is suicidal in the long run … a cumulative poison, all the more dangerous because it has a sweet taste at first."[41]

Browns president Donald Barnes was so miffed about the uniform seven-game restriction on night games that he spent considerable time surreptitiously arranging for the transfer of the Browns from St. Louis to Los Angeles for the 1942 season. At the time Los Angeles was the fifth largest city in the country, with a population of 1.5 million residents, making it a likely lucrative untapped market for major-league baseball. The only problem was that Los Angeles was 1,500 miles from the nearest existing major-league city, creating massive logistical transportation and scheduling issues.[42]

With five clubs now hosting night games, the American League denoted night games on its official 1941 schedule released in January as well as 16 Sunday doubleheaders, to eliminate a significant portion of the mid-season runaround to designate an off-day following a night game and move the once-scheduled game to form a Sunday twin bill. With improved certainty to the schedule released before spring training, ballpark spectators could make better plans to attend both night games as well as daylight games. From this point forward, having an open date on the day following a night game was no longer deemed necessary or even desirable, in an attempt to prop up the attendance at the next subsequent daylight game.[43]

In May 1941 Connie Mack floated the idea of having a special league meeting to increase the number of allowable night games. Mack, though, received little support from the other club owners, who wished to continue the policy that a night game was a special event and conducting more than seven per year "would ruin the novelty of night baseball." Then there was the logistics of such a decision. "I would have to oppose any movement to allow more [night] games," Yankees president Ed Barrow declared. "This was settled in Chicago last winter when Commissioner Landis himself voted against more than seven games."[44]

The timing was also off for Mack's plea for more night games, since the federal government was then actively promoting energy conservation as part of its national defense initiatives. In the southern states where electrical power was especially in short supply, several minor-league ball clubs in the Southern Association and Southeastern League curtailed the number of night games they staged while the Class D Georgia–Florida League reverted to an entirely daylight schedule. Secretary of the Interior Harold Ickes said in a speech in late May that electricity needs were so critical to national defense that "it's more important to make aluminum than to have night baseball."[45]

"Naturally the major leagues want to do everything in their power to help national defense, but I can't see where abandoning night baseball would provide much assistance," Mack responded to the government's position on night games as articulated by Ickes. "In the first place, we play so few night games and use so little power comparatively that I don't think the turning of it over to defense purposes would offset the recreational advantages now provided by our playing under lights."[46]

As the federal government was weighing in on the recreational tradeoffs required for its national defense programs, the Washington Senators staged their first home night game on May 28, 1941, on an oppressively hot evening against the Yankees before 25,000 spectators. Legendary Washington pitcher Walter Johnson participated in the pre-game ceremony by throwing a pitch through a light beam set up at home plate, which automatically released a switch that flooded Griffith Stadium in bright light from the Westinghouse floodlights atop the towers surrounding the field.

The lights gave no home-field advantage to the lowly Senators in the augural night game in Washington, as they lost their tenth consecutive game. "If Griffith Stadium's spiffy new lighting system could spare the loan of a faint flicker off its 180,000,000 candle-power beams, the Nats would appreciate its aid in guiding them out of the dim, clammy atmosphere of the American League cellar," the *Washington Evening Star* characterized the plight of Clark Griffith's ball club. The cartoon accompanying the game story showed Griffith basking in a light beam filled with dollar signs and shouting "Ah! The Wonders of Electricity!" as a Washington ballplayer lay prostrate on the ground with "10th Straight Loss" circling his head. The cartoon aptly demonstrated the "bright light" to the woes of the Senators on the playing field, as money could amply be made from night baseball hosted by a losing team.[47]

The merits of night baseball in producing sufficient revenue to build a pennant-winning ball club was demonstrated for a third consecutive year, as the Brooklyn Dodgers won the National League championship in 1941 on the heels of the pennants won by the Cincinnati Reds the prior two seasons. There was no better argument for the conducting of night games than having the two pioneering night-baseball clubs in the majors, the Reds and the Dodgers, build a championship club to replace their prior lowly status in the league standings during their daylight-only days.

The 77 night games played in the major leagues during the 1941 season represented 6.2 percent of all major-league games played that season, in stark contrast to the estimated 70 percent of minor-league games that were conducted as night games. This major-league ratio would double during the 1942 season, then continue at an accelerated growth rate thereafter (see Appendix D), in the aftermath of the Japanese bombing of Pearl Harbor on December 7, 1941, which established the setting to forever convert professional baseball from a daylight game into a night sport.[48]

◆ 11 ◆

The War Years

On December 9, 1941, the winter meetings of the two major leagues were slated to start in Chicago, where two items on the preliminary agenda would have expanded night baseball during the 1942 season. However, due to the Japanese attack on Pearl Harbor on December 7 that plunged the United States into World War II, both of those agenda items were scuttled.

The more dramatic of the two night-game issues was the proposed relocation of the St. Louis Browns to Los Angeles, California. If the transfer were approved (as painstakingly pre-negotiated with the American League club owners), the relocated Browns almost certainly would have pushed for a significant exception to the seven-game limitation on night games, since the Los Angeles Angels, the minor-league farm club of the Chicago Cubs in the Pacific Coast League, played a substantial schedule of night games during the previous dozen years.

The second night-game issue was the expected announcement that two more ball clubs would install lighting systems to play night baseball, the Chicago Cubs at Wrigley Field and the Detroit Tigers at Briggs Stadium. During the fall of 1941, both clubs had reached the decision to play night home games in 1942, with the Cubs having already purchased an expensive, telescoping system that would retract when not in use and thus not spoil the scenery for daylight games.[1]

Both agenda items were shelved following the public announcement of the Pearl Harbor incident, which changed the course of night-baseball history. The Browns abandoned the carefully crafted plan to move to Los Angeles, while the Tigers and Cubs delayed their plans to install lights for the duration of the war. The Tigers and the Cubs became the last clubs in their respective major leagues to finally adopt night baseball, Detroit in 1948 and Chicago four decades later in 1988.

Cubs owner Phil Wrigley donated the lighting equipment, once destined for Wrigley Field, to the federal government. "We felt that this material could be more useful in lighting flying fields, munitions plants or other war defense plants under construction," Wrigley explained his decision to forego night baseball. The course of baseball history in Chicago would have been vastly different had lights been installed in 1942 at Wrigley Field.[2]

Given the uncertainty of operating during wartime, the National League club owners voted to retain the existing seven-game limit for the 1942 season, while the American League voted for unlimited night games to support the lobbying by the owners of the Washington Senators and St. Louis Browns for a 14-game limit. At the joint-league meeting, Landis had to break the deadlock again, as he had to do one year earlier at the

December 1940 joint meeting, siding once more with the National League to retain the existing seven-game limitation on night games. However, most ball club owners thought this limit was merely theoretical, since the prevailing attitude was that "war conditions next summer might force abandonment of all night baseball in the majors."[3]

The retention of the 1941 night-game policy exacerbated the abandonment of the Browns' move to Los Angeles. The Browns were again financially desperate, now without the benefit of either the relocation to Los Angeles or the reinstitution of the 14 night games that the club had been allowed to conduct during the 1940 season. Browns president Donald Barnes, unable to obtain forbearance on the number of allowable night

While the FDR green-light letter has been often reproduced and its text frequently quoted in regard to night baseball, the original letter from Commissioner Landis has received much less acclaim. However, this hand-written letter provides many clues to understanding the genesis of why President Roosevelt advocated the expansion of night baseball in his green-light response letter (National Archives, Collection FDR-PPF, Papers as President, President's Personal File: 1933–1945, PPF 227: Baseball, Item Identifier 6997538).

games for the 1942 season, appears to have worked a backchannel of Democratic Party politics in Washington as a way to obtain more flexibility on night baseball.

President Franklin Roosevelt, as historians have amply established, was instrumental in enabling professional baseball to survive the war years, when he issued his "green light" letter in January 1942. Commissioner Landis had written a letter to Roosevelt to inquire that "inasmuch as these are not ordinary times, I venture to ask what you have in mind as to whether professional baseball should continue to operate." Landis got much more than he had hoped for in the response from Roosevelt.[4]

Roosevelt replied to Landis with a morale argument: "I honestly feel that it would be best for the country to keep baseball going. There will be fewer people employed, and everybody will work longer hours and harder than ever. And that means that they ought to have a chance for recreation and for taking their minds off their work even more than before." He added that this was his personal point of view and not an official government position. Roosevelt also famously added this unanticipated sentence: "And incidentally, I hope that night games can be extended because it gives an opportunity to the day shift to see a game occasionally." While professional baseball got its go-ahead from the president, the approval came with the implied quid pro quo of more night games.[5]

At the time, Landis received all the public credit for enticing Roosevelt into blessing the continued existence of professional baseball during the war, which is interesting in retrospect since Landis, a staunch Republican, was about as far right from a New Deal Democrat as anyone in America. Over time, Washington Senators owner Clark Griffith got more of the credit, due to his relationship with Roosevelt that originally involved the "first pitch" duties on opening day at Griffith Stadium. Based on the future developments in night baseball that largely benefited his ball club, Griffith appears to have used his conduit to the Roosevelt administration to not only persuade the president to issue a positive perspective on baseball's continuation during the war, but also to seek an increase in night baseball. Griffith never publicly took that much credit. In an autobiographical essay he wrote in 1952, Griffith humbly said of that task, "I pride myself on having had something to do with the continuance of the game during World War II." While his approach in that statement was humble, he also might have been indicating that he shared the credit with another individual, who had died in 1949.[6]

Only three decades later did the name Bob Hannegan enter the conversation about the Roosevelt green-light letter, when Bill DeWitt, the general manager of the St. Louis Browns in 1942, revealed Hannegan's role during an interview with William Mead for his 1978 book *Even the Browns: The Zany, True Story of Baseball in the Early Forties*. "Griffith was the one who persuaded Roosevelt to take action. Another fellow that had a lot to do with it was Robert Hannegan. Don Barnes and Hannegan were very close," DeWitt said about his boss's relationship with the Democratic boss in St. Louis. "He was in great shape with the president. Did he talk to Roosevelt about the green light? Yeah, absolutely. Griffith helped, but the guy who really put it over was Hannegan." DeWitt added that the newspapers never found out about Hannegan's involvement, so he was divulging "a dead man's secret."[7]

Politics was the connection that produced the green-light letter, through what author Mead called "a coup engineered behind the scenes by two astute baseball lobbyists." While Griffith had the baseball relationship with Roosevelt, Hannegan more importantly had the political pull to interact with Roosevelt in those early days of the wartime administration. A non-war issue had to be vital to make it to Roosevelt's desk during the tumultuous first few weeks following the attack on Pearl Harbor. On its own, the Landis letter was unlikely to gain Roosevelt's attention, despite Griffith's rapport with the White House. Hannegan, though, had the political acumen to turn the ostensible baseball-only issue into a war-related issue that deserved the president's attention, especially since he could also meld in a secondary benefit for the president within domestic politics. The combination of Hannegan and Griffith as a team made the green-light letter happen.[8]

Rather than the random act of the president merely replying to one of the many letters he received each week, the six-paragraph green-light letter seemed to be part of a well orchestrated scheme, not a simple off-the-cuff reply to the Landis letter. In the first place, the handwritten Landis letter is dated January 14 and the typewritten Roosevelt reply is dated January 15. The letter could not have traveled to Washington from Chicago in one day, and less possibly in one day from Florida where Landis was, in fact, wintering for the entire month of January. Since the "4" in the date "14" is written in very different handwriting than the "4" in the year "1942," the Landis letter appears to have been penned at the league meetings in December 1941 for transmittal to the White House when convenient, with Griffith the likely courier of the "fill in the date" letter. This would also explain why such an important letter was handwritten, not typewritten, as was normally the case for business correspondence in that era, when even short thank-you notes were conveyed in typewritten format. The compressed nature of the one-page letter's final paragraph also indicates that the letter was crafted in a rush.

The guts of the green-light letter, which followed the first three paragraphs that sound very much like Roosevelt talking, seem to have been also pre-drafted. The fourth paragraph about night baseball and the long fifth paragraph about ballplayers and military service look to be the work of Griffith. The crucial sixth paragraph, which lays out the political explanation for continuing baseball during wartime, seems to have been crafted by Hannegan: "Here is another way of looking at it—if 300 teams use 5,000 or 6,000 players, these players are a definite recreational asset to at least 20,000,000 of their fellow citizens—and that in my judgment is thoroughly worthwhile." These numbers did not just leap from Roosevelt's mind in the haste of dictating an immediate reply to the Landis letter, if its January 14 date is to be believed as the letter's actual date of creation.[9]

Hannegan had access to President Roosevelt and his staff at the White House because he had been instrumental in delivering the 15 electoral votes of Missouri into the Roosevelt column in the 1940 election (as well as assisting in the re-election of Missouri senator Harry Truman). The big-city political machines were vital to the Roosevelt victory. Many Democrats had soured on Roosevelt for running for a third term in violation of the precedent, set by George Washington, for a two-term maximum. There was fear that the country would not re-elect any man to a third term. Other Democratic voters had serious concerns that Roosevelt would eventually involve the United States in the war then being fought in Europe, a stance that the isolationist Republican candidate, Wendell Willkie, vowed never to do.[10]

Although the final election returns indicated a landslide victory, 449 electoral votes to 82 with Roosevelt carrying 38 of the 48 states, the presidential race was considerably closer during the fall as Willkie actively campaigned while Roosevelt remained close to Washington to reinforce that he was the commander-in-chief in war-preparation mode. To counter the impact of Willkie on the campaign trail, Ed Flynn, the chairman of the Democratic National Committee, focused the Roosevelt strategy on the big-city vote, where working-class and lower-middle-class voters were heavily influenced by their city's political boss. St. Louis, where Hannegan was the boss, turned out to be important in helping Roosevelt to carry Missouri and ward off an extension of Willkie's message eastward from the other Midwestern states that were Willkie's stronghold in the electoral-college voting.[11]

There were two reasons why Hannegan was motivated to help orchestrate the green-light letter. First, he was a St. Louis baseball fan and wanted to assist Barnes now that the Browns' move to Los Angeles was aborted. Second, he was looking for a new role in politics, since in 1941 he had failed to get the mayor of St. Louis re-elected. Hannegan seemed to be amply rewarded for his efforts, by both the political and baseball establishments. In March 1942, Roosevelt nominated Hannegan to be the collector of revenue in St. Louis, and by 1943 Hannegan was in Washington as the head of the Internal Revenue Service. Hannegan was then appointed DNC chairman in 1944, to replace Flynn, where he marshaled Roosevelt to re-election for a fourth term after having engineered Truman to be the vice presidential running mate. In baseball circles, Hannegan was seriously considered in 1945 as a candidate to become the next commissioner, as successor to the deceased Landis, and in 1947 he did become president of the St. Louis Cardinals. Barnes likely arranged for a suitable recompense in local ways back in St. Louis.

Hannegan almost certainly crafted the essence of the political argument to justify the continuation of baseball during wartime, by explicitly positioning the national pastime as a morale booster for war-production workers and others supporting the war effort on the home front as well as servicemen on the front lines. Implicitly, the morale argument, especially its night baseball element, also contained

President Franklin Roosevelt (left) and Washington Senators owner Clark Griffith (right) met annually for the ceremonial presentation of a season pass to ball games at Griffith Stadium. This relationship created the foundation for Roosevelt's green-light letter in January 1942 that expanded night baseball during the war years (Library of Congress, Prints & Photographs Division, LC-DIG-hec-47563).

a significant dose of "raw politics" designed to maintain public support for Roosevelt's wartime policies in a nation whose population still largely possessed an isolationist attitude. The green-light letter was a good demonstration of Roosevelt's political acumen, which Briley described in his "Don't Let Hitler (or the Depression) Kill Baseball" essay as "his ability to understand the values and passions of the American people as he adroitly used the spirit of baseball as a metaphor and morale booster" to rally their support through the war years. The ask for night baseball also secondarily furthered Roosevelt's New Deal social agenda, which became the lasting legacy of the green-light letter and thus averted its consignment to a mere footnote in World War II history.[12]

The timing of the Roosevelt response letter was certainly well engineered with its January 15 release date, which was perfectly timed to meet the editorial deadlines of the weekend newspapers. This showed the hand of Stephen Early, Roosevelt's press secretary, who held a press conference on Friday morning, January 16, to announce the release of the green-light letter and elaborate on its contents. Since there was substantial censorship of military-related news following Pearl Harbor, the news about the continuation of baseball was desirable positive news from the White House as well as a welcome reprieve for Early, who avoided once again needing to tell reporters that there was no news to report from the White House. Interestingly, the Associated Press story about the green-light letter not only quoted Early but also prominently included quotations from both Griffith and Barnes, which silently signaled their roles in the crafting of the green-light letter. Overall, these details help to support the pre-drafting of the green-light letter and an engineering of its public release, rather than being left to the whims of bureaucracy in its development.[13]

Landis could scarcely accept the nod from President Roosevelt to continue professional baseball during the war and at the same time disavow the president's expressed desire that more night games be conducted. The green-light letter put Landis in a difficult political position with the 16 major-league ball-club owners. On January 20, Landis announced that special league meetings would be held on February 2 to 3 to discuss the night baseball situation for the 1942 season.

In the separate league meetings in February, the stance of the National League continued to differ from the policy desired by the American League, just as it had in the earlier league meetings in December 1941. Consistent with Roosevelt's text in the green-light letter, the National League club owners now voted to increase the limit on a club's home night games from 7 to 14 games. The American League also concurred with a 14-game restriction, but with an exception for Washington to stage 28 night games. Griffith seemed to use leverage gained from his working on the green-light letter to seek 28 night games for his Washington club, a doubling of his original ask made just two months earlier. His public logic was that Washington should be treated comparably to the single-city total allowed in both Philadelphia and St. Louis, where the two clubs could each hold 14 night games for a city-wide total of 28 night games.[14]

In the joint-league meeting on February 3, Landis struck a compromise to break the deadlock, rather than vote with one league over the other as he had done twice before in regard to night-game policy in December 1940 and December 1941. The compromise was a 14-game limit on night games for the 1942 season, with an exception for the Washington Senators to stage 21 night games. Landis supported his decision by citing some unusual scheduling gymnastics that Griffith would have to do to actually arrange for 28 night games, but also added his own opinion that "after all, there still must be some fans in Washington who would like to see a ball game in the afternoon."[15]

By granting this exception to Griffith, did Landis merely curry favor with the politicians and government bureaucrats who inhabited wartime Washington? Or did Landis provide a reward to Griffith for his efforts to orchestrate the green-light letter? The exact reasoning of Landis was, of course, left unsaid and never revealed, but it just might have been a combination of both angles. But what of a reward for the behind-the-scenes role of the St. Louis Browns? While not the higher limit of 21 games for the Washington club, St. Louis could conduct 14 night games in 1942, which was enough for Barnes to entice new investors to infuse capital into the ball club.

In describing the new policy for night baseball, *New York Times* baseball writer John Drebinger quipped: "So the major leagues, which only a few years ago had accepted night baseball with considerable skepticism, committed themselves to a program whereby a total of 161 games, 77 in the American and 84 in the National, may be played under artificial lights next summer if all clubs avail themselves of stocking up to the full quota." To minimize scheduling issues with the expanded number of night games to be played in 1942 by the 11 ball clubs with a lighting system in their home ballpark, the two leagues voted to eliminate restrictions on Sunday doubleheaders.[16]

One issue not overly addressed at the time was whether the increased limit on night baseball was just for the duration of the war and therefore would be rolled back when the war ended. National League president Ford Frick talked about "suspending" the seven-game rule during wartime, which seems to have become the general understanding of most ball-club owners. The concept that the 14-game limit might be considered a precedent for peacetime in the postwar period appears to have eluded baseball executives.[17]

This expansion of night baseball hit a snag just a few weeks into the 1942 season, when the U.S. Army issued dim-out regulations in late April "to curb both the direct rays of shore lights and the shore glow that silhouette ships at sea and make them 'easy targets' for enemy submarines." In cities located within 15 miles of the seacoast, the regulations required that every light higher than 15 stories be shaded or turned out. Since ballpark lights appeared to be covered by the regulation, a few major-league ball clubs were impacted as well as several minor-league clubs in the International League, Pacific Coast League, and South Atlantic League.[18]

At the major-league level, only the ball clubs in New York City were directly impacted by the dim-out regulations. Washington and Philadelphia were far enough inland so that night games there were not affected. Boston would have been impacted, but lights had yet to be installed in either Braves Field or Fenway Park. New York City police commissioner Lewis Valentine ordered the lights shut off at Ebbets Field and the Polo Grounds, effectively ending night baseball in 1942 for the Brooklyn Dodgers and New York Giants (Yankee Stadium then had no lights). Both the Dodgers and Giants initially tried to substitute twilight games, but these contests proved to be sparsely attended.[19]

In the minor leagues, the Pacific Coast League initially received a reprieve on the dim-out regulations, which were not applied until August. In the South Atlantic League, the Jacksonville, Florida, and Savannah, Georgia, clubs discontinued night games and tried to squeeze in twilight games by enforcing hurry-up tactics to complete games before sunset. In the International League, only the Jersey City and Newark clubs in New Jersey were impacted, being so close to New York City. The dim-out regulations in those two cities were enforced beginning in early June.[20]

Larry MacPhail, general manager of the Brooklyn Dodgers, solved the dim-out dilemma for the ball clubs in the New York City area by obtaining permission from Major General Thomas Terry to begin a game during daylight hours and use the stadium lights for one hour after sunset to complete the game. For a game that began at 7:00, this new policy provided two and a half hours to finish the game, since sunset in June was at 8:30 or so. The combination was referred to as a "twilight-night" game or "twight" for short. The Jersey City club first tried the combination technique on June 12. The Brooklyn Dodgers and New York Giants quickly adopted the approach, as did the Newark club. The major-league All-Star Game played at the Polo Grounds in 1942 was also conducted under the twilight-night technique, temporarily dispatching its previous all-daylight stature.[21]

The twilight-night game was awkward from several perspectives. First, there was the timing, with its 7:00 start and a fixed ending time, when the lights were turned off. Second, there was the game's artistic merit, since the game was played in three different lighting conditions. The first innings were played in daylight, the next one or two innings in dusk conditions somewhat mitigated by artificial light, and the last few innings in darkness under the lights. However, the twilight-night game initially appealed to weary war workers, who swelled the attendance figures at Ebbets Field and Polo Grounds for these quasi-night games. Once the popularity of twilight-night games was established, the Dodgers and Giants converted their original 14-game night calendar to this scheduling technique. Since the rule counting a daylight game completed under lights as a night game still applied, both clubs had a maximum of 14 possible twilight-night games.

Clark Griffith, already with an exception for his Washington Senators to conduct 21 night games in 1942, sought approval at the July league meetings to stage an additional 14 night games for a total of 35 for the season. This new exception would allow him to conduct all remaining home games at night, except for Sundays and holidays. His argument was that weekday daylight games in wartime Washington were a poor draw, while demand for evening activities was extremely high, given the stressful daytime working conditions due to the war. Since the restriction on the number of night games a ball club could conduct required joint approval of both leagues, Griffith's proposal seemed a long shot for approval.[22]

At the league meetings in July 1942, the American League club owners approved Griffith's proposal, but the National League owners voted against it, citing the same St. Louis issue that had undermined mutual agreement on the uniform night-game restriction back in December 1940. Once again, Landis had to break the tie at the joint-league meeting, again siding with the National League, which sportswriters attributed to Landis's "fear of setting a trend for all night games," i.e., the concept of unlimited night baseball.[23]

After the rebuff, Griffith announced that he would convert the remaining non–Sunday daylight games in Washington to the twilight-night approach used in the National League by the Dodgers and Giants, since he was told he needed no approval to stage a twilight game. The first such contest was conducted on July 17. However, either through a misunderstanding or a miscommunication, Griffith ran afoul of the rule prohibiting the completion of a daylight game under lights, with its associated penalty that the game would count toward the club's limited number of night games. With his twilight-night plan quashed by American League president Harridge, Griffith reluctantly returned to conducting just his original quota of 21 night games.[24]

The concept of the twilight-night game soon dropped from favor following the

August 3 game at the Polo Grounds. The large crowd of 57,000 people saw the Giants–Dodgers game suddenly halted in the ninth inning, with the Giants mounting a rally to overtake a Brooklyn lead, when the lights were abruptly turned off. The crowd booed vociferously when it was announced that the score reverted to the last completed inning, giving the Dodgers the victory. After the game, Giants president Horace Stoneham stated there would be no more twilight games at the Polo Grounds for the duration of the war. The Dodgers, though, continued playing twilight-night games at Ebbets Field through the 1943 season.

A bigger issue for night baseball than the dim-out regulations was gasoline rationing, which the federal government instituted in May 1942. The limit of four gallons of gasoline per week for car with an "A" sticker enabled people to get to work, but it didn't leave much in the gas tank for pleasure trips to the ballpark. Many spectators for a ball game, whether in the daylight or at night, needed to take public transportation to the ballpark. With restrictions on automobile travel and people working longer hours, ball clubs needed to exercise creativity to attract spectators to a ball game.

Doubleheaders multiplied on the 1942 baseball calendar (40 percent of all major-league games played that year), providing two games for the price of one to encourage attendance at daylight games. For those ball clubs able to host night baseball, the twilight-night doubleheader became a staple of wartime baseball, which was a combination of a twilight game starting at 5:30 or 6:00 followed by a night game starting at 8:30 or 9:00. Much like the Sunday doubleheader of the 1930s, these twin bills were fashioned either naturally, to make up an earlier postponed game, or in a synthetic manner, by canceling a future daylight game. The first twilight-night doubleheaders, soon to be known as a twi-night doubleheader, were played in the American League on July 24 in St. Louis and Cleveland. The approach was quickly imitated by other American League clubs with a lighting system in their home ballpark. The National League, though, eschewed the night-time doubleheader concept.[25]

The initial twi-night doubleheader in St. Louis attracted the largest audience for a Browns game in more than two years. "Twilight-floodlight doubleheader baseball had its premiere at Sportsman's Park last night, and it was a smash hit," the *St. Louis Post-Dispatch* reported. "More than 20,000 persons paid at the gate, and the show, lasting five hours and 52 minutes, was all that the most critical could have demanded." The biggest concern for spectators was when and how to eat dinner. The Browns anticipated this by stocking up on hamburgers and hot dogs as well as by laying in box lunches and sandwiches, much of it consumed during the 45-minute intermission between games.[26]

Depending on the actual length of the first game, there could be a significant break between the two games of a twi-night doubleheader. Since daylight games could not yet be completed under lights, the opener needed an early start time to allow for extra innings if needed, and night games needed to begin after sunset. In the worst-case scenario, darkness could end the opener in a tie, as occurred on August 11 in Cleveland.

The attendance-challenged Browns also experimented with pairing a daylight game with a night game, soon to be known as a day-night doubleheader, with one admission providing entrance to both games. Pass-out privileges applied at the day game so that spectators could re-enter the ballpark for the night game. This type of twin bill, first staged on September 4, was not nearly as popular as the twi-night doubleheader.

The Detroit Tigers, one of the five ball clubs still without a lighting system, engaged in numerous twilight games at Briggs Stadium. Since Detroit was located on the western edge of the Eastern Time Zone, sunset was approximately an hour later than in Boston. Under the federal War Time Act of 1942 that required daylight savings time to be observed year-round across the nation in order to conserve energy, the Tigers could conduct twilight games as quasi-night games without lights, with a 6:00 dinner-time start that allowed for the game to be played during evening hours yet be completed before darkness.[27]

By the end of the 1942 season, 12 percent of all major-league games had been conducted as night games. When MacPhail left the Dodgers for military service after the 1942 season and Branch Rickey was hired to replace him, major-league baseball lost its moderating voice when it came to policy-making about night baseball. Although the two major leagues retained the night-game limits agreed to in February 1942 for the 1943 season, expansion of night baseball was on the imminent horizon.[28]

Attendance prospects for baseball in 1943 dwindled further with a ban on all pleasure driving by limiting gasoline rations for people with an "A" sticker to three gallons per week. While the major leagues coped with that fallout, the minor leagues seriously contracted for the remainder of the war to a dozen leagues or less, nearly all at the Class B level or higher. Saturated with night baseball by the late 1930s, the minor leagues were now less influential in the trends evolving in night baseball. With two-thirds of major-league clubs now playing home games in ballparks with lighting systems (soon to be 94 percent in the immediate postwar period), the story of night baseball during the postwar decades was largely within the major leagues.

During the 1943 season, doubleheaders continued to thrive in the major leagues (48 percent of all games) as an incentive for the war weary to attend a ball game. Experiments were conducted with morning games to try to attract war workers on the swing shift, who normally couldn't attend a game during the workweek because they worked from 3:00 in the afternoon to 11:00 in the evening. The morning game debuted in the majors on May 3, when Cincinnati hosted Pittsburgh in a game that started before lunch at 11:30. A natural extension was the morning-afternoon doubleheader, dubbed the "swing-shift doubleheader," where the first game began at 10:30 in the morning and the second game around 12:30 in the early afternoon. The Philadelphia Phillies initiated the swing-shift doubleheader on June 15 and combined it with a Ladies Day promotion to optimize attendance. These war-worker accommodations only marginally increased attendance, though, never approaching the ability of night baseball to fill a ballpark.[29]

During the spring of 1943, Clark Griffith once again lobbied his fellow club owners for more night games than his existing 21-game allotment, already an exception to the 14-game limitation that applied to all other ball clubs. Griffith pointed out that he had averaged 14,000 spectators for nine night games so far that year, easily 10,000 more than would pay to attend a game played in daylight, thus providing hefty checks to visiting clubs for their road-game share of the proceeds. His broader argument was that "night games are more suitable for war-jammed Washington," which was largely comprised of government workers absorbed in war-related activities. Griffith, once the arch-enemy of night baseball, now apparently saw the light, pun intended. "It has to come sooner or later and we might as well recognize it," Griffith told the *Washington Evening Star* about his stance on night baseball. "That's when fans want to see ball and it's our job to please the public."[30]

Griffith was speaking like a proprietor of entertainment, not as the traditional baseball mogul with the old-fashioned attitude that a ball club was in the unique business of the national pastime, so people should inherently find the time to go to the ballpark, day or night. While Griffith had his fellow American League owners at "hefty checks," he could still count on non-support from his National League compatriots, so he needed to convince Commissioner Landis, holder of the tie-breaking vote in the joint-league meeting, to reverse his position from 1942.

Griffith succeeded at the joint-league meeting of club owners at the 1943 All-Star Game, which was conducted as a night game at Shibe Park in Philadelphia, an event that itself signaled a softening of night-game policy. At the meeting, Griffith's proposal passed, making the Washington ball club "the first real 'owls' of major league baseball" with the ability to stage unlimited night games for the rest of the 1943 season, on dates other than Sunday or a holiday. "I think we'll prove major league teams in the future must play more night games," Griffith told reporters. "The fans want them."[31]

Landis, by casting the deciding vote, uncharacteristically supported Griffith's proposal for unlimited night games, in light of the commissioner's long-standing scorn for night baseball. In reversing his opinion, Landis told reporters, "Wartime conditions of employment in Washington make it worth while to have more night games." Much like he had swallowed the expanded night-game proviso contained in President Roosevelt's green-light letter in 1942, Landis accepted the reality of Washington, where Griffith functioned as baseball's unofficial emissary and lobbyist to the federal government. One clue to Landis's thinking was a second item approved at the joint-league meeting, the formation by major-league baseball of the War Relief and Service Fund, Inc., with funds raised to go to the American Red Cross.[32]

Landis was not simply deciding between the differing night-baseball positions of the two leagues as much as he was appeasing multiple constituencies with this decision. One faction that Landis wanted to keep content was the federal government, especially the upper-echelon bureaucrats at the government agencies that controlled manpower and transportation issues, which baseball desperately needed support from in order to continue operating during wartime. An unhappy Griffith, who had marshaled the green-light letter, would not serve that end, nor would a disenchanted Roosevelt, the authorizer of baseball's continuation via the green-light letter. The "wartime conditions of employment" that Landis referred to were not just the large throng of government workers seeking a recreational break from their stressful war jobs, which Griffith sought as customers at the night games. Landis was also appeasing the levers of government that baseball depended upon. So the expanded exception for night baseball in Washington was good for Griffith as well as beneficial for baseball.

For the rest of the 1943 season, the Washington Senators only played Sunday doubleheaders and night games at Griffith Stadium. One outgrowth of unlimited night baseball was that Washington became the first big-league club to play a steady diet of night games on Saturday as well as during the month of September. With no concern about the usual restriction on completing a daylight game under artificial lights, Griffith could now stage twi-night doubleheaders with games that were played back-to-back rather than disconnected by a long intermission. Twi-night doubleheaders in Washington now began at 7:00, with the second game starting shortly after the conclusion of the first game.

Whether he was merely maximizing a wartime exigency or had envisioned a postwar change in the audience for baseball, Griffith was perilously close to jettisoning the civic component of the civic/profit business basis and fully concentrating on the money-making aspect of it. He seemed to eviscerate the remaining boosterism element in the civic component, which now was largely the perceived special nature of the national pastime. Worse, Griffith was virtually operating his ball club on the minor-league model, further cheapening, in the eyes of his fellow club owners, the game of baseball.

Not that Griffith should be chastened for this action. He did have an accurate picture of the postwar future where this business balance would be necessary to effectively compete, as an entertainment business rather than a baseball business. However, Griffith was essentially a renegade, forsaking the desired audience that the other club owners believed necessary to support the elevated cachet of the business.

Major-league ball clubs had quickly gravitated away from the day-of-game scheduling mix toward the time-of-day mix that the minor leagues had been absorbed in for a decade trying to compete as an entertainment business. Fundamentally, this is where the major leagues needed to shift toward, but most club owners still loathed the idea of concentrating on night baseball, even after two years of enforced adaptation by Roosevelt's green-light letter. Many owners still recollected Larry MacPhail's words of wisdom back in 1939, when he warned them about the perils of normalizing night baseball. However, MacPhail's reason for sounding the alarm then was linked to the exclusivity of baseball, not to the fundamental shifts that were beginning to occur in the nature of occupational employment and residential location. In the postwar environment, these substantive trends in work and housing would greatly impact professional baseball.

Griffith was not the only ball club owner who wanted to embrace the impending new world of professional baseball. Sam Breadon of the St. Louis Cardinals was also on that train. "You can't overlook the experience of the Washington club," he told reporters in November 1943 as he lobbied for more night baseball. "The Senators have a small park, but by playing night games they attracted 600,000 persons. That's more than the Cardinals drew with a pennant winner. If the people want night baseball, let's give it to them," although he then added a disclaimer, "in this emergency." Breadon was not quite ready to break ranks with his fellow club owners, although he did tell the sportswriters that the Cardinals in their night games in 1943 outdrew their weekday games, including doubleheaders, by five to one.[33]

Breadon and Griffith were the first major-league club owners to pursue policies that implicitly contemplated the ballpark audience as having the tri-level composition of frequent, periodic, and occasional fans. Wartime baseball at night appealed not just to war workers, but also made new fans of women and school-age children, which helped to democratize the audience at the ballpark, especially at night games. Family units were the up-and-coming audience at the ballpark, not male businessmen who had dominated the audience for prewar baseball. As Breadon further noted in his comments in the preceding paragraph, if promoted properly, night baseball could effectively wean people off the winning-team attitude as their primary reason for more often going to the ballpark. This is exactly what Griffith demonstrated with his last-place Washington Senators team during the 1944 season.

In his 1952 autobiographical essay, Griffith expressed his appreciation for "Mr. Edison's invention of the electric light" and the changes it had brought to baseball. "Why not give the greatest number of people what they want, since recreations offered after 8 o'clock in the evening appeal to more persons than they do during our workday hours," Griffith told J.G. Taylor Spink, the publisher of *The Sporting News*. "Tradition and all that goes with it are wonderful assets for baseball. But many years have passed since I saw a horse and buggy driven into the Washington ball park."[34]

Women and children line up during the war years to buy tickets for a day game at Briggs Stadium in Detroit. The Detroit Tigers played only daylight games during the war, as the club did not install a lighting system until 1948, the last ball club in the American League to do so (Library of Congress, Prints & Photographs Division, LC-USW3-007097-D).

Neither of these enlightened attitudes about night baseball had yet to broadly emerge among ball club owners when Breadon and Griffith were publicly making the case for greater exceptions to the 14-game standard for night baseball to propose at their respective league meetings in December 1943.

In the American League, club owners voted for two exceptions to the 14-game restriction, with the Washington Senators to have unlimited nights games after May 5 and the St. Louis Browns the same number as the crosstown Cardinals were granted by the National League. However, in the National League meeting, the owners declined to support Breadon's request for an exception to the 14-game limitation, while concurring with the unlimited exception for Washington in the American League. Without a common policy passed by both leagues, Commissioner Landis would once again cast the deciding vote at the joint-league meeting.[35]

The National League club owners tried to hold the line on a massive expansion of night-baseball policy, as only the Boston and Philadelphia clubs supported Breadon's proposal. The five dissenting clubs apparently assumed Landis would uphold the National League rule that required unanimous consent to increase the league's night-game limit (a MacPhail condition imposed back in 1934), as a governance issue if not simply given Landis's aversion to night baseball in principle. However, Landis stunned the National League owners by siding with the American League and unilaterally stipulating a limit of 21 night games for both St. Louis clubs. Landis, as usual, gave little public insight into his decision, other than to say he considered his power as commissioner to override a league rule.[36]

This vote on night baseball indicates just how much Landis was willing to compromise in order for major-league baseball to remain in the good graces of the federal government. Landis appeared to pursue a wartime policy vis-à-vis the Roosevelt Administration that called for minimal direct interaction to influence policy-making and instead sufficient overt actions to achieve favorable rulings from government agencies.

While the exceptions to night baseball policy pursued for the 1942 and 1943 seasons favored the Washington ball club, an overt action to accommodate government workers, the additional night games approved for Griffith Stadium were not specifically responsive to the war-worker concern expressed in the Roosevelt green-light letter. The audience for Washington night games was largely office workers, since there were few war plants in the area, so Landis took action to more directly align the night-game policy exceptions to war workers. Why was St. Louis important to this endeavor? St. Louis had a significant number of defense plants, in particular a plant of the Curtiss–Wright Corporation that was the primary supplier of aircraft to the United States military, as well as the appetite to conduct a substantial number of night games. This combination did not exist in any of the other nine major-league cities.

Providing an extra seven games to the St. Louis Browns might be perceived as a deferred reward to the ball club for Bob Hannegan's role in the Roosevelt green-light letter. The former political boss of St. Louis was now in Washington as the IRS commissioner and was soon to be the head of the Democratic National Committee in President Roosevelt's re-election campaign in the 1944 election. That's probably not the case, although the political acumen of Hannegan might have been relayed through Griffith to Landis to help ensure baseball's smooth continuance during the third year of the war, when rosters for the 1944 season were expected to be more replete with 4–F ballplayers (ruled unfit for military duty) due to limited draft deferments for, and additional enlistments by, more physically able men.

On the 1944 schedule, all ball clubs scheduled their maximum limit of night games, with Washington initially establishing its "unlimited" capacity as 43 night games. Detroit also pre-planned seven twilight games. Dim-out restrictions were lifted for the 1944 season, which resulted in an uptick in night games played in the major leagues, with the Giants and Dodgers now able to resume nocturnal scheduling in New York City. Night games also returned to the neighboring New Jersey minor-league cities of Newark and Jersey City in the International League as well as to the Pacific Coast League on the other side of the country.[37]

The War Production Board, one of those government entities that Landis wished to appease by expanding night baseball, signaled in May 1944 that it was receptive to inquiries from the five major-league ball clubs without lighting systems to seek approval for such installations to increase the opportunity for more war workers to see ball games. However, when the Chicago Cubs did apply, the WPB rejected the club's application, which postwar soured the Cubs on pursuing night baseball.[38]

During the first half of the 1944 season, 1.1 million people attended night games, producing an average 13,900 crowd for a night game, compared to just 4,900 for a daylight game during the workweek. Sunday games and night games accounted for two-thirds of total attendance. At the league meetings in Pittsburgh in July at the 1944 All-Star Game, the second consecutive one to be played as a night game, both leagues supported unlimited night baseball for all ball clubs for the remainder of the 1944 season.[39]

However, the discussion about night-baseball policy "was not as sweet and serene as later was advertised," Dan Daniel wrote in his recap of the meetings in *The Sporting News*. "There was a red-hot fight" in the National League meeting, where Breadon of the Cardinals announced that even with a first-place team "he had outdrawn 31 day games with ten night attractions," but still couldn't turn a decent profit even with the 21 night games he was accorded for the season. Counting abstainers as against unlimited night ball, the National League would have voted no to that proposition. The Browns were in no better financial shape as the first-place team in the American League. Despite three die-hard opponents of night baseball (Boston, Detroit, and New York), the league acquiesced to the night-hosting clubs playing as many evening games as they wanted. Accompanying Daniel's article was a *New York World–Telegram* cartoon that very aptly anticipated baseball's future, showing a ballplayer sporting the uniform of "daytime baseball" bound in an electric chair for execution, with a business-suited man ready to flick the switch denoted "unlimited night games" while another man tells the player "sit back and relax, we're just turning up the lights a little."[40]

Club owners were more focused on financially surviving the 1944 season, while Commissioner Landis was concerned about the sport's ultimate survival through the 1945 season and into the postwar era, whether that was 1946 or a later year. Although Landis did not have to cast a deciding vote in the joint-league meeting in July 1944, he no doubt would have sided with the American League's thumbs-up on unlimited night games to enable baseball's policy to be maximum war-worker consideration for night games, consistent with the green-light letter that was the ultimate source of the sport's survival through the war years.

Night baseball became standard at Sportsman's Park in St. Louis, as both the Browns and Cardinals, both in first place in their respective league standings, took maximum advantage of the revised night-game policy for the 1944 season. However, a vote of the club owners at that July joint-league meeting decreed that if both of the St. Louis clubs qualified for the World Series, then all of the games at Sportsman's Park would be played in daylight.[41]

The 1944 World Series contested between the St. Louis Browns and St. Louis Cardinals was the sixth consecutive fall classic to feature a National League champion that was a night-hosting club as well as the first one to involve an American League champion that conducted night games in its home ballpark. For the St. Louis Browns, the 1944 pennant was its first, and only, championship flag, a reward for its ever-vigilant quest to conduct as much night baseball as possible in one of the smallest two-club cities in the major leagues. After both St. Louis clubs played hefty night-game schedules at Sportsman's Park during the 1944 regular season, it must have seemed very odd to play six consecutive daylight games there in the World Series.

Twi-night doubleheaders increased in volume in 1944 after the lifting of restrictions on the number of night games. Just like the Sunday doubleheader, spectators loved the twi-night doubleheader's combination of two games for the price of one played at a time best convenient to them. For that reason, many club owners despised the giveaway as a cheapening of the night game. However, by 1944, more National League clubs now participated in twi-night twin bills, not just clubs in the American League. For single night games, some clubs now used a Ladies Night promotion to increase attendance.

Many feared that night baseball would lose it special nature and become so common that, like the now obligatory Sunday doubleheader, it would "strangle the goose which has been laying the golden eggs." Arthur Daley of the *New York Times* alleged in June 1944 that if night baseball became the rule rather than the exception, "baseball will find itself competing with the movies, the radio and manifold other amusements." Daley missed the memo, however, because baseball was already competing with those types of entertainment activities. There was no going back to the 1910 era of weekday daylight games played before an audience of businessmen.[42]

The strategic issue for major-league baseball clubs was to determine the best way to adapt to this competitive environment once the war was over. "Certainly the 1944 American League figures bore out the contention that night play was needed to accommodate war workers," an Associated Press writer blatantly analyzed the issue confronting baseball executives. "When peace comes that argument will disappear, but the wartime precedent may make it difficult for owners to return to strictly a sunshine diet." The afternoon ball game played in daylight during the workweek seemed to be an already-dead dinosaur, not a hibernating bear waiting to be awoken.[43]

Night-game policy for 1945 was "home rule," under the tacit understanding that club owners would not abuse the privilege, especially the St. Louis Browns and Washington Senators which both had played a hefty night-game calendar during the 1944 season. Due to the death of Commissioner Landis in November 1944, the club owners had much bigger issues to discuss than an extended debate about possible restrictions on night baseball.[44]

The instincts of Landis to have taken several steps to good-faith comply with the night-baseball clause in the Roosevelt green-light letter as the war unfolded in 1943 and 1944, not just early on in February 1942, paid off posthumously in January 1945 when major-league baseball faced existential threats to its continuation for the 1945 season. As the nation adopted stringent energy conservation measures, the War Production Board determined that cutbacks to non-essential lighting would not impact night baseball. Baseball also staved off the impact of work-or-fight legislation that Congress was considering during the winter of 1945, which if enacted into law would have produced a dire manpower shortage and exacerbated baseball's status as a "useful, but not essential" industry that was a desirable morale booster and recreational outlet for war workers.[45]

Hannegan re-emerged on the baseball scene in January 1945, this time in a more public mode as a follow-up to his earlier behind-the-scenes role. Hannegan, now a well-known Democratic insider well-connected to the White House following the re-election of Roosevelt, met with reporters to reinforce Roosevelt's wishes for baseball's position in the war effort, since "baseball provides a vital uplift to the morale of both servicemen and civilians and should be continued in 1945." After meeting with Hannegan and Griffith, Roosevelt personally met with reporters a few days later to pitch wartime baseball. "People must have some recreation and baseball is a great American game," Roosevelt said, but only gave a conditional green-light by acknowledging that "perfectly healthy young men should not be playing baseball at this time." Roosevelt clearly was not going to interfere with the working of government officials, particularly those involved with manpower decisions, to accomplish his recreational motives for baseball.[46]

Two months later, with baseball still in limbo, Roosevelt met with Griffith in the annual ceremony of presenting a season-pass to the president. He then went to bat one more time for baseball at a subsequent news conference, where he reiterated that he was "all in favor of baseball so long as it did not require perfectly healthy people who could be doing more useful war work." In response to a reporter's questioning if that proposition was possible in 1945, Roosevelt sharply replied, "Why not?" and then added that "while baseball under wartime conditions might not be quite so good," he would be willing to go out and watch such competition. Roosevelt also confirmed Griffith's statement the previous day that the president approved of the continuation of night baseball, crowing that "I was one of the fathers of it," referring to his green-light letter of January 1942. A week later the War Manpower Commission officially announced that baseball was the principal business of ballplayers, not their off-season job in a war plant, to give the green-light to baseball for the 1945 season. Roosevelt, however, never got a chance to throw out the first pitch at opening day, as he died in early April.[47]

Roosevelt left a substantial legacy to the history of night baseball. With his sign-off on the sentence in the green-light letter encouraging professional baseball to conduct more night games for war workers, Roosevelt undeniably established the foundation for the postwar expansion of night baseball, despite the protestations of many ball-club owners. Roosevelt's focus on the war-worker audience for night games created the path to acceptance of a more diversified audience for major-league ball games beyond the tolerated one on Sunday afternoons. Roosevelt's re-definition of the American Dream, which played out in many societal changes in postwar America, made it nearly impossible for professional baseball to ignore those changes when it came to night baseball.

On April 24, less than two weeks after Roosevelt's funeral, the major-league ball club owners picked Albert "Happy" Chandler to be the new commissioner of baseball. Larry MacPhail had nominated the U.S. senator from Kentucky, and acolyte of President Roosevelt, to replace the deceased Landis. MacPhail was at the special owners meeting to pick the new commissioner because he was now president of the New York Yankees, one of the trio of men who had recently purchased the ball club from the Ruppert estate. With Harry Truman now in the White House, Bob Hannegan, who had secretly assisted Griffith with the Roosevelt green-light letter back in 1942, finished in second place in the balloting, given his close connection to the new president. In fact, nearly all of the men initially considered to become baseball commissioner were Democrats, given that party's control of the federal government for the next two years and likely all four years before the 1948 presidential election. If there was one thing the ball-club owners learned from their wartime experience, it was good to have friends in the federal government.[48]

One of Chandler's first stops after being named commissioner was the White House, where he talked with Truman. After Chandler emerged from his meeting with the president, he announced, "The President thinks baseball has justified its right to continue and that it has made a maximum contribution to the war effort." The ball-club owners thought Chandler would be a go-along-to-get-along kind of commissioner, from whom they could retract the power that Landis had seized from their hands (and from Griffith as de facto ambassador to the government). Curiously, the owners failed to interview Chandler before offering him the job, apparently presuming that the talkative politician would be content to be promoter-in-chief of the sport.[49]

During the 1945 season, wartime restrictions on civilian train travel and perpetual rainy weather combined to create enormous challenges in scheduling major-league baseball games, which led to a vast number of twi-night doubleheaders played in 1945. A bit of skullduggery in St. Louis painted the twi-night doubleheader in a sinister light, which caused Brooklyn Dodgers president Branch Rickey and several other club owners to cast the twi-night doubleheader as an evil element in baseball scheduling during the postwar period.

In mid–September the Dodgers played back-to-back road series against the St. Louis Cardinals and Chicago Cubs, the two teams left contending for the National League pennant. On September 12 the planned twi-night doubleheader in St. Louis was shortened to just the opener as the nightcap was doused out by rain. When the twi-night doubleheader slated for September 13 was also rained out, a brouhaha erupted regarding the timing of the make-up doubleheader to be played on September 14. In today's parlance, September 14 was a getaway day, since the Dodgers had to travel to Chicago after the doubleheader to play a daylight game on September 15 against the league-leading Cubs in no-lighting-system Wrigley Field. The Dodgers obviously preferred to play a conventional daylight doubleheader in St. Louis on September 14 that started early in the afternoon, so that the ballplayers could reach Chicago in time to get some sleep before the next day's game.

St. Louis owner Sam Breadon, though, insisted the two teams play a twi-night doubleheader on September 14, ostensibly to maximize attendance (and gate receipts) but also seemingly to give the Cardinals an advantage to overtake the first-place Cubs. "Since no sleeper accommodations are available, the Dodgers are going to face the team the Cards are trying to beat for the pennant after sitting up in a coach all night," one wire-service writer aptly characterized the forthcoming sleepless-in-Chicago situation. At the September 14 twi-nighter, only 2,378 spectators showed up and the Dodgers won both games, partially squelching the apparent deviousness by Cardinals management. However, the tortuous evening continued for the Dodgers as the team traveled through the early morning hours to Chicago. The train crashed into a gasoline tanker truck and caused an explosion on the railroad tracks, delaying the team's arrival in Chicago by several hours. No Dodgers were injured, but the accident further contributed to lack of rest for the ballplayers. Brooklyn lost not only the afternoon game on September 15 but also both games of the Sunday doubleheader the next day.[50]

The Chicago Cubs went on to win the National League pennant in 1945, the last National League ball club with an all-daylight home schedule to accomplish that feat.

As a result of the scheduling shenanigans in St. Louis on September 14, 1945, the twi-night doubleheader, considered by many then to be an "in-the-gloaming monstrosity," had a significant impact upon the deliberations about night-game policy for getaway days during the postwar years when Happy Chandler served as the commissioner of baseball.

During the 1945 season, night baseball continued its expansive scope, as 18 percent of all major-league games were played as night games. Following the end of the war that summer, few people thought that Chandler, just getting his feet wet as commissioner, would be the accelerant for an even greater escalation of night baseball during the 1946 season.

✦ 12 ✦

Postwar Expansion

As World War II came to an end during the 1945 baseball season, two of the five major-league ball clubs that had weathered the four wartime seasons without ballpark lighting decided to install lighting systems for the 1946 season. This decision by the New York Yankees and Boston Braves brought the total of night-game hosts to 13 of the 16 ball clubs.

The New York Yankees, under the new ownership of Larry MacPhail and his two partners Dan Topping and Del Webb, jettisoned the club's long-time daylight-only policy under the tenure of now-retired general manager Ed Barrow. MacPhail, as he had done in his previous three stops where he introduced night baseball, sought to pursue a seven-game agenda of night games at Yankee Stadium to maintain the special novelty of baseball under artificial lighting, which had been the prewar tradition. On the other hand, the Boston Braves, under the new leadership of Lou Perini, sought to gain an advantage over the Red Sox in two-club Boston by playing as many night games as possible at Braves Field, in essence continuing the wartime policy of unlimited night baseball.[1]

Of the three remaining ball clubs without a lighting system at their home ballpark, the Chicago Cubs were the most insistent about retaining an all-daylight home schedule. "Wrigley Field will be the last outpost of 100 percent daytime baseball," Cubs owner Phil Wrigley said during the fall of 1945, since he believed that "baseball is a daytime sport to be played in the sunshine." The Boston Red Sox, still on the fence about night baseball for 1946, announced in May that lights would be installed at Fenway Park for the 1947 season. The Detroit Tigers continued to believe there was a future in twilight games as an alternative to night baseball.[2]

MacPhail went all out for the most modern lighting system he could have installed at Yankee Stadium, spending $250,000 for lights under the engineering guidance of the General Electric Company and its lead illumination engineer Robert Swackhamer, who before the war had worked on the lights for MacPhail at the Cincinnati and Brooklyn ballparks. The project was so expensive because MacPhail decreed that there be a uniform 200 foot-candles of illumination over the entire playing field, much higher than the best-lighted ballpark at the time, and mandated the use of only the six light banks placed atop the upper deck to produce this brilliance with no light towers bordering the outfield fence. This lighting standard required the use of 1,409 reflectors (each with a 1,500-watt lamp), when no ballpark at the time utilized more than 900. As part of "the last word in scientific lighting and intensity," Swackhamer also deployed the newly developed L–69 floodlight that had an impact-resistant glass cover, another lighting innovation from General Electric.[3]

Perini took a more thrifty approach to illuminating Braves Field, spending $150,000 and hiring the Crouse–Hinds Company to engineer the lighting using the conventional eight-tower approach to encircle the entire playing field with lamps. "We will play at least 14 games at night and as many as the public wants," Perini told sportswriters in the fall of 1945, "but probably not as many as Griffith played in Washington last season." Perini was the first of the coming wave of new ball-club owners who sported a different attitude about night baseball that markedly clashed with the philosophy of MacPhail.[4]

On the eve of the first postwar winter meetings in December 1945, the club owners that planned to play night baseball were splintered into three camps regarding the night-game policy to be applied for the 1946 season. Several owners still viewed night baseball with skepticism and the recent expansion of night games as a mere wartime exigency. All three clubs in New York City (the Giants, Dodgers, and Yankees) wanted to revert to the seven-game limitation imposed during the prewar years; Washington and the two St. Louis clubs (and, quietly, the Boston Braves) wanted to retain the unlimited policy permitted during the later war years; the remaining clubs were amenable to the 14-game restriction that had initially applied in the early war years. The divergence of opinion on night baseball led to the emergence of two different league policies on the matter.

In the American League, there were heated discussions about what the night-game policy should be in the postwar era. Clark Griffith, owner of the Washington Senators, led the progressive wing by proposing the continuation of unlimited night baseball, with the consent of the visiting club. It was the opportunity to establish night games as a permanent replacement for poorly-attended weekday afternoon games and respond to a changing American society. At a minimum, the wartime conditions that had led to the exceptions granted to Washington and the St. Louis Browns to stage a greater number of night games still existed.[5]

MacPhail led the hard-liners who sought a return to the original prewar seven-game restriction. It was the last stand for the concept of night baseball as a novelty to be rationed in order to subsidize weekday afternoon baseball. MacPhail reportedly "fought Griffith's plan bitterly from the time it was presented" and "stubbornly refused to consider more than seven night games a season on any club's home schedule." However, MacPhail could marshal no further support for the seven-game restriction beyond one owner, either Yawkey in Boston or Briggs in Detroit. A majority of the American League owners voted for the compromise of a 14-game limit, with a 33-game exception for the Washington Senators and St. Louis Browns, all subject to consent by the visiting club.[6]

In the National League, there was a greater consensus among the club owners, after St. Louis Cardinals owner Sam Breadon made his pitch for unlimited night baseball. Breadon presented a statistics-based argument that 58 percent of his club's total attendance in 1945 came from night games and 39 percent came from Sunday doubleheaders. Almost nobody came to the few daylight games conducted in St. Louis. "Our customers have shown unmistakingly they prefer night ball," Breadon concluded. The National League owners showed more support for Breadon's position than they had during the war years, in fact reversing their majority position articulated in December 1943 to now support unlimited night baseball, with visiting-club consent. It is unclear how this reversal came about; possibly an abstention by the Pittsburgh club due to its impending change in ownership tipped the balance of voters, with the New York Giants reportedly the sole dissenter.[7]

Once again, the conflicting positions of the two leagues forced the issue into the joint-league meeting, where Happy Chandler would face his first tie-breaking vote as the new commissioner. In the joint-league meeting on December 12, Commissioner Chandler broke the tie by siding with the National League for unlimited night games, thus eliminating all specific numerical limitations or exceptions. The one proviso to Chandler's decision was that, in all cases, the consent of the visiting club must be obtained to conduct a night game, a restriction "expected to take care of any objectional features, particularly night games on a getaway day." The usual stipulations to prohibit Sunday and holiday night games and to enforce an 11:50 curfew (adjusted for daylight savings time) still applied.[8]

While MacPhail quietly accepted the new restrictions on night baseball, he certainly did not like them. He not only revered the old seven-game restriction, he was cemented into the primacy of daylight baseball in the majors. "I think any increase in the number of night games is a mistake. I believe if the number is hopped up from seven to 14, the leagues will have struck a severe blow at afternoon baseball for all time," MacPhail had told the *Brooklyn Eagle* back in January 1942. "The moment they schedule 14 night games, they'll never get the number back to seven. The next step will be to schedule 21. And mid-week afternoon baseball will be a dead pigeon." MacPhail could not have been more prophetic about the future of night baseball.[9]

Both leagues were in agreement that they did "not approve of" twi-night doubleheaders, a wartime bugbear that many owners wanted to prohibit in the postwar environment. However, they disagreed on the implementation of this policy. The National League interpreted disapproval to mean a complete ban on twi-night doubleheaders, which required postponed games to be made up in a daylight game. The American League left the door open a bit by allowing twi-night doubleheaders to be utilized "when necessary" to make up a postponed game, such as in the last series of the season played by the visiting club in the home club's city.[10]

Larry MacPhail, as president of the New York Yankees, installed lights in Yankee Stadium for the 1946 season. By scheduling just 14 night games, MacPhail continued his philosophy of rationing night baseball in order to preserve baseball as a daylight event on weekdays (National Baseball Hall of Fame Library, Cooperstown, New York).

Chandler's decision set the stage for a dramatic increase in night baseball. As a Democrat and fervent follower of the Roosevelt administration's New Deal societal agenda, Chandler supported baseball policies that benefited the average person. "As commissioner, A.B. Chandler was neither a visionary nor a crusading reformer," William Marshall described Chandler in his book *Baseball's Pivotal Era, 1945–1951*. "He was at heart a baseball fan, a man who wanted to take the commissioner's position off its pedestal, to humanize it, and to share himself and the game with its followers." Since he concurred with President Roosevelt's broad social agenda that was behind the desire for more night games inserted into the 1942 green-light letter, Chandler simply applied that philosophy to his decision in December 1945 concerning night baseball.[11]

However, Chandler's ruling on night baseball did not end the debate about night-game policy. While hard limits on the number of night games were ostensibly eliminated, the visiting-club consent clause became the battleground in formulating policy for night baseball over the next several years. This clause, present from the inception of night baseball in the majors in 1935, was not much of an issue during the prewar years when the number of night games was severely limited, and had been virtually discarded in the blur of the wartime efforts to ensure baseball's survival. Visiting-club consent emerged as a substantive issue for "unlimited" night baseball in the 1946 season, because the clause put control of the night-game schedule in the hands of the visiting clubs, not the home clubs that had invested in ballpark lighting systems. Night baseball was not really "unlimited" if visiting clubs could effectively impose caps through their withheld consent.

There was a degree of inherent cooperation between ball clubs in the scheduling of night games, in the spirit of structured mutualism that bound together clubs within a league. All clubs usually agreed to play two road night games with each night-hosting club. The conflict emerged when some clubs insisted upon a lower level of road night games that contradicted the desire of home clubs to conduct a large volume of night games. Typically, this was just a problem for clubs that wished to schedule more than 14 home night games during the season. Rather than play an even number of night games with each visiting club, prolific night-game schedulers had to convince some clubs to book an overload to compensate for the clubs that refused to consent to a full slate of night games. In 1946, the New York Giants in the National League and the New York Yankees in the American League were the most persnickety clubs about limiting their booking of road night games.

In the schedules for the 1946 season, only four of the 13 clubs hosting night games had grander ambitions for night baseball than the nine clubs that adhered to an informal 14-game standard. In the National League, the St. Louis Cardinals scheduled 38 night games and the Boston Braves slated 20 night games. However, the Giants refused to schedule more than two night games in either city. To compensate for this shortfall, Cardinals booked nine night games with the Philadelphia Phillies and the Braves slated one less night game. In the American League, the St. Louis Browns carded 42 night games while Washington listed 32 night games. However, the Yankees capped their road night games at four in St. Louis and three in Washington. To compensate, the Browns scheduled overloads of nine games each with Washington and Boston, while Washington carded overloads of seven games each with the Browns and Detroit Tigers, to cover the fewer bookings with some clubs.[12]

As clubs increased the number of night games they wished to stage during the late 1940s, the visiting-club consent issue became thornier with each successive season.

The 42 night games planned by the St. Louis Browns began to approach the natural limit of night baseball within the 77 home games played by clubs in the 154-game season. Under the conventions of that era, a maximum of 48 night games would be conceivable, because the other 29 games had a special place in daylight baseball: 12 Sunday double-headers (24 games), two holiday twin bills (four games), and a single game on opening day. Since Sunday was the only specific day of the seven-day week when daylight games were mandated, the outer limit of night baseball, in theory, was 65 night games, presuming a club scheduled all single games on its 12 Sunday dates and staged its holiday and opening-day games as night events. Jettisoning some of these premium daylight games was one aspect of night baseball growth in the coming years.

The first night game at Braves Field was staged on Saturday, May 11, and attracted a crowd of 35,000 spectators, the club's largest one-day attendance since the 1933 season. There were fireworks before the game, the introduction of neon foul poles, and the use of special sateen uniforms by the Braves for better spectator visibility at night. Perini targeted occasional ballpark attendees, who were listeners of radio broadcasts and readers of the sports page, but infrequent visitors to either Braves Field or Fenway Park in two-club Boston, mostly for Saturday or Sunday daylight games. Indicative of a more modern approach to marketing night baseball, the front office of the Braves club organized a bus package to transport fans to Braves Field from cities in the outer suburbs of Boston to make it easier for fans to get to night games who likely otherwise would not attend. A three-dollar ticket on the Braves Field Express provided round-trip transportation and a reserved grandstand seat. Thirty buses brought 1,000 fans to that first night game.[13]

The first night game at Yankee Stadium on May 28 drew just 49,000 people rather than the anticipated 65,000 spectators, due to cool and soggy weather. Highlighting the importance of the lighting engineers to the success of night ball, the president of the General Electric Company threw out the first ball to illustrate "the true synthesis of sunshine, the utmost in the approximation of daylight" at Yankee Stadium that evening. "May 28 is too early for night ball in the North," MacPhail explained the low turnout, quietly knocking his fellow club owners for abandoning his original principle for staging night baseball. "However, just so long as the club owners insist on a minimum of 14 night contests, we will have to risk cold weather. When we get down to seven under the lights, we will be able to hold off until June."[14]

Demonstrating the proliferation of night baseball, all eight ball games played on August 9 were conducted as night games, the first time this had occurred in the major leagues since the inception of night baseball back in 1935. Another boost to night ball was the rescheduling of postponed games into games that came as a package with a night game. In the American League, the St. Louis Browns hosted the first postwar twi-night doubleheader on August 13, while in the National League, which prohibited twi-night twin bills, the Brooklyn Dodgers inaugurated the playing of a day-night doubleheader on August 14, which required separate admissions to the afternoon and evening contests. Both techniques greatly improved the attendance for make-up doubleheaders, compared to the crowd for the usual daylight twin bill that had been used for decades to make up a postponement. American League clubs soon began to select among the three options of twi-night, day-night, and day-day to create a twin bill to best handle a postponed game.[15]

With 13 of 16 ball clubs conducting night baseball in the 1946 season, 81 percent of major-league baseball clubs had lighting systems to stage night games. During the 1946

The Boston Braves wore special sateen uniforms for night games at Braves Field, illustrated in this photograph by Tommy Holmes (left), Bama Rowell (center), and Johnny Hopp (right). The sateen uniforms were designed for fans to see the ballplayers better under artificial lighting, since the fabric, cotton using a satin weave structure, improved their visibility (courtesy Boston Public Library, Leslie Jones Collection).

season, minor-league baseball reached 100 percent saturation of night-baseball capability within its higher-classification leagues, when the Beaumont, Texas, club in the Texas League installed a lighting system at its ballpark in May, ending the ball club's stigma as "one of the last strongholds of continuous daylight play in the high minors."[16]

The Boston Red Sox captured the American League championship in 1946, the last time a ball club with an all-daylight home schedule qualified for the World Series. Beyond fielding a winning team, Boston club owner Tom Yawkey had a number of factors in his favor that enabled him to pursue a calendar of all-daylight baseball in Boston and still attract a reasonable volume of spectators. Fenway Park was still a relatively new ballpark, only a dozen years removed from its renovation overhaul for the 1934 season. The ballpark also had intimacy, as spectators sat close to the action on the field. The Red Sox had a star ballplayer, Ted Williams, and the team was built in the American League style, with a number of home-run hitters in addition to Williams. Both aspects attracted people to the ballpark. Then there was the rivalry with the New York Yankees. Yawkey appealed to baseball purists as his customer base. The publicity men in the Red Sox organization were the ballplayers in uniform on the field, not former sportswriters wearing a business suit in the front office. All of these components still produced good-sized crowds at weekday afternoon games in Fenway Park, especially during the warm-weather months of July and August, while filling the stands for Saturday, Sunday, and holiday games.[17]

During the 1946 season, the American League drew 9.6 million spectators while the National League attracted 8.9 million people, shattering the previous high-water marks for attendance, as postwar crowds packed the major-league ballparks. Ten of the 16 ball clubs drew more than one million spectators as "night and twilight games were a big factor in the record breaking." Publicists in the league offices left the numerical impact of night baseball unspecified, perhaps to continue to protect daylight baseball by not overly promoting the popularity of night games. A few ball clubs divulged their total gate from night baseball. The New York Yankees led the majors with 2.3 million customers in 1946, with about 675,000 attending the club's night games. The Boston Braves, with the northernmost ballpark in majors, attracted 600,000 people to their night games, which represented two-thirds of the club's overall attendance that season.[18]

This popularity of night games among ballpark spectators in 1946, now 21 percent of all games played in the majors, led not only to revenue growth in gate receipts but also spurred revenue growth in rights payments for radio broadcasts of the ball games. Although only a nominal input into the revenue component of the civic/profit business basis during the late 1930s, broadcasting rights rapidly increased in percentage composition of the average ball-club revenue in the late 1940s, rising from 3 percent in 1946 to an estimated 7 percent by 1948 on its way to 10 percent by 1950. The rise in broadcasting revenue necessarily depressed the shares represented by gate receipts (85 percent in 1946) and the "other" category (e.g., concessions and stadium rentals for football), reducing ownership's once-solitary focus on spectatorship.[19]

As more ball clubs enhanced their radio strategy to include the broadcast of both home and road games (6 of 16 clubs in 1946), the value of radio rights increased as more consumers listened to the ball games and consequently drove up demand among advertisers to reach this growing postwar audience. The increasing value of radio broadcasts put pressure on ball-club management to balance the two distinct audiences, the ballpark spectators that generated gate receipts and the non-ballpark radio listeners that drove broadcast rights fees. Night baseball further exacerbated this dichotomy, since night games were the key to increasing the value of both of these revenue components. This put additional pressure on the continuation of weekday daylight ball games, which were generally subsidized by Sunday gate receipts (or now by night games) to further the boosterism element of the civic/profit business balance.

At the league meetings in December 1946, the two leagues had no difference of opinion on the night-game limitations, agreeing on a continuation of unlimited night baseball for the 1947 season. The ball-club owners did codify the existing process by establishing a "normal quota" of night games that a club could book without obtaining the consent of the visiting club, set at 14 games, thus for the first time establishing absolute control by the home club to schedule a certain number of night games. The club owners also agreed to avoid playing a night game on the day preceding a doubleheader, which had become a growing issue during the 1946 season with Saturday night games that were followed by a Sunday doubleheader. Sunday night games continued to be prohibited and the 11:50 evening curfew (adjusted for daylight saving time) still applied to curtail lengthy night games.[20]

The heavy schedulers of night baseball, Washington and the two clubs in St. Louis, were joined in 1947 by the Boston Braves, who slated 29 night games, based on the results of its fan poll during the 1946 season that indicated a significant desire for more night games. In the Braves' survey, 70 percent of fans wanted 28 or more night games (38 percent wanted 28 and 32 percent wanted more than 28) while 22 percent favored 21 night games and just 8 percent were content with just 14 games.[21]

The Cleveland Indians and Pittsburgh Pirates both abandoned the 14-game quota for night games to schedule 21 night games during the 1947 season. Both clubs had new ownership, headed by Bill Veeck in Cleveland and Frank McKinney in Pittsburgh, which spurred them to expand night baseball since they had little allegiance to the former limited approach to night baseball. However, eight of the 14 clubs that hosted night games in 1947 still continued to schedule just 14 evening games, including the Boston Red Sox that inaugurated night baseball that year.[22]

One new trend in night baseball was evident in the 1947 schedule. There were fewer Sunday doubleheaders, as clubs determined that the old twosome of a Saturday afternoon game and a two-for-one Sunday doubleheader was less popular than the new three-part combination of a Saturday night game, Sunday single game, and a weekday night game (conversion of the second free game of the Sunday doubleheader). The St. Louis Cardinals were a leader in this approach, with just one Sunday doubleheader slated for 1947.

Another trend in 1947 was increased flexibility to purchase tickets for reserved seats prior to the date of a night game. At the time, only a limited number of tickets were sold prior to the day of a game, either on a per-game reserved basis or as part of a season ticket, and only applied to box seats or a small portion of the grandstand seating (so-called "reserved grandstand," which varied in volume by the expected demand to see the game). Most seats in the grandstand, pavilion, and bleacher sections of a ballpark were sold on the day of the game. However, due to the increasing popularity of night games in 1946, many potential customers were shut out at the box office for high-demand night games. For the 1947 season, the Brooklyn Dodgers decided to pre-sell a more significant block of grandstand seats at Ebbets Field for night games so that fans could be assured of being able to attend.[23]

In addition, some clubs offered season ticket packages specifically designed for night games. The Philadelphia Phillies sold six different types of season-ticket plans, most containing the club's 14 night games in the package; for instance, Plan A covered opening day, the Independence Day holiday, and the 14 night games. Among the several plans offered by the Boston Braves, one applied solely to the 29 night games at Braves Field. As an added bonus, all Braves season tickets came with the right to buy World Series tickets if the Braves won the National League pennant.[24]

Interestingly, many clubs began to use earlier start times for their weekday daylight games, abandoning the traditional 3:00 or 3:30 commencement. For the 1947 season, the Chicago Cubs, Cleveland Indians, and Pittsburgh Pirates all used a 1:30 start time, while the New York Yankees, Brooklyn Dodgers, Boston Braves, and Boston Red Sox started their daylight games at 2:00. Night games continued to have a typical start time of 8:30, although the Philadelphia Athletics had a 9:00 time for the first pitch of its night games.[25]

The reasoning behind the earlier start time seemed to be the recognition that most attendees of a weekday afternoon game intended to devote half a day to going to the ballpark, such as stay-at-home wives or out-of-town businessmen, rather than consist of a preponderance of local businessmen leaving their office early to catch the game on the way home for dinner, who for decades had been the desired audience for weekday daylight baseball.

With their first night game on June 13, 1947, the Boston Red Sox became the 14th major-league ball club to host night baseball. Red Sox owner Tom Yawkey invested $250,000 to install a state-of-the-art lighting system at Fenway Park (1,120 floodlights atop seven towers) and hired General Electric to engineer 200 foot-candles of illumination across the playing field. While he was a stickler for daylight baseball, Yawkey recognized the cross-town competition at Braves Field and the changing dynamics of the baseball audience. "It became apparent last year, from the many letters we received asking for night ball and also from the success the Braves were having with their new plant, that the demand for lights at Fenway Park was much too great to be ignored," Yawkey told reporters. "Men would write to say that the only free afternoons they had away from work were on Saturdays, Sundays, and holidays, and that they would like to see our games, but felt they should take the family to the country or the beach. The only solution, therefore, was night ball."[26]

After seeing the introduction of night ball at Yankee Stadium and Fenway Park, the Detroit Tigers decided to install lights at Briggs Stadium for the 1948 season.[27]

In the fall of 1947, there was some progress on the thorny issue of the prohibition on completing a daylight game under artificial lighting. During the era of the seven-game limit on night games, this rule made some sense in order to distinguish night games from daylight games. But in the era of double-digit night games, the rule had much less logic.

Boston, Detroit, and New York, the three American League ball clubs strongly opposed to night baseball in the prewar years, all installed top-of-the-line lighting systems during the immediate postwar period. Light stanchions like the one in this photograph provided 200 foot-candles of illumination over the playing field in these three cities (courtesy Boston Public Library, Leslie Jones Collection).

When the second game of the 1947 World Series appeared as though it might end in a tie due to impending darkness, Commissioner Chandler and the two league presidents collaborated to decide that there should be no more tie games in baseball's premier event, and authorized the umpires "to turn on the lights if necessary to complete the contest."[28]

After the Yankees won the 1947 World Series, MacPhail retired as owner, selling his share of the ball club to his two partners, and left the game of baseball. "MacPhail, in his startling brief thirteen-year period as a baseball executive, had dramatically enhanced the vistas for baseball attendance and profitability," historian Jules Tygiel summarized MacPhail's impact on baseball in his book *Past Time: Baseball as History*, adding that he "redefined the ways in which millions of fans experienced the game." While Tygiel also accurately described MacPhail as having "reshaped the baseball marketplace, establishing a new order for a modern age," it was not exactly the order that MacPhail wished it to be. He never relented on the primacy of the daylight game and insisted that night baseball should be promoted as a novelty. MacPhail became a gadfly who periodically commented publicly during the 1950s and 1960s on important issues in major-league baseball.[29]

The night-game policy for the 1948 season remained the same as in 1947, after the club owners at the league meetings in December 1947 quashed a movement to allow truly unlimited night-game scheduling. Bill DeWitt, general manager of the St. Louis Browns, had proposed eliminating the requirement for visiting-club consent for more than two road night games.[30]

The 1948 schedule included Detroit as the eighth American League club, and 15th major-league club, to host night baseball. Like the other five ball clubs with a distinct preference for daylight baseball, the Tigers scheduled just 14 night games for Briggs Stadium. The special pageantry of night baseball, as now observed through the 14-game de facto minimum, was recognized in 1948 by just six ball clubs: Detroit, New York, and Boston in the American League and Brooklyn, New York, and Cincinnati in the National League. More than half of the ball clubs that hosted night baseball now conducted at least 21 night games during the season, with the Chicago White Sox and the two Philadelphia clubs booking more than 14 games for the 1948 season.

The days of weekday daylight baseball now were numbered. "Night baseball is not a novelty. It is a necessity," Sam Breadon said soon after selling his St. Louis Cardinals club to a consortium of investors headed by Bob Hannegan, the former head of the Democratic National Committee who was close to President Roosevelt and had aided the continuation of the sport through the war years. "Now baseball is actually the national pastime of the common people. Whole families come out under the lights. It used to be only those who wanted to be idle, or who were favored financially, could attend workday sunshine contests."[31]

As more ball clubs expanded their schedule of night games, a three-tier pattern emerged among the nine ball clubs that carded more than 14 night games in 1948. At the highest level were the two St. Louis clubs (Cardinals with 45 and Browns with 40) and Washington with 38. In the middle tier were the Boston Braves with 32 and Philadelphia Athletics with 28. The lowest level of owl ball, with slates ranging from 21 to 25 games, contained the Chicago White Sox, Cleveland Indians, Pittsburgh Pirates, and Philadelphia Phillies.[32]

The St. Louis Cardinals, now led by Hannegan as president, preferred even more than the club's league-leading 45 night games planned for 1948, but was vexed by the visiting-club consent clause. "It seems ridiculous that certain clubs, such as the Giants and Dodgers, can refuse to play us an unlimited number of night games in St. Louis," manager Eddie Dyer told reporters. "In short, that simply means that the visiting team is telling the Cardinals when they can or cannot play their night games." DeWitt of the St. Louis Browns echoed those thoughts. "Three clubs in the American League have refused to play as many night games in St. Louis as we would like," DeWitt remarked, citing the Tigers and Yankees as the major culprits with the Red Sox capping their allotment at five night games.[33]

The initial night game in Detroit was played before 50,000 spectators on June 15, under a $400,000 lighting system that General Electric engineers provided the latest in illumination science to facilitate top-notch playing conditions for night games. This inaugural night game did not begin until sunset at 9:30, though, due to daylight savings time being observed in Detroit.[34]

Albert "Happy" Chandler, the commissioner of baseball in the late 1940s, had a significant impact on the expansion of night baseball within the major leagues, when he cast the deciding vote at the joint-league meeting in December 1945 to institute unlimited night baseball during the 1946 season (Library of Congress, Prints & Photographs Division, LC-DIG-hec-28633).

An article in *Popular Science* in July 1948 detailed how Swackhamer and the lighting engineers at General Electric used illumination science on the Briggs Stadium project. "With slide rule, protractor, stadium blueprints—and a good deal of past experience—he calculated just where each of the 1,386 individual floodlight lamps should be placed and aimed to provide shadowless illumination for players and spectators." In order to provide 200 foot-candles of even illumination, every spot on the field received light from six lamps on at least two light towers. To accomplish this, the engineer created "a series of aiming charts, one for each of the stadium's eight lighting towers, which gave the aiming angle for each lamp, the number of degrees it should be turned to right or left, up or down." Workmen then set the calibration dials on each floodlight mounting to adjust that lamp precisely to the engineer's specifications.[35]

General Electric was the illumination engineer for three of the four postwar lighting installations to initiate night baseball in a major-league ballpark. Of the 13 major-league ballparks with lights by 1948, General Electric had been the lighting engineer for six parks (Cincinnati Reds, Brooklyn Dodgers, Cleveland Indians, New York Yankees, Boston Red Sox, and Detroit Tigers). Westinghouse did the lighting for six ballparks (Shibe Park in Philadelphia, Sportsman's Park in St. Louis along with the parks of the Chicago White

Sox, Pittsburgh Pirates, New York Giants, and Washington Senators), while Crouse–Hinds handled one (Braves Field). General Electric also engineered the lighting of 150 minor-league ballparks. Swackhamer was featured in a General Electric advertisement in *The Sporting News*, which included a photo of him along with his engineering qualifications. However, absent a major reversal in policy by the Chicago Cubs, there were no more major-league ballparks in the foreseeable future in which to install a high-end lighting system.[36]

Swackhamer had spent two decades establishing General Electric as one of the premier experts in the field of outdoor sports lighting. It was not a bad career for a boy who grew up on a dairy farm in Upstate New York and worked his way through Syracuse University to earn an "applied science" degree, a forerunner to today's engineering program. Following the completion of the Briggs Stadium project, Swackhamer took a new job within General Electric, transferring from the Schenectady, New York, location to the facility in Lynn, Massachusetts. He worked in Lynn for half a dozen years, before transferring in 1955 to a job at the company's facility in Hendersonville, North Carolina, near the city of Asheville in the Blue Ridge Mountains. Swackhamer retired in 1958 after 36 years with General Electric. He and his wife, Mattie, continued to reside in Hendersonville during his retirement years. Swackhamer died in 1978 and is buried in Shepherd Memorial Park in Hendersonville.[37]

Although Walter Briggs had installed lights at his Detroit ballpark, he continued to take a very conservative approach to the Tigers playing night games on the road, capping those at three per ball club in 1948. That level was just one above the minimum

Braves Field in Boston was illuminated for night games in 1946 using the classic eight-tower system first deployed by lighting engineers at the General Electric Company in 1927 in their experiments conducted in the city of Lynn, ten miles north of Boston (Boston Public Library, Arts Department, Tichnor Brothers Collection).

the Detroit club was obligated to play under the visiting-club consent clause in the night-baseball policy. Clark Griffith openly complained about the lack of consent given by the Detroit club for a three-game series in Washington in mid–July, when the Senators had to play three consecutive daylight games on Wednesday through Friday rather than conduct them as night games. Attendance at the three daylight games totaled only 8,000 spectators, when three night games would have drawn at least 45,000 people. Perpetuating daylight baseball on the weekday made no sense in this situation, Griffith argued, since both clubs lost money from an economic perspective and many Washington baseball fans were deprived of a chance to watch a ball game. "Baseball as a daytime sport belongs to the past," Griffith contended. "There's nothing to do but admit it."[38]

The demise of daylight baseball was also echoed that summer by Cleveland Indians farm-system director Hank Greenberg. "I believe we are moving fast toward a situation in which we will have daylight baseball only on Sundays," Greenberg told sportswriter Dan Daniel. "I know that shocks you. But how long do you think those who keep shouting that baseball is a game primarily for the sunshine are going to be able to hold out? Well, you draw 15,000 in the afternoon and 50,000 or better under the arcs. In which direction is your conscious, or unconscious, pull?"[39]

The total attendance for American League games in 1948 was 11 million people, 40 percent of which came at night games. The pennant-winning Cleveland Indians drew 2.6 million customers, with 1.2 million of them attending the club's 26 night games for an average night-game crowd of 46,000 people. Cleveland owner Bill Veeck used a number of promotions to maximize his night-game attendance, most famously staging "Good Old Joe Early Night" to honor the average fan.[40]

Night games during the 1948 season represented 29 percent of all major-league ball games played that season, which was a 60 percent increase over the 18 percent ratio experienced just three years earlier in 1945. With such dynamic growth, major-league baseball's unlimited, although partially restricted, policy for night baseball was liberalized at the winter meetings in December 1948. The St. Louis Browns, often abused by the visiting-club consent provision of the night-game policy, led the charge for greater control of night games by the home ball club. "After all, we must realize that baseball is in the amusement field," a member of the Browns front office said in advance of the league meetings. "You have to cater to the wishes of the people who would like to patronize you."[41]

At the joint-league meeting, Chandler opted to discontinue the past practice to mandate a common night-game policy in both leagues, which all too frequently involved a testy exchange among club owners to hammer out a compromise between the different policies voted at the two separate league meetings. Rather than vote with one league over the other, Chandler let the differing league policies stand. For the 1949 season, ball clubs were free to schedule night games without the consent of the visiting club for up to four games in the American League and up to five games in the National League. These limits replaced the previous two-game maximum for non-consent scheduling. The existing prohibition of night games on Sunday continued to apply, as did the avoidance of night games on the day before a doubleheader and on a getaway day. The latter two items, more optional than mandated, were often flaunted by the club owners through the use of visiting-club consent.[42]

Night baseball was not a prominent topic anymore at the annual winter meetings held every December, as executives in professional baseball confronted more complex, perplexing issues that were beginning to tear at the fabric of the sport. Publicity about any new nuances in night-game policy rarely made newspaper headlines and the details were often buried deep in the articles published about the conclusions reached at the meetings. An example is this lede paragraph after the 1948 meetings: "Although sidestepping television and radio changes for another year and arranging for further study of the bonus issue, the major-league owners made some concessions to the unlimited night-ball advocates at their annual meeting here."[43]

The new night-game policies for the 1949 major-league season fostered a greater concentration in evening events in the time-of-day model, which had already been happening in the minor leagues. As clubs in the majors pared back their Sunday games from a doubleheader to a single game in order to create more room for night games, many minor-league clubs were replacing the traditional daylight game on opening day with a night game. In the American Association and the Texas League, all four games to start the 1949 season were conducted as night games. Minor-league clubs were also transforming holiday dates into night games. On the Independence Day holiday in 1949, one-half of the holiday games in the International League, American Association, Southern Association, and Texas League were conducted as twi-night doubleheaders. This complete transformation in the minor leagues of the premier events of Sunday, holiday, and season-opener from daylight games into night games soon began to creep into the major leagues.[44]

A significant change in the night calendar for the 1949 season was the Brooklyn Dodgers abandoning the rationing of night games to book 21 night games at Ebbets Field, leaving just five ball clubs now at the 14-game minimum level. "The real reason for playing night ball is quite obvious: it pays so much better," Rickey, now a night-baseball convert, acknowledged the business consideration that drove the decision. "Night ball is no longer merely a spectacle. Surveys show that more people can attend at night. The sustained audience proves it." Another noticeable change in the 1949 schedule was the encroachment of night games into cool weather dates near opening day and the last regular-season games before the World Series. The St. Louis Cardinals scheduled an April 23 night game, while the Pittsburgh Pirates carded a September 30 night game.[45]

Two games late in the 1949 season put pressure on the ball-club owners to legislate greater flexibility to use lighting systems to complete games during the 1950s. Although the league policies that contained a night-game curfew generally had minimal impact to the playing season, the game on September 3, 1949, between the Cincinnati Reds and the league-leading St. Louis Cardinals was one of the rare instances where it did apply. The game was stopped by the curfew, which resulted in a 9–9 tie after 15 innings of play. The second incident occurred at the fifth game of the 1949 World Series, when Commissioner Chandler ordered the lights to be turned on in the ninth inning, once again rendering a public decision that a daylight game in the majors should be able to be completed under lights when darkness threatened its stoppage.[46]

The ball-club owners would finally change these archaic rules for the 1950 season, just in time to confront a serious impediment to night baseball that had been lurking on the horizon. The negative impact of television on the ballpark audience would be one of baseball's greatest concerns in the coming decade.

◆ 13 ◆

Twi-Night Doubleheaders

Night baseball experienced an uptick during the early years of the 1950s when ball-club owners sought to reverse the sizeable decline in major-league attendance that followed the postwar ballpark-spectator boom from 1946 through 1949. Attendance at games hit its peak in 1948, when 20.9 million people went to the ballpark, a level that would be unsurpassed until the 1960s. Attendance then dropped significantly to 17.4 million in 1950 and continued its downward spiral to 14.6 million in 1952. This precipitous decline in ballpark attendance was, in large measure, caused by the urban exodus of the middle class to the suburbs and the impact of television on recreational habits.

Residents in the suburbs depended on the private automobile, not public transportation (railroad or streetcar) around which the now-obsolete major-league ballparks (most built between 1909 and 1915) were located in the early 1950s. The automobile substituting for mass transit reinforced the emphasis of suburban home as a place for family leisure in a private space, replacing the prior emphasis on leisure activities in the community space. Limited-access highways in the 1950s were inefficient at best and non-existent in many major-league cities, while the paucity of automobile parking proximate to the ballpark also discouraged suburban treks to the ballpark. The automobile was one reason that sociologist Lewis Mumford called the suburbs "a collective effort to lead a private life." The other reason was television, the new postwar communication medium that captured society.[1]

Television provided private entertainment in the comfort of the suburban home, making it an easy option to community-based entertainment at the ballpark or the movie theater. Soon after television's arrival in private homes in 1947, "the normal way to enjoy a community experience was at home in your living room at your TV set." While many club owners allowed some major-league ball games to be televised, the picture quality in the early 1950s was deplorable and thus had little, if any, impact on ballpark attendance. The screen was very small and the reception quality of the black-and-white picture depended entirely upon the adequate positioning of the "rabbit ears" antenna. There wasn't much for viewers to see even if there was a quality TV picture, just the pitcher and the batter, and portions of those players might be cut off. There were only two cameras to follow the ball once it was in play, and the cameras were often late in capturing the action. Announcers added little to what viewers saw on the television screen.[2]

It was entertainment programming on television that kept suburban fans glued to their comfortable chairs at home and stifled their ambition to travel to the ballpark. In 1950, when just nine percent of American households owned a TV set, the three major television networks (NBC, CBS, and ABC) first had a full lineup of shows during the evening on Monday through Friday. The most popular shows at this time featured Milton Berle on Tuesday night and Arthur Godfrey on Monday night; both shows disrupted night-game attendance at the ballpark on those two evenings. By 1952, when one-third of American households owned one, television was not just a new technology, but also an instrument of broader social transformation. "People seemed to go out less for entertainment once they bought a television," Richard Butsch wrote in his book *The Making of American Audiences: From Stage to Television*, as steady declines occurred in the 1950s not just at the ballpark but also at movie theaters and other places of amusement.[3]

The more fundamental reason for the scheduling of more night games in the 1950s was a general change in the nature of employment, which altered the potential ballpark audience for weekday games. Attending a daylight baseball game on a weekday was less of an option for the shrinking number of self-made business owners and others with autonomy and time flexibility. Civic capitalism, with its associated boosterism for the city, was no longer the rule for many local businesses, replaced by an emphasis on national capitalism that dominated ownership mentality. More workers were wage or salary earners, not owners whose compensation was based on the firm's profit.

"The Great Depression and World War II changed the way Americans thought about individuals, communities, and society," Jillson wrote in *Pursuing the American Dream*. "The decreasing importance of strong backs and the rising importance of strong minds had changed the meanings of freedom, equality, and opportunity." In the postwar economy, "the American Dream came to focus on a high-consumption, leisure-oriented, and pleasure-filled private life." While many more Americans could now pursue a middle-class life, all too often that came with a loss of independence. Blue-collar workers no longer had the "feeling of autonomy, security, and personal pride of the master craftsman," while white-collar workers climbing the career ladder at a corporation "rarely had the independence and control that goes with ownership."[4]

A shift in American ideology, which President Roosevelt began to foster in the 1930s, was now more evident in the 1950s, as individualism was replaced by collectivism as a means for most people to earn a living. Achievement through individual pursuit gave way to the anonymity of achievement through group effort, in what author William Whyte in his 1956 book *The Organization Man* called "a bureaucratic ethic" in contrast to the Protestant work ethic that drove individualism. Creativity and initiative moved from an individual to a corporate mode. Whyte believed "a generation of bureaucrats" was being groomed in the corporate office buildings of America, reinforced by the relative "classlessness in suburbia," where tiny differences in social rank were measured by mass consumption of consumer goods, overshadowing the merits of the classic approach to upward social mobility through entrepreneurism. "The great majority of small business firms cannot be placed on any continuum with the corporation. For one thing, they are rarely engaged in primary industry," Whyte observed, contrasting that economic function to a variety of service industries such as insurance agencies, restaurants, lumber yards, and automobile dealers. "The corporation is forever a threat to the economics of the small businessman," Whyte wrote, accurately forecasting that the security-seeking denizen of the corporation, the Organization Man, not the risk-taking entrepreneur, would largely be the future of employment status.[5]

In the early 1950s the average American worked a five-day, 40-hour workweek and had one week of paid vacation time. This provided ample time to pursue recreational opportunities, both on the weekend and evenings on the weekdays. However, how those hours were devoted to recreation changed between 1946 and 1953, when expenditures for private endeavors (radio or television, books and magazines, etc.) increased from 58 percent of the recreational dollar to 70 percent, while expenditures for public pursuits (movies, sports, etc.) decreased from 42 percent to 30 percent.[6]

Major-league baseball was now battling for the entertainment dollar. If the club owners had not moved significantly into night-baseball scheduling in the immediate postwar years, major-league baseball as an enterprise would have been in serious trouble during the early 1950s as it grappled with all these societal changes.

While the Organization Man did not have the general time flexibility to take the afternoon off to attend a ball game, he could make it to a night game, though, and often would bring along his family. Since the potential weekday audience for night games was much larger than the audience that could attend daylight games, a number of club owners responded by conducting more night games. Some owners responded faster than others, though, depending upon whether their philosophy of the baseball business was sport or entertainment. With this backdrop, the two major leagues began to liberalize their policies for the use of artificial lighting systems at the ballpark.

At the winter meetings in December 1949, the two major leagues made no modification to their general policy for night games in the 1950 season, as both retained the visiting-club consent parameters used for the 1949 season (no consent for up to four games in the American League and up to five games in the National League). However, the two leagues did vote to authorize the completion of daylight games under artificial lighting, an issue that had confounded the sport since the beginning of the night-baseball era. Since common policy for night baseball in both leagues had been eliminated at the winter meetings in December 1948, the two leagues now adopted different policies to accomplish the goal of using lights to complete daylight games.

"The National League club owners, in as drastic a move as the majors have known since the advent of night ball, decided to allow the turning on of lights for afternoon games that run into darkness with the score tied or before a regulation nine-inning contest has been completed," the *New York Times* reported. "The American League voted to allow this only if necessary in a final series of the season involving teams still in the running for first, second, third, or fourth-place World Series shares." The American League would later adopt the National League policy at its league meeting in December 1950 for use during the 1951 season.[7]

The first major-league daylight game where this new policy was implemented occurred at Braves Field on April 23, 1950, which the *Boston Globe* commemorated the next day with the headline "Braves Game Ends Under Lights; Move Makes N.L. History."

Commissioner Chandler pushed this rule change for the regular season, after he had ushered in the policy on an impromptu basis at the 1949 World Series. "There are nothing but frustrated fans leaving the parks whenever a game has to be called and the score is tied," Chandler told reporters. "They feel they have wasted their time." Even if some of the owners did not see it, Chandler recognized the fundamental shift in the audience composition at the ballpark, for both daylight and night games. Chandler said that public acceptance of night baseball "has made it mandatory upon us to give them as much of it as they want."[8]

National League club owners voted for two additional night-game rule changes in December 1949, eliminating the curfew for night games and permitting twi-night doubleheaders. The American League voted to retain the curfew, but needed to take no action on twi-night twin bills, since these had been legitimate in that league for several years. Both leagues agreed that a night game preferably should not be played on a get-away day, unless the consent of the visiting club was obtained. This was a softening of the previous stance, which had been phrased in terms of general avoidance. As a concession to the concern of ballplayers, the National League agreed that its clubs would avoid such consent for a night game when the departing team could not reach its next destination at least four hours before its next scheduled game. Night-game scheduling on getaway days would remain a persistent problem into the 1970s.[9]

The differing night-game policies of the two leagues created confusion among base-ball fans. While the major provision regarding the number of night games that the home club controlled in scheduling was digestible, the differing details concerning minor pro-visions, such as the application of the curfew and exactly when lights could be used to finish a daylight game, easily could elude the recall by an ardent follower of base-ball. Sometimes even baseball executives got confused about proper implementation of night-game policy, particularly when it involved the rules for determining a suspended game or the integration of state-specific laws.

There were several complications with the policies about completing a daylight game under lights and the night-game curfew. Games on Monday through Friday normally could continue into the evening hours, or into the early hours of the next day, without concern. Games on Saturday in several cities, though, could not proceed past midnight due to state laws that precluded the playing of ball games on Sunday prior to a certain time on Sunday afternoon. Those same state laws also prohibited Sunday games from being played after a certain hour on Sunday evening, which introduced a great amount of complexity into the completion of Sunday doubleheaders under lights. Both leagues tinkered with their policies throughout the 1950s to respond to these complications and other concerns that arose during the decade.

During the 1950 season, major-league ball clubs first took action to transform the three premium daylight playing dates of Sunday, holiday, and opening day into a night game. While Sunday night games were specifically outlawed by league rule, there was no direct prohibition of night games on opening day or on the three national holidays. Club owners in that era did not believe a formal prohibition was required, since opening day and holidays were such lucrative events because they inherently attracted a large audi-ence to the ballpark. Therefore, no specific rule was required to dissuade clubs from con-sidering these dates for night games. That was logic from the 1930s, though. From the perspective of the 1950s, a "large" attendance was good for these premium daylight dates, but a bigger crowd likely would be achieved by staging them as a night game, since the daylight games on these dates did not necessarily maximize the attendance.

Opening day was the first premium daylight date to be converted into a night game by an enterprising ball-club owner. St. Louis Cardinals owner Fred Saigh, who had succeeded the late Bob Hannegan as club president, scheduled opening day at Sportsman's Park in 1950 to be a night game on an expected chilly evening in mid–April. "The fans want night ball, and they're the only ones we have to consider," Saigh said in defense of his unorthodox decision. He added that women were 40 percent of the attendance in St. Louis and "the ladies want night ball." Saigh clinched his argu-ment by citing the general change in the nature of the daytime audience, which before the war would have packed the ballpark on opening day. "St. Louis is a hard-working city, but the natural industrious character of the population makes day games conflict with the bread-winning of too many," Saigh said. "Night ball has made the national pastime a family relaxation here."[10]

On April 18, 1950, the St. Louis Cardinals hosted the first night game on opening day in the major leagues, defeating the Pittsburgh Pirates before an opening-night crowd of 20,871 spectators at Sportsman's Park. It was reportedly the largest attendance ever achieved by the Cardinals at the club's first home game of the season. The Cardinals played night games at their home opener from 1950 through 1953 (official opening day or the secondary one as home opener). The Philadelphia Athletics in 1951 also experimented with night ball on opening day.[11]

Saigh proposed to transform a second premium daylight playing date by conducting a Sunday night game on July 16, 1950, when the night game between the Cardinals and Brooklyn Dodgers on June 3 was rained out. The make-up game was slated to be part of a separate-admission day-night doubleheader, since the two clubs already had a single game scheduled for that Sunday afternoon.

"The movies, municipal (summer) opera, legitimate theatre, basketball and hockey operate on Sunday night," Saigh declared, "and I see no reason why we shouldn't play baseball then too." Branch Rickey, president of the Dodgers, had initially consented to this arrangement, but then backed off when Commissioner Chandler expressed his disapproval. "It's my judgment that we should not play Sunday night baseball at a time when people are going to church," Chandler told reporters. "We could forfeit a great deal of good will in that way that I am very anxious to keep."[12]

Despite a thumbs-down by National League president Ford Frick, Saigh was insistent that the Sunday night game be played. "The Cardinals have not received one objection from a churchman or a layman to the Sunday night setting," Saigh countered Chandler. "To the contrary, the ticket sale is unprecedented, which indicates that the people, the fans, most of whom are church members, are for it 100 per cent." Saigh also cited the commissioner-approved practice of minor-league clubs frequently playing Sunday night games. When a lawyer for the National League cited chapter and verse that a Sunday night game would violate league rules, Saigh, under pressure from Baptist ministers in St. Louis, relented and canceled the game. Sunday night baseball would have to wait another dozen years before its arrival in the major leagues.[13]

These two forays by Saigh to schedule night games in contravention of major-league norms were all part of a concerted plan by the St. Louis Cardinals to make a big leap forward toward a saturation point of night games within the club's 77-game home schedule. The Cardinals booked 54 night games on the 1950 schedule, the first time that a ball club had exceeded the 50-game threshold for night baseball. The club's remaining 23 daylight games broke down as follows: 13 on Sunday (11 single games, one doubleheader), two on holidays (Independence Day doubleheader), five on Saturday, and three on weekdays. With its slated 54 night games, St. Louis planned to play 40 more night games than the New York Giants, which scheduled the lowest level in the National League with 14. In the American League, Washington was still the leader with 43 scheduled night games, 29 more than the lowest-tier of 14 night games carded by the trio of Boston, Detroit, and New York Yankees.[14]

Night games were now so prevalent that some ball clubs began to offer inducements for spectators to buy tickets. Several clubs, notably the Cleveland Indians, promoted Ladies Night to offer discounted tickets for certain night contests and the Brooklyn Dodgers sponsored community nights to attract a block of customers from a particular suburban community.

Twi-night doubleheaders surged during the 1950 season, when the National League joined the American League in authorizing the technique. As ballpark attendance plummeted during the early 1950s, many clubs resorted to playing twi-night doubleheaders, which offered the promotion of watching two games for the price of one. The double feature started with the twilight game at 6:00, with the night game commencing soon after its conclusion, usually around 8:30 or 9:00. For late-arriving spectators seeking primarily the main event, the one-and-a-half games for the price of one was considered a bonus to the night game.

While virtually forgotten today, the twi-night doubleheader was instrumental in bridging the postwar transformation of scheduling from primarily daylight baseball to predominately night baseball. The twi-night doubleheader was an interlude strategy that reduced daylight afternoon games through the substitution of a twilight game as the opener of the doubleheader. While this transformation of a daylight game was not per se into a night game, the resulting twilight game was directly connected to the subsequent night game and thus served as an effective middle ground in the ongoing process to eliminate the daylight ball game in favor of a full slate of night games on weekdays.

Completing the opening twilight game under lights was the key to staging a

Boston Red Sox infielder Vern Stephens crosses home plate after hitting a home run in a night game played at Fenway Park, as several teammates gather to congratulate him (courtesy Boston Public Library, Leslie Jones Collection).

fan-friendly twi-night doubleheader, to avoid a lengthy delay between the end of the twilight game and the start of the night game. This had been an issue before 1944, when the opener of a twi-night twin bill had to finish in daylight to avoid having the game count against a club's limited night-game allocation. When unlimited night baseball was in its most expansive wartime mode from mid-season of 1944 through the end of the 1945 season, the second game could begin soon after the end of the first game.

During the postwar years of 1946 through 1949, when the twi-night doubleheader was authorized only in the American League, the opening twilight game was usually completed under lights, using the visiting-club consent provision to approve the additional "night" game. This consent was generally easy to obtain, since the alternative was to play the make-up game as a sparsely-attended afternoon game on an open date or as the afternoon portion of a day-night doubleheader. Neither alternative was typically very appealing to the visiting club. The daylight-game completion rule adopted by the leagues for the 1950 season largely eliminated this technical issue of needing to justify the completion of the twilight game under lights.

Before 1951, the twi-night doubleheader was largely viewed as just an arcane technique to schedule the make-up of a postponed game. During the 1951 and 1952 seasons, the single-admission twi-night doubleheader approach gained popularity in comparison to the traditional single-admission day-day afternoon doubleheader and the nouveau separate-admission day-night doubleheader. The object for many clubs was to determine which of the three approaches would produce the largest audience for the make-up date. For clubs with increasingly paltry attendance at daylight weekday games, the twi-night doubleheader was the winning solution. The weaker franchise in two-club cities also had a distinct preference for twi-night doubleheaders, as evidenced by the large volume conducted by the Boston Braves, Philadelphia Athletics, and St. Louis Browns.

Clubs pursuing a night-game policy that scheduled only the 14-game standard often used the traditional day-day doubleheader approach, while a club in hot pursuit of the pennant or playing a hated rival often used the day-night doubleheader approach. The contrast in New York City for the two games slated for August 12, 1952, illustrates the choice. The postponed game at Yankee Stadium against the Washington Senators was rolled into a day-day doubleheader the next day, while the postponed game at Ebbets Field between the Dodgers and the New York Giants was turned into one-half of a day-night doubleheader the next day. More typical was the rescheduling of

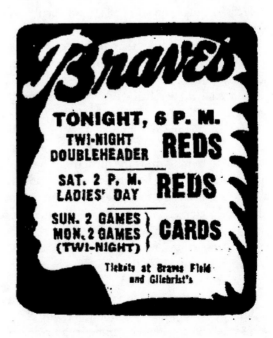

The Boston Braves were prolific schedulers of twi-night doubleheaders and other promotions to try to attract spectators to Braves Field, as shown in this four-day schedule contained in a 1951 newspaper advertisement.

the game at Comiskey Park in Chicago on June 28, 1951, when rain fell in the first inning and "after a wait of thirty-seven minutes the game was postponed. It will be played as part of a twilight-night doubleheader Sept. 7."[15]

There were suspicions that not all postponements were "natural" in the creation of the twi-night doubleheader. In some quarters, the twi-night doubleheader was as maligned as the Sunday doubleheader had been in the 1930s, as a "synthetic" creature created by a trumped-up rather than legitimate rationale. "Wet grounds" at a daylight afternoon game sometime served as the public rationale for the home club to postpone the game and reschedule it into the opener of a twi-night twin bill. Better to seek a larger night crowd through promotion of the twi-nighter two months hence than to accept the meager receipts from a tiny crowd at the rainy daylight game. Of course, no ball club ever admitted to this pretext, at least not for public consumption.

While nearly all twi-night doubleheaders were staged to replay a postponed game, they did make an appearance on the 1952 National League schedule, when the Brooklyn Dodgers, now under the leadership of Walter O'Malley, booked three twi-night doubleheaders on the club's original schedule. By 1953 it was not uncommon for an entire slate of league games to be all conducted as twi-night doubleheaders, which first occurred on August 25, 1953, when all four National League contests were staged as twi-night doubleheaders.[16]

Twi-night doubleheaders helped to stem the tide of the declining ballpark attendance in the early 1950s, providing a stopgap measure to ease the transition from the demise of the daylight game to the saturation of night games on the weekday calendar. Over the next two decades, the twi-night doubleheader would serve additional duty for relocated and expansion ball clubs to enable efficient scheduling in the face of wider geographic distances between major-league cities.

Because overall attendance declined significantly between the 1949 and 1952 seasons, the two major leagues only reluctantly publicized a modicum of season-long attendance figures, given their negative public-relations value. This obscured the impact of increased night baseball. For the 1951 season, the American League did announce that 8.8 million people attended games played by its eight ball clubs, with night games drawing 3.6 million people, or 40 percent of the overall total. This was the same percentage experienced during the 1948 season, the high-water mark of major-league attendance. The Cleveland Indians drew the most night-game spectators, with 830,000 attending its night games, representing 49 percent of the club's 1.7 million in total attendance. The Chicago White Sox had the second-best night attendance at 560,000 customers, which was 43 percent of the club's 1.3 million in overall attendance. The National League did not divulge its night-game attendance.[17]

At the winter meetings in December 1951, the American League club owners voted to expand night baseball, "which has been encroaching steadily on the daylight version as the game's pioneers played it," by allowing all night games to be scheduled without regard to any consent or non-consent parameters. The National League held fast to its existing policy of five night games that the home club could schedule without the visiting club's consent, with any higher number requiring consent.[18]

Clark Griffith, owner of the Washington Senators, and Bill Veeck, now owner of the St. Louis Browns, pushed for the new night-game policy in the American League. The issue they sought to resolve involved the threesome of the Boston, Detroit, and New York clubs, all resistant to extensive night baseball, which often utilized their right as the visiting club to veto road night games once the club reached its obligation to play four such night games. The vote to pass the new rule reportedly was five owners affirmative and three owners negative. The home ball club now fully controlled the scheduling of night games in the American League.[19]

Both leagues now had the same curfew rule for night games played Monday through Saturday during the 1952 season, since the National League voted to readopt such a curfew (now expressed in daylight savings time). No inning could start after 12:50 in the morning and any inning in progress at that time had to be completed. However, the two leagues differed on the use of lights to complete a Sunday game. The American League voted to allow "local option" to complete Sunday afternoon games under lights, allowing lights to remain on until 7:00 in the evening (subject to earlier stop times under the Sunday statutes in Massachusetts and Pennsylvania). Each club had to announce prior to the start of the season whether it would use lights to complete Sunday games. On the other hand, the National League voted to no longer allow lights to complete Sunday games, believing that such a policy effectively allowed for Sunday night games in contravention of baseball tradition.[20]

In the 1952 league schedules, the two Philadelphia ball clubs became prolific hosts of night games, joining the ranks of Washington and the two St. Louis clubs in booking more than 35 night games. The Phillies, with 41 night games, were the second largest proponent of night baseball in the National League, well ahead of the 28 night games carded by Pittsburgh and Boston. The Athletics, with 38 night games, were the third largest scheduler in the American League, well in front of the 29 night games slated by Cleveland. There were now only four diehard minimalists in night baseball, the American League triumvirate with just 14 night games that had opposed the move to pure unlimited baseball, both home and road, and the New York Giants in the National League with 15 games. Cincinnati left that group, as the Reds now booked 25 night games.[21]

In the midst of the rapid postwar growth of night baseball, the Chicago Cubs were the last bastion of all-daylight baseball, playing without lights in Wrigley Field. Owner Phil Wrigley had a strong conviction that he could successfully apply the merchandising strategies used in his chewing-gum business to the baseball business. Wrigley advertised the experience of attending a ball game at the "friendly confines" of Wrigley Field, with its ivy-covered outfield walls.[22]

As a sportsman and avowed steward of the sport, Wrigley felt he had a civic commitment not just to sponsor the national pastime on the north side of Chicago but also to avoid disrupting the residential neighborhood where Wrigley Field was located. Wrigley had almost a minor-league perspective concerning civic boosterism, which enabled him to have a lower emphasis on profit-making in his ball club's business basis and thus insulate the owner from the siren call of night baseball to maintain an adequate bottom line.

In the early 1950s Wrigley embraced television to advertise Wrigley Field, seeking to attract new occasional customers to his ballpark and convert them into periodic visitors if not frequent customers. "The team's unique position of playing all of its home games during the day became a means of developing new fans among daytime television viewers," James Walker and Robert Bellamy observed in their book *Center Field Shot: A History of Baseball on Television.* "A generation of Cubs fans was born when they came home from school and turned on the game, unless mom already had it on."[23]

"This night ball is like a drug," Wrigley remarked in 1952. "I have studied every angle of night baseball and I have come to the conclusion that it's nothing more than a shot in the arm to attendance. The novelty wears off and then we find that attendance isn't any higher than it was originally playing day ball." Wrigley was convinced he had an advantage relative to night baseball. "Daylight baseball should be more successful than ever since the rise of television. There is more competition at night. Furthermore, in a large community like Chicago, the rotation of days off makes more people available to watch daytime games than years ago." It would be another three decades before lights would be installed at Wrigley Field and even then there would be only limited night baseball played there.[24]

Wrigley was unlike the other 15 ball-club owners in the major leagues, since he had a decidedly different outlook on the civic/profit business basis, which was undergoing a significant long-term shift in the early 1950s. As the owners within the old cadre of "family business" ball clubs (Washington Senators, Philadelphia Athletics, Chicago White Sox, and New York Giants) and those who were sportsmen (Chicago Cubs, Boston Red Sox, Detroit Tigers, and Cincinnati Reds) lost their influence, the newer club owners that were more purely capitalists (Brooklyn Dodgers, Philadelphia Phillies, Cleveland Indians, and Pittsburgh Pirates) increasingly dominated policy-making in the league meetings.

The civic component, whether oriented to city boosterism or national-pastime mythology, was now much more minimal, if not wholly negligible, in the civic/profit business basis of a ball club. Promotion to drive revenue was a larger element of the profit component, as the business transformed from selling baseball to hawking entertainment. Television broadcasts became a factor to stem the attendance decline, as many clubs used broadcasting rights payments to offset lower gate receipts. Club owners increasingly needed to consider not just the gate receipts from ballpark spectators (now about 80 percent of revenue for the average ball club), but also rights fees associated with television viewers (now about 15 percent of revenue, including radio rights), since arguably, for night games, one body in the ballpark was equivalent to several bodies in front of the TV. Finding the appropriate balance between the two factors, though, remained complicated.[25]

Television revenue increasingly dictated the time-of-day model for the scheduling of games, as the weekday afternoon game evaporated and was replaced by a night game or, on an interim basis, by a twilight game tagged onto a night game in the form of a twi-night doubleheader.

The imprimatur of the national pastime as the driving boosterism element for major-league baseball started to lose its luster. As a legal matter, the U.S. Supreme Court in its 1953 decision in *Toolson vs. New York Yankees* "preserved baseball's immunity from the anti-trust laws," but the court swung open the door for Congress to modify baseball's "unique legal status as a sport that was not a business." From the fan's perspective, major-league baseball continued to be America's favorite sport, according to a 1948 Gallup Poll survey, but pro football and pro basketball both had sizeable followings as America's second and third favorite sports (baseball at 39 percent, with football at 17 percent and basketball at 10 percent).[26]

In the early 1950s the meaning of "big league" began to expand beyond just baseball, as professional leagues now operated in three other team-based sports that had franchises in more cities than just those with major-league baseball clubs. The National Football League, established in 1920 and a veritable youngster as a pro sport compared to baseball, was a legitimate threat to baseball's once unassailable position as the nation's number one sport. Up-and-coming potential threats were the National Basketball Association, a newcomer to pro sports with its 1946 establishment, and, to a lesser degree, the National Hockey League, a regional league comprised of two Canadian clubs and four American clubs. By 1953 the NFL had anointed big-league status to three minor-league baseball cities (Los Angeles, San Francisco, and Baltimore), all of which were among the dozen largest cities in the 1950 federal census. The NBA also bestowed big-league status on several smaller cities, most notably Minneapolis and Milwaukee, in addition to Baltimore, the nation's sixth-largest city.

Pro football and pro basketball gained popularity because their games almost always were staged at spectator-friendly times, with NFL games on Sunday afternoon and NBA games on week nights and weekend afternoons. Big-league baseball, on the other hand, still had a healthy dose of weekday afternoon ball games in several of its larger cities.

From a broader perspective, a city's standing among big-league entities could now be defined not just by baseball but by its depth of penetration into the other three pro team sports. This outlook created new tiers of status among the 10 cities with major-league baseball, an unchanged ten-some for half a century. New York City, still at the top, was the only city with clubs in all four pro team sports in 1953. Things got fuzzier from there, though. Chicago had two clubs in two sports, baseball and football (Bears and Cardinals), but had clubs in just three of the four sports (the other was hockey, not basketball). Boston, Detroit, and Philadelphia each also had clubs in three of four sports for consideration in the second tier. At the lower end were Cleveland, Pittsburgh, and Washington that each had baseball and football clubs, while St. Louis, a two-club baseball city, and Cincinnati both lacked a foothold in any of the other three sports.

With baseball on the brink of moving into new locales, the boosterism element was now arguably a city's multi-sport orientation, not just its desire for baseball via the national pastime mythology. Additionally, population within city borders was no longer the driving force for success potential, replaced by a new government statistic in 1950, the Metropolitan Statistical Area, which measured the number of people in the city plus its suburbs.

In 1952, one-third of all major-league ball games were conducted as night games, which set the foundation for an even more expansive growth of night baseball during the mid–1950s when the major leagues experienced their first franchise relocations since the turn of the century. Night ball played a key role in making those relocated ball clubs financially successful and helped to usher in the expansion era in the early 1960s.

Boosting Night Games
in the 1950s

In December 1952, *The Sporting News* reported that the "preference of fans for night ball in the majors was revealed by the release of the official 1952 attendance figures," which told the grim story of another substantial decline in overall attendance, a 10 percent drop from the 1951 turnout. The good news was that 41 percent of the 1952 combined attendance in both leagues came from night games, which represented 34 percent of all games played that season. Night games in the American League averaged 17,758 per game compared to 6,572 for daylight games, while the National League averaged 12,636 per night game and 9,115 per day game.[1]

Night baseball was poised to dominate the major-league playing schedule in the near future, as neither league took action to try to rein in what sportswriters oxymoronically called "arc ball," after the now-archaic arc lighting technology that long ago had been replaced by incandescent lamps. "Both the American and National Leagues agreed to hold the line," *The Sporting News* reported about the league meetings along with its 1952 attendance analysis, "with the American going for unlimited night ball except on Sundays and holidays, while the National retained its previous rule of no more than five night games with each club without permission." There was no further modification by either league in their general night-game policy until the 1960s.

The big baseball trend in the 1950s was the relocation of five of the 16 major-league ball clubs to new cities, which helped to stem the attendance decline and accelerate the already rising level of night baseball. The first wave of relocations involved the two-club cities of Boston, St. Louis, and Philadelphia, when the Boston Braves moved to Milwaukee for the 1953 season, the St. Louis Browns transferred to Baltimore in 1954, and the Philadelphia Athletics went to Kansas City in 1955.

The ball-club owners acted as if the national pastime, or at least their cartel devoted to it, was dependent upon the original 10 great cities with ball clubs in 1903 that had not changed in five decades. By 1952 the demise of the two-club city was abundantly clear and that the format could only possibly survive in the nation's two largest urban areas, New York City and Chicago. In the other three less-populous cities, the two clubs were merely splitting one potential patronage. Relocation or bankruptcy was inevitable for the weaker club in Boston, St. Louis, and Philadelphia.

Growth patterns within the nation only exacerbated the challenges associated with the geographic concentration of major-league baseball. "The dramatic movement of American population from the Northeast and Midwest cities to the Southwest and Far

West suggested the existence of potentially lucrative markets of new major-league baseball fans," White observed in *Creating the National Pastime*. "A game could hardly claim to be the national pastime if those who ran it deliberately excluded large numbers of Americans from the opportunity to participate in it directly as local fans of a hometown franchise." Los Angeles and San Francisco, two of the three cities within the top dozen largest American cities without a major-league baseball club, clearly had the population base to support one. However, because the Pacific Coast League harbored an ambition for major-league status, politics initially stymied baseball's relocation to the West Coast.[2]

The transfer of the Braves from Boston to Milwaukee for the 1953 season by owner Lou Perini was the first break in the linkage of major-league baseball with its half-century-old alignment of cities. The Milwaukee Braves in their first season attracted 1.8 million spectators to their ball games at County Stadium, located several miles west of downtown Milwaukee and having 10,000 available parking spaces adjacent to the ballpark. In the next two years, the Braves drew a combined 4.1 million spectators, which transformed the former decline into a trend of increasing attendance. Night games produced 55 percent of the 1.8 million customers in Milwaukee during 1953, as the Braves attracted 1.0 million spectators to their 33 night dates (29 single games and four twi-night doubleheaders), averaging a capacity crowd of 33,000 for each night event.[3]

While 50 percent of the National League attendance in 1953 came from night games, the rate in the American League was slightly lower, at 44 percent, since the attendance numbers for the night games of the Philadelphia Athletics and St. Louis Browns significantly lagged the other ball clubs, even though both clubs played far more night games than their competitors (other than the Washington Senators). The American League also had three ball clubs that were night-baseball minimalists.

For the 1954 season, the St. Louis Browns transferred to new ownership in Baltimore, where the moribund ball club was renamed the Orioles to expunge all evidence of its prior lowly existence. Baltimore scheduled 38 night games for the 1954 season, the second highest in the American League behind the Washington Senators with 45 night games. Although the Orioles were not much better on the playing field than the old Browns, Baltimore drew 1.1 million spectators to its refurbished Memorial Stadium, where its night games attracted 632,000 customers, or 60 percent of its total attendance. This night-game ratio was the highest in the American League for 1954. In the National League, the St. Louis Cardinals, that circuit's top night-game club (53 home games) and now the sole club in that city, had a night-game attendance ratio of 65 percent, far ahead of the 53 percent that transpired in Milwaukee that season.[4]

The last of the initial trio of ball club relocations occurred for the 1955 season, when the Mack family sold the Philadelphia Athletics to Arnold Johnson, who moved the club to Kansas City. The Athletics scheduled 40 night games in their new locale, the highest number in the American League. The Athletics attracted 827,000 spectators to their night games in Municipal Stadium, which represented 60 percent of the club's total attendance of 1.4 million people, the highest percentage among the eight American League clubs.[5]

Each of the three ball clubs that relocated for the 1953 to 1955 seasons left an old privately-owned ballpark located in the central city to play in a newer municipally-owned stadium located on the outskirts of the city, closer to the suburbs. While attendance in Milwaukee, Baltimore, and Kansas City was admittedly juiced by the twin honeymoon effects of new club and new or refurbished ballpark, the new ball clubs were instrumental in thrusting night baseball into the primary slot of the time-of-day model, bumping

Sunday afternoon from its top perch as lead attendance generator. Daylight baseball had no rich tradition in these former minor-league outposts now transformed into major-league cities.

The new ballparks not only created a favorable atmosphere to generate a proliferation of night games in the baseball schedule, but also modified the civic/profit business balance for ball clubs, due to the urge of the citizenry of Milwaukee, Baltimore, and Kansas City to achieve status as a city possessing a major-league sports franchise. "The terms 'big league' and 'major league' have become metaphors for excellence," William Mullins wrote in his book *Becoming Big League*. "Woe to the municipality that is described as 'minor league' or, worse, 'bush league.'"[6]

These three club relocations reinvigorated boosterism, which sixty years earlier had helped to form the two major leagues and more recently during the last several decades had been an important ingredient of minor-league baseball. Business executives in Milwaukee, through the Greater Milwaukee Committee for Community Development, began in 1948 to lobby local government to revitalize the city (the 13th largest in the 1950 census) through $200 million in public works projects, including highway and airport improvements as well as a new zoo, library, and ballpark. The ground breaking at the former Story Quarry site, on the western edge of Milwaukee, occurred in 1950 and the new stadium was ready for the 1953 season. The city of Baltimore (the sixth largest city) converted its municipally-owned football stadium in 1950 for baseball use, while Kansas City (the 20th largest city) renovated its existing stadium in 1954. All three cities made sweeping concessions in their stadium-rental deals to entice the ball clubs to relocate there. These newer stadiums ushered in a wave of new ballparks with suburb-friendly automobile access.[7]

Ball clubs no longer needed to sacrifice profits to gain the backing of civic boosters. As numerous cities within the top two dozen in population sought "big league" status, municipalities built modern stadiums to entice a major-league club to relocate to there. Clubs wishing to stay in their current city could use these potential opportunities as leverage to secure tax incentives and other municipal benefits to remain in the city. Despite its poor performance on the playing field, the St. Louis Browns had considerable perceived value as a baseball franchise if under new ownership in a new location. So did every other major-league ball club. Suddenly there was inherent value in the offers a city would ante up to acquire, or keep, a major-league club. Boosterism transformed from business-produced to government-induced, or in some cases citizenry-induced.

With the elimination of the three weak links in the two-club cities, major-league attendance in 1955 started to reverse its previous decline and by 1958, with the West Coast relocations, attendance climbed back to its 1950 level. The spectators who flocked to the night games in the newer stadiums in Milwaukee, Baltimore, and Kansas City helped to offset the general attendance decline experienced in many of the aging ballparks used by the other ball clubs. However, it also magnified the problem of many older urban areas in the 1950s, which were experiencing changing racial composition in the areas near the ballpark. Paradoxically, night games in many of the older ballparks increased ballpark attendance, over the comparable expectation for a daylight game, but at the same they depressed that attendance due to spectator safety concerns.

The inner-city environment was often uncomfortable for suburban fans, in the opposing cultural landscapes that Eric Avila termed "chocolate cities and vanilla suburbs" in his book *Popular Culture in the Age of White Flight*. "As old families, mostly

Memorial Stadium in Baltimore (center) was one of the first major-league ballparks located on the outskirts of the city, which made it more convenient for suburban fans to drive there by automobile during the 1950s to attend night games (Library of Congress, Prints & Photographs Division, HABS MD-1111-83 (CT).

white, moved out, new groups, many Black and Puerto Rican, moved in as older urban neighborhoods increasingly lost their appeal as an appropriate venue for professional baseball." Kuklick in *To Every Thing a Season: Shibe Park and Urban Philadelphia* provided a vivid description of the safety concern in the area around that ballpark. "Motorists did not want to endure intimidation or 'gangster mob damage' to their cars," Kuklick wrote about the increasingly rough neighborhood near the Phillies ballpark. Once their automobile was parked, suburban fans felt "the isolating experience" of having to walk to the ballpark through "the hostile stare of street-corner youth, the boarded up and vandalized houses, [and] abandoned and stripped cars."[8]

As the United States converted from a manufacturing to a service economy during the 1950s, American cities had to grapple with how that economic change would impact the already modified structure of the city that had begun back in the 1930s. The general trend was for residential dispersal, with upper- and middle-class residents moving to the periphery and suburbs, while "the lower class, many of whose members belonged to one or another of the nation's ethnic and racial minorities, were staying put," some voluntarily but many others because they could not afford to leave. The general trend for the central city was a deteriorating central business district in the downtown area that was bordered by residential neighborhoods "filled with dilapidated dwellings, often mixed with run-down warehouses and factories." Most ballparks were located in the intermediate zone between the deteriorating downtown and the thriving suburbs.[9]

Federal government initiatives of the era were geared to developing the suburbs rather than redeveloping inner-city areas. While the 1949 federal housing act had initially encouraged redevelopment, this law was quickly supplanted by the 1954 housing act that focused on urban renewal. Older cities in the Northeast and Midwest, the heartland of major-league baseball, "faced problems metropolitan in scope with only the resources of one municipality to address them." While baseball's attendance issue was a perfect example of a problem "metropolitan in scope" that was addressable only by "one municipality," a new baseball stadium was often not near the top of the list of urban-renewal issues to tackle in the 1950s.[10]

No longer simply a task handled by a few people seeking to attract industry to a city, urban planning in the 1950s was a mosaic of diverse "highly technical and highly professionalized" city-planning staffers, whose full-time government job was to integrate business interest with human issues to revitalize a city. It was no easy task, especially when federal money to accomplish that goal was based on the theory that "well-to-do Americans would return to the center city only if the slums and blighted areas were eliminated and replaced by safe, healthy, and attractive middle- and upper-middle-class neighborhoods."[11]

The complex politics of urban renewal ultimately forced the Brooklyn Dodgers and New York Giants to leave New York City and relocate to the West Coast. While Walter O'Malley of the Dodgers enthusiastically tried to keep the ball club in Brooklyn, he was stymied by Robert Moses, New York's city-planning czar, in his attempt to use federal funds to secure land upon which to build a privately financed ballpark. Despite his perceived legacy as a money-grubbing pariah in Brooklyn, "O'Malley stated repeatedly that he intended to construct a new ballpark with his own capital, but that he needed government assistance to acquire suitable land," Neil Sullivan summarized the situation in his book *The Dodgers Move West*. "New York officials were unwilling to furnish him with the site he wanted in Brooklyn, at Atlantic and Flatbush Avenues, while Los Angeles offered three hundred acres in Chavez Ravine, centrally located in the Los Angeles basin."[12]

O'Malley's preferred site in Brooklyn was the Fort Greene Market, adjacent to the Long Island Rail Road depot, which was the nexus of a train line and nine subway lines and less than a mile from a planned automobile expressway. O'Malley tried to interest Moses in the redevelopment of that area as a project under the federal housing act, which provided funding "to purchase property in desolate areas and either construct a public project or else sell the land to a private developer whose construction would conform to a large 'public purpose.'" O'Malley fervently believed that his proposed ballpark and parking facility, built with private funds on publicly-acquired land transferred to him at a low cost, satisfied the "public purpose" requirement. Moses vehemently disagreed with O'Malley's contention. And, as they say, the rest is history. The Los Angeles Dodgers, nee Brooklyn Dodgers, significantly changed the course of night baseball history.[13]

While O'Malley verbally sparred with Moses to build a new ballpark in Brooklyn, he and the other club owners who had not relocated to a new city grappled with how to best attract suburban spectators to night games. By the mid–1950s there was little confusion that suburban residents were the majority of the spectator composition at the ballpark. The movement to the suburbs corresponded with a rise in leisure time and consequent change in spending habits, as Americans shifted their recreational dollars from public to private forms of leisure. The baby boom, which started in 1946 and continued until 1964, altered the leisure patterns of young married adults during the 1950s. The emergence of the baby boomers would greatly impact the baseball industry, first with their desire to play Little League baseball and later with their fixation on television, as alternatives to attending a major-league game.[14]

In a survey conducted in 1954, the ownership of the Baltimore Orioles discovered that ballpark spectators largely came from suburban areas, "drawing disproportionately from the middle and higher income groups." The survey found that the average crowd was 60 percent white-collar workers, 27 percent blue-collar workers, and 13 percent non-workers (about equally divided among student, wife, retiree, and unemployed). Four of five spectators came to the game by automobile, while one of four spectators traveled more than 45 minutes to get to the game, many driving from Pennsylvania. Nearly nine of ten spectators polled wanted the Orioles to schedule 31 or more night games.[15]

Surveys conducted by the New York Giants and Commissioner Ford Frick concluded that the number one reason why people declined to attend a baseball game was the lack of adequate automobile parking near the ballpark. "People expressed the feeling that it was more comfortable in their living rooms," Frick told reporters about his office's survey of fans, "than it was making a long trip to a ball park and sitting in inferior seats." Therefore, ball clubs scrambled to acquire parking rights in the proximate area of the

Suburban families flocked to weekday night games during the 1950s, which created a stark contrast to the predominantly male businessmen audience who had attended weekday daylight games that dominated the baseball calendar in the 1930s (courtesy Boston Public Library, Leslie Jones Collection).

ballpark. Some of the new parking arrangements came about by leveraging the new civic boosterism concept to have government create more public parking, which was an initial step toward resolving the broader issue of ballparks located near rundown neighborhoods of the central city.[16]

By 1955, on the 20th anniversary of night baseball in the major leagues, there was a changing of the guard among baseball executives, and consequently in policy related to night baseball. Both Connie Mack and Clark Griffith, once the leading advocates for night games in the American League, left club ownership and died in the mid–1950s. Larry MacPhail, the night-baseball pioneer in the National League and avowed night-game minimalist, had been out of baseball ownership for half a dozen years. Walter O'Malley, owner of the Brooklyn Dodgers, replaced these gentlemen as the chief architect of philosophy regarding night baseball.

MacPhail, never bashful in expressing his opinions, continued to pontificate his thesis about the economic merits of night baseball, which he felt were best served by a 14-game maximum each season. "The big league clubs are overdoing it and creating problems they never had before. I didn't think greedy club owners would take it to such lengths," MacPhail remarked in a 1955 interview about clubs greatly exceeding his night-game limit. "That would add the equivalent of 14 Sundays to each club's home schedule and they would all get fat. But they wanted to gorge themselves and look what happened." MacPhail believed ball-club owners were now in an entirely different business. "When they expanded this thing to stage as many as 45 night games in some parks, they went out of the baseball business and into the show business. Now they're learning what it's like to be in show business." No doubt shaking his head as he said it, MacPhail concluded, "They dissipated the pulling power of night ball as a novelty by pouring it on."[17]

"It is economics," O'Malley defended the proliferation of night baseball. "We cannot retreat, whatever our sentiment may be for the day game. The turnouts [for night games] are still better than corresponding day crowds." The multiple for

Ticket stubs like this one from a 1957 night game at Ebbets Field (the N watermark signifies a night game) became collector's items when Walter O'Malley, owner of the Brooklyn Dodgers, moved the ball club to Los Angeles for the 1958 season, where he escalated the scheduling of night games to 63 games for the 1959 season.

a night game in 1955 was generally three times the size of a day crowd. Nearly half of the 1955 attendance at major-league games (47 percent) came from night games, which represented just 36 percent of all ball games. For some clubs, night games were essential to survival. In Philadelphia and St. Louis, more than two-thirds of the club's attendance came from night games, at 72 percent and 68 percent, respectively.[18]

MacPhail was right in that night games needed to be seen as special, but not in his narrow sense of their comparison to daylight baseball. Instead, in a broader perspective, baseball itself, whether by night or by day, now needed to be seen as special compared to all the other alternatives available to Americans in the Eisenhower era. "Baseball is no longer the national pastime, but just another form of entertainment that must compete for the consumer's dollar with horse racing, the theatre and air-conditioned movies," Murray Schumach observed in 1955, "or to the increasing desire of Americans to spend their leisure time at golf, fishing, swimming, driving, or home carpentry."[19]

O'Malley was also correct in his economic assessment, because night baseball was now the new normal for the operation of a ball club. Baltimore and Kansas City both booked more than 40 night games for the 1957 season, to become the top nocturnal schedulers in the American League. St. Louis, Cincinnati, and Philadelphia also slated more than 40 night games in the National League. Detroit and Boston were the last holdouts for MacPhail's 14-game maximum for night games, as both clubs (and the New York Yankees) maintained a sizeable audience of businessmen to stage numerous daylight games during the workweek through the 1956 season. However, when the Detroit ball club was sold in 1956 to settle the estate of deceased owner Walter Briggs, the new owners announced that the Tigers would host 21 night games in the 1957 season. Boston Red Sox owner Tom Yawkey then approved a schedule of 18 night games.[20]

Ball clubs took action to make their night games more suburban-spectator friendly. Several clubs moved up the start of their night games to 8:00 rather than the traditional 8:30 start, so that suburban fans could return home at a more convenient time to get some sleep before going to work the next morning. The Boston Red Sox offered "Family Night" promotions in 1956 against weaker opposition, such as Kansas City on July 17 and Baltimore on August 8. The Chicago White Sox, under new owner Bill Veeck, famously staged various group nights with reduced admission for teachers, cab drivers, and transit workers. The Brooklyn Dodgers had the most novel strategy, scheduling seven night games to be played at Roosevelt Stadium in Jersey City, New Jersey, as a supplement to the 30 night games planned for their regular ballpark, Ebbets Field.[21]

Small changes in the staging of premium daylight games began to emerge during the mid–1950s, led by the St. Louis Cardinals, now owned by August Busch, who also owned the Anheuser–Busch brewery. In 1955 the Cardinals decided not to host a holiday doubleheader, "as one oddity in the schedule shows Cincinnati in St. Louis for a single game on Labor Day." This single game began a trend for ball clubs to forego playing a holiday doubleheader, which soon led to clubs staging their single holiday game as a night game. In 1956 the Cardinals reinstituted their former policy of playing their home-opener as a night game, which cleared the way for other ball clubs to modify their game-time policy for opening day. This trend established another night-baseball oxymoron: night game on opening day.[22]

For the 1958 season, New York City was no longer a three-club city as both the Dodgers and the Giants relocated to the West Coast, to Los Angeles and San Francisco, respectively. This left Chicago as the only multi-club city in the major leagues. Owners

O'Malley and Horace Stoneham were the first to galvanize the new boosterism to their club's benefit as the move of their clubs to the West Coast was premised on public funding to assist in the building of a new ballpark. The national pastime component took a back seat to a new gold-rush attitude of a city to be considered "big league" (or to retain that status) through the use of public money to fund a sports stadium.

This next wave of club relocations dramatically accelerated the growth of night base-ball, which changed the perception of the sport on the East Coast, since results of the West Coast night games that started at 8:00 Pacific time rarely made the morning news-papers in the Eastern Time Zone. Both the Dodgers and Giants maintained their 1957 night-game policies for the 1958 season, when they began staging ball games in their temporary home ballparks, Seals Stadium for the Giants and the Los Angeles Coliseum for the Dodgers. The Giants planned to hold just 21 night games in 1958, maintaining a sizeable daylight calendar, while the Dodgers carded double that number with 42 night games on the schedule. Both clubs, though, encountered lighting challenges in their tem-porary ballparks.[23]

There were several issues with the night games in San Francisco at Seals Stadium, where the existing minor-league lighting system was sub-standard for major-league play. Even with the addition of several banks of lights, shadows still cropped up in the out-field. The weather was also a persistent concern, due to the traditionally cool evenings that occurred in the City by the Bay. At the first night game on April 16, 1958, "expe-rienced sportsgoers came with overcoats, sweaters and blankets for temperatures that dropped well below 50 degrees." San Francisco would turn out to be a leader throughout the 1960s in scheduling daylight games, particularly after the Giants moved into Candle-stick Park in 1960 where the wind made night games especially cold during mid-summer evenings. This weather phenomenon reduced turnout there for night games, despite the state-of-the-art lighting system engineered by Westinghouse to deliver 400 million can-dlepower of light to illuminate the playing field from the 1,417 floodlights atop the eight towers encircling the ballpark.[24]

The Los Angeles Coliseum was constructed as a football stadium (and venue for the 1932 Olympic Games), which resulted in a very odd layout for baseball, asymmetrical to say the least. O'Malley shoehorned a baseball field onto the gridiron by having a tiny left field (with a 40-foot-high fence to prevent easy home runs) and an expansive right field. While the Coliseum had an enormous seating capacity of 95,000 people, most of the seat-ing for baseball games was located far from the infield diamond, requiring occupants to bring binoculars to get the best glimpse of the action. Because the lighting system at the Coliseum was only sufficient for football games, the Dodgers had to install addi-tional light towers with several banks of light to adequately illuminate their night games there. An additional challenge was that all the seats in the Coliseum were in the open air, as there was no roof. While this was fine for football games played in the cool autumnal weather, it was a distinct problem for daylight baseball games played during the hot sum-mer months.[25]

O'Malley, as he moved forward to build Dodger Stadium on the Chavez Ravine land, increased the schedule of night games at the Coliseum, given the uncovered nature of the seating there and the cool summer nights that prevailed following the hot afternoons in the city. For the 1959 season, O'Malley scheduled the Dodgers for the then-radical level of 63 night games, which included the club's home opener and its two holiday dates. The Dodgers slated just 14 daylight games, 13 on Sunday (11 single games and one

The Los Angeles Dodgers initially played their home games at the Los Angeles Coliseum, where the ball club tolerated an inferior playing surface (note the extremely constrained left-field area) laid over a football gridiron. However, the 95,000-person seating capacity at the Coliseum produced huge attendance figures for the voluminous night-game schedule of the Dodgers (courtesy ievenlostmycat).

doubleheader) and one on a weekday (Tuesday afternoon, September 15, against Milwaukee). Getaway days were generally not a scheduling issue for the Dodgers, since visiting clubs traveling east usually had an off-day before their next ball game. However, the Braves had a daylight game on September 16 in San Francisco, which precipitated the day game at the Coliseum on September 15.[26]

There was also one unplanned daylight game played by the Dodgers at the Coliseum in 1959, when Los Angeles and Milwaukee finished in a tie for first place in the National League standings. The second playoff game for the league championship was at the Coliseum on September 29, when the Dodgers defeated the Braves in extra innings to advance to the World Series. This game was an extension of major-league baseball's all-daylight postseason policy, which did not consider night games to be appropriate for the determination of a championship.

The Dodgers 63-game night calendar for the 1959 season set the pace for change in two of the three premium daylight playing dates. Relocated clubs and the soon-to-be-minted expansion clubs were more amenable to foregoing tradition on the premium daylight dates, because the audience in those new big-league cities were not nearly as wedded to traditions established by the mores of the owners of the Original Sixteen clubs. While Sunday remained a sacred daylight-only playing date, change occurred in the staging of opening day and holiday games as night games.

In 1959 the Dodgers were one of three ball clubs to conduct their home-opener as a night game rather than the traditional afternoon daylight game. The other two opening-day night games in 1959 were played in St. Louis and Philadelphia, which also had the distinction of being the earliest night games (by calendar date) ever played in the major leagues. The Dodgers also slated a night game on two holidays in 1959, Memorial Day and Labor Day, while the Philadelphia Phillies hosted a night game on the Independence Day holiday. More ball clubs would soon arrange night games for their season-opening home game and holidays. By 1959 the holiday schedule had already gravitated away from doubleheaders, which now comprised just half the usual holiday calendar, with single games comprising the other half.

By substantially breaching the previous 50-game upper bound on night games, O'Malley was a trailblazer who motivated other ball clubs to expand their night-game schedules. By the end of the 1960 season, the 25th anniversary of night baseball in the majors, nearly one-half of all games (49.4 percent) were conducted as night games, up substantially from the one-third of all games played at night in 1952.

For the 1960 season, the three-tier pattern among ball clubs in their night-game scheduling was still in place, but the volume of games had adjusted upward. In the National League, the Dodgers were alone in the top tier with 64 night games. However, there was a robust middle tier with five clubs: Philadelphia (52), St. Louis (48), Cincinnati (45), Pittsburgh (42), and Milwaukee (38). San Francisco was the lone minimalist with 23 night games. In the American League, Baltimore and Kansas City were in the top tier, with 59 and 55 night games, respectively. The middle tier was inhabited by three clubs: Washington (45), Cleveland (35), and Chicago (34). The traditional minimalists continued to be Detroit (24), New York (22), and Boston (19).[27]

The time-of-day model by 1960, in round numbers, had gravitated to 50 percent night games and 50 percent daylight games, just 25 years since home-club scheduling, except for the Cincinnati Reds, was 100 percent daylight. The Los Angeles Dodgers were in the extreme of time-of-day scheduling, with its 82 percent night games and 18 percent daylight games (nearly all on Sunday). For the average ball club in 1960, the 50 percent of daylight games broke down approximately into one-half Sunday games, one-quarter Saturday games, and one-quarter weekday (including holiday and opening-day games).

All the changes in major-league baseball during the 1950s, including the explosion of activity in night baseball, occurred when the club owners were relatively unrestrained by the laissez-faire attitude of Commissioner Frick, who had replaced Happy Chandler as baseball commissioner in 1951. Frick held a weak hand on the tiller in contrast to his predecessors, Judge Landis who held a firm grip on baseball and Chandler who actively (but unsuccessfully) tried to do what he thought was best for the baseball business.

Frick infamously characterized most baseball-related issues as a "league matter" in order to avoid public meddling. Even when he dove into weighty matters, he informed rather than suggested action. Frick's biographer John Carvalho illustrated this tepidness by citing the 1954 example of Frick telling the club owners there were three important long-term challenges: "financial, with related discussion of relocation and expansion; the minor-league problem; and radio and television." Carvalho, in describing Frick's subsequent words on those substantive issues, wrote: "Addressing all three, Frick did not provide much guidance, but did cite geographic data and minor-league franchise survey results to the owners." When it came to baseball being the national pastime, Frick was quick to validate that impression. "I look upon this job as the protection and fostering of a great American institution," he said in 1956. "Baseball is not only organized baseball; it's much broader than that. And it is, emphatically, the American national pastime." Others, though, had a different perspective on the future of baseball.[28]

"The national pastime has lost some of its old magic along with paying spectators," Roger Kahn wrote in his 1959 essay "Something's Changing About Baseball" published in the *New York Times*. "The game is not in danger of extinction, but neither is it likely ever again to dominate a great portion of our national scene." Kahn blamed televised baseball, with its "mixed mission of reporting and of selling beer," as the culprit. "By televising indiscriminately, baseball has made itself infinitely available," Kahn espoused, which he believed "has cooled the love affair between the public and the game" and made the trip to the ballpark, once a highly-sought adventure, now only happenstance when the television needed to be repaired.[29]

Unfortunately, the national pastime was all but mythology by the late 1950s, even though baseball still nominally held that title. In 1960 the Gallup Poll surveyed Americans about their favorite sport and found baseball to be number one, at 34 percent, but with football gaining popularity, at 21 percent. Since the initial survey on the topic in 1948, the gap in the Gallup Poll results between the top two sports had narrowed by nine percentage points, from 22 points in 1948 to 13 points in 1960. In truth, the gap was accelerating to zero, not just narrowing.[30]

The aspirations differed between pro football and pro baseball. Major-league baseball had an enduring attachment between its clubs and their local populations, which caused the club owners to be more interested in local fan loyalty and local broadcast rights than any national viewpoint. The NFL, trying to gain a profitable foothold in the more leisure-oriented society of the 1950s, was more amenable to national exposure. Baseball's fruitful "early prototype" for success, though, was not the "modern prototype" for a successful major league. According to Eric Leifer in his book *Making the Majors: The Transformation of Team Sports in America*, the NFL "sought to capture the involvement of national publics," not just the local publics in team cities, by actively courting broadcasting rights fees from television networks.[31]

Twenty years after the New Deal altered the American nation by transforming a society based on individualism into one based largely on collectivism, the same ideology played out in the 1950s between baseball and football. The baseball business was rooted in individualism, while the football business was based on collectivism. Television money would drive a wedge between the two sports, and their respective followers, during the 1960s.

Football was the sport of national television, which enhanced its popularity following the exciting 1958 NFL championship game when the Baltimore Colts defeated the New York Giants in an overtime victory. Ironically, that game was played at Yankee Stadium, with the football gridiron laid out over the baseball field. Many ball-club owners viewed the rental of their ballparks in the fall to NFL teams as supplemental revenue to increase their profits, tragically missing the angle that they were enabling the competition to surpass their sport in popularity.

National television exposure skyrocketed after that 1958 NFL title game, which is universally acclaimed to be either the "greatest game" or the "best game ever" in NFL history. That's not just because it was a thrilling game or that 40 million people watched it on black-and-white TV. "The NFL had staged a championship contest that was more than just another game," John Eisenberg wrote in his history of the NFL. "It had been a dramatic, unpredictable spectacle, just as compelling on television as it was in person."[32]

The suspense of live-action drama on television, with its do-or-die nature, completely changed the nature of championship games in sports, especially when football's one-game, three-hour spectacle was compared to baseball's week-long, multi-game encounter in the World Series. "In the 1958 title game, pro football had arrived as a viable alternative to baseball, not merely as the most popular sport, but the one that best defined America," Michael MacCambridge wrote in his book *America's Game: The Epic Story of How Pro Football Captured a Nation*. While baseball's survival-of-the-fittest approach to a league championship appealed to self-made men who had built a successful business, the corporate Organization Man enjoyed the do-or-die approach of the football playoffs.[33]

Major-league baseball had a hard time jettisoning its local nature to adopt a national perspective to fully embrace the money-making potential of its civic/profit business basis, since to do so required dropping individualism and accepting collectivism. With the 1961 passage of the federal Sports Broadcasting Act, the NFL took full advantage of the law's provision to legalize revenue-sharing of national-television money among a league's clubs to leverage the 87 percent of households that now owned a television set. Baseball club owners were content with their individual local-TV broadcasting revenue.

National television was one of several boundaries that major-league baseball had to breach in the 1960s in its quest to optimize the use of night baseball to further the business basis of its ball clubs.

◆ 15 ◆

Pushing Boundaries

Night games represented one-half of all major-league ball games played in 1961, crossing an invisible threshold that firmly established night baseball as the dominant mode of conducting professional baseball. During the decade of the 1960s, ball-club owners tested several other boundaries, both geographic and philosophical, to further expand the role of night games within the business of baseball.

Expansion of the two major leagues from eight to ten clubs in 1961 and 1962 was the first planned attempt to broaden the geographic reach of major-league baseball to cities outside its historical footprint in the Northeast and Midwest. However, it was a half-hearted effort, since each league positioned one of its two expansion clubs to make amends for relocations that had vacated the nation's capital and downsized the nation's most highly populated metropolis to a one-club city.

The American League, under the direction of new league president Joe Cronin, re-established a club in Washington for the 1961 season, since the Senators had relocated to Minneapolis to become the Minnesota Twins, enticed by the recently built Metropolitan Stadium in suburban Bloomington. The National League returned a ball club to New York City for the 1962 season, as the Mets filled the void left by the departed Dodgers and Giants to play in the soon-to-be-constructed Shea Stadium in the borough of Queens. Since the American League also moved into Los Angeles in 1961 to make it a two-club city, the addition of Houston (the nation's seventh largest city) to the National League in 1962 was the only "new city" to enter major-league baseball via expansion among the several cities seeking "big league" status.

With the baseball calendar expanded to a 162-game schedule from its former 154-game schedule, the perspective on night baseball by the two new ball clubs in each league could not have been more polar, since pairs of prolific and minimalist clubs produced an offsetting effect vis-à-vis incremental night baseball. In 1961 in the American League, the Los Angeles Angels carded 60 night games on its schedule, while the Minnesota Twins were minimalist with 32 night games. In 1962 in the National League the Houston Colts scheduled a league-high 62 night games while the New York Mets carded a league-low 23 night games. The Mets, who temporarily used the Polo Grounds until the club's new ballpark was completed in 1964, continued the tradition of daylight baseball games that the Stoneham family had pursued when the Giants called New York home.[1]

Night baseball did play a prominent role in scheduling during the early expansion years through the deployment of twi-night doubleheaders. The Angels, the only American League club on the West Coast, often needed to book twi-night doubleheaders to make the travel gymnastics work for the visiting club leaving Los Angeles on getaway day.

For example, on Friday, May 19, 1961, there was a twi-night doubleheader in Los Angles between the Angels and the Chicago White Sox, followed by an open date on Saturday to enable the White Sox to traverse the 3,000 miles and three time zones to get to Boston for a Sunday afternoon game on May 21. The schedule-maker tried to card an off-day following the California visit or have the club travel to the closest league locations of Kansas City or Minneapolis for the next series, but this was not always possible.

By 1963 there were two dozen twi-night doubleheaders on the American League schedule, as *The Sporting News* remarked, "The twi-night doubleheader, which was once a contrivance used only when other efforts to reschedule a game failed, now appears as a standard part of the American League summer." The Angels and Senators each carded five twi-nighters in 1963, with six other clubs booking at least one. Both games of a twi-night doubleheader were now counted as night games, rather than one game being tabulated as daylight as was often done in the 1950s, which added to the growth of night baseball in a numerical manner (any game that started at 6:00 or later) beyond its structural impact.[2]

One philosophical boundary that geographic expansion exacerbated was the use of publicly-operated stadiums by the Mets at Shea Stadium and by the expansion Senators at District of Columbia Stadium in Washington, the first of the so-called "concrete doughnut" multi-purpose stadiums. Baseball had a difficult time sharing with football the newfound public boosterism, because the politics of publicly-operated stadiums favored football, which increasingly was the public's favorite sport. "So it was not surprising that stadiums built for both baseball and football were almost without exception round and large, huge concrete doughnuts surrounded by acres of parking lots," Paul Goldberger wrote in his architectural treatise *Ballpark: Baseball in the American City*. Concrete-doughnut stadiums generally had spectator sight lines that favored football over baseball. In the 1970s these stadiums also tended to install artificial turf rather than grass, which again favored football over baseball. Dodger Stadium in Los Angeles, which opened in 1962, was purely a baseball stadium and thus offered a different spectator experience.[3]

One benefit of the new wave of stadium construction was improved lighting systems for night games. When the Mets moved into Shea Stadium for the 1964 season, the ballpark had the new lighting technology of mercury-vapor lights in combination with incandescent floodlights. Mercury-vapor lamps produce light by passing an electric arc through vaporized mercury under high pressure. In a way, baseball had returned to its past, since arc lights had been used in the 1909 and 1910 experiments with artificial lighting to stage night baseball games before scientists had sufficiently improved the technology of incandescent lighting. Mercury-vapor lamps were more efficient than incandescent ones, with a longer lifetime and higher intensity, but they also emitted light that had a bluish tint rather than pure white. The lamps also required a five-minute warm-up period before reaching their full intensity.[4]

Houston played an important role in the history of night baseball as the first ball club to break the philosophical barrier of conducting night games on Sunday, the last of the three premium daylight dates to convert to night baseball. National League club owners approved this once-sacrilegious scheduling technique, not just because of the intense summer heat in Houston, but also due to the health hazard posed by the club's use of a temporary ballpark that lacked a roof to cover the seating area. A Sunday doubleheader on June 10, 1962, against the Dodgers drew a capacity crowd to Colt Stadium, where 78 people were treated for heat prostration, one umpire was incapacitated, and pitcher Don

Drysdale lost 12 pounds due to the heat and humidity of the 90-degree temperature that afternoon. At a special meeting of the National League club owners in late July, the Houston Colts received permission to play Sunday night games during the 1963 season and start their Sunday games at 4:00 in the afternoon for the remainder of the 1962 season.[5]

For the 1963 season, Houston scheduled 69 night games in total, with seven slated for Sunday evening. For the 1964 season, Houston went all-out with night baseball, scheduling 77 night games, the most ever by a major-league ball club. There were just four daylight games on the Houston schedule, one on a Sunday early in the season and the other three on Saturday getaways days. During the 1964 season, the Houston Colts became the first major-league club to conduct night home games on all three premium daylight dates of opening day, holiday, and Sunday. When the ball club moved into its new domed stadium in 1965 and renamed itself as the Astros, the club maintained a hefty night-game schedule but discontinued the Sunday night games since the Astrodome was an air-conditioned facility. Fittingly, the 1965 home-opener in the Astrodome was a night game.[6]

Because the 1949 National League rule limiting home-club control of night baseball to just five games with each club was still in effect, the other nine league clubs would have had to consent to Houston's prolific night-game schedule for games in excess of five. It is unclear when the National League extinguished this night-baseball restriction and adopted the unlimited policy used by the American League since the 1952 season. The visiting-club consent limitation does not seem to have hindered clubs in the National League from conducting more than 45 night games in a season, given the hefty schedule of the Houston ball club and numerous other clubs during the 1960s that carded more than 50 night games in a season.[7]

By 1964, to better accommodate suburban attendees, ball clubs now generally started night games at 7:30 or earlier rather than at 8:00 or later. In Kansas City, "the Athletics have changed their starting times for night games to 7 o'clock through the week and 6 o'clock on Saturdays," to allow the large number of spectators that travel 50 or more miles to the ballpark to return earlier to their homes in the Missouri and Kansas countryside.[8]

In addition to the earlier start time for night games, Charlie Finley, who now owned the Kansas City ball club following the death of previous owner Arnold Johnson, pursued a number of non-conventional promotions to try to fill ballpark seats beyond the nearly ubiquitous Bat Day giveaway. The bombastic Finley outfitted the team in colorful uniforms (Kelly green and Fort Knox gold), gave newly acquired pitcher Jim Hunter a fictitious nickname (Catfish), and put a live mule (named Charlie O.) in a petting-zoo area at the ballpark. Ever the salesman, Finley also created numerous promotions for night games, such as Farmers Night where the ballplayers participated in cow-milking contests. The Kansas City A's had just a short-term future, though. Finley actively courted several cities that sought to become "big league," including Dallas–Fort Worth and Oakland, but was forced by the American League to commit to Kansas City through the 1967 season before the club encamped to Oakland.[9]

One great idea by Finley failed to capture the imagination of his fellow club owners. In the fall of 1964 Finley pitched the idea of playing World Series games at night, based on the disconnect between "the working man who supports baseball throughout the entire [regular] season" and the vastly different audience for the weekday afternoon games of the World Series. "We are going to stage it at the most inconvenient and unreasonable time for you to see it [on television]," Finley wrote about the situation to Commissioner

Night baseball made significant inroads into premium daylight playing dates during the 1960s, particularly for opening day of the season, where the pre-game introduction of ballplayers now occurred less often in afternoon daylight, such as this opening day scene at DC Stadium in Washington (Library of Congress, Prints & Photographs Division, LC-DIG-ds-04926).

Frick. "We are going to start it on Wednesday afternoon when you are working at the steel mills, coal mines, factories, or offices. You can get the details when you get home from work."[10]

The concept of World Series night games was well ahead of its time, despite the logic in Finley's argument. First, he confronted the long-standing national pastime attitude of most club owners that drove the all-daylight presentation of the World Series. Second, there was little money for the owners in making the change to night games, because the bulk of the television money from the World Series (and All–Star Game) was pre-destined to the players' pension fund. This reality began with the 1954 deal orchestrated by Frick and was reinforced in 1960 when Frick negotiated an extension of the television contract with NBC to broadcast baseball's two premier events from 1962 through 1966. Third, there was little interest by the television networks, which were very content with the money they made from their evening programming on weekday nights, which would be disrupted by night World Series games.[11]

John Fetzer, owner of the Detroit Tigers, was more successful in his pursuit of national television exposure for night games played during the regular season. In 1963, Fetzer headed a committee of club owners set up to negotiate baseball's first national television contract in light of the 1962 deal between CBS and the NFL to telecast weekly pro football games and share the $4.6 million in annual revenue equally among all the league clubs, as now legally permitted under the Sports Broadcasting Act of 1961. The challenge for the baseball committee was to do a national deal but yet protect the local television revenue of the ball clubs.[12]

While baseball had a national television contract for the World Series and All–Star Game, the national Game of the Week telecasts then were a mishmash of deals negotiated between TV networks and individual ball clubs. These Saturday afternoon ball games had limited national exposure because the telecasts were blacked out in most major cities, as a tariff to protect the local TV deals of the ball clubs. With the games seen largely just in rural areas of the country, the Game of the Week telecasts produced meager overall revenue. Fetzer looked to remediate this problem by copying the concept of the CBS football deal.

During 1963 and 1964, Fetzer pitched all three television networks on the idea of a "Monday Night Baseball Spectacular," so named because the network would be broadcasting an exclusive ball game. The plan involved limiting major-league scheduling to just two ball games, the national telecast and a standby game in case of weather issues, with all the other clubs idle and no local black-outs. Fetzer believed his idea would fetch $20 million in national television revenue over a three-year period, to provide about $350,000 annually to each ball club. However, the idea was stillborn, because no network was interested in this experiment of delivering sports during the prime-time hours of evening television.[13]

"Fetzer pushed boldly to stretch baseball's boundaries with television further than anyone imaged," Dan Ewald wrote in his biography *John Fetzer: On a Handshake*. "Although it achieved only fragmentary success, his dream for a network prime-time Monday Night Baseball Spectacular never quite developed into the image he had envisioned." Fetzer had to settle for a $5 million deal with ABC to televise a national Game of the Week on Saturday afternoons during the 1965 season, with an option for the network to continue the deal for a second season in 1966. While Fetzer did arrange "the first regular-season share-the-wealth television plan" for major-league baseball, his Monday night baseball idea took a few more years before it came to fruition.[14]

Baseball's Game of the Week national TV deal, though, paled in comparison to the CBS football deal for NFL games consummated earlier in 1964, which paid the NFL club owners a combined $14 million each year. This translated into $1 million annually for each NFL club, more than double what baseball owners received from the Game of the Week deal. This was one of the first public indications that football had surpassed baseball as the nation's favorite sport, a bitter conclusion for baseball ownership that had depended upon the national pastime concept being the foundation of their civic/profit business basis. By 1965 the approximate crossover point occurred in the Gallup Poll surveying of the nation's favorite sport, demonstrating that football was now the top sport. Although the follow-up to the 1960 survey did not occur until 1972, by then football had long been the nation's favorite sport, not baseball, 38 percent to 19 percent.[15]

Favorite sport was increasingly defined by people as watching it on national television, not by viewing the game in person at the ballpark. Baseball's local television contracts did fill the gap somewhat, but these deals, while remunerative to ball clubs (on average three times what they got from their share of the Game of the Week proceeds), did not provide a great deal of national prestige as a substitute for the waning belief in the national pastime concept.[16]

Football club owners had a collectivism attitude that largely directed their business philosophy, while baseball owners still were mostly motivated by individualism. The limited collectivism within baseball was a minority portion of the World Series television revenue and a small stake in the new Game of the Week television deal. This put baseball at a distinct disadvantage as the fortunes of its business were too dependent on ballpark spectators, whose employment nature and pursuit of the American Dream were more oriented to collectivism than individualism. Baseball was too slow to react to national television revenue becoming a major component of the business basis of all professional sports. Fortunately, night baseball would eventually be the catalyst for baseball's growth in national television revenue, but football had a big head start and baseball would always lag behind.

Television motivated the Milwaukee Braves, now owned by an investor group headed by William Bartholomay that had bought the club from Lou Perini in 1962, to relocate to Atlanta, Georgia, for the 1966 season. Television revenue, the local variety, spurred this relocation, since Atlanta was just the 24th largest city in the country, with a population barely larger than Kansas City. "No act of corporate boosterism, however, could compete with Atlanta's broadcast appeal," historian Glen Gendzel wrote in "Competitive Boosterism: How Milwaukee Lost the Braves," a journal article published in 1995. "Milwaukee's advertising market of 2.5 million television households halted at Chicago to the south, Minneapolis to the west, Canada to the north, and Lake Michigan to the east. Around Atlanta sprawled a seven-state empire of six million baseball-deprived households between the Atlantic Ocean and the Mississippi River." For its first season in Atlanta, the Braves negotiated a television deal worth five times what the club had commanded back in Milwaukee. Of course, night games were an essential ingredient to that television package.[17]

Walter O'Malley, who dabbled with the prospect of pay-TV, combated the decline of baseball as the national pastime by taking a different approach to the marketing of the Los Angeles Dodgers. He saw Los Angeles as a way to market baseball that was not focused on winning games, but as entertainment, where "an enjoyable ballpark experience could outweigh the outcome of the game itself," with "the final score only part of the value his customers would receive for their money." As history professor Jerald Podair wrote in his book *City of Dreams: Dodger Stadium and the Birth of Modern Los Angeles*, Dodger Stadium offered "a day of excitement, fun, and adventure, even if the Dodgers lost the game." Using Disneyland as his model, O'Malley was engaged in marketing baseball, not just selling baseball. As a marketer, he also tried to appeal to every segment of the local population. Dodger Stadium was "class- and gender-inclusive," with design elements to attract the Mexican American community and women in addition to movie stars and males. Podair described O'Malley's ballpark as "a combination of a secular church where devoted Dodger fans came together in a common spirit and a theme park offering entertainment, fulfillment, and connection."[18]

By 1965, at the time of the 30th anniversary of night baseball in the majors, the term "night baseball" was now passé, used mostly in reference to its early years of adoption during the 1930s and 1940s. "Night game" was the common parlance now, although nicknames related to stadium lighting such as "arc ball" and "under the mazdas" persisted, vestiges of technical terms once used to define artificial lighting.

Night games were so common by 1965 that many newspapers in their game summaries just added the abbreviation "(n)" to differentiate them from their daylight brethren, rather than designate them by the complete term. The installation of lighting systems was no longer a highlight of articles discussing the amenities of new ballparks, with just very general reporting and no mention of the company that did the lighting engineering, which had occurred in the 1930s and 1940s when General Electric and Westinghouse were often noted prominently for their work in lighting installations. Subtle changes in night-game policy voted by the leagues now generally went unreported, even as both leagues tinkered with their night-game curfew rule during the decade.

Sportswriters lionized Larry MacPhail in 1965, three decades after he had brought night baseball into the major leagues. "Violent was the opposition from the horse-and-buggy thinkers in the room, but the persuasive MacPhail was in so desperate a monetary bind that the owners had little choice except to grant him reluctant permission," Arthur Daley wrote in the *New York Times*. "So the first night game in the majors took place in Cincinnati 30 years ago last week. It has revolutionized the sport." Even though there were now more night games than day games played in the majors (57 percent to 43 percent), MacPhail still insisted that "limitless after-dark play is a serious mistake and that its novelty appeal should have been preserved." However, there was no going backwards. Night baseball had enriched the club owners and transformed the structure of baseball, all because "MacPhail had the imagination and daring to propose a radical departure from all previous concepts." Beginning in 1966, night baseball also began to rescue the club owners by establishing a viable basis for them to sufficiently cash in on national television revenue.[19]

The national Game of the Week television deal fell apart after the 1965 season, when ABC declined its option to renew for the 1966 season, since the Saturday afternoon ball games were so unprofitable. NBC, which had the existing contract to televise the World Series and All-Star Game through the 1966 season, stepped in to take the Game of the Week telecasts for three years (1966 through 1968) as part of an extension into 1967 and 1968 of its existing television arrangement.[20]

To make the Game of the Week attractive to the television networks and more lucrative to the ball-club owners, Fetzer packaged together the World Series, All–Star Game, and Game of the Week into one deal. In essence, the business strategy was that networks would overpay for the Game of the Week in order to acquire rights to the World Series and All–Star Game, the only truly valuable baseball properties for national television.

In the combined deal worth a total of $30.6 million, NBC agreed to pay $12.6 million for two years of the World Series and All–Star Game (an average of $6.3 million each year) and $18 million for three years of the Game of the Week ($6 million each year). This was an absurdly high price for the rights to televise the demonstrably unprofitable Game of the Week property, making the price for the World Series and All–Star Game wildly undervalued. These reported figures likely were finagled beyond their true economic representation, since "the individual clubs will profit only from the game-of-the-week, because 95 percent of the All–Star Game and radio–TV receipts go to the player pension fund and 60 percent of the World Series radio–TV money goes into that fund."[21]

The possibility for night games in the Game of the Week package was a minor aspect of the public reporting of the virtually all-daylight television deal in an era when more than one-half of all ball games were played as night games. "Most 'game of the week' broadcasts next season, about 25 in all, will be presented on Saturday afternoons," the *New York Times* reported. "But Carl Lindemann Jr., vice president of sports for NBC, said he had agreed that NBC would carry some games on Monday, Tuesday, Wednesday or Thursday evenings. The number of night games is still to be determined, Mr. Lindemann said."[22]

NBC agreed to televise three night games during the 1966 season, on the Monday evenings of the Memorial Day, Independence Day, and Labor Day holidays. These night games, as well as the Saturday afternoon games, were broadcast in color, rather than black-and-white, to increase the demand to watch the ball games (among viewers who owned a color TV set) and hopefully make the Game of the Week a somewhat profitable venture.[23]

While the first nationally televised night baseball game was the game between the Braves and Dodgers on Monday, May 30, 1966, the Labor Day night telecast of the game between the Dodgers and Giants on Monday, September 5, 1966, drew what was then the largest national-television audience for a regular-season baseball game. The Labor Day game started at 4:00 West Coast time so that the national telecast could begin at 7:00 East Coast time, to capture the largest possible viewing audience across the entire country. Based on the early success of the televised night games in 1966, NBC decided to telecast three night games in 1967 as well as experiment with a night telecast of the All–Star Game via a late-afternoon start on the West Coast.[24]

This was the rather innocent beginning of night baseball on national television. While continuing to increase its share of the playing season, night baseball now began to serve a more important function to elevate the monetary value of national television contracts. The term "night game" soon needed to put into a pragmatic context of whether it was ballpark time (local time) or national-television time (East Coast time).

Lindemann is a little-recognized pioneer in the history of night baseball. Fetzer, as the other portion of this early nexus among baseball and television executives, can also be lauded for his contributions to initiate night games on national television. Fetzer, though, had a more important place in baseball history through his role in convincing the club owners to agree to equal sharing of the national television revenue, which eventually supplanted gate receipts as the foundation of the profit component within the baseball business basis.

It was Lindemann's deep understanding of the television business that enabled televised night baseball to gain some traction in the late 1960s. He began with dates that would least disrupt NBC's revenue stream from entertainment programming in the prime-time schedule, slotting the night games on dates that had lower natural audience levels and used little original programming. Lindemann first used holiday dates, then switched to weekdays during the June to August period of reruns of previous shows, to avoid interfering with the first-run entertainment during the lucrative September to May period. Given the seemingly inflated payment for the Game of the Week component of the package, Lindemann had the incentive to find ways to improve the profitability of televised baseball at night. Since NBC also had the contract to televise AFL football games, Lindemann had knowledge of the different audience dynamics for football relative to baseball.

In 1967 a Harris Poll indicated that baseball was still preferred over football (39 percent to 29 percent), but the poll's overall conclusion revealed a conflict vis-à-vis its potential for television revenue: "Although baseball leads overall, there are sharp differences by age and income. Baseball has lost out to football among young people and those with higher incomes." Only 25 percent of sports fans under age 35 preferred baseball (41 percent preferred "other" and 34 percent preferred football), while 55 percent of those age 50 or older preferred baseball. More devastating to baseball's comparable position to football was the income breakdown. Baseball was overwhelmingly popular with those having an income less than $5,000, while football was tops with those earning $10,000 or more. Based on these demographics, football was more profitable to the television networks than baseball, since advertisers were more interested in reaching younger people with a high income than older people with a low income.[25]

A greater homogenization of night-game scheduling among the ball clubs existed by 1967, the last season before a Basic Agreement with the Players Association, rather than the three-tier pattern that had evolved during the 1950s. Most clubs now had a hefty schedule (at least 45 night games) with a small group of clubs with a more conservative schedule (between 35 and 44 night games) and only one club booking less than 35 night games. Twi-night doubleheaders were extensively scheduled in the American League (nearly three dozen), while the National League carded a less prolific number of twin bills involving a night game.

Seven of the ten clubs in the National League were hefty schedulers, led by Houston (63) and Philadelphia (62) and including Atlanta (59), Los Angeles (59), St. Louis (58), Pittsburgh (51), and Cincinnati (50). There was one more conservative club, the New York Mets (44), and one minimalist club in the San Francisco Giants (23). The Chicago Cubs remained an all-daylight ball club at home. The American League had five hefty schedulers, led by California (63) and Baltimore (58) and followed by Washington (51), Kansas City (48), and Detroit (47). There was an equally sized more conservative grouping, comprised of New York (43), Cleveland (41), Chicago (39), Boston (39), and Minnesota (38).[26]

By 1967 one-third to one-half of the premium daylight dates on the holidays and opening day were conducted as night games. Atlanta, Los Angeles, and Philadelphia in the National League and California and Kansas City in the American League were frequent night-game hosts on these dates.

Although the ratio of night games played during the regular season had risen to 58 percent in 1967 from 51 percent in 1961, baseball's marquee events, the All–Star Game and World Series, continued to be conducted as daylight games. Converting these super-premium daylight playing dates into a night-time extravaganza was a huge philosophical barrier for major-league baseball to abandon. The All–Star Game was the first to break the night-game barrier when the 1967 event was played at Anaheim Stadium in suburban Los Angeles, the home ballpark of the California Angels.

"The game will be the first in All–Star history to be beamed at an evening television audience over much of the United States," the *New York Times* reported. "It will begin at 4:15 Pacific daylight time, which will be 7:15 and 'prime time' on the Eastern seaboard." The evening telecast of the 1967 All–Star Game was not only a ratings hit on the East Coast. When the game lasted 15 innings, the telecast was also a prime-time event on the West Coast.[27]

The ratings bonanza associated with the telecast of the 1967 All–Star Game encouraged Lindemann at NBC to arrange for a true night-game telecast of the 1968 game to be played at the Astrodome in Houston. The promotional efforts for the 1968 game focused on it being the first All–Star Game to be played indoors, with little note that it was the first All–Star Game played as a night game since the wartime contests during World War II. Beginning with the 1969 event, the All–Star Game was always scheduled to be a night game, a policy only interrupted by the rainout of the 1969 All–Star Game in Washington.[28]

Soon after the 1967 All–Star Game, Fetzer and the television committee quietly announced a three-year extension of the NBC television contract to cover the 1969 through 1971 seasons worth $50 million. The deal provided for 28 weekly Game of the

The Astrodome in Houston was the site of the first All-Star Game played as a night game since World War II. The air-conditioned indoor stadium, which made Sunday night games at Colt Stadium obsolete, conducted a full six-day slate of night games on Monday through Saturday (Library of Congress, Prints & Photographs Division, HAER TX-108–1).

Week telecasts each season, although no details were specified about the number of night games. NBC elected to stay with the three-game night schedule for 1969 and 1970, but moved off the holidays. "The problem on more [night] games is the movie schedule that our network is committed to for next year," Lindemann admitted about the challenge in 1970 to expand the Monday night baseball programming. NBC did bump the night calendar to five games for the 1971 season following ABC's successful introduction of its *Monday Night Football* show in the fall of 1970, which broke the ground for more sports to be televised in prime-time slots on national television.[29]

This new television deal coincided with the club owners breaking precedent to funnel to the players' pension plan 60 percent of the World Series television money and 95 percent of the All-Star Game television money. By creating an independent negotiation of a dollar amount to be the pension-plan contribution, this unilateral move allowed more television money to flow to the club owners. This came at the expense of enflaming the Players Association and its new executive director, Marvin Miller, who was then negotiating the first-ever collective bargaining agreement between the players and owners. The result was difficult labor relations, including work stoppages, over the next several decades as baseball's marriage to television, or at least its lust for television money, increasingly favored the quest to attract eye balls to the television screen rather than a focus on attracting spectators to the ballpark.

Additional national television revenue was generated by the second wave of expansion that occurred for the 1969 season, when the two major leagues enlarged from 10 to 12 clubs and adopted a two-division format. The expansion of the American League to add the Seattle Pilots (soon to move to Milwaukee) and Kansas City Royals (the Athletics had moved to Oakland) and the National League to add the Montreal Expos and San Diego Padres created the impetus to add another level of postseason play prior to the World Series, with the League Championship Series contested by the division winners. Three new cities were accorded "big league" status, the American cities of San Diego (18th largest) and Seattle (19th largest) and Canada's largest city, Montreal.

To enlarge the national broadcasting money, the club owners agreed to begin both the League Championship Series and the World Series on a Saturday. This upended the longstanding baseball philosophy to conclude the regular season on a Sunday (it now would end on a Thursday) and begin the World Series on the following Wednesday (it would now begin on a Saturday). The new symbiotic relationship between major-league baseball and television networks soon instituted more change to the postseason baseball landscape, when the World Series began its transformation from an all-daylight affair with its entrée in night baseball.

Expansion of the two major leagues in 1969 coincided with the installation of a new baseball commissioner, Bowie Kuhn, who would later be elected to the Baseball Hall of Fame, where his plaque in Cooperstown notes that he "introduced night-time baseball to the World Series" and "expanded television coverage with dual network broadcasts and a variety of baseball programming."

Kuhn signaled his intent to become the television commissioner when he immediately created the post of director of broadcasting in the commissioner's office. In his autobiography, Kuhn wrote that this job was designed "to use network television more effectively to stimulate increased interest in baseball and to increase the dollar value of network television." Kuhn hired Tom Dawson to fill this position, and acknowledged that "Tom was soon talking about the introduction of night games in the World Series" to accomplish both of those goals.[30]

Kuhn and Lindemann moved cautiously to introduce night baseball into the World Series, since the weather for a night game in mid–October in the northeastern portion of the country could be quite chilly, if not downright frigid conditions. Kuhn notified the club owners at the winter meetings in December 1970 that he and NBC were exploring the idea of having one night game played in the 1971 World Series.[31]

The decision was finalized in January 1971 and announced in a joint statement between the dynamic duo of night baseball on national television. "This innovation will make it possible for additional millions of fans to see baseball's annual postseason classic," Kuhn was quoted. "All of us at NBC feel certain that a World Series game at night bears witness to the increasing popularity of sports on nighttime television," Lindemann was quoted.[32]

Before the first night game in World Series history was even played, Kuhn and Lindemann negotiated a four-year extension to the existing NBC contract to cover the 1972 through 1975 seasons, which expanded the night baseball portion of televised coverage as one component of the $70 million deal. In May 1971 NBC and baseball announced that the three weekday games of the World Series would be conducted as night games beginning in 1972. In addition, the Game of the Week coverage would be expanded to 35 regular-season games, 10 as night games and the remaining 25 on Saturday afternoon. John Fetzer's original vision for a Monday Night Baseball Spectacular was inching closer to reality.[33]

"The new deal will mark the end of an era for a generation of men who annually either delay or stretched their lunch hours during the World Series for a glimpse of the daytime games," one writer observed. "Instead, they will have something to look forward to those nights." Indeed, the average working person now would be able to see every one of the seven possible games of the World Series, since the three weekday night games were book-ended by two weekends of afternoon games.[34]

Discussions with the other two national networks, ABC and CBS, seemed to provide the incentive for NBC to expand the Monday night baseball program to 10 games in 1972, up from five in 1971 and just three in 1970. Kuhn reportedly weighed splitting the television deal two or even three ways, "but we just couldn't work it out," Dawson told sportswriters. ABC seemed to be itching to apply its success with *Monday Night Football* to baseball telecasts on that evening during the summer months.[35]

The first postseason night game in major-league history was staged in the fourth game of the 1971 World Series on Wednesday, October 13, in Pittsburgh. When the television audience for that night game produced the highest rating ever for a televised evening sports event, the train started barreling down the track for night baseball to dominate the network television coverage and produce future contracts worth hundreds of millions of dollars to enrich the ball-club owners. Through its partnership with network television, baseball now clearly recognized that the sport had transcended into entertainment and that night baseball had far greater economic value than the daylight game.[36]

The television appetite for World Series night games accelerated after the 1975 World Series. When rain postponed all weekend attempts to play the sixth game in 1975, Kuhn arranged for that game to be played as a night game on Tuesday, October 21. Following an epic sixth game, which the Boston Red Sox won by a walk-off home run by Carlton Fisk in extra innings, the seventh game was played as a night game the following day. Therefore, five of the seven World Series games in 1975 were played at night.

Based on the phenomenal television ratings for the night games in the 1975 World Series, Kuhn then arranged for a Sunday game to be played as a one-year experiment in the 1976 World Series, to avoid competition on television with the afternoon NFL football games. He also introduced night baseball into the League Championship Series that year. However, there was very cold weather at the Sunday night game played in 1976 at Riverfront Stadium in Cincinnati.

Kuhn famously sat through the chilly weather at that night game, which some baseball writers labeled as "arctic," wearing just a sport coat in an attempt to visually portray that it was not that cold. "Everyone else who was shivering that Sunday night in Cincinnati was bundled in an overcoat, a parka or several sweaters," Dave Anderson of the *New York Times* later wrote. "But to Bowie Kuhn, if it was the World Series, it had to be warm." Secretly, though, Kuhn had on thermal underwear to stay warm. Anderson, tongue only partially planted in cheek, suggested that "his thermal underwear should be retired and sent to the Hall of Fame at Cooperstown," given Kuhn's role "as a TV producer who arranged for World Series games to be played in prime time."[37]

The idea of Sunday night games in the World Series was abandoned, temporarily. For the remainder of the 1970s and into the early 1980s, the only World Series games played at night were those played on weekdays, with daylight games played on Saturday and Sunday.

Despite the colder weather for night games in mid–October, major-league baseball was insatiably drawn by the money available from selling national television rights. "The networks were paying big money for postseason baseball; they demanded the best opportunity to maximize their audience," Walker and Bellamy wrote in *Center Field Shot: A History of Baseball on Television*. "The nighttime postseason was here to stay. More than ever, television was influencing baseball." Television revenue enabled the ball-club owners to elevate night baseball to its maximum level during the late 1970s.[38]

◆ 16 ◆

Maximizing Night Baseball

Night baseball reached a saturation point in the major leagues during the 1970s, at two-thirds of all games played in the regular season in 1979, up from a three-fifths ratio in 1969. The volume of night baseball conducted during the postseason had a greater impact to major-league baseball during the 1980s and 1990s, because it translated into rapidly rising national television revenue. Maximizing night baseball in the postseason became more important, which diminished the need for club owners to relentlessly hunt for additional night-game opportunities during the regular season.

During the 1970s, continued conversion of daylight games to night games occurred in the Monday-through-Saturday schedule as well as the three, once sacrosanct, premium daylight dates of holidays, opening day, and Sunday. Several broad trends defined this final push to the night-game saturation point for the regular season.

Early-season afternoon games conducted in cold-weather states were a ripe area for the conversion of daylight games, as clubs such as the New York Yankees, Boston Red Sox, and Minnesota Twins gradually relaxed their reluctance to stage night games in April. The American League expansion from 10 to 12 clubs in 1977 helped this trend. The Seattle Mariners, playing its games indoors at the Kingdome, had no reluctance to stage night games in April, although the Toronto Blue Jays, then playing outdoors in Canada's second-largest city, preferred daylight times for its home games in April.

Opening-day games increasingly were conducted as night games, especially in warm-weather cities inhabited by relocated or expansion clubs. The Houston Astros, California Angels, and San Diego Padres typically conducted their home openers as a night game. Among the old-guard clubs, the St. Louis Cardinals, the originator of the opening-day night game back in 1950, also often opened with a night game.

Saturday night games became more popular during the 1970s, especially in the summer months, when there was substantial competition from other entertainment options on Saturday afternoon. Expansion clubs in the West and relocated clubs in the South were most likely to stage Saturday night games. The Texas Rangers (the relocated expansion Washington Senators), Los Angeles Dodgers, and Atlanta Braves were heavy Saturday-night schedulers, in addition to the three clubs noted in the preceding paragraph that usually opened the home season at night.

Monday night games on national television increased in volume during the decade. NBC did 15 telecasts in 1975, five times the number in 1970. ABC acquired the rights to televise the Monday night games in the national television contract for the 1976 through 1979 seasons, which elevated the number of telecasts to 18 by the end of that deal.[1]

Doubleheaders on the day following a night game were prohibited in the 1970 Basic

Agreement negotiated between the club owners and the Players Association, headed by labor-negotiator Marvin Miller. This provision of the collective-bargaining agreement resulted in a substantial contraction in the volume of games conducted on premium daylight dates. Doubleheaders on holidays and Sunday converted to single games, with the aborted second game transferred to a normal weekday playing date and staged as a night game.[2]

The demise of the holiday doubleheader had already begun in the 1960s, and by 1967 one-half of the holiday calendar consisted of single games rather than twin bills. During the 1970s generally 75 percent of the holiday card was played as single games, with at least one-half staged at night rather than in daylight. Night games on the Independence Day holiday in steamy July were very popular in both relocated and expansion cities as well with old-guard clubs. In 1975 night games on the Fourth of July holiday were conducted by newcomers Oakland Athletics and Los Angeles Dodgers as well as by old-guard clubs Detroit Tigers and Cleveland Indians. Games on Memorial Day began to be treated as a normal playing date, when the Monday holiday law in 1971 shifted the celebration of Memorial Day from May 30 to the last Monday in May. By 1985 the holiday doubleheader would completely disappear from the major-league baseball schedule.[3]

Sunday doubleheaders became obsolete in the 1970s, as a response to the prohibition on doubleheaders following a Saturday night game but also because most local television contracts with ball clubs declined to telecast the second game, thereby reducing revenue to the ball club. By the mid–1970s big-market ball clubs such as the Boston Red Sox and Los Angeles Dodgers had abandoned the Sunday doubleheader. Following the negotiation of free-agent rights for ballplayers in the 1976 Basic Agreement, club owners accelerated the death of the doubleheader in order to have 81 single-admission home games to help pay the skyrocketing salaries that ballplayers now commanded in the era of free agency. By 1979 the Sabbath twin bill survived mostly at small-market ball clubs like the Pittsburgh Pirates, Cleveland Indians, and Oakland A's. There were less than a dozen Sunday doubleheaders on the major-league baseball schedule each year by the early 1980s.[4]

While the single daylight game on Sunday remained a fixture of the baseball schedule, there was also a modified attitude toward Sunday night games, which had not been conducted in the majors since 1964 when the Houston Colts staged an extensive number before moving into the Astrodome for the 1965 season. In 1972 the Texas Rangers initiated evening play on the Lord's Day with the club's July 16 game in its Arlington, Texas, ballpark. Even with late-afternoon start times for Sunday games in June, daylight baseball in the Dallas–Fort Worth area was just too hot for players and spectators (at the inaugural Sunday night game it had been 115 degrees during the afternoon). The Rangers conducted four Sunday night games in 1972 and then adopted the concept on a regular basis with the 1973 season. Several other ball clubs experimented with Sunday night games, indicating that the earlier church-centric prohibition on such scheduling no longer carried as much weight. The Atlanta Braves began to stage Sunday night games in 1976 and Seattle and Philadelphia also conducted them in 1980.[5]

Night-baseball pioneer Larry MacPhail died in October 1975, whose life paralleled the ascension of night baseball in the 1930s to its ultimate saturation point in the late 1970s. His death occurred a few months after the 40th anniversary of the arrival of night baseball in the major leagues, when newspapers heralded him as being personally responsible for its introduction through his convincing arguments to overcome the deep-seated objections of ball-club owners. Now four decades after its debut in Cincinnati in May

1935, night baseball had experienced a complete role reversal. In 1935 the daylight game was the norm and the night game was a novelty, whereas in 1975 the night game was the norm and the daylight game, other than on Sunday, was a novelty. MacPhail was posthumously inducted into the Baseball Hall of Fame in 1978, with the script on his plaque noting that he was a "dynamic, innovative executive" and "pioneered night baseball at Cincinnati in 1935; also installed lights at Ebbets Field and Yankee Stadium."[6]

Daylight games, so cherished by MacPhail to maintain the novelty of night baseball, had become an endangered species by the 1970s, although not quite on their way to extinction. Of course, the Chicago Cubs still played an all-daylight home schedule in Wrigley Field, where light towers remained non-existent. Sunday remained a premium daylight game date, as the large majority of games on Sunday were played in the afternoon, despite the inroads made by the Texas Rangers and other clubs that were Sunday-night experimenters. Saturday afternoon and a small selection of weekday daylight games were still popular in a few coastal cities, particularly with the San Francisco Giants, Oakland A's, and New York Mets.

However, the apparent inexorable disappearance of most daylight games from the baseball schedule was thwarted by the yeoman efforts of Marvin Miller, who tenaciously fought for improved working conditions for the ballplayers in his negotiations on behalf of the Players Association. In addition to negotiating contract provisions that restricted the club owners from excessive use of doubleheaders that involved night games (both twi-night and day-night varieties), Miller also was persnickety about negotiating the rules involving games on getaway days to minimize impact to the health of ballplayers. The getaway-day provision in the 1976 contract read: "Games shall not be scheduled or rescheduled to start later than 5 p.m. on a getaway day if either Club is required to travel for a day game, scheduled the next day, between cities in which the in-flight time is more than one and one-half hours." The getaway game date, which was a very small percentage of daylight games in the 1970s, became the one growth area of daylight ball games during the next several decades.[7]

As night baseball reached its saturation point for regular-season games during the 1970s, the bigger trend associated with night baseball was the rise in national television revenue. TV money changed the ratio of gate receipts to broadcasting fees within the profit component of the civic/profit business basis of major-league baseball, which made attracting spectators to the ballpark less of a consideration for the club owners. By the mid–1970s the civic/profit business balance had morphed into virtually a total focus on profit, with merely a when-needed usage of the civic component.

The civic component had substantially dropped in significance, now largely tied to big-league-city boosterism and lacking a helpful connection to the national pastime element, which had long been the cornerstone of the civic component. In the 1972 Gallup Poll survey of favorite sport, Americans preferred watching football as their favorite sport, by a 2-to-1 margin over baseball (38 percent to 19 percent). Basketball, now a close third to second-place baseball, was the pick of 10 percent of Americans polled. Ice hockey, at 5 percent, was gaining in popularity.[8]

During the 1970s the composition of the profit component changed fairly dramatically. Television revenue, both the club's share of the national television contract and the full amount of the club's local television and radio deals, grew rapidly and combined to approach the revenue produced by gate receipts, while the "other sources" such as concessions and parking grew in importance. In 1975 television money represented 25 percent of overall baseball revenue, for the average ball club, while 62 percent came from gate receipts and 13 percent from other sources. New national television contracts over the next dozen years would reverse this ratio.[9]

Commissioner Bowie Kuhn negotiated a two-network deal for national television rights for the 1976 through 1979 seasons, worth a combined $92 million to the club owners. With the decoupling of World Series and All–Star Game television revenue from the players' pension fund, the TV money from baseball's marquee events now inured wholly to the club owners. Each ball club received $0.9 million annually during the four years of the new contract, up from $0.7 million per year under the previous deal. The 1976–1979 contract was split between NBC and ABC, with the networks alternating postseason telecasts each year between the League Championship Series and World Series (as well as alternating the All–Star Game). ABC won the Monday night telecasts and NBC got the consolation prize of the Saturday afternoon Game of the Week telecasts.[10]

The increased television revenue came with strings, though, on the postseason scheduling. The most lucrative ball games to the networks were now the weekday night games, since they drew the largest audiences and thus generated the most lucrative commercial advertisements, compared to the weekend afternoon games that had to directly compete with college and pro football games. Kuhn revised the schedule for the World Series, beginning in 1977, so that the World Series started on a Tuesday. This ensured at least three night games would always be conducted, with a possibility of five night games if the series went the full seven games. The Saturday and Sunday games in daylight were now the fourth and fifth games of the World Series. The same logic applied for the best-of-five-games League Championship Series, which now also had staggered starts to minimize both leagues playing on the same day in order to optimize the number of televised night games in the prelude competition to the World Series.

The national television money rose exponentially thereafter. The four-year contract for the 1980 through 1983 seasons was worth $175 million to the club owners (doubling the annual per-club take to $1.8 million) and the six-year deal for the 1984 through 1989 seasons was worth a whopping $1.1 billion (quadrupling the annual per-club payment to $7.2 million). The billion-dollar television contract came with more postseason scheduling modifications, which saturated the postseason with night games as much as possible. Beginning with the 1985 World Series, all World Series games were conducted as night games, both weekday and weekend. The League Championship Series was also lengthened from a best-of-five-games contest to a best-of-seven-games match.[11]

One danger of this collaboration was that revenue associated with postseason telecasts now subsidized not just the Saturday edition of Game of the Week but also regular-season games in general. For the six-month regular season, this was a dangerous dependency upon a few weeks in autumn in the midst of the football season. This was the dark side of how night baseball influenced the financial underpinnings of baseball. Scholars still debate whether the relationship between television and sports has been symbiotic (each gaining something) or parasitic (television benefiting at the expense of sports).

The crossover point when television revenue exceeded gate receipts within the profit component of the business basis occurred in the mid–1980s for the big-market ball clubs and by the end of the 1980s for the average ball club, since the value of local television contracts varied widely according to the market size of the city where the ball club was located.

For the Boston Red Sox, the estimated crossover point was the 1984 season. Jack Craig, a Boston writer who specialized in sports media issues, estimated the club's revenue in 1983 from broadcasting contracts to be $6.0 million, comprised of $2.7 million from local TV, $1.5 million from local radio, and the $1.8 million per-club from national TV. The total media payments equaled about 60 percent of the club's projected $10.0 million in gate receipts in 1983, which Craig characterized as "the final one in which teams make more money from gate receipts than from television and radio." For the 1984 season, the total broadcasting revenue was anticipated to be $11.4 million, increased by the $7.2 million per-club network TV payment, which exceeded the club's projected revenue from gate receipts.[12]

By 1988, the composition of the average ball club's revenue was 42 percent from television, 40 percent from gate receipts, and 18 percent from other sources, according to the computations of economist Andrew Zimbalist in his treatise *Baseball and Billions: A Probing Look Inside the Big Business of Our National Pastime*.[13]

Night baseball, which had economically diversified the ballpark audience for weekday ball games in the 1950s and 1960s, now enabled an even broader diversification of viewership through local and national telecasts of ball games in the 1970s and 1980s. Shedding its earlier skepticism of the mass-market audience, baseball ownership now embraced the broad array of viewers, both at the ballpark and in front of the TV set, to fuel their business. Or at least they embraced the vast repository of revenue that flowed their way from their television contracts.

Changes in the postseason structure that accompanied the television money were designed to appeal more to the newest generations within the mass audience, which broadly shared little preference for baseball in contrast to their parents. In the 1990 Gallup Poll survey of favorite sport, football continued to be rated as America's favorite, still by a 2-to-1 margin over the next most popular sport (35 percent to 16 percent). However, baseball was now in a statistical tie for second place with basketball (16 percent to 15 percent) as the second most favorite sport. By the next such Gallup Poll in 2001, baseball decidedly would be America's third most favorite sport.[14]

Baseball was clearly at a disadvantage to football and basketball among younger adults. To the baby boomer generation born between 1946 and 1964, and those of the previous unnamed generation born between 1933 and 1945 who became adults in the postwar years, baseball was less appealing than it was to their parents, and didn't neatly integrate into their perspective of the American Dream as it had for their parents. This was understandable given the rise of income inequality during the 1980s that extinguished, to a large degree, the classic American Dream that through hard work, sacrifice, and initiative anyone could attain upward social mobility. Both generations had a change of heart in sports as well as in work.

Baseball rewarded hard work and individual responsibility for success, which equated with the changelessness within its heritage of the yeoman farmer and self-made business owner. Football, on the other hand, was industrial in nature, so it was more open to change to redeploy its collective, hierarchical effort to enhance the sport's competitiveness. "Change in the game of football is normal, natural, deliberate, and constant," Michael Mandelbaum wrote in his 2004 book *The Meaning of Sports*. "For football, unlike in baseball, change has a positive connotation. It is deemed progress." The wild card introduced into football's playoff format in 1970 was accepted as an improvement to the sport. Basketball was post-industrial in nature, based on knowledge (not land or capital), which had continuous action, unlike the sporadic action in football and baseball, and required on-the-fly decisions by players and less strategy by management. To the baby boomers and non-veterans in the previous generation that came of age in postwar America, football and basketball were much more akin to their life experiences than baseball.[15]

Boomers, the first generation to grow up with television, defined success in life differently than their parents did. To boomers the American Dream was less likely to mean "success is the end result of competitive (occupational) achievement" to be "measured by indexes of personal merit such as property and wealth and first-place ribbons." Instead, boomers embraced "success as a process of self-actualization in which one develops and utilizes physical, intellectual, and creative talents to become the best that one can be." Bettering yourself replaced striving to be the best. Boomers also applied this philosophy to sports.[16]

The championship structure of football and basketball, with many teams achieving "success" merely by qualifying for the playoffs to compete for the championship, was more appealing to boomers sitting in front of the television set than the mode of baseball, where just a few teams vied to be the sole team to achieve "success" by winning the World Series. The compelling action drama and suspense in football and basketball games attracted viewers to watch those games on television, while baseball struggled to attract a similar voluminous viewership for its less intense, slower-moving postseason contests.

With the business basis of a ball club increasingly driven by television revenue, night baseball overwhelmed the league schedules for the 1979 season. Of the 25 ball clubs that hosted night games (the Cubs were still all-daylight), all but one club scheduled at least one-half of their home games as night games (40 of the 81 home games). The exception was the San Francisco Giants, which scheduled only 36 night games for wind-swept Candlestick Park. The Texas Rangers with 75 night games and the Atlanta Braves with 73 night games were the top owl schedulers in each league. One-half of the ball clubs (14 of 25) planned to play at least 67 percent of their home games (54 or more) as night games.[17]

During the early 1980s, equilibrium was reached regarding the relative allotment of night and daylight games in the major-league baseball schedule. During the 1979 baseball season, 67 percent of all ball games were conducted as night games, the first time that two-thirds of the major-league schedule was comprised of night games. Three years later in 1982, 70 percent of all ball games were played at night. This was the plateau for the night-game ratio. During the next thirty years this ratio did not stray from the 65 to 70 percent banding.[18]

Effectively, the time-of-day model was now retired from schedule consideration. The "night game" designation in newspaper summaries of game results was now an anachronism, as editors determined that it was superfluous to differentiate a night game from the once-standard daylight game. Once highly promoted in marketing a ball club's schedule during the winter preseason, night games, along with holiday and doubleheader dates, disappeared from the content in marketing material, replaced by giveaway promotions.

The saturation of night games on the regular-season baseball schedule contributed to the dramatic increase in overall attendance at major-league games, from 38 million in 1977 to 55 million in 1989 and up to 72 million by 2000, as night baseball fulfilled the "utopian hope" of the 1930s rather than collapse to "dystopian fear" as a result of the changing nature of the ballpark audience. "While night baseball helped to break down class barriers, it simultaneously bridged the gap between the traditional values and ethics which the game professes and new ideas of the industrial age," Sheila Schroeder wrote in her 1994 article "When Technology and Culture Collide: The Advent of Night Baseball." Because night baseball "reconciled the traditional virtue of rugged individualism with the new ethic of teamwork," its growing dominance of the baseball schedule not only paralleled the expansion of the American Dream concept but also accommodated modification in how the American Dream was achieved. This was reflected in the changing nature of the ballpark audience, which had shifted its focus over the decades from self-employed business owner to middle-class corporate employee to a variety of people seeking success simply through a job that helps people or improves society.[19]

The universality of night baseball even impacted nostalgia for the sport that was an offshoot of the national pastime concept. *Shoeless Joe*, the 1982 novel written by W.P. Kinsella, was ostensibly a nostalgic visit to baseball's mythical idyllic past, when ball games were only played in daylight. Kinsella, though, used artificial lighting to stage the ball games played by the deceased ballplayers who returned from the afterlife to play baseball at night in an Iowa cornfield. In the movie *Field of Dreams*, the wildly popular 1989 film adaptation of Kinsella's book, the novel's real theme of redemption was consummated on screen when a father and his alienated son (the Iowa farmer) reunited to play catch under the lights on the cornfield turned baseball diamond, as the camera dramatically zoomed out to show the illuminated section of cornfield set against the darkening sky.[20]

Daylight baseball was still popular at Wrigley Field in Chicago during the 1990s, since night baseball was limited by city-council ordinance. At the upper far right is one bank of the lighting system installed in 1988 to conduct night baseball at Wrigley Field (Library of Congress, Prints & Photographs Division, LC-DIG-highsm-18121).

During the late 1980s, night baseball crashed through the once-impenetrable barrier of the last bastion of daylight baseball, Wrigley Field, and made further inroads into the once-sacrosanct domain of the daylight game, Sunday afternoon.

In 1988 the last major-league ballpark without a lighting system, Wrigley Field, finally hosted night games. Following the 1977 death of Phil Wrigley, the long-time owner of the Chicago Cubs and die-hard advocate for daylight baseball, Wrigley's heirs sold the ball club in 1981 to the Tribune Company. However, it took seven years for the new owner to overcome neighborhood and legislative resistance to playing night baseball at Wrigley Field.

Neighborhood groups in the Wrigley Field area protested the plan to install a lighting system and formed an organization called Chicagoans United for Baseball in the Sunshine, or CUBS for short, which effectively lobbied the Chicago City Council to intervene in the situation. In 1983, the City Council passed an ordinance that prohibited a sporting event between 8:00 at night and 8:00 in the morning in an enclosed stadium that contained more than 15,000 seats and was located within 500 feet of 100 or more dwelling units. The wordsmithing of the ordinance artfully tried to hide the fact that the only stadium impacted by the ordinance was Wrigley Field.[21]

In 1984 the lack of lights at Wrigley Field became not just a local business issue but also a national baseball issue, when the Cubs finished first in the East Division to qualify for the National League Championship Series. Commissioner Kuhn ruled that if the Cubs won the NLCS, the middle three games of the World Series to be played on Friday through Sunday would be played in the daylight at Wrigley Field, negating the club's home-field advantage since it was the National League's turn that year to host the first two games (and last two games, if needed) of the World Series.[22]

Given the situation with the network-television contract, Kuhn could not afford to have the opening games of the World Series played on Tuesday and Wednesday be conducted as daylight games rather than as night games, since baseball would have to rebate some of the television money it had already received. As it turned out, the Cubs did not qualify for the World Series. The Cubs won the first two games of the NLCS, played in daylight at Wrigley Field, but then lost the next three games in San Diego to send the Padres to the World Series.

During the fall of 1984, the Cubs went to court to challenge the Chicago City Council ordinance, since, if the Cubs qualified for the World Series, the club would have to move all of its home games to another ballpark, because all World Series games would be played as night games beginning in 1985. The Cubs challenged the ordinance on the grounds that it was a single-target law, having been blatantly crafted to apply just to Wrigley Field and none of the other arenas in Chicago that hosted professional sports.[23]

As the Cubs waited in 1985 for the Illinois Supreme Court to rule on their appeal, the baseball media quietly celebrated the 50th anniversary of night baseball in the major leagues. The anniversary of the first night game in Cincinnati in 1935 was recognized by Ohio-area newspapers and a nationally distributed Associated Press story, but otherwise there was little fanfare. The Cubs then faded from contention for the playoffs, rendering moot their participation in night games in the World Series that fall. In October 1985, the Illinois Supreme Court upheld the validity of the Chicago City Council ordinance that effectively banned night games at Wrigley Field.[24]

Following the court defeat, the Cubs entered into serious discussions with the CUBS, the neighborhood organization that had successfully blocked night games at

Wrigley Field. It took two years to reach a compromise solution. In February 1988, the Chicago City Council passed a new ordinance that permitted night games at Wrigley Field under a number of conditions, which included (1) no night games on Friday or Sunday, with a maximum of two on Saturday, (2) start time of 7:05 at the latest, and (3) eight night games in 1988 after July 1 and a maximum of 18 night games each season beginning in 1989, plus any postseason games if applicable.[25]

In the spring of 1988, construction of the lighting system began at Wrigley Field to prepare for the ballpark's first night baseball game, which was held on August 9, 1988. Six 33-foot steel towers were erected on top of the upper-deck roof, three on the third-base side and three on the first-base side, each with a bank of lights containing 90 metal-halide 1,500-watt lamps, which spread 150 to 250 foot-candles of light over various portions of the playing field. Metal-halide lamps were the latest in lighting technology for sports venues. A metal-halide lamp produces light by having an electric arc pass through a gaseous mixture of vaporized mercury and a metal halide, such as sodium iodine. This type of lamp emits five times the light of the incandescent floodlights previously used to illuminate ballparks. However, it does take 10 to 15 minutes for a metal-halide lamp to warm-up to full capacity.[26]

Once night baseball had invaded Wrigley Field, two years later the Sunday night game, then only conducted by the Texas Rangers, was popularized via a television contract with ESPN, then a little-known cable-television network.

The term "night baseball" re-entered sports lexicon in 1989, when Commissioner Peter Ueberroth negotiated new television contracts for the 1990 through 1993 seasons. Ueberroth negotiated a $1.1 billion contract with CBS that covered the network television rights for the World Series, All–Star Game, all other postseason games, and just a few regular-season games. As an adjunct to that contract, Ueberroth negotiated a deal with ESPN, which agreed to pay $400 million to televise 175 regular-season games annually. The vast majority of the ESPN telecasts were night games, in a package comprised of two games each on Tuesday and Friday nights and exclusive rights to one designated game on Wednesday and Sunday nights. The most ground-breaking, and longest lasting, element of this television contract was its Sunday night programming, which ESPN branded as the *Sunday Night Baseball* show.[27]

ESPN, founded in 1979, was heralded at that time by *Sports Illustrated* with the august forecast that "ESPN may become the biggest thing in TV sports since Monday Night Football and night-time World Series games." Ten years later in 1989, while the network had established itself as being known generically as "cable sports TV," ESPN wished to have a stronger brand and have its acronym "become synonymous with sports the way Kleenex means tissues." The initial foray toward that lofty recognition came in 1987 with its first contract with the NFL, where ESPN acquired the rights to telecast eight regular-season football games on Sunday nights during the 1987 through 1989 seasons.[28]

Following its deal for NFL football, ESPN looked to expand its major-league sports platform and found a willing compatriot in Commissioner Ueberroth. Together, they devised a plan to expand baseball's third and last-converted premium daylight playing date, Sunday, into a night-time gala attraction on television. The *Sunday Night Baseball* show debuted on ESPN in April 1990 and well into the twenty-first century continued to showcase night games on the Lord's Day. There was no greater symbol of the modern business basis of baseball than *Sunday Night Baseball* on ESPN.

In addition to its telecasts increasing the conversion of the Sunday premium daylight games into night events, ESPN also contributed to the further conversion of holiday games, through its tripleheader telecasts on the three national holidays that culminated with a night game. In 1994 ESPN also accelerated the transformation of opening-day games through its inauguration of an Opening Night telecast, which showcased a game on Sunday evening that preceded all the other opening-day games on Monday.

The ESPN contract for a large package of night games, particularly the Sunday night games, gave major-league baseball a better position to compete for television viewers with football and basketball, which were more popular with fans given the drama and suspense of those games. Baseball club owners also modified their business basis by elevating the principal function of the business from providing "compelling entertainment" to creating an "emotional bond" with consumers. Savvy owners further intensified those emotional ties through an "experience," which Goldberger in his book *Ballpark: Baseball in the American City* called "the ballpark as theme park," where the stadium is surrounded by urban development, such as shops, hotels, and restaurants, in a managed environment to produce multiple other sources of income beyond gate and television revenue.[29]

Night baseball remained a key driver of all three categories of baseball revenue into the twenty-first century, when the three categories underwent seismic change, as television and other sources increasingly were more valuable components than gate receipts, which had once been the largest element of revenue. One economist pegged the revenue composition for the average ball club in 2001 to be 39 percent gate receipts, 36 percent television, and 25 percent other sources. By 2015 the breakdown likely approximated

Night baseball in the twenty-first century was part of the modern "ballpark as theme park" experience, where shops, hotels, and restaurants are directly integrated with a ballpark, exemplified by SunTrust Park in suburban Atlanta (Library of Congress, Prints & Photographs Division, LC-DIG-highsm-46700).

30 percent gate receipts, 40 percent television, and 30 percent other sources. The big growth areas were television, a category that now also included internet content, and other sources, which now encompassed luxury-box rental, in-park advertising, and merchandise sales among an ever-expanding array of items beyond beer and hot dogs at the concession stand.[30]

With the percentage of night games remaining remarkably consistent for the 35 years from 1980 to 2015, at two-thirds of all ball games played in the regular season, the more intriguing story was how daylight baseball maintained equilibrium at one-third of games played and the shift within the composition of those daylight games. The approximate breakdown in 2015 of daylight games was 50 percent Sunday, 15 percent Saturday, 25 percent weekday getaway, and 10 percent other weekday (holiday, home opener, and non-getaway games, notably rescheduled postponements but also those intentionally scheduled).

While Sunday was still the dominant source of daylight ball games in 2015, there were offsetting trends in the other daylight dates from those in the 1970s. Saturday afternoon games, once a hefty portion of the daylight game, had substantially converted into night games, while many weekday night games had converted into getaway daylight games, once a tiny portion of the schedule. For example, on June 20, 2015, the Saturday schedule showed just six of 15 games played in daylight with the other nine as night games, while five days later on June 25 the Thursday schedule showed eight daylight games and just three night games on the 11-game getaway-day calendar.

Robust advancements in conditions associated with getaway-day scheduling negotiated by the Players Association are the primary rationale for daylight baseball today, designed to lessen the negative effects of the constant travel to stage ball games across the country. In 2018, all ball clubs were required to stage more afternoon games on getaways days, in response to a provision in the 2017–2021 Basic Agreement that imposed greater restrictions on starting times when either club was traveling to another destination. Getaway dates account for roughly three-fourths of all daylight games, when factoring in Sunday, which is effectively a getaway date because most series that involve weekend games conclude on Sunday.[31]

The other one-fourth of daylight games survives largely on its economic merits, either by an immediate payoff (such as a capacity crowd at a holiday game) or as a marketing expenditure that will generate future income or build the brand (such as a Saturday afternoon game with a substantial attendance by youngsters). The Chicago Cubs continue to play a sizeable weekday daylight schedule, due to the legal restrictions imposed on night games at Wrigley Field. In 2015 nights games there were capped at 35, up from the original 18-game limit. Surprisingly, several ball clubs still voluntarily schedule some weekday games for daylight rather than as a night game.[32]

There is an environmental appeal to daylight baseball that drives the occasional scheduling of a weekday daylight game. The term "day baseball," once reserved exclusively to refer to games played at daylight-only Wrigley Field, is now conveyed with nostalgic warmth as a matinee game to describe the novelty of a daylight game in the largely night-game world of major-league baseball.

Commentators ascribe this newfound euphoria to the different feeling of attending a day game. "Night games, especially those during the week, are rushed affairs. Get off of work, fight traffic to the game, eat there or speed through dinner somewhere close to the park, down a couple of beers before last call and by 9:30, it's time to think about the commute home, getting ready for the following day," Peter Bernstein observed in an *ESPN: The Magazine* article. "Day games are more relaxed and time is rarely the issue. If it's the weekend, you've got your free evening ahead of you; if it's during the week, well, is there anything better than playing hooky at the ballpark?"[33]

"Nowadays, all but a few Monday-through-Friday games are played at night, and a business suit is as rare at the Stadium as the day game itself. But a few businesspeople still play hooky to come to the weekday game," Charlie LeDuff wrote about a group of spectators at a Thursday afternoon game at Yankee Stadium for the *New York Times*. Much like the businessmen of an earlier era when daylight baseball was the norm, spectators in the box seats had first gone to the office and attended a morning meeting, then left to go out to lunch. "The 2 o'clock starts allowed a man to put a half-day's work in, step out for lunch and never come back," LeDuff wrote, noting that lunch was comprised of a hot dog and beer at the ballpark.[34]

Night baseball will continue to dominate the major-league baseball schedule during the twenty-first century, due to its favorable nature within the business basis of baseball to produce optimal revenue from gate receipts, television broadcasts, and other sources of revenue, especially in merchandise. Night baseball, though, is unlikely to ever comprise 100 percent of the major-league schedule, given the bargaining power of the Players Association and the revenue sources that do not heavily rely on night games, such as internet content.

As night baseball in the major leagues approaches its 100th anniversary in 2035, night-baseball pioneer Larry MacPhail, who preached the rationing of night games to maintain the decorum of the sport through daylight baseball, would no doubt smile at the continued resiliency of daylight baseball to resist a total influx of night baseball.

Appendix A

*First Night Games
in the Minor Leagues in 1930*

League	Class	Ball Club	Date
American Association	AA	Indianapolis, Indiana	June 7
Arizona State League	D	Phoenix, Arizona	June 19
Blue Ridge League	D	Hagerstown, Maryland	August 12
Cotton States League	D	Jackson, Mississippi	May 29
Eastern League	A	Allentown, Pennsylvania	July 17
International League	AA	Buffalo, New York	July 3
Middle Atlantic League	C	Wheeling, West Virginia	July 15
Mississippi Valley League	D	Waterloo, Iowa	June 17
Nebraska State League	D	Lincoln, Nebraska	May 19
New York–Pennsylvania	B	Binghamton, New York	July 22
Pacific Coast League	AA	Sacramento, California	June 10
Piedmont League	C	High Point, North Carolina	July 8
South Atlantic League	B	Asheville, North Carolina	July 24
Southeastern League	B	Montgomery, Alabama	June 21
Southern Association	A	Little Rock, Arkansas	July 21
Three-I League	B	Decatur, Illinois	May 14
Texas League	A	Waco, Texas	June 20
Western Association	C	Independence, Kansas	April 30
Western League	A	Des Moines, Iowa	May 2

Appendix B

First Night Games
by Class AA Minor-League Ball Clubs

American Association	
Ball Club	*Date*
Columbus, Ohio	June 17, 1932
Indianapolis, Indiana	June 7, 1930
Kansas City, Missouri	July 6, 1932
Louisville, Kentucky	May 25, 1932
Milwaukee, Wisconsin	June 6, 1935
Minneapolis, Minnesota	July 16, 1937
St. Paul, Minnesota	July 15, 1937
Toledo, Ohio	June 23, 1933
International League	
Ball Club	*Date*
Baltimore, Maryland	Sept. 11, 1930
Buffalo, New York	July 3, 1930
Jersey City, New Jersey	July 24, 1930
Montreal, Canada	June 7, 1934
Newark, New Jersey	August 6, 1930
Reading, Pennsylvania	August 14, 1930
Rochester, New York	August 7, 1933
Toronto, Canada	June 29, 1934
Pacific Coast League	
Ball Club	*Date*
Hollywood, California	August 5, 1930
Los Angeles, California	July 22, 1930
Mission, California	May 5, 1931
Oakland, California	August 5, 1930
Portland, Oregon	July 22, 1930
Sacramento, California	June 10, 1930
San Francisco, California	April 23, 1931
Seattle, Washington	July 22, 1930

Note: Clubs existing in 1930 at time of initial night game in the minor leagues

Appendix C

First Night Games
by Major-League Ball Clubs

American League	
Ball Club	***Date***
Boston Red Sox	June 13, 1947
Chicago White Sox	August 14, 1939
Cleveland Indians	June 27, 1939
Detroit Tigers	June 15, 1948
New York Yankees	May 28, 1946
Philadelphia Athletics	May 16, 1939
St. Louis Browns	May 24, 1940
Washington Senators	May 28, 1941

National League	
Ball Club	***Date***
Boston Braves	May 11, 1946
Brooklyn Dodgers	June 15, 1938
Chicago Cubs	August 9, 1988
Cincinnati Reds	May 24, 1935
New York Giants	May 24, 1940
Philadelphia Phillies	June 1, 1939
Pittsburgh Pirates	June 4, 1940
St. Louis Cardinals	June 4, 1940

Note: Clubs existing in 1935 at time of first night game in the major leagues

Appendix D

Major-League Night Games, 1935–1985

				Night Games			
Year	Games	Season	Percent	Year	Games	Season	Percent
1935	7	1,228	1%	1961	732	1,430	51%
1936	7	1,238	1%	1962	836	1,621	52%
1937	7	1,239	1%	1963	870	1,619	54%
1938	14	1,223	1%	1964	892	1,626	55%
1939	42	1,231	3%	1965	917	1,623	57%
1940	77	1,236	6%	1966	919	1,615	57%
1941	77	1,244	6%	1967	943	1,620	58%
1942	150	1,224	12%	1968	969	1,625	60%
1943	156	1,238	13%	1969	1,175	1,946	60%
1944	247	1,242	20%	1970	1,233	1,944	63%
1945	224	1,230	18%	1971	1,202	1,938	62%
1946	260	1,242	21%	1972	1,164	1,859	63%
1947	322	1,243	26%	1973	1,255	1,943	65%
1948	361	1,237	29%	1974	1,243	1,945	64%
1949	384	1,240	31%	1975	1,282	1,934	66%
1950	396	1,238	32%	1976	1,257	1,939	65%
1951	410	1,239	33%	1977	1,390	2,103	66%
1952	423	1,239	34%	1978	1,390	2,102	66%
1953	441	1,240	36%	1979	1,404	2,099	67%
1954	450	1,237	36%	1980	1,420	2,105	68%
1955	445	1,234	36%	1981	918	1,394	66%
1956	469	1,239	38%	1982	1,487	2,107	71%
1957	493	1,235	40%	1983	1,453	2,109	69%
1958	504	1,235	41%	1984	1,435	2,105	68%
1959	543	1,238	44%	1985	1,376	2,103	65%
1960	611	1,236	49%				

Note: From 1986 to 2018, the percentage of night games remained about two-thirds, ranging from 65% to 70%.

Source: Retrosheet database

Chapter Notes

Introduction

1. Dave Smith, e-mail to author on April 19, 2019, with Retrosheet data tabulation of year-by-year totals of night games played in the major leagues.

Chapter 1

1. Jane Brox, *Brilliant: The Evolution of Artificial Light* (Boston: Houghton Mifflin Harcourt, 2010), 46, 61.

2. Peter Baldwin, *In the Watches of the Night: Life in the Nocturnal City, 1820–1930* (Chicago: University of Chicago Press, 2012), 104; John Jakle, *City Lights: Illuminating the American Night* (Baltimore: Johns Hopkins University Press, 2001), 5; David Nasaw, *Going Out: The Rise and Fall of Public Amusements* (New York: Basic Books, 1993), 2.

3. Tom Melville, *Early Baseball and the Rise of the National League* (Jefferson, NC: McFarland, 2001), 2–8.

4. Steven Riess, *City Games: The Evolution of American Urban Society and the Rise of Sports* (Urbana: University of Illinois Press, 1989), 195; Stephen Guschov, *The Red Stockings of Cincinnati: Base Ball's First All-Professional Team and Its Historic 1869 and 1870 Seasons* (Jefferson, NC: McFarland, 1998), 9, 96.

5. Rowland Berthoff, "Independence and Enterprise: Small Business in the American Dream" in *Small Business in American Life*, ed. Stuart Bruchey (New York: Columbia University Press, 1980), 33; Cal Jillson, *Pursuing the American Dream: Opportunity and Exclusion Over Four Centuries* (Lawrence: University Press of Kansas, 2004), 55.

6. Daniel Boorstin, *The Americans: The National Experience* (New York: Random House, 1965), 116.

7. Boorstin, *The Americans: The National Experience*, 117, 123; Eric Daniels, "A Brief History of Individualism in American Thought," in *For the Greater Good of All: Perspectives on Individualism, Society, and Leadership*, ed. Donelson Forsyth and Crystal Hoyt (New York: Palgrave Macmillan, 2011), 72–73; Berthoff, "Independence and Enterprise: Small Business in the American Dream," 35; John Cumbler, *A Social History of Economic Decline: Business,* Politics, and Work in Trenton (New Brunswick: Rutgers University Press, 1989), 3.

8. Cindy Aron, *Ladies and Gentlemen of the Civil Service: Middle-Class Workers in Victorian America* (New York: Oxford University Press, 1987), 3; Wright Mills, *White Collar: The American Middle Classes* (New York: Oxford University Press, 1951), 63; Stuart Blumin, *The Emergence of the Middle Class: Social Experience in the American City, 1760–1900* (New York: Cambridge University Press, 1989) 83–84, 137.

9. David Surdam, *Century of the Leisured Masses: Entertainment and the Transformation of Twentieth-Century America* (New York: Oxford University Press, 2015), 46; Charlie Bevis, *Sunday Baseball: The Major Leagues' Struggle to Play Baseball on the Lord's Day, 1876–1934* (Jefferson, NC: McFarland, 2003), 11–20.

10. Mansel Blackford, *A History of Small Business in America* (New York: Twayne, 1991), 36.

11. Benjamin Rader, *Baseball: A History of America's Game* (Urbana: University of Illinois Press, 1992), 27–30; Michael Haupert, "William Hulbert and the Birth of the National League," *Baseball Research Journal*, Spring 2015, 83.

12. John Thomas, "Holding the Middle Ground" in *The American Planning Tradition: Culture and Policy*, ed. Robert Fishman (Washington: Woodrow Wilson Center Press, 2000), 44; Rader, *Baseball: A History of America's Game*, 26.

13. Charles Glaab and Theodore Brown, *A History of Urban America* (New York: Macmillan, 1967), 115–116.

14. Riess, *City Games: The Evolution of American Urban Society and the Rise of Sports*, 68; Gregg Carter, "Baseball in Saint Louis, 1867–1875: An Historical Case Study in Civic Pride," *Missouri Historical Society Bulletin*, July 1975, 258.

15. *Acts and Resolves Passed by the General Court of Massachusetts in the Year 1871* (Boston: Wright & Potter, 1871), 508; George Tuohey, *A History of the Boston Base Ball Club* (Boston: M.F. Quinn, 1897), 62.

16. "The Boston Base-Ball Club," *Boston Daily Advertiser*, January 21, 1871.

17. "The Professional Base Ball Association— What It Must Do to Be Saved," *Chicago Tribune*, October 24, 1875.

18. Sam Bass Warner, *Streetcar Suburbs: The Process of Growth in Boston, 1870–1900* (Cambridge: Harvard University Press, 1962), 53; Mills, *White Collar*, 63.

19. Baldwin, *In the Watches of the Night: Life in the Nocturnal City*, 104.

20. Melville, *Early Baseball and the Rise of the National League*, 128.

Chapter 2

1. Harold Passer, *The Electrical Manufacturers, 1875–1900: A Study in Competition, Entrepreneurship. Technical Change, and Economic Growth* (New York: Arno Press, 1972), 14–16; Mel Gorman, "Charles F. Brush and the First Public Electric Street Lighting System in America," *Ohio Historical Quarterly*, April 1961, 135–136.

2. Gorman, "Charles F. Brush," 141.

3. "Lighting Towns by Electricity," *Boston Daily Advertiser*, September 3, 1880; "Electric Light," *Boston Globe*, September 3, 1880.

4. "Jordan, Marsh & Co.," *Boston Daily Advertiser*, November 23, 1880; "The Electric Light," *Boston Post*, September 3, 1880.

5. Neil Sullivan, *The Minors: The Struggles and Triumphs of Baseball's Poor Relation from 1876 to the Present* (New York: St. Martin's Press, 1991), 137; Edward White, *Creating the National Pastime: Baseball Transforms Itself, 1903–1953* (Princeton: Princeton University Press, 1996), 160.

6. Gorman, "Charles F. Brush," 142.

7. "The Sporting World," *Milwaukee Sentinel*, May 30, 1883.

8. "Baseball by Electric Light," *Milwaukee Sentinel*, June 3, 1883; "Sporting Matters," *Milwaukee Daily Journal*, June 4, 1883.

9. "Sporting Matters," *Milwaukee Daily Journal*, May 30 and June 4, 1883.

10. "New Light on Base Ball," *Boston Daily Advertiser*, May 31, 1883.

11. Passer, *The Electrical Manufacturers*, 56.

12. Arthur Bright, *The Electric-Lamp Industry: Technological Change and Economic Development from 1800 to 1947* (New York: Macmillan, 1949), 34; Bernard Carlson, *Innovation as a Social Process: Elihu Thomson and the Rise of General Electric* (New York: Cambridge University Press, 1991), 73.

13. Carlson, *Innovation as a Social Process*, 181–182, 192–193.

14. "Solved at Last: Play by Electric Light Possible," *Sporting Life*, March 30, 1887.

15. "A Novel Project Considered," *Indianapolis Journal*, August 14, 1888; "The New Light Contract," *Indianapolis Journal*, July 24, 1888.

16. "Playing by Gaslight," *Indianapolis Journal*, August 22, 1888.

17. "Base-Ball Notes," *Indianapolis Journal*, September 1, 1888; "Not Very Successful," *Indianapolis Journal*, September 6, 1888.

18. Carlson, *Innovation as a Social Process*, 216; Passer, *The Electrical Manufacturers*, 53–56.

19. Passer, *The Electrical Manufacturers*, 322;

Bright, *The Electric-Lamp Industry*, 101; Carlson, *Innovation as a Social Process*, 296.

20. David Pietrusza, *Lights On! The Wild Century-Long Saga of Night Baseball* (Lanham, MD: Scarecrow Press, 1997), 7–8.

21. "Baseball News," *Wilmington Daily Republican*, July 6, 1896.

Chapter 3

1. "The Boston Club's Finances," *Boston Globe*, August 19, 1881.

2. "Boston vs. Chicago," *Chicago Inter Ocean*, July 5, 1881.

3. Charlie Bevis, *Doubleheaders: A Major League History* (Jefferson, NC: McFarland, 2011), 21.

4. Dean Sullivan, "Faces in the Crowd: A Statistical Portrait of Baseball Spectators in Cincinnati, 1886–1888," *Journal of Sport History*, Winter 1990, 359–362.

5. Chad Seifried and Donna Pastore, "The Temporary Homes: Analyzing Baseball Facilities in the United States Pre-1903," *Journal of Sport History*, Summer 2010, 266.

6. David Nye, *Electrifying America: Social Meanings of a New Technology, 1880–1940* (Cambridge: MIT Press, 1991), 3; Ernest Freeberg, *The Age of Edison: Electric Light and the Invention of Modern America* (New York: Penguin Press, 2013), 49.

7. William Flanagan, *Urban Sociology: Images and Structure* (Lanham, MD: Rowman & Littlefield, 2010), 199.

8. Steven Riess, *Sport in Industrial America, 1850–1920* (Wheeling, IL: Harlan Davidson, 1995), 26.

9. Blake McKelvey, *The Urbanization of America, 1860–1915* (New Brunswick: Rutgers University Press, 1963), 34, 37.

10. Charles Glaab, "Historical Perspectives on Urban Development Schemes," in *Social Science and the City: A Survey of Urban Research*, ed. Leo Schnore (New York: Praeger, 1967), 197–198.

11. Kenneth Land, "Organizing the Boys of Summer: The Evolution of Minor-League Baseball, 1883–1990," *American Journal of Sociology*, November 1994, 792.

12. Charlie Bevis, "Sunday Baseball Adoption in the Minor Leagues," *Base Ball 11: New Research on the Early Game*, 2019, 55; Bevis, *Sunday Baseball*, 131.

13. Scott Cline, "To Foster Honorable Pastimes: Baseball as a Civic Endeavor in 1880s Seattle," *Pacific Northwest Quarterly*, Fall 1996, 171; David Martin, "Baseball and Boosterism: Henry W. Grady, the Atlanta Constitution, and the Inaugural Season of the Southern League," Masters thesis, University of Tennessee, 2006, 3.

14. James Quigel and Louis Hunsinger, *Gateway to the Majors: Williamsport and Minor League Baseball* (University Park: Pennsylvania State University Press, 2001), 2, 46.

15. Charlie Bevis, "Economic Anatomy of an

1891 Minor League Ball Club," *Base Ball: A Journal of the Early Game*, Fall 2007, 78–92.

16. "To Be Reorganized," *Wichita Daily Eagle*, August 11, 1898.

17. "A Double Dose: New Orleans Wins Two Games on Sunday by Brilliant Playing," *New Orleans Picayune*, August 29, 1887; "The Sporting Calendar," *Milwaukee Journal*, July 26, 1889.

18. Lloyd Johnson, ed., *The Encyclopedia of Minor League Baseball* (Durham, NC: Baseball America, 1997), 107.

19. Mark Eberle, *Kansas Baseball, 1858–1941* (Lawrence: University Press of Kansas, 2017), 32–34, 211–212.

20. Johnson, *Encyclopedia of Minor League Baseball*, 131.

21. Johnson, *Encyclopedia of Minor League Baseball*, 136.

22. Thomas, "Holding the Middle Ground," 44.

23. McKelvey, *The Urbanization of America*, 43; Nye, *Electrifying America*, 16.

24. Cumbler, *A Social History of Economic Decline*, 5–6.

25. Freeberg, *The Age of Edison*, 210, 256–257.

26. Nasaw, *Going Out*, 8; Jakle, *City Lights*, 43.

27. Stephen Hardy, "Polo at the Rinks: Shaping Markets for Ice Hockey in America, 1880–1900," *Journal of Sport History*, Summer 2006, 160.

28. Steven Riess, *Touching Base: Professional Baseball and American Culture in the Progressive Era* (Westport, CT: Greenwood Press, 1980), 19.

29. "National Baseball Agreement," *New York Times*, August 30, 1903.

30. Bevis, "Sunday Baseball Adoption in the Minor Leagues," 63.

31. Bevis, "Sunday Baseball Adoption in the Minor Leagues," 56, 58.

32. Bevis, *Sunday Baseball*, 173; Bevis, "Sunday Baseball Adoption in the Minor Leagues," 58.

33. F.C. Lane, "The Greatest Problem in the National Game: The Critical Situation in Sunday Baseball," *Baseball Magazine*, October 1911, 26.

34. Harold Livesay, "Lilliputians in Brobdingnag: Small Business in Late-Nineteenth-Century America," in *Small Business in American Life*, ed. Bruchey, 342.

35. Blackford, *A History of Small Business in America*, 36.

36. Maury Klein, *The Genesis of Industrial America, 1870–1920* (New York: Cambridge University Press, 2007), 131, 133, 137, 145.

37. Jillson, *Pursuing the American Dream*, 127.

38. Aron, *Ladies and Gentlemen of the Civil Service*, 5, 15, 144, and 187.

39. Melanie Aucher and Judith Blau, "Class Formation in Nineteenth-Century America: The Case of the Middle Class," *Annual Review of Sociology*, 1993, 28–32.

40. Jon Peterson, *The Birth of City Planning in the United States, 1840–1917* (Baltimore: Johns Hopkins University Press, 2003), 151, 204; Glaab, "Historical Perspectives on Urban Development Schemes," 214–215.

Chapter 4

1. Jerry Kuntz, *Baseball Fiends and Flying Machines: The Many Lives and Outrageous Times of George and Alfred Lawson* (Jefferson, NC: McFarland, 2009), 93; "Baseball by Electric Light," *Buffalo Enquirer*, August 3, 1901; "Last Night's Game by Electric Light," *Harrisburg Independent*, August 30, 1901.

2. "Baseball by Electric Light," *New York Times*, September 18, 1901.

3. "Baseball by Electric Light," *Chicago Tribune*, September 13, 1900.

4. "First Base Ball Game," *Scranton Tribune*, April 15, 1902.

5. "Night Ball Game: Immense Crowd Sees Scranton and Lancaster Play the National [Game] by Electric Light," *Scranton Tribune*, May 15, 1902; "Electric Light Game," *Scranton Times*, May 15, 1902.

6. Quigel and Hunsinger, *Gateway to the Majors*, 27.

7. "Baseball by Electric Light," *New York Times*, June 10, 1902; "Root for the Rooters," *Amsterdam* (New York) *Evening Recorder*, June 10, 1902.

8. Jerry Kuntz, "Tramping Through the Baseball Subculture: The Career of Alfred W. Lawson," *Base Ball: A Journal of the Early Game*, Fall 2007, 93.

9. Jeffrey Powers-Beck, *The American Indian Integration of Baseball* (Lincoln: University of Nebraska Press, 2004), 51, 60; Barbara Gregorich, "John Olsen and His Barnstorming Baseball Teams," *Michigan History*, May/June 1995, 39–40.

10. "Baseball by Electric Light," *Boston Globe*, September 12, 1907.

11. "To Try Baseball at Night: Electric Light Scheme to Be Tested at Cincinnati," *Chicago Tribune*, August 30, 1908.

12. Patent number 755,447 granted by the United States Patent Office on March 22, 1904.

13. "Baseball at Night!" *Washington Sunday Star*, July 4, 1909.

14. "Baseball at Night!"

15. "Baseball at Night!"

16. Reynold Weidenaar, *Magic Music from the Telharmonium* (Metuchen, NJ: Scarecrow Press, 1995), xiv–xv; "Telharmonic Co. in Trouble," *New York Times*, June 6, 1908.

17. Patent number 1,235,527 granted by the United States Patent Office on July 31, 1917.

18. "Baseball at Night Under Powerful Electric Lights," *Popular Mechanics*, August 1909, 129–130.

19. "Baseball Played at Night: Experiment in Artificial Light at Cincinnati a Big Success," *New York Times*, June 19, 1909; "Night Baseball Tested in Cincinnati and Huge Tower and Lamps at League Park," *Los Angeles Herald*, June 19, 1909.

20. "Cahill Triumphant," *Sporting Life*, June 26, 1909; "Night Ball at Reds' Park," *The Sporting News*, June 24, 1909.

21. "Baseball at Night Under Powerful Electric Lights," 130.

22. "Night Base Ball Game Series Great Success," *Washington Evening Star*, July 8, 1909.

23. "Pittsburgh's First Hippodrome Opens on Forbes Field Tomorrow Night," *Pittsburgh Press*, July 25, 1909.

24. "Baseball Games at Night," *Independence* (Kansas) *Daily Reporter*, April 14, 1909.

25. "A Circuit of Hippodromes: Harry Davis to Start One on Twenty Ball Parks," *New York Times*, September 13, 1909; "New Use for Ball Parks," *New York Times*, May 31, 1910.

26. "Electric Light Ball," *Sporting Life*, September 10, 1910.

27. "Electric Lighting of a Baseball Field," *Electrical Review and Western Electrician*, September 3, 1910, 473–474; "Initial Night Baseball Game at Sox Park Proves Success," *Chicago Inter Ocean*, August 28, 1910.

28. "Baseball at Night," *Chicago Tribune*, August 29, 1910.

29. "Necrology," *The Sporting News*, October 24, 1935.

30. Bright, *The Electric-Lamp Industry*, 194–197.

31. Bright, *The Electric-Lamp Industry*, 322; patent number 1,180,159 granted by the United States Patent Office on April 18, 1916.

32. Gail Fenske, *The Skyscraper in the Sky: The Woolworth Building and the Making of Modern New York* (Chicago: University of Chicago Press, 2008), 284–285; Henry Magdsick, "Flood Lighting the World's Tallest Building," *Electrical World*, August 26, 1916, 412; Dietrich Neumann, *Architecture of the Night: The Illuminated Building* (New York: Prestel, 2002), 102.

33. "Is It Baseball at Night?" *Brooklyn Eagle*, September 4, 1915; "Baseball at Night Starts September 29," *Brooklyn Eagle*, September 11, 1915; "No Night Baseball Just Yet," *Brooklyn Eagle*, September 30, 1915.

34. "Night Baseball Tried at Last," *Brooklyn Eagle*, October 27, 1915; patent number 1,235,527 granted by the United States Patent Office on July 31, 1917.

Chapter 5

1. "Twilight Baseball Makes Big Hit Here," *Minneapolis Star Tribune*, May 25, 1918; "Wichita Booms With Team Showing Heels," *The Sporting News*, June 20, 1918; "Twilight Baseball Proves a Success," *New York Herald*, June 12, 1918.

2. "Braves Win With Twilight Missing," *Boston Globe*, July 2, 1918.

3. Bill Phelon, "Here's More Cheer by Cheery Phelon," *The Sporting News*, September 19, 1918.

4. John Mollenkopf, *The Contested City* (Princeton: Princeton University Press, 1983), 12–13; Cumbler, *A Social History of Economic Decline*, 70–71.

5. Robert Fogelson, *Downtown: Its Rise and Fall, 1880–1950* (New Haven: Yale University Press, 2001), 14.

6. Peterson, *The Birth of City Planning in the United States*, 16.

7. David Nye, *American Illuminations: Urban Lighting, 1800–1920* (Cambridge: MIT Press, 2018), 137; Nasaw, *Going Out*, 143.

8. Fogelson, *Downtown: Its Rise and Fall*, 186.

9. Fogelson, *Downtown: Its Rise and Fall*, 206, 208, 216.

10. Blandford, *A History of Small Business*, 36.

11. James Palmer, "Economic and Social Aspects of Chain Stores," *Journal of Business of the University of Chicago*, July 1929, 272.

12. Jillson, *Pursuing the American Dream*, 157.

13. Jillson, *Pursuing the American Dream*, 171; Herbert Hoover, *American Individualism* (Garden City, NY: Doubleday, 1922), 9.

14. Jules Tygiel, *Past Time: Baseball as History* (New York: Oxford University Press, 2000), 63.

15. Bevis, *Doubleheaders*, 111, 213.

16. "Brown Starts Seven-Run Rally for Giants in 10th," *Brooklyn Eagle*, June 19, 1921; "Women Have Chance to See Braves Free Today," *Boston Globe*, July 20, 1923; "First Ladies Day at Fenway Park Thursday," *Boston Globe*, August 7, 1923; "Ladies Day at Ball Games Found Success in West," *New York Times*, August 4, 1929.

17. Tygiel, *Past Time: Baseball as History*, 66, 73.

18. Bevis, "Sunday Baseball Adoption in the Minor Leagues," 63.

19. "Results of Yesterday's Minor League Games," *New York Times*, July 13, 1925; "Texas League," *The Sporting News*, July 23, 1925.

20. "First Ladies Day of Season Today," *Buffalo Times*, July 16, 1920; advertisement for Indianapolis vs. Minneapolis game, *Indiana Daily Times*, June 10, 1920; "Double-Header Booster Day Feature Tomorrow," *Rock Island Argus*, August 17, 1920; "Booster Day Here Thursday, *Joplin Globe*, July 10, 1921; Richard Beverage, *The Los Angeles Angels of the Pacific Coast League, 1903–1957* (Jefferson NC: McFarland, 2011), 43.

21. Johnson, *Encyclopedia of Minor League Baseball*, 239, 253, 259.

22. Bruce Kuklick, *To Every Thing a Season: Shibe Park and Urban Philadelphia, 1909–1976* (Princeton: Princeton University Press, 1991), 25–26.

23. David Surdam and Michael Haupert, *The Age of Ruth and Landis: The Economics of Baseball During the Roaring Twenties* (Lincoln: University of Nebraska Press, 2018), 280–281.

24. White, *Creating the National Pastime*, 58.

25. Stuart Banner, *The Baseball Trust: A History of Baseball's Antitrust Exemption* (New York: Oxford University Press, 2013), 36–37.

26. Banner, *The Baseball Trust*, 52, 68–69, 72.

27. Banner, *The Baseball Trust*, 86–87.

28. White, *Creating the National Pastime*, 58, 80.

29. Edgar Wolfe, "The Benevolent Brotherhood of Baseball Boys," *Literary Digest*, July 7, 1923, 68.

30. Eberle, *Kansas Baseball*, 124–126.

31. Surdam and Haupert, *The Age of Ruth and Landis*, 4, 5, 237; "Shift of Minors to Major Control Silent but Sure," *The Sporting News*, January 12, 1928.

32. "Purchase of Columbus Club as Farm Appears Near," *The Sporting News*, December 9, 1926.

33. "Pro Football Men Favor 2 Divisions," *New*

York Times, February 6, 1927; "Basketball Dates Set," *New York Times*, March 3, 1928.

34. "Minor League Club Values," *The Sporting News*, January 15, 1925; "Shift of Minors to Major Control Silent but Sure."

35. "Jersey City Back in International," *New York Times*, January 17, 1928.

36. Jamie Selko, *Minor League All-Star Teams, 1922–1962* (Jefferson NC: McFarland, 2007), 2.

Chapter 6

1. Neumann, *Architecture of the Night*, 54, 108.

2. George Waltz, "Behind the Lights at a Night Ball Game," *Popular Science*, July 1948, 104.

3. Jakle, *City Lights*, 94.

4. Weidenaar, *Magic Music from the Telharmonium*, 264–265; "Cahill Bros.," *New York City Directory*, 1922.

5. "Firpo Felled Ten Times," *New York Times*, September 15, 1923.

6. Joseph Durso, *Madison Square Garden: 100 Years of History* (New York: Simon & Schuster, 1979), 140; Colleen Aycock, *Tex Rickard: Boxing's Greatest Promoter* (Jefferson, NC: McFarland, 2012), 153.

7. Guy Bartlett, "Baseball at Night," *Baseball Magazine*, September 1927; "Frederick W. Ralston: Father of Night Baseball," *Boston Globe*, May 29, 1953.

8. "Lynn Plays Ball by Electric Light," *Boston Globe*, August 25, 1923; Polish National Alliance vs. Midnight Wanderers, *Lynn Evening Item*, August 28, 1923.

9. "Baseball Played by Electric Light," *Christian Science Monitor*, August 25, 1923.

10. "Football at Night Impresses Coaches," *Boston Globe*, November 23, 1923; "Night Soccer Test a Success," *Boston Globe*, December 20, 1923.

11. "Sun Outwitted by Electricians: New Inventions Permit Playing of All Games at Night," *Schenectady Gazette*, December 24, 1923.

12. "Play Baseball and Football at Night," *Council Grove* (Kansas) *Republican*, March 6, 1924.

13. "Game Tonight by Artificial Light," *Boston Globe*, June 23, 1927; "Lynn G.E. Wins Battle to Get Out of Cellar," *Boston Globe*, June 18, 1927.

14. "Rain Halts Night Baseball Game," *New York Times*, June 24, 1927.

15. "Floodlight Baseball Game at G.E. Field Draws 5000 Fans, *Lynn Evening Item*, June 25, 1927; "Baseball at Night Proves Successful," *New York Times*, June 25, 1927.

16. "Johnson Faces Red Sox in Contest Here Today," *Washington Sunday Star*, June 26, 1927.

17. Lynn vs. Cornets, *Lynn Evening Item*, September 15, 1927.

18. Robert Payne, *Let There Be Light: A History of Night Baseball* (Bloomington, IN: Author House, 2010), 14–15.

19. Jakle, *City Lights*, 103; Waltz, "Behind the Lights at a Night Ball Game," 104.

20. "Future Points to Baseball by Electric Light,"

Brooklyn Eagle, July 10, 1927; "New England League," *The Sporting News*, June 30, 1927.

21. Sheila Schroeder, "When Technology and Culture Collide: The Advent of Night Baseball," *NINE: A Journal of Baseball History and Social Policy Perspectives*, Fall 1994, 90–91.

22. Schroeder, "When Technology and Culture Collide," 91.

23. Weidenaar, *Magic Music from the Telharmonium*, 264–265; "George F. Cahill, 66, Inventor, Dies Here," *New York Times*, October 15, 1935.

24. "Gives Lights for Stadium," *New York Times*, May 3, 1926; "2 Colleges to Test Football at Night," *New York Times*, September 20, 1927; "National Eleven Wins Night Match," *New York Times*, May 13, 1928.

25. "Drake Considers Plan to Play Its Football Games at Night," *New York Times*, September 14, 1928; E.C. Lytton, "Night Football at Drake University," *Athletic Journal*, January 1929, 15.

26. Sec Taylor, "No Grass Ever Grows Under Keyser's Feet," *The Sporting News*, March 3, 1933; Robert Burnes, "First O.B. Lamplighter Still Carrying the Torch," *The Sporting News*, December 15, 1948.

Chapter 7

1. Taylor, "No Grass Ever Grows Under Keyser's Feet."

2. "Record Number of Player Deals Completed By Club Owners," *The Sporting News*, December 12, 1929.

3. Sec Taylor, "Keyser Gets Permit for Games at Night," *The Sporting News*, February 13, 1930.

4. "Night Ball May Provide Better Days for Minors," *The Sporting News*, March 20, 1930.

5. "12,000 Fans See Night Ball Game," *New York Times*, May 3, 1930.

6. Sec Taylor, "Test at Des Moines Regarded as Success," *The Sporting News*, May 8, 1930.

7. "12,000 Fans See Night Ball Game."

8. Advertisements for General Electric Company, *The Sporting News*, May 15 and 22, 1930.

9. Burnes, "First O.B. Lamplighter Still Carrying the Torch."

10. Larry Bowman, "'I Think It Is Pretty Ritzy, Myself': Kansas Minor League Teams and Night Baseball," *Kansas History*, Winter 1995/1996, 254–255.

11. Eberle, *Kansas Baseball*, 140–141.

12. Larry Bowman, "The Monarchs and Night Baseball," *The National Pastime*, 1996, 81–82.

13. Larry Bowman, "To Save a Minor League Team: Night Baseball Comes to Shreveport," *Louisiana History*, Spring 1997, 195–198; "Arc Lights Turn Waco Into Flag Contender," *The Sporting News*, August 7, 1930.

14. "Commodores Defeat Quincy Indians in Night Opener," *Decatur Herald*, May 15, 1930; "Lincoln Loses Night Contest," *Lincoln Star*, May 20, 1930; "Senators Again Lose Night Baseball Tilt," *Jackson Clarion-Ledger*, May 31, 1930.

15. "Western League," *New York Times*, May 14, 1930.

16. Advertisement for Giant Manufacturing Company, *The Sporting News*, May 29, 1930.

17. Clyde Harding, "Manufacturers Anticipate that 80 Per Cent of Minors Will Play at Night This Year," *The Sporting News*, April 16, 1931.

18. Dennis Snelling, *The Greatest Minor League: A History of the Pacific Coast League, 1903–1957* (Jefferson, NC: McFarland, 2012), 134.

19. "Night Baseball Games on Pacific Coast Draw Three Times the Attendance of Day Contests," *New York Times*, September 7, 1930.

20. "Baseball Magnates, Fans Declare Night Baseball a Success," *Buffalo Courier-Express*, July 4, 1930; "Jersey City Sees Night League Game," *New York Times*, July 25, 1930; "12,000 See Baltimore Night Game," *New York Times*, September 5, 1930.

21. "Night Tilt Will Close Saint Stay," *Indianapolis Times*, June 9, 1930; advertisement for General Electric Company, *The Sporting News*, February 26, 1931.

22. "Afternoon and Night Twin Bill," *Indianapolis Times*, June 11, 1930; "Night Twin Bill Results in Two More Tribe Defeats," *Indianapolis Times*, August 6, 1930.

23. "Initial Night Baseball Game Here Tonight," *Allentown Morning Call*, July 17, 1930; "Night Baseball Thrills Fans at Little Rock," *Atlanta Constitution*, July 22, 1930; "Night Baseball Wins Approval of 1,500 Fans," *Binghamton Press and Sun-Bulletin*, July 23, 1930; William Akin, *The Middle Atlantic League, 1925–1952: A Baseball History* (Jefferson, NC: McFarland, 2015), 51; "Night Baseball Proves Success in Debut in N.C.," *Asheville Citizen-Times*, July 9, 1930.

24. Advertisement for General Electric Company, *The Sporting News*, February 26, 1931.

25. "Burch Tells How Arcs Aided Game," *The Sporting News*, April 16, 1931; advertisement for Giant Manufacturing Company, *The Sporting News*, July 31, 1930.

26. David Ogden, "Black Baseball at Forbes Field," in *Forbes Field: Essays and Memories of the Pirates' Historic Ballpark, 1909–1971*, ed. David Cicotello and Angelo Louisa (Jefferson, NC: McFarland, 2007), 57.

27. "Breadon Confers With Keyser, Night Baseball Pioneer; May Install a Plant at Houston," *St. Louis Post-Dispatch*, May 22, 1930; "Two Big Innings Give Tribe 17–5 Win Over Reds in Exhibition Tilt," *Indianapolis Times*, July 31, 1930.

28. "Night Baseball Edging Nearer to Majors," *New York Times*, July 27, 1930; "10,000 See Giants Take Night Game," *New York Times*, August 7, 1930.

29. "Night Baseball Tried at the Polo Grounds," *New York Times*, August 2, 1930; "Paterson Silk Sox Win," *New York Times*, September 10, 1930; "Bushwicks Beaten in Night Ball Game," *New York Times*, July 24, 1930.

30. "National League Having Best Year," *New York Times*, August 7, 1930.

31. "Jersey City Sees Night League Game."

32. "Night Baseball Games on Pacific Coast";

"Indianapolis Night Games Triple Attendance Figures," *New York Times*, July 20, 1930; "Banner Year in Western League Brightened by Night Arc Lights," *The Sporting News*, November 13, 1930.

33. "Landis, Club Heads, Praise Night Ball," *The Sporting News*, April 16, 1931.

Chapter 8

1. "Mazdas Burn in 56 Parks This Season," *The Sporting News*, April 16, 1931; "Lights Treble Attendance in San Francisco," *The Sporting News*, June 11, 1931.

2. "Mazdas Burn in 56 Parks This Season."

3. "Nine Mid-Atlantic Clubs All Set to Play at Night," *The Sporting News*, March 19, 1931; Akin, *The Middle Atlantic League*, 108–109; advertisement for Giant Manufacturing Company, *The Sporting News*, March 26, 1931.

4. Advertisements for Giant Manufacturing Company, *The Sporting News*, January 29, March 12, and April 16, 1931; advertisements for General Electric Company, *The Sporting News*, January 15 and February 26, 1931.

5. Advertisement for Giant Manufacturing Company, *The Sporting News*, January 29, 1931; advertisement for General Electric Company, *The Sporting News*, January 15, 1931.

6. Author-calculated percentages based on the 136 minor-league clubs that began the 1931 season and night-game-hosting clubs specified in "Mazdas Burn in 56 Parks This Season" article.

7. John Drebinger, "Giants Turn Back White Sox, 17 to 8," *New York Times*, March 26, 1931.

8. F.C. Lane, "The Romance of Night Baseball," *Baseball Magazine*, October 1930, 484.

9. Francis Powers, "Popularity of Night Baseball Wanes," *Washington Evening Star*, January 31, 1933; Fred Lieb, "Minor Leagues Hard Hit by Depression," *Boston Globe*, February 7, 1933; "Night Ball Wearing Off," *The Sporting News*, June 16, 1932.

10. Lane, "The Romance of Night Baseball," 484.

11. "Night Baseball Liked by Head of Cardinals," *Brooklyn Eagle*, September 29, 1932.

12. White, *Creating the National Pastime*, 8, 188.

13. Schroeder, "When Technology and Culture Collide," 91.

14. Quigel and Hunsinger, *Gateway to the Majors*, 81–83; Edgar Brands, "Minors' Night Game Experience Lights Way for Majors," *The Sporting News*, January 24, 1935.

15. "To Play 7 Night Games," *Indianapolis Star*, June 8, 1932; "Limited Night Play for Columbus Club," *The Sporting News*, February 8, 1934.

16. Don Warfield, *The Roaring Redhead: Larry MacPhail—Baseball's Great Innovator* (South Bend, IN: Diamond Communications, 1987), 24–25; Tygiel, *Past Time: Baseball as History*, 96–102.

17. Irven Scheibeck, "Larry MacPhail, Columbus President, Takes Club Owners to School in Making Things Go," *The Sporting News*, February 23, 1933.

18. "Reds in Form, Fall Before Columbus," *Cincinnati Enquirer*, September 20, 1932.

19. "Giants Beat Seals in Night Game," *New York Times*, April 1, 1932; "20,000 See Giants Defeat Bushwicks," *New York Times*, September 24, 1932.

20. Christopher Siriano, *The House of David* (Charleston, SC: Arcadia, 2007), 104, 109; Robert Fogarty, *The Righteous Remnant: The House of David* (Canton: Kent State University Press, 1981), 121.

21. Dave Egan, "Braves Win in First Night Game," *Boston Globe*, August 2, 1932.

22. "Night Baseball Liked by Head of Cardinals."

23. Bevis, *Doubleheaders*, 123; Bevis, *Sunday Baseball*, 262.

24. "Synthetic Double-Headers," *The Sporting News*, May 25, 1933.

25. "Big Leagues Vote for Uniform Ball," *New York Times*, December 15, 1933.

26. Robert Ehrgott, *Mr. Wrigley's Ball Club: Chicago and the Cubs During the Jazz Age* (Lincoln: University of Nebraska Press, 2013), 3, 51.

27. "This 13 Not Unlucky," *Brooklyn Eagle*, November 13, 1933.

28. Nicholas Lemann, *Transaction Man: The Rise of the Deal and the Decline of the American Dream* (New York: Farrar, Straus and Giroux, 2019), 40, 45; Jordan Schwarz, *Liberal: Adolf A. Berle and the Vision of an American Era* (New York: The Free Press, 1987), 56, 83.

29. "Radical Move to Help Baseball," *New York Times*, December 8, 1932.

30. Charlie Bevis, "How the Shaughnessy Plan Redefined Success in Sports," *NINE: A Journal of Baseball History & Culture*, Fall 2011, 32–33.

31. "Joe Carr to Promote Game," *The Sporting News*, January 19, 1933; "New Deal in Baseball," *The Sporting News*, March 16, 1933; "Carr Sets Ultimate Goal at 50 Minor Leagues," *The Sporting News*, February 15, 1934.

32. David Surdam, *Wins, Losses, and Empty Seats: How Baseball Outlasted the Great Depression* (Lincoln: University of Nebraska Press, 2011), 318.

33. "Landis Predicts Baseball Revival," *New York Times*, November 14, 1933.

34. James Truslow Adams, *The Epic of America* (Boston: Little, Brown, and Company, 1931), 404.

35. Jillson, *Pursuing the American Dream*, 158, 177.

36. Brands, "Minors' Night Game Experience Lights Way for Majors."

37. "More Nocturnal Games in Int[ernational] Loop This Year," *The Sporting News*, March 8, 1934; "Sunday Night Game Carded," *New York Times*, June 22, 1934.

38. Brands, "Minors' Night Game Experience Lights Way for Majors."

39. Brands, "Minors' Night Game Experience Lights Way for Majors."

40. Paul Dickson, *Bill Veeck: Baseball's Greatest Maverick* (New York: Walker & Company, 2012), 42; Rusty McClure, *Crosley: Two Brothers and a Business Empire That Transformed the Nation* (Cincinnati: Clerisy Press, 2006), 254, 290.

Chapter 9

1. McClure, *Crosley*, 234, 272, 279.

2. John Drebinger, "Night Baseball on Limited Scale Adopted Unanimously by National League," *New York Times*, December 13, 1934.

3. McClure, *Crosley*, 291.

4. Bevis, *Sunday Baseball*, 204, 250.

5. John Drebinger, "Shedding a Little Light," *New York Times*, December 27, 1934.

6. Advertisements for Giant Manufacturing Company, *The Sporting News*, February 21 and March 7, 1935.

7. Drebinger, "Night Baseball on Limited Scale."

8. John Lardner, "Bulb Baseball Better Show, But MacPhail Prefers Sun," *New York Evening Post*, March 16, 1935.

9. Dick Farrington, "Cardinals in Dark on Nocturnal Play," *The Sporting News*, December 20, 1934.

10. "New York Giants Will Not Play Night Baseball," *Boston Globe*, December 21, 1934.

11. Lee Allen, *The Cincinnati Reds* (Kent, OH: Kent State University Press, 2006), 236; Dan Daniel, "Reds Likely to Be Alone in Experiment with Night Baseball," *The Sporting News*, December 20, 1934; Tom Swope, "MacPhail Lights on A.L. Critics as Reds Light Way for Night Ball," *The Sporting News*, December 20, 1934.

12. H.I. Phillips, "Night Baseball and Hot Dogs," *Boston Globe*, December 15, 1934.

13. "McCarthy Opposed to Night Baseball," *New York Times*, February 17, 1935; "Cronin Disapproves of Night Baseball," *Boston Globe*, February 12, 1935.

14. James O'Leary, "Baseball Is a Game for Daylight Only," *Boston Globe*, February 16, 1935; F.C. Lane, "Will the Major Leagues Adopt Night Baseball?" *Baseball Magazine*, October 1935, 489.

15. "Night Ball Games Are Passing Fad, Says Connie Mack," *Boston Globe*, February 16, 1935.

16. Ford Frick, "Frick Sees 5 Clubs in Race for Flag," *New York Times*, January 6, 1935; John Carvalho, *Frick*: *Baseball's Third Commissioner* (Jefferson, NC: McFarland, 2016), 66.

17. John Drebinger, "Rule Permitting Night Baseball with Restrictions Passed by National League," *New York Times*, February 6, 1935.

18. Warfield, *The Roaring Redhead*, 58.

19. Payne, *Let There Be Light*, 30–40.

20. Tom Swope, "Cincinnati Lights Way in Big League Style," *The Sporting News*, May 23, 1935.

21. "Reds' Night Game Draws 25,000 Fans," *New York Times*, May 25, 1935.

22. "Turning on the Lights," *The Sporting News*, May 16, 1935.

23. Payne, *Let There Be Light*, 179; advertisements for General Electric Company, *The Sporting News*, October 31 and November 21, 1935.

24. Advertisements for General Electric Company, *The Sporting News*, February 20, 1936, and March 11, 1937.

25. Tommy Holmes, "Quinn Against Arcs," *Brooklyn Eagle*, October 24, 1935.

26. "Flashy Uniforms, Night Baseball, Planned

for Braves by Marshall," *New York Times*, August 8, 1935.

27. Payne, *Let There Be Light*, 179.

28. "Added Drama in Night Play Pleases Fans," *Brooklyn Eagle*, January 31, 1937.

29. "League Approves Sale of Browns; Permits Night Ball in St. Louis," *New York Times*, November 13, 1936; "No Night Baseball in St. Louis," *New York Times*, December 16, 1937.

30. "Night Ball Plan Fails," *New York Times*, October 21, 1937.

31. Red Smith, "Connie Sees Light, May Play at Night," *The Sporting News*, November 19, 1936.

32. Norman Macht, *The Grand Old Man of Baseball: Connie Mack in His Final Years, 1932–1956* (Lincoln: University of Nebraska Press, 2015), 196–198.

33. "Night Ball Spreads in '37," *The Sporting News*, December 30, 1937.

34. George Barton, "St. Paul Held Scoreless for Six Innings in Night Baseball Inaugural," *Minneapolis Star Tribune*, July 16, 1937.

35. "Business Boom in Baseball Predicted for This Season," *Charleston Mail*, April 12, 1936.

36. "A.L. Turns Down Tribe on Night Ball," *The Sporting News*, December 9, 1937.

37. Fogelson, *Downtown: Its Rise and Fall*, 222, 227.

38. "No Night Ball, Says MacPhail," *Brooklyn Eagle*, January 20, 1938.

39. Tommy Holmes, "MacPhail Sees Night Ball Pulling Dodgers Out of Red," *Brooklyn Eagle*, May 29, 1938; Tommy Holmes, "Brooklyn to Light Up with $110,000 Mazdas," *The Sporting News*, May 26, 1938.

40. Robert Swackhamer, "Lighting Major League Baseball Fields," *General Electric Review*, September 1939, 388–389.

41. "Dodgers List Dates for Six Night Games," *New York Times*, June 8, 1938.

42. Tommy Holmes, "Lights Shed Bright Ray on 700,000 Dodger Gate," *The Sporting News*, September 15, 1938.

43. Tommy Holmes, "Dodgers Open the Last Word in Night Ball Plants," *Brooklyn Eagle*, June 15, 1938.

44. "Harridge Sees Night Baseball for All in Majors," *Brooklyn Eagle*, July 3, 1938.

45. Smith, e-mail to author, with Retrosheet data. All future references to percentage of major-league games played as night games are from this source.

46. "Mack for Night Ball," *New York Times*, October 19, 1938.

Chapter 10

1. "Mack Indorses Night Baseball," *Philadelphia Inquirer*, October 18, 1938.

2. Francis Shea, "Win, Lose or Draw," *Washington Evening Star*, December 13, 1938; "Club Used on Fox Griffith To Win Night Game Backing," *New York Evening Post*, December 15, 1938; Macht, *Grand Old Man of Baseball*, 199–200. Newspaper reports varied

on which ball club actually blocked waivers on Bonura; the Associated Press reported that both Cleveland and Philadelphia held up the trade, while a few papers reported that Mack was the sole culprit (which would have been out of character for him).

3. John Drebinger, "Indians and Athletics to Introduce Night Ball to American League Next Year," *New York Times*, December 15, 1938; "A's and Indians Win Nocturnal Privilege," *The Sporting News*, December 22, 1938.

4. "Phils Join Brooklyn, Reds in Owl Contests," *The Sporting News*, December 22, 1938; "Arcs Give N.L. More Sunday Twin Bills," *The Sporting News*, February 9, 1939.

5. "Mack, 76 Tomorrow, Out to Win Another Flag Before He Retires," *New York Times*, December 22, 1938; "Daylight Baseball Not in Danger," *Boston Globe*, February 10, 1939.

6. Advertisement for General Electric Company, *The Sporting News*, January 26, 1939.

7. "780 Lights for Stadium," *New York Times*, January 26, 1939; Kuklich, *To Every Thing a Season*, 76.

8. Shirley Povich, "This Morning," *Washington Post*, May 18, 1939.

9. "Yankees to Appear Twice in Night Games This Year," *New York Times*, May 18, 1939.

10. Macht, *Grand Old Man of Baseball*, 224.

11. "White Sox to Play Night Home Games," *New York Times*, June 23, 1939; Bevis, *Doubleheaders*, 135.

12. "Warning Is Issued by MacPhail Against Night Ball Overloading," *New York Times*, July 16, 1939.

13. Dan Daniel, "Over the Fence," *The Sporting News*, August 31, 1939.

14. Daniel Wann and Nyla Branscombe, "Sports Fans: Measuring Degrees of Identification with Their Team," *International Journal of Sport Psychology*, January–March 1993, 1–17.

15. "Wide Range in Lighting as Game Grows Night-Minded," *The Sporting News*, May 11, 1939.

16. Advertisements for Westinghouse, *The Sporting News*, May 25 and August 10, 1939; "Powerful Lights for Tribe," *The Sporting News*, June 15, 1939.

17. Swackhamer, "Lighting Major League Baseball Fields," 389–390; "Major Parks Seating 100,000 Seen as Result of Night Ball," *The Sporting News*, July 13, 1939; "Engineer Predicts Roofed Parks, Indirect Lighting," *The Sporting News*, December 7, 1939.

18. Ron Briley, "Don't Let Hitler (or the Depression) Kill Baseball: Franklin D. Roosevelt and the National Pastime, 1932–1945," in *Franklin D. Roosevelt and the Shaping of American Political Culture*, eds. Nancy Beck Young et al (Armonk, NY: M.E. Sharpe, 2001), 119.

19. Briley, "Don't Let Hitler (or the Depression) Kill Baseball," 122–124; Curt Smith, *The Presidents and the Pastime: The History of Baseball and the White House* (Lincoln: University of Nebraska Press, 2018), 78.

20. "Wide Range in Lighting as Game Grows Night-Minded."

21. "21-Player Limit Voted by League," *New York Times*, November 28, 1939; "Minor Leagues Take

Heart," *Literary Digest*, August 20, 1932; Doug Taylor, "A Community and Its Team: The Evangeline League's Lafayette White Sox, 1934–1942," *Louisiana History*, Spring 1995, 165.

22. "New Men and Kleinke's Arm Spark Red Wings," *The Sporting News*, August 12, 1937.

23. "Red Wings and Buffalo Herd Meet in Night Doubleheader," *Rochester Democrat and Chronicle*, August 21, 1935; "Baseball Tonight: Twilight-Night Doubleheader," *Rochester Democrat and Chronicle*, August 15, 1939.

24. "Fans Share Pay-Off from Cincy Lights," *The Sporting News*, January 4, 1940.

25. John Drebinger, "Giants Will Play Night Baseball Here," *New York Times*, November 15, 1939.

26. John Drebinger, "American League Bars Champion's Trades with Rival Clubs Except on Waiver," *New York Times*, December 8, 1939; "Aid to Pitcher Seen in New Rule," *New York Times*, February 13, 1940.

27. "Owl Ball Hurdles Cleared in St. Louis," *The Sporting News*, February 1, 1940; "42 Night Contests to Be Played in N.L.," *The Sporting News*, February 8, 1940; "No Night Baseball in Senators' Park," *New York Times*, March 12, 1940.

28. Advertisement for Westinghouse, *The Sporting News*, October 3, 1940.

29. "Recommendations for Lighting Crosley Field, Cincinnati, Ohio," in *A History of Baseball in 100 Objects*, by Josh Leventhal (New York: Black Dog & Leventhal, 2015), 218; Brands, "Minors' Night Game Experience Lights Way for Majors."

30. Advertisements for Westinghouse, *The Sporting News*, May 25 and November 30, 1939; "Great Arc Lamps to Brighten Fair," *New York Times*, March 26, 1939.

31. Macht, *The Grand Old Man of Baseball*, 199.

32. "Ten Years in Night Ball History," *The Sporting News*, May 2, 1940; "Wide Range in Lighting as Game Grows Night-Minded."

33. Advertisement for General Electric Company, *The Sporting News*, November 28, 1940.

34. Hal Borland, "Night Baseball Packs 'Em In," *New York Times*, June 9, 1940.

35. John Drebinger, "Champions Crush Browns by 12 to 3," *New York Times*, June 15, 1940.

36. "Night Games Seen by 1,558,021 in Major League Parks This Year," *New York Times*, September 7, 1940; "Night Game Figures Tell the Story," *The Sporting News*, September 19, 1940.

37. "Night Ball for Senators," *New York Times*, November 9, 1940; advertisement for Westinghouse, *The Sporting News*, November 28, 1940.

38. Francis Stan, "Now Arc Addict, Inconsistent Griff Is a Man of Mystery," *Washington Evening Star*, November 9, 1940.

39. "N.L. Refuses to Lift the Limit on Seven Night Games," *The Sporting News*, July 11, 1940; "Browns Head Hits Night Game Limit," *New York Times*, December 14, 1940.

40. John Drebinger, "Joint Session Action Limits Each Club in Majors to Seven Home Night Games," *New York Times*, December 12, 1940; White, *Creating the National Pastime*, 116.

41. John Kieran, "The Day Side and the Night Shift," *New York Times*, June 28, 1940.

42. "Majors Gird to Carry On During U.S. Emergency," *The Sporting News*, December 18, 1941; J.G. Taylor Spink, "Full Story of Browns' Near Shift in '41," *The Sporting News*, August 31, 1949.

43. "16 Sabbath Twins Scheduled by A.L.," *The Sporting News*, January 30, 1941.

44. "Barrow Opposes More Night Games," *New York Times*, May 17, 1941.

45. "Arc-Light Games Voluntarily Curtailed to Conserve Power," *The Sporting News*, June 5, 1941; "Ickes Favors Extension of Daylight Time," *Boston Globe*, May 30, 1941.

46. "Mack Says Giving Up Night Baseball No Help to Defense," *Boston Globe*, May 30, 1941.

47. Burton Hawkins, "New Arcs No Aid to Nats in Hunt for Triumph," *Washington Evening Star*, May 29, 1941.

48. "70 Pct. of Minor-League Ball Now Played at Night," *The Sporting News*, December 7, 1939.

Chapter 11

1. "Detroit to See Night Ball," *The Sporting News*, November 13, 1941; Dickson, *Bill Veeck*, 61–62.

2. "Majors Will Discuss More Night Baseball," *New York Times*, January 21, 1942.

3. John Drebinger, "Ott Pays $50,000 for First Baseman," *New York Times*, December 12, 1941.

4. Letter from Commissioner Landis to President Roosevelt, January 14, 1942, in President's Personal Files 1933–1945, PPF 227: Baseball, at Franklin D. Roosevelt Library, Hyde Park, New York.

5. Letter from President Roosevelt to Commissioner Landis, January 15, 1942, in Correspondence Collection of Manuscript Archives, BA MSS 044: Box 1, Folder 46, at National Baseball Hall of Fame, Cooperstown, New York.

6. Clark Griffith, "Clark Griffith's 50 Golden Years in the American League," *The Sporting News*, August 8, 1952.

7. William Mead, *Even the Browns: The Zany, True Story of Baseball in the Early Forties* (Chicago: Contemporary Books, 1978), 37.

8. Mead, *Even the Browns*, 36.

9. Letter from President Roosevelt to Commissioner Landis, January 15, 1942; Smith, *The Presidents and the Pastime*, 83.

10. Susan Dunn, *1940: FDR, Willkie, Lindbergh, Hitler—the Election amid the Storm* (New Haven: Yale University Press, 2013), 61–62, 128–129.

11. John Jeffries, *A Third Term for FDR: The Election of 1940* (Lawrence: University Press of Kansas, 2017), 171–172; Edward Flynn, *You're the Boss: The Practice of American Politics* (New York: Collier, 1962), 171.

12. Briley, "Don't Let Hitler (or the Depression) Kill Baseball," 129–130.

13. Linda Levin, *The Making of FDR: The Story of Stephen T. Early, America's First Modern Press Secretary* (Amherst, NY: Prometheus, 2008), 274–275;

Hal Cooper, "Roosevelt OK's Baseball Continuation," *Wilmington* (NC) *Morning Star*, January 17, 1942.

14. John Drebinger, "Baseball Drafts Wartime Program," *New York Times*, February 3, 1942.

15. John Drebinger, "Big Leagues Lift Seven-Game Quota," *New York Times*, February 4, 1942.

16. Drebinger, "Big Leagues Lift Seven-Game Quota."

17. John Drebinger, "More Night Games Expected by Frick," *New York Times*, January 18, 1942.

18. "Army to Dim Coast to 15-Mile Depth Effective Tonight," *New York Times*, April 28, 1942.

19. "Valentine Orders Cancellation of Night Baseball in City During Wartime," *New York Times*, May 19, 1942.

20. Snelling, *The Greatest Minor League*, 191; Mead, *Even the Browns*, 80; "Baseball at Night Banned in Jersey," *New York Times*, June 10, 1942.

21. Tommy Holmes, "Arc Setup Finds Dodgers Stuck on Horns of Dilemma," *Brooklyn Eagle*, June 13, 1942; James Dawson, "Dodgers Book Five 7 P.M. Games; Lights May Be Used for an Hour," *New York Times*, June 13, 1942.

22. Burton Hawkins, "14 Extra Night Games for Nats at Home Sought by Griffith," *Washington Evening Star*, July 4, 1942.

23. Louis Effrat, "Senators Plea for More Night Games Denied," *New York Times*, July 7, 1942.

24. Shirley Povich, "Defiant Griff Turns to Twi-Night Ball," *The Sporting News*, July 16, 1942; Shirley Povich, "Harridge Dims Nats' Twilight-Glimmer Tilts," *The Sporting News*, July 30, 1942.

25. Bevis, *Doubleheaders*, 141.

26. Roy Stockton, "Laabs' 19th Home Run Gives Browns Split with Red Sox," *St. Louis Post-Dispatch*, July 25, 1942.

27. "Tiger Twilight Tilt Ticks at Turnstiles," *The Sporting News*, July 2, 1942.

28. John Drebinger, "Night Game Limit of 14 Is Retained," *New York Times*, December 4, 1942.

29. Bevis, *Doubleheaders*, 146–147.

30. Burton Hawkins, "Griff's Plea for More Night Games Makes Sense," *Washington Evening Star*, June 16, 1943.

31. "Nats Become 'Owls' as They Get Unlimited Night Games," *Washington Evening Star*, July 14, 1943.

32. Shirley Povich, "Griff Now Runs Biggest 'Night Spot' in Majors," *The Sporting News*, July 22, 1943.

33. "St. Louis Ball Clubs Want More Than 14 Night Games in 1944," *Boston Globe*, November 28, 1943.

34. Griffith, "Clark Griffith's 50 Golden Years."

35. "American League for Short Season," *New York Times*, December 2, 1943.

36. Edward Murphy, "National Leaguers Assail Decision on Night Baseball," *New York Sun*, December 4, 1943; Dan Daniel, "Majors Speed Their Postwar Plans," *The Sporting News*, December 9, 1943.

37. "Giants and Dodgers Join Arc Parade" *New York Times*, March 6, 1944; "Jersey City Toppled, 3–2," *New York Times*, May 20, 1944; "West Coast Gets Night Sports Back," *New York Times*, October 10, 1943.

38. "WPB May Lift Ban on Light Equipment in Big League Parks," *Boston Globe*, May 1, 1944; "WPB Chief Forbids Lights in Cubs Park," *New York Times*, May 9, 1944.

39. "Night Baseball Brings Pot of Gold to Owners," *Boston Globe*, July 4, 1944; "Night Ball Limit Ends on Weekdays," *New York Times*, July 12, 1944.

40. Dan Daniel, "Night Ball Fight Stirs Majors' Meetings," *The Sporting News*, July 20, 1944.

41. "No Night Contests for World Series," *New York Times*, July 13, 1944.

42. Arthur Daley, "Dead Geese Lay No Golden Eggs," *New York Times*, June 10, 1944.

43. "A.L. Saw Big Gain in Night Baseball," *New York Times*, December 3, 1944.

44. John Drebinger, "Majors Set Plans to Pick New Head," *New York Times*, December 13, 1944.

45. "WPB Night Game Sanction Raises Baseball's Hopes," *Boston Globe*, January 15, 1945; "Proposed Work-or-Fight Order Figures to Hit Baseball Hardest," *New York Times*, January 5, 1945.

46. "Baseball's Role Praised," *New York Times*, January 11, 1945; "Wartime Baseball Is Put on 'If' Basis," *New York Times*, January 17, 1945; Dan Daniel, "Game Sees No Hint in Washington of Stop Order," *The Sporting News*, January 25, 1945.

47. "Roosevelt Wants Baseball to Go On," *New York Times*, March 14, 1945; "WMC Decision Lets Baseball Players Leave War Plants," *New York Times*, March 22, 1945.

48. William Marshall, *Baseball's Pivotal Era, 1945–1951* (Lexington: University Press of Kentucky, 1999), 19–22.

49. "Truman's Anxious for Baseball to Keep Going, Chandler Reports," *New York Times*, April 29, 1945.

50. "Dodgers and Cards Are Upset by Rain," *New York Times*, September 14, 1945; "Dodgers Escape Injury in Wreck," *Brooklyn Eagle*, September 15, 1945.

Chapter 12

1. James Dawson, "Yankees to Introduce Twilight Ball to Stadium," *New York Times*, May 18, 1945; "Braves Will Play Night Baseball Next Year," *Boston Globe*, July 19, 1945.

2. "No Lights in '46 for Cubs, Says Wrigley," *Chicago Tribune*, October 21, 1945; "Lights for Fenway Park," *New York Times*, May 3, 1946.

3. John Drebinger, "Yankee Stadium Lights to Eclipse Those at All Other Sports," *New York Times*, January 16, 1946; advertisement for General Electric Company, *The Sporting News*, June 5, 1946.

4. "Braves Will Install Night Game Lights," *Boston Globe*, November 8, 1945; advertisement for Crouse-Hinds Company, *The American City*, August 1949.

5. "Unlimited Night Game Issue at Major Leagues," *New York Times*, December 1, 1945; John Keller, "Majors Held Likely to Concede Washington, St. Louis Clubs Heavy Night Play at Home," *Washington Evening Star*, December 11, 1945.

6. John Keller, "Chandler's Vote Wins Griffith's Battle for Night Baseball," *Washington Evening Star*, December 13, 1945; John Drebinger, "Chandler Blocks Night Game Limit," *New York Times*, December 13, 1945.

7. Fred Lieb, "St. Louis Clubs to Battle Against Cut in Arc Tilts," *The Sporting News*, December 6, 1945; Edward Murphy, "Baseball Fuss Ends in Victory for Czar Happy," *New York Sun*, December 13, 1945; Drebinger, "Chandler Blocks Night Game Limit."

8. Drebinger, "Chandler Blocks Night Game Limit."

9. Tommy Holmes, "More Night Games? Larry Still Says No!" *Brooklyn Eagle*, January 21, 1942.

10. "Twi-Night Twin Bills Explained," *The Sporting News*, January 24, 1946; "Twi-Night Bargain Bills Barred in National Loop," *The Sporting News*, August 21, 1946.

11. Marshall, *Baseball's Pivotal Era,* 395.

12. Official league schedules, *The Sporting News*, March 7, 1946.

13. Charlie Bevis, *Red Sox vs. Braves in Boston: The Battle for Fans' Hearts, 1901–1952* (Jefferson, NC: McFarland, 2017), 178–179; Harold Kaese, "Braves Field Express, Home to Game to Home, Newest Fan Convenience," *Boston Globe*, May 14, 1946.

14. Dan Daniel, "First-Nighters at Yanks' New Arc Show," *The Sporting News*, June 12, 1946.

15. Steven Gietschier, ed., *Complete Baseball Record Book* (St. Louis: Sporting News Publishing, 2004), 123; Bevis, *Doubleheaders*, 154–155.

16. "Texas League," *The Sporting News*, May 23, 1946; "Beaumont Group to Buy Franchise From Tigers," *The Sporting News*, September 4, 1941.

17. Bevis, *Red Sox vs. Braves in Boston*, 179, 184.

18. "Baseball Crowds Rose 63 Per Cent," *New York Times*, October 19, 1946; Warfield, *The Roaring Redhead*, 177; "Braves Night Crowds Surpass Attendance of Previous Seasons," *Boston Globe*, September 8, 1946.

19. Andrew Zimbalist, *Baseball and Billions: A Probing Look Inside the Big Business of Our National Pastime* (New York: Basic Books, 1992), 48.

20. John Drebinger, "Braves Ask Unlimited Night Baseball as Majors Convene," *New York Times*, December 6, 1946; John Drebinger, "Braves Purchase Pitcher Barrett from the Cards," *New York Times*, December 8, 1946.

21. "Braves-Sox Night Game Battle Looms," *Boston Globe*, November 27, 1946.

22. Official league schedules, *The Sporting News*, February 19, 1947.

23. Harold Burr, "New Dodger Ducat Plan Reserves Entire Grandstand at Ebbets Field," *Brooklyn Eagle*, December 7, 1946.

24. Advertisement for the Philadelphia Phillies, *The Sporting News*, December 11, 1946; "Braves to Issue Tickets Covering All 29 Night Tilts," *Boston Globe*, January 31, 1947.

25. "Many Major Clubs Start Afternoon Games Earlier," *The Sporting News*, April 23, 1947.

26. Ed Rumill, "Yawkey, Opposed to Arcs, Gives Fans the Best," *The Sporting News*, June 25, 1947.

27. "Tigers Surrender to Night Baseball," *New York Times*, July 1, 1947.

28. "Stadium Lights Were Ready," *New York Times*, October 6, 1947.

29. Tygiel, *Past Time: Baseball as History*, 115.

30. "Browns Move to Permit Unlimited Night Ball Fails," *The Sporting News*, December 17, 1947.

31. Dan Daniel, "Breadon Still Dazed by Sale of Cards," *The Sporting News*, December 10, 1947.

32. Official league schedules, *The Sporting News*, February 11 and 25, 1948.

33. Ray Gillespie, "Give Cards More Home Night Games," *The Sporting News*, May 19, 1948.

34. H.G. Salsinger, "Hal Newhouser Star of First Mazda Contest," *The Sporting News*, June 23, 1948.

35. Waltz, "Behind the Lights at a Night Ball Game," 102.

36. Advertisements for General Electric Company, *The Sporting News*, December 3, 1947, and April 21, 1948.

37. "R.J. Swackhamer Retires from General Electric After 36 Years," *Illuminating Engineering*, Volume 53 (1958), 708; various documents at the Ancestry.com website concerning Robert J. Swackhamer who was born in Turin, New York, in 1900 and married Mattie Shobe in 1935.

38. Shirley Povich, "Griff Finds Rich His Arc-Enemies," *Baseball Digest*, January 1949, 47.

39. Dan Daniel, "Greenberg Favors Full Night Card, Except on Sundays," *The Sporting News*, July 8, 1948.

40. "More Night Games Wanted in Majors," *New York Times*, December 12, 1948; Dickson, *Bill Veeck*, 153–155.

41. Ray Gillespie, "50–50 Night-Game Chart, But St. Louis Asks More," *The Sporting News*, December 8, 1948.

42. John Drebinger, "More Night Games Voted," *New York Times*, December 14, 1948.

43. Edgar Brands, "Majors Expand Night-Game Program," *The Sporting News*, December 22 1948.

44. "Minor Leagues," *New York Times*, April 14, April 20, and July 5, 1949.

45. Official league schedules, *The Sporting News*, January 26 and February 9, 1949; Harold Burr, "Rickey Goes to Bat for Arc Light Tilts," *Brooklyn Eagle*, January 25, 1949.

46. "Reds and Cards Tie in 15 Innings, 9–9," *New York Times*, September 4, 1949; Bert Hochman, "That Old Bromide's Here Again as Flock Gets 6 to Yankees' 10," *Brooklyn Eagle*, October 10, 1949.

Chapter 13

1. Eric Avila, *Popular Culture in the Age of White Flight* (Berkeley: University of California Press, 2004), 2–3; Neil Sullivan, *The Dodgers Move West*

(New York: Oxford University Press, 1987), 38–40; Robert Putnam, *Bowling Alone: The Collapse and Revival of American Community* (New York: Simon and Schuster, 2001), 210.

2. James Walker and Robert Bellamy, *Center Field Shot: A History of Baseball on Television* (Lincoln: University of Nebraska Press, 2008), 34, 71.

3. Lynn Spigel, *Make Room for TV: Television and the Family Ideal in Postwar America* (Chicago: University of Chicago Press, 1992), 100; Richard Butsch, *The Making of American Audiences: From Stage to Television, 1750–1990* (New York: Cambridge University Press, 2000), 246–247; Christopher Sterling and John Kittross, *Stay Tuned: A Concise History of American Broadcasting* (Belmont, CA: Wadsworth, 1990), 657.

4. Jillson, *Pursuing the American Dream*, 197, 203–204.

5. William Whyte, *The Organization Man* (New York: Simon and Schuster, 1956), 4–6, 19–20, 63, 298.

6. Surdam, *Century of the Leisured Masses*, 46, 83.

7. John Drebinger, "National League Votes Afternoon Lights, Ends Night-Game Curfew," *New York Times*, December 13, 1949; "Two-Day Playoff Period Provided by New American League Ruling," *New York Times*, December 12, 1950.

8. "Public Forces Night Ball: Chandler," *Boston Globe*, December 14, 1949.

9. Dan Daniel, "Spitball's Return Rejected; N.L. Scraps Night Curfew," *The Sporting News*, December 21, 1949.

10. Bob Broeg, "Women Want Arc Ball, Saigh Finds," *The Sporting News*, February 15, 1950.

11. "Cards Trip Pirates Under Lights," *New York Times*, April 19, 1950.

12. "Sunday Night Game at St. Louis Declined by Rickey, Chandler Says," *New York Times*, June 9, 1950.

13. "Cards, Ignoring Order by Chandler, Ask Hearing on Sunday Night Ball," *New York Times*, June 10, 1950; "Cardinals Call Off Sunday Night Game with Dodgers," *New York Times*, June 13, 1950.

14. Official league schedules, *The Sporting News*, February 8, 1950.

15. Louis Effrat, "Dodgers to Use Erskine and Wade Against Giants in Day-Night Bill," *New York Times*, August 13, 1952; "White Sox Rained Out," *New York Times*, June 29, 1951.

16. "Dodgers Serve Notice There's No Biz Like Show Biz at Ebbets," *Brooklyn Eagle*, January 6, 1952; Gietschier, *Complete Baseball Record Book*, 123.

17. "16,126,676 Watched Big League Games," *New York Times*, December 9, 1951.

18. John Drebinger, "American League Ends Limitation on Night Baseball," *New York Times*, December 9, 1951.

19. "Players Propose Liaison Office for Their Affairs," *The Sporting News*, December 5, 1951; Burton Hawkins, "Griffith and Veeck Win Campaign for Unlimited Night Baseball," *Washington Evening Star*, December 9, 1951.

20. Dan Daniel, "Majors Agree on Curfew, But Differ on Sunday Arcs," *The Sporting News*, April 2, 1952.

21. Official league schedules, *The Sporting News*, February 13, 1952.

22. Paul Angle, *Philip K. Wrigley: A Memoir of a Modest Man* (Chicago: Rand McNally, 1975), 63, 113.

23. Walker and Bellamy, *Center Field Shot*, 53.

24. Edgar Munzel, "'Night Ball Like Drug' Declares Holdout Wrigley," *The Sporting News*, February 20, 1952.

25. Zimbalist, *Baseball and Billions*, 50.

26. Banner, *The Baseball Trust*, 123; Jim Norman, "Football Still Americans' Favorite Sport to Watch," *Gallup News Service*, January 4, 2018.

Chapter 14

1. "Gate Report: More at Night, Fewer by Day," *The Sporting News*, December 17, 1952.

2. White, *Creating the National Pastime*, 307–308.

3. "N.L. Attendance Up Million, A.L. Dips 1,080,573," *The Sporting News*, December 16, 1953.

4. "Majors' Gate Up 1,552,084 in '54," *The Sporting News*, December 15, 1954.

5. "1,049,288 A.L. Gate Dip Due to Yank Waltz to Flag," *The Sporting News*, December 12, 1956.

6. William Mullins, *Becoming Big League: Seattle, the Pilots, and Stadium Politics* (Seattle: University of Washington Press, 2013), 7.

7. Tygiel, *Past Time: Baseball as History*, 172–177.

8. Avila, *Popular Culture in the Age of White Flight*, 153; Kuklick, *To Every Thing a Season*, 121, 131, 158.

9. Fogelson, *Downtown: Its Rise and Fall*, 318–319.

10. Lizabeth Cohen, *Saving America's Cities: Ed Logue and the Struggle to Renew America in the Suburban Age* (New York: Farrar, Strauss and Giroux, 2019), 177.

11. Glaab, "Historical Perspective on Urban Development Schemes," 198; Cohen, *Saving America's Cities*, 101; Fogelson, *Downtown: Its Rise and Fall*, 319.

12. Sullivan, *The Dodgers Move West*, 3–4.

13. Andy McCue, *Mover and Shaker: Walter O'Malley, the Dodgers, & Baseball's Westward Expansion* (Lincoln: University of Nebraska Press, 2014), 135; Sullivan, *The Dodgers Move West*, 48–51.

14. David Surdam, *The Postwar Yankees: Baseball's Golden Age Revisited* (Lincoln: University of Nebraska Press, 2008), 87–88.

15. Herb Heft, "Orioles' Out-of-Town Fans Spent $5,500,000," *The Sporting News*, January 12, 1955.

16. Harold Rosenthal, "Giants' Poll Brings More Parking, Earlier Arc Play," *The Sporting News*, March 3, 1955; Carl Lundquist, "Game to Act on Fan Ideas Revealed in Survey: Frick," *The Sporting News*, December 14, 1955.

17. Shirley Povich, "Majors Overdo Arc Ball, Pioneer MacPhail's View," *The Sporting News*, June 1, 1955.

18. Joe King, "Major Arc Ball to Hit New High in '56," *The Sporting News*, December 14, 1955.

19. Murray Schumach, "Big League Baseball Facing Shutout by Television," *New York Times*, September 18, 1955.

20. "Cardinals Will Be Night Owls of National League This Year," *New York Times*, January 15, 1957; "American League Adds Night Tests," *New York Times*, January 18, 1957; Hy Hurwitz, "Sox' 18 Night Games Big Baseball Surprise," *Boston Globe*, January 1, 1957.

21. Dickson, *Bill Veeck*, 232; Joseph Sheehan, "City Officials to Help Dodgers Get New Stadium and Stay Here," *New York Times*, August 18, 1955.

22. "250 Night Games Set by National League," *New York Times*, January 12, 1955; National League schedule, *New York Times*, January 26, 1956.

23. "Giants Schedule 21 Night Games," *New York Times*, November 21, 1957; "42 Mazda Dates on Dodger Chart for Los Angeles," *The Sporting News*, February 12, 1958.

24. Gladwin Hill, "Cheers Rub Chill Off Coast Night," *New York Times*, April 17, 1958; "Lights Will Be Bright at Giants' New Park," *New York Times*, July 19, 1959; Giants' Park Dazzling Diamond Palace," *The Sporting News*, April 6, 1960.

25. Frank Finch, "Dodgers Rush Plans for Coliseum Play," *The Sporting News*, January 29, 1958.

26. Frank Finch, "Dodgers to Set Arc-Game High With 63 in '59," *The Sporting News*, January 14, 1959.

27. Official league schedules, *The Sporting News*, February 3, 1960.

28. Carvalho, *Frick*: *Baseball's Third Commissioner*, 176; William Conklin, "Commissioner Frick Gives Needle to LP Baseball Games," *New York Times*, April 15, 1956.

29. Roger Kahn, "Something's Changing About Baseball," *New York Times*, April 5, 1959.

30. Norman, "Football Still Americans' Favorite Sport to Watch."

31. Eric Leifer, *Making the Majors: The Transformation of Team Sports in America* (Cambridge: Harvard University Press, 1995), 126–127.

32. John Eisenberg, *The League: How Five Rivals Created the NFL and Launched a Sports Empire* (New York: Basic Books, 2018), 326.

33. Michael MacCambridge, *America's Game: The Epic Story of How Pro Football Captured a Nation* (New York: Random House, 2004), 113.

Chapter 15

1. Official league schedules, *New York Times*, February 10, 1961, and *The Sporting News*, February 7, 1962.

2. Bob Burnes, "One-Day Stands, 24 Twi-Night Twin Bills, on A.L. Chart," *The Sporting News*, February 16, 1963.

3. Paul Goldberger, *Ballpark: Baseball in the American City* (New York: Alfred A. Knopf, 2019), 174.

4. "New York to Play 29 Night Games," *New York Times*, November 22, 1963.

5. Associated Press article in *Corpus Christi Times*, quoted in Bill McCurdy, "Houston's Role in the Initiation of Sunday Night Baseball," *The National Pastime*, 2014, 6–7; Dan Daniel, "Houston Gets Green Light on Sunday Arc Schedule Next Year," *The Sporting News*, August 11, 1962.

6. "Houston Colts to Play Sunday Night Baseball," *New York Times*, January 25, 1963; "77 Colt Contests Set Under Lights," *New York Times*, January 21, 1964.

7. The visiting-club consent rule remained in effect at least through the 1965 season ("DeWitt Heads N.L. Group to Set Up Disaster Plan," *The Sporting News*, December 19, 1964).

8. "Red Sox Moving Most Night Tilts Ahead to 7:30," *Boston Globe*, June 20, 1965; "Swatters Take Dim View of Dusk Starts for Kaycee Games," *The Sporting News*, February 23, 1963.

9. Michael Green and Roger Launius, *Charlie Finley: The Outrageous Story of Baseball's Super Showman* (New York: Walker & Company, 2010), 79–88.

10. "World Series Games at Night?" *Boston Globe*, November 7, 1964; Green and Launius, *Charlie Finley*, 66–67.

11. Charlie Bevis, "Baseball Players' Pension Plan: A Home Run by Any Measure," *Employee Benefits Journal*, September 1991, 9.

12. Val Adams, "C.B.S. Gets Rights to Pro Football," *New York Times*, April 27, 1961.

13. C.C. Johnson Spink, "$6.5 Million Jackpot Seen in Video Plan," *The Sporting News*, October 12, 1963; Leonard Koppett, "Majors Finally Catch Up to 60's During Chicago Summer Talks," *New York Times*, August 12, 1964.

14. Dan Ewald, *John Fetzer: On a Handshake: The Times and Triumphs of a Tiger Owner* (Champaign, IL: Sagamore, 1997), 94; Leonard Koppett, "19 Major League Clubs Expected to Sign Television Pact Today," *New York Times*, December 15, 1964.

15. Val Adams, "C.B.S.–TV to Pay $28.2 Million for 2-Years Pro Football Rights," *New York Times*, January 25, 1964; Norman, "Football Still Americans' Favorite Sport to Watch."

16. "Majors' Revenue From Radio–TV Hits $29 Million," *The Sporting News*, March 4, 1967.

17. Glen Gendzel, "Competitive Boosterism: How Milwaukee Lost the Braves," *Business History Review*, Winter 1995, 548.

18. Jerald Podair, *City of Dreams: Dodger Stadium and the Birth of Modern Los Angeles* (Princeton: Princeton University Press, 2017), 75, 247, 256.

19. Arthur Daley, "Revolution by Electricity," *New York Times*, May 31, 1965.

20. "N.B.C. Will Pay $30.6 Million for Baseball TV in New Pact," *New York Times*, October 20, 1965.

21. Edgar Munzel, "Majors Pluck $30 Million Plum in Three-Year NBC Video Deal," *The Sporting News*, October 30, 1965.

22. Val Adams, "NBC in Baseball Package Deal," *New York Times*, October 24, 1965.

23. Advertisement of NBC, *New York Times*, April 16, 1966.

24. Walker and Bellamy, *Center Field Shot*, 126.

25. "Baseball Remains Top Sport, But Fans Ask Faster Pace," *New York Times*, July 11, 1967.

26. Official league schedules, *The Sporting News*, February 11 and 18, 1967.

27. Joseph Durso, "Marichal and Chance Chosen to Start in All–Star Game at Anaheim Today," *New York Times*, July 11, 1967; Walker and Bellamy, *Center Field Shot*, 137.

28. "50,000 Expected for Indoor Game," *New York Times*, July 7, 1968.

29. Edgar Munzel, "N.L. Blocks Move by A.L. to Install Two-Division Play," *The Sporting News*, August 19, 1967; Jack Craig, "sporTView," *The Sporting News*, October 3, 1970.

30. Bowie Kuhn, *Hardball: The Education of a Baseball Commissioner* (Lincoln: University of Nebraska Press, 1987), 42.

31. Joseph Durso, "Owners Considering Plan for Series Night Games," *New York Times*, December 5, 1970.

32. Stan Isle, "Wednesday Series Game Slated for Night This Year," *The Sporting News*, January 23, 1971.

33. "Night Schedule Will Grow for World Series in 1972," *New York Times*, May 7, 1971.

34. Jack Craig, "Baseball Pact Victory for All," *Boston Globe*, May 9, 1971.

35. Craig, "Baseball Pact Victory for All."

36. "63 Million, a Record, Saw Series Night Game," *New York Times*, October 15, 1971.

37. Dave Anderson, "The Thermal Man," *New York Times*, November 2, 1982.

38. Walker and Bellamy, *Center Field Shot*, 138.

Chapter 16

1. Jack Craig, "Huge Gain in Baseball TV Swag," *The Sporting News*, April 5, 1975.

2. Article IV, Section D, "1970 Basic Agreement," 3.

3. Bevis, *Doubleheaders*, 176–177, 207.

4. Bevis, *Doubleheaders*, 180–181.

5. "Rangers Take Heat Off Fans," *New York Times*, July 17, 1972; "Braves to Play 2 Sunday Night Games," *New York Times*, November 18, 1975.

6. "40 Years of Night Ball—What a Meal Ticket!" *The Sporting News*, March 29, 1975; "MacPhail, Majors' Night Ball Pioneer, Dies at 85," *The Sporting News*, October 18, 1975; "Mathews, MacPhail and Joss Enter Shrine," *The Sporting News*, August 19, 1978.

7. Bevis, *Doubleheaders*, 180–181; Article IV, Section D, "1976–1979 Basic Agreement," 5.

8. Norman, "Football Still Americans' Favorite Sport to Watch."

9. Zimbalist, *Baseball and Billions*, 48–51.

10. Craig, "Huge Gain in Baseball TV Swag"; Paul Staudohar and James Dworkin, "The Impact of Baseball's New Television Contracts," *NINE: A Journal of Baseball History and Culture*, Spring 2002, 103.

11. Jack Craig, "Baseball Lands $175-Million TV Contract," *Boston Globe*, April 26, 1979; Neil Amdur, "Baseball Gets Billion-Dollar TV Deal," *New York Times*, April 8, 1983; Staudohar and Dworkin, "The Impact of Baseball's New Television Contracts"; "Series to Be at Night," *New York Times*, May 30, 1985.

12. Jack Craig, "Changing Picture of Baseball on TV," *Boston Globe*, April 2, 1983.

13. Zimbalist, *Baseball and Billions*, 48–51.

14. Norman, "Football Still Americans' Favorite Sport to Watch."

15. Michael Mandelbaum, *The Meaning of Sports: Why Americans Watch Baseball, Football, and Basketball and What They See When They Do* (New York: Public Affairs, 2004), 107, 124.

16. Leah Vande Berg and Nick Trujillo, "The Rhetoric of Winning and Losing: The American Dream and America's Team," in *Media, Sports, & Society*, ed. Lawrence Wenner (Oaks, CA: Sage, 1989), 206–207.

17. Official league schedules, *The Sporting News*, February 17, 1979.

18. Dave Smith, e-mail to author on April 19, 2019, with Retrosheet data tabulation of year-by-year totals of night games played in the major leagues.

19. Schroeder, "When Technology and Culture Collide," 93, 100.

20. Suzanne Prestien, "Past [Im]Perfect: Mythology, Nostalgia, and Baseball," in *Baseball and the American Dream: Race, Class, Gender and the National Pastime*, ed. Robert Elias (Armonk, NY: M.E. Sharpe, 2001), 165; W.P. Kinsella, *Shoeless Joe* (Boston: Houghton Mifflin, 1982), 13, 16; Dwier Brown, *If You Build It …* (Ojai, CA: Elsie Jean Books, 2014), 187–188.

21. Dave Nightingale, "Special Situation, Special Legislation," *The Sporting News*, May 30, 1988.

22. "Cubs Win With 5-Run 10th; Lights Issue Is Settled," *New York Times*, August 31, 1984.

23. Ira Berkow, "Cubs Still Can't Pull Switch to Night," *New York Times*, June 17, 1985.

24. "Night Baseball Celebrates 50th," *St. Joseph* (Missouri) *News–Press*, May 25, 1985; "Court Keeps Cubs in the Dark," *Boston Globe*, October 4, 1985.

25. Nightingale, "Special Situation, Special Legislation."

26. Dave Nightingale, "Let There Be Lights!" *The Sporting News*, May 30, 1988.

27. Joseph Durso, "A Billion-Dollar Bid by CBS Wins Rights to Baseball Games, *New York Times*, December 15, 1988; Jeremy Gerard, "ESPN Will Pay $400 Million for Baseball-Game Rights," *New York Times*, January 6, 1989.

28. Travis Vogan, *ESPN: The Making of a Sports Media Empire* (Urbana: University of Illinois Press, 2015), 28–30, 40.

29. Vince Gennaro, *Diamond Dollars: The Economics of Winning in Baseball* (Hingham, MA:

Maple Street Press, 2007), 193–197; Goldberger, *Ballpark: Baseball in the American City*, 306–314.

30. Gennaro, *Diamond Dollars*, 6–7. The percentages cited in the text are a remix of this book's statistics, which were presented as 20% nationally derived revenue shared among ball clubs (network television and internet) and 80% locally controlled and fully retained revenue (broken down as 49% gate receipts, 20% local television, and 31% other).

31. Article V, Section C, "2017–2021 Basic Agreement," 7–8.

32. John Byrne, "City Council Gives Cubs Go-Ahead for More Night Games," *Chicago Tribune,* June 5, 2013.

33. Peter Bernstein, "Night and Day: What's the Baseball Difference?" *ESPN: The Magazine,* August 5, 2008.

34. Charlie LeDuff, "Office Dress: Baseball Casual," *New York Times,* July 27, 2001.

Bibliography

Adams, James Truslow. *The Epic of America.* Boston: Little, Brown, and Company, 1931.

Akin, William. *The Middle Atlantic League, 1925–1952: A Baseball History.* Jefferson, NC: McFarland, 2015.

Angle, Paul. *Philip K. Wrigley: A Memoir of a Modest Man.* Chicago: Rand McNally, 1975.

Aron, Cindy. *Ladies and Gentlemen of the Civil Service: Middle-Class Workers in Victorian America.* New York: Oxford University Press, 1987.

Aucher, Melanie, and Judith Blau. "Class Formation in Nineteenth-Century America: The Case of the Middle Class." *Annual Review of Sociology,* 1993.

Avila, Eric. *Popular Culture in the Age of White Flight.* Berkeley: University of California Press, 2004.

Aycock, Colleen. *Tex Rickard: Boxing's Greatest Promoter.* Jefferson, NC: McFarland, 2012.

Baldwin, Peter. *In the Watches of the Night: Life in the Nocturnal City, 1820–1930.* Chicago: University of Chicago Press, 2012.

Banner, Stuart. *The Baseball Trust: A History of Baseball's Antitrust Exemption.* New York: Oxford University Press, 2013.

Bartlett, Guy. "Baseball at Night." *Baseball Magazine,* September 1927.

Berthoff, Rowland. "Independence and Enterprise: Small Business in the American Dream." In *Small Business in American Life,* ed. Stuart Bruchey. New York: Columbia University Press, 1980.

Beverage, Richard. *The Los Angeles Angels of the Pacific Coast League, 1903–1957.* Jefferson NC: McFarland, 2011.

Bevis, Charlie. *Doubleheaders: A Major League History.* Jefferson, NC: McFarland, 2011.

_____. "Economic Anatomy of an 1891 Minor League Ball Club." *Base Ball: A Journal of the Early Game,* Fall 2007.

_____. "How the Shaughnessy Plan Redefined Success in Sports." *NINE: A Journal of Baseball History & Culture,* Fall 2011.

_____. *Red Sox vs. Braves in Boston: The Battle for Fans' Hearts, 1901–1952.* Jefferson, NC: McFarland, 2017.

_____. "Sunday Baseball Adoption in the Minor Leagues." *Base Ball 11: New Research on the Early Game,* 2019.

_____. *Sunday Baseball: The Major Leagues' Struggle to Play Baseball on the Lord's Day, 1876–1934.* Jefferson, NC: McFarland, 2003.

Blackford, Mansel. *A History of Small Business in America.* New York: Twayne, 1991.

Blumin, Stuart. *The Emergence of the Middle Class: Social Experience in the American City, 1760–1900.* New York: Cambridge University Press, 1989.

Boorstin, Daniel. *The Americans: The National Experience.* New York: Random House, 1965.

Bowman, Larry. "'I Think It Is Pretty Ritzy, Myself': Kansas Minor League Teams and Night Baseball." *Kansas History,* Winter 1995/1996.

_____. "The Monarchs and Night Baseball." *The National Pastime,* 1996.

_____. "To Save a Minor League Team: Night Baseball Comes to Shreveport." *Louisiana History,* Spring 1997.

Brands, Edgar. "Minors' Night Game Experience Lights Way for Majors." *The Sporting News,* January 24, 1935.

Bright, Arthur. *The Electric-Lamp Industry: Technological Change and Economic Development from 1800 to 1947.* New York: Macmillan, 1949.

Briley, Ron. "Don't Let Hitler (or the Depression) Kill Baseball: Franklin D. Roosevelt and the National Pastime, 1932–1945." In *Franklin D. Roosevelt and the Shaping of American Political Culture,* eds. Nancy Beck Young et al. Armonk, NY: M.E. Sharpe, 2001.

Brox, Jane. *Brilliant: The Evolution of Artificial Light.* Boston: Houghton Mifflin Harcourt, 2010.

Butsch, Richard. *The Making of American Audiences: From Stage to Television, 1750–1990.* New York: Cambridge University Press, 2000.

Carlson, Bernard. *Innovation as a Social Process: Elihu Thomson and the Rise of General Electric.* New York: Cambridge University Press, 1991.

Carter, Gregg. "Baseball in Saint Louis, 1867–1875: An Historical Case Study in Civic Pride." *Missouri Historical Society Bulletin,* July 1975.

Carvalho, John. *Frick*: Baseball's Third Commissioner.* Jefferson, NC: McFarland, 2016.

Cline, Scott. "To Foster Honorable Pastimes: Baseball as a Civic Endeavor in 1880s Seattle." *Pacific Northwest Quarterly,* Fall 1996.

Cohen, Lizabeth. *Saving America's Cities: Ed Logue and the Struggle to Renew America in the*

Suburban Age. New York: Farrar, Strauss and Giroux, 2019.

Cumbler, John. *A Social History of Economic Decline: Business, Politics, and Work in Trenton.* New Brunswick: Rutgers University Press, 1989.

Daniels, Eric. "A Brief History of Individualism in American Thought." In *For the Greater Good of All: Perspectives on Individualism, Society, and Leadership,* ed. Donelson Forsyth and Crystal Hoyt. New York: Palgrave Macmillan, 2011.

Dickson, Paul. *Bill Veeck: Baseball's Greatest Maverick.* New York: Walker & Company, 2012.

Drebinger, John. "Baseball Drafts Wartime Program." *New York Times,* February 3, 1942.

_____. "Chandler Blocks Night Game Limit," *New York Times,* December 13, 1945.

_____. "Indians and Athletics to Introduce Night Ball to American League Next Year." *New York Times,* December 15, 1938.

_____. "Night Baseball on Limited Scale Adopted Unanimously by National League." *New York Times,* December 13, 1934.

Dunn, Susan. *1940: FDR, Willkie, Lindbergh, Hitler—the Election amid the Storm.* New Haven: Yale University Press, 2013.

Durso, Joseph. *Madison Square Garden: 100 Years of History.* New York: Simon & Schuster, 1979.

Eberle, Mark. *Kansas Baseball, 1858–1941.* Lawrence: University Press of Kansas, 2017.

Ehrgott, Robert. *Mr. Wrigley's Ball Club: Chicago and the Cubs During the Jazz Age.* Lincoln: University of Nebraska Press, 2013.

Eisenberg, John. *The League: How Five Rivals Created the NFL and Launched a Sports Empire.* New York: Basic Books, 2018.

Elias, Robert, ed. *Baseball and the American Dream: Race, Class, Gender and the National Pastime.* Armonk, NY: M.E. Sharpe, 2001.

Ewald, Dan. *John Fetzer: On a Handshake: The Times and Triumphs of a Tiger Owner.* Champaign, IL: Sagamore, 1997.

Fenske, Gail. *The Skyscraper in the Sky: The Woolworth Building and the Making of Modern New York.* Chicago: University of Chicago Press, 2008.

Flanagan, William. *Urban Sociology: Images and Structure.* Lanham, MD: Rowman & Littlefield, 2010.

Fogelson, Robert. *Downtown: Its Rise and Fall, 1880–1950.* New Haven: Yale University Press, 2001.

Freeberg, Ernest. *The Age of Edison: Electric Light and the Invention of Modern America.* New York: Penguin Press, 2013.

Gendzel, Glen. "Competitive Boosterism: How Milwaukee Lost the Braves." *Business History Review,* Winter 1995.

Gennaro, Vince. *Diamond Dollars: The Economics of Winning in Baseball.* Hingham, MA: Maple Street Press, 2007.

Gietschier, Steven, ed. *Complete Baseball Record Book.* St. Louis: Sporting News Publishing, 2004.

Glaab, Charles. "Historical Perspectives on Urban Development Schemes." In *Social Science and the City: A Survey of Urban Research,* ed. Leo Schnore. New York: Praeger, 1967.

Glaab, Charles, and Theodore Brown. *A History of Urban America.* New York: Macmillan, 1967.

Goldberger, Paul. *Ballpark: Baseball in the American City.* New York: Alfred A. Knopf, 2019.

Gorman, Mel. "Charles F. Brush and the First Public Electric Street Lighting System in America." *Ohio Historical Quarterly,* April 1961.

Green, Michael, and Roger Launius. *Charlie Finley: The Outrageous Story of Baseball's Super Showman.* New York: Walker & Company, 2010.

Gregorich, Barbara. "John Olsen and His Barnstorming Baseball Teams." *Michigan History,* May/June 1995.

Griffith, Clark. "Clark Griffith's 50 Golden Years in the American League." *The Sporting News,* August 8, 1952.

Guschov, Stephen. *The Red Stockings of Cincinnati: Base Ball's First All-Professional Team and Its Historic 1869 and 1870 Seasons.* Jefferson, NC: McFarland, 1998.

Hardy, Stephen. "Polo at the Rinks: Shaping Markets for Ice Hockey in America, 1880–1900." *Journal of Sport History,* Summer 2006.

Haupert, Michael. "William Hulbert and the Birth of the National League." *Baseball Research Journal,* Spring 2015.

Holmes, Tommy. "MacPhail Sees Night Ball Pulling Dodgers Out of Red." *Brooklyn Eagle,* May 29, 1938.

Hoover, Herbert. *American Individualism.* Garden City, NY: Doubleday, 1922.

Jakle, John. *City Lights: Illuminating the American Night.* Baltimore: Johns Hopkins University Press, 2001.

Jeffries, John. *A Third Term for FDR: The Election of 1940.* Lawrence: University Press of Kansas, 2017.

Jillson, Cal. *Pursuing the American Dream: Opportunity and Exclusion Over Four Centuries.* Lawrence: University Press of Kansas, 2004.

Johnson, Lloyd, ed. *The Encyclopedia of Minor League Baseball.* Durham, NC: Baseball America, 1997.

Klein, Maury. *The Genesis of Industrial America, 1870–1920.* New York: Cambridge University Press, 2007.

Kuhn, Bowie. *Hardball: The Education of a Baseball Commissioner.* Lincoln: University of Nebraska Press, 1987.

Kuklick, Bruce. *To Every Thing a Season: Shibe Park and Urban Philadelphia, 1909–1976.* Princeton: Princeton University Press, 1991.

Kuntz, Jerry. *Baseball Fiends and Flying Machines: The Many Lives and Outrageous Times of George and Alfred Lawson.* Jefferson, NC: McFarland, 2009.

_____. "Tramping Through the Baseball Subculture: The Career of Alfred W. Lawson." *Base Ball: A Journal of the Early Game,* Fall 2007.

Land, Kenneth. "Organizing the Boys of Summer: The Evolution of Minor-League Baseball, 1883–1990." *American Journal of Sociology,* November 1994.

Lane, F.C. "The Greatest Problem in the National Game: The Critical Situation in Sunday Baseball." *Baseball Magazine,* October 1911.

_____. "The Romance of Night Baseball." *Baseball Magazine,* October 1930.

_____. "Will the Major Leagues Adopt Night Baseball?" *Baseball Magazine,* October 1935.

Leifer, Eric. *Making the Majors: The Transformation of Team Sports in America.* Cambridge: Harvard University Press, 1995.

Lemann, Nicholas. *Transaction Man: The Rise of the Deal and the Decline of the American Dream.* New York: Farrar, Straus and Giroux, 2019.

Levin, Linda. *The Making of FDR: The Story of Stephen T. Early, America's First Modern Press Secretary.* Amherst, NY: Prometheus, 2008.

Livesay, Harold. "Lilliputians in Brobdingnag: Small Business in Late-Nineteenth-Century America." In *Small Business in American Life,* ed. Stuart Bruchey. New York: Columbia University Press, 1980.

Lytton, E.C. "Night Football at Drake University." *Athletic Journal,* January 1929.

MacCambridge, Michael. *America's Game: The Epic Story of How Pro Football Captured a Nation.* New York: Random House, 2004.

Macht, Norman. *The Grand Old Man of Baseball: Connie Mack in His Final Years, 1932–1956.* Lincoln: University of Nebraska Press, 2015.

Mandelbaum, Michael. *The Meaning of Sports: Why Americans Watch Baseball, Football, and Basketball and What They See When They Do.* New York: Public Affairs, 2004.

Marshall, William. *Baseball's Pivotal Era, 1945–1951.* Lexington: University Press of Kentucky, 1999.

Martin, David. "Baseball and Boosterism: Henry W. Grady, the Atlanta Constitution, and the Inaugural Season of the Southern League." Masters thesis, University of Tennessee, 2006.

McClure, Rusty. *Crosley: Two Brothers and a Business Empire That Transformed the Nation.* Cincinnati: Clerisy Press, 2006.

McCue, Andy. *Mover and Shaker: Walter O'Malley, the Dodgers, & Baseball's Westward Expansion.* Lincoln: University of Nebraska Press, 2014.

McCurdy, Bill. "Houston's Role in the Initiation of Sunday Night Baseball." *The National Pastime,* 2014.

McKelvey, Blake. *The Urbanization of America, 1860–1915.* New Brunswick: Rutgers University Press, 1963.

Mead, William. *Even the Browns: The Zany, True Story of Baseball in the Early Forties.* Chicago: Contemporary Books, 1978.

Melville, Tom. *Early Baseball and the Rise of the National League.* Jefferson, NC: McFarland, 2001.

Mills, Wright. *White Collar: The American Middle Classes.* New York: Oxford University Press, 1951.

Mollenkopf, John. *The Contested City.* Princeton: Princeton University Press, 1983.

Mullins, William. *Becoming Big League: Seattle, the Pilots, and Stadium Politics.* Seattle: University of Washington Press, 2013.

Nasaw, David. *Going Out: The Rise and Fall of Public Amusements.* New York: Basic, 1993.

Neumann, Dietrich. *Architecture of the Night: The Illuminated Building.* New York: Prestel, 2002.

Norman, Jim. "Football Still Americans' Favorite Sport to Watch." *Gallup News Service,* January 4, 2018.

Nye, David. *American Illuminations: Urban Lighting, 1800–1920.* Cambridge: MIT Press, 2018.

_____. *Electrifying America: Social Meanings of a New Technology, 1880–1940.* Cambridge: MIT Press, 1991.

Ogden, David. "Black Baseball at Forbes Field." In *Forbes Field: Essays and Memories of the Pirates' Historic Ballpark, 1909–1971,* ed. David Cicotello and Angelo Louisa. Jefferson, NC: McFarland, 2007.

Palmer, James. "Economic and Social Aspects of Chain Stores." *Journal of Business of the University of Chicago,* July 1929.

Passer, Harold. *The Electrical Manufacturers, 1875–1900: A Study in Competition, Entrepreneurship. Technical Change, and Economic Growth.* New York: Arno Press, 1972.

Payne, Robert. *Let There Be Light: A History of Night Baseball.* Bloomington, IN: Author House, 2010.

Peterson, Jon. *The Birth of City Planning in the United States, 1840–1917.* Baltimore: Johns Hopkins University Press, 2003.

Pietrusza, David. *Lights On! The Wild Century-Long Saga of Night Baseball.* Lanham, MD: Scarecrow Press, 1997.

Podair, Jerald. *City of Dreams: Dodger Stadium and the Birth of Modern Los Angeles.* Princeton: Princeton University Press, 2017.

Povich, Shirley. "Griff Finds Rich His Arc-Enemies." *Baseball Digest,* January 1949.

Powers-Beck, Jeffrey. *The American Indian Integration of Baseball.* Lincoln: University of Nebraska Press, 2004.

Prestien, Suzanne. "Past [Im]Perfect: Mythology, Nostalgia, and Baseball." In *Baseball and the American Dream: Race, Class, Gender and the National Pastime,* ed. Robert Elias. Armonk, NY: M.E. Sharpe, 2001.

Putnam, Robert. *Bowling Alone: The Collapse and Revival of American Community.* New York: Simon & Schuster, 2001.

Quigel, James, and Louis Hunsinger. *Gateway to the Majors: Williamsport and Minor League Baseball.* University Park: Pennsylvania State University Press, 2001.

Rader, Benjamin. *Baseball: A History of America's Game.* Urbana: University of Illinois Press, 1992.

Riess, Steven. *City Games: The Evolution of American Urban Society and the Rise of Sports.* Urbana: University of Illinois Press, 1989.

_____. *Sport in Industrial America, 1850–1920.* Wheeling, IL: Harlan Davidson, 1995.

_____. *Touching Base: Professional Baseball and American Culture in the Progressive Era.* Westport, CT: Greenwood Press, 1980.

Schroeder, Sheila. "When Technology and Culture Collide: The Advent of Night Baseball." *NINE: A*

Journal of Baseball History and Social Policy Perspectives, Fall 1994.

Schwarz, Jordan. *Liberal: Adolf A. Berle and the Vision of an American Era.* New York: The Free Press, 1987.

Seifried, Chad, and Donna Pastore. "The Temporary Homes: Analyzing Baseball Facilities in the United States Pre-1903." *Journal of Sport History,* Summer 2010.

Siriano, Christopher. *The House of David.* Charleston, SC: Arcadia, 2007.

Smith, Curt. *The Presidents and the Pastime: The History of Baseball and the White House.* Lincoln: University of Nebraska Press, 2018.

Snelling, Dennis. *The Greatest Minor League: A History of the Pacific Coast League, 1903–1957.* Jefferson, NC: McFarland, 2012.

Spigel, Lynn. *Make Room for TV: Television and the Family Ideal in Postwar America.* Chicago: University of Chicago Press, 1992.

Stan, Francis. "Now Arc Addict, Inconsistent Griff Is a Man of Mystery." *Washington Evening Star,* November 9, 1940.

Staudohar, Paul, and James Dworkin. "The Impact of Baseball's New Television Contracts." *NINE: A Journal of Baseball History and Culture,* Spring 2002.

Sterling, Christopher, and John Kittross. *Stay Tuned: A Concise History of American Broadcasting.* Belmont, CA: Wadsworth, 1990.

Sullivan, Dean. "Faces in the Crowd: A Statistical Portrait of Baseball Spectators in Cincinnati, 1886–1888." *Journal of Sport History,* Winter 1990.

Sullivan, Neil. *The Dodgers Move West.* New York: Oxford University Press, 1987.

_____. *The Minors: The Struggles and Triumphs of Baseball's Poor Relation from 1876 to the Present.* New York: St. Martin's Press, 1991.

Surdam, David. *Century of the Leisured Masses: Entertainment and the Transformation of Twentieth-Century America.* New York: Oxford University Press, 2015.

_____. *The Postwar Yankees: Baseball's Golden Age Revisited.* Lincoln: University of Nebraska Press, 2008.

_____. *Wins, Losses, and Empty Seats: How Baseball Outlasted the Great Depression.* Lincoln: University of Nebraska Press, 2011.

Surdam, David, and Michael Haupert. *The Age of Ruth and Landis: The Economics of Baseball During the Roaring Twenties.* Lincoln: University of Nebraska Press, 2018.

Swackhamer, Robert. "Lighting Major League Baseball Fields." *General Electric Review,* September 1939.

Swope, Tom. "Cincinnati Lights Way in Big League Style." *The Sporting News,* May 23, 1935.

Taylor, Doug. "A Community and Its Team: The Evangeline League's Lafayette White Sox, 1934–1942." *Louisiana History,* Spring 1995.

Thomas, John. "Holding the Middle Ground." In *The American Planning Tradition: Culture and Policy,* ed. Robert Fishman. Washington: Woodrow Wilson Center Press, 2000.

Tygiel, Jules. *Past Time: Baseball as History.* New York: Oxford University Press, 2000.

Vande Berg, Leah, and Nick Trujillo. "The Rhetoric of Winning and Losing: The American Dream and America's Team." In *Media, Sports, & Society,* ed. Lawrence Wenner. Oaks, CA: Sage, 1989.

Vogan, Travis. *ESPN: The Making of a Sports Media Empire.* Urbana: University of Illinois Press, 2015.

Walker, James, and Robert Bellamy, Jr. *Center Field Shot: A History of Baseball on Television.* Lincoln: University of Nebraska Press, 2008.

Waltz, George. "Behind the Lights at a Night Ball Game." *Popular Science,* July 1948.

Wann, Daniel, and Nyla Branscombe. "Sports Fans: Measuring Degrees of Identification with Their Team." *International Journal of Sport Psychology,* January–March 1993.

Warfield, Don. *The Roaring Redhead: Larry MacPhail—Baseball's Great Innovator.* South Bend, IN: Diamond Communications, 1987.

Warner, Sam Bass. *Streetcar Suburbs: The Process of Growth in Boston, 1870–1900.* Cambridge: Harvard University Press, 1962.

Weidenaar, Reynold. *Magic Music from the Telharmonium.* Metuchen, NJ: Scarecrow Press, 1995.

White, Edward. *Creating the National Pastime: Baseball Transforms Itself, 1903–1953.* Princeton: Princeton University Press, 1996.

Whyte, William. *The Organization Man.* New York: Simon & Schuster, 1956.

Zimbalist, Andrew. *Baseball and Billions: A Probing Look Inside the Big Business of Our National Pastime.* New York: Basic Books, 1992.

Digital Archives of Newspapers

Brooklyn Newsstand (*Brooklyn Eagle*)
Chronicling America: Historic American Newspapers
Gale Nineteenth Century U.S. Newspapers
Newspapers.com
Old Fulton New York Post Cards
Paper of Record (*The Sporting News*)
ProQuest Historical Newspapers (*New York Times, Boston Globe*)

Index

Numbers in **bold** *italics* indicate pages with illustrations